John Costello's previous books include *D-Day* (with Warren Tute), *The Battle of the Atlantic* and *Jutland 1916* (both with Terry Hughes) and *The Pacific War*. He was educated at Fitzwilliam College, Cambridge, and worked as a producer in British television for many years. He currently divides his time between London and New York.

On first publication of *The Pacific War*, Sir William Stephenson ('Intrepid') wrote, 'It provides the most comprehensive and accurate background to the complexity of events, including diplomatic manoeuvres, leading to the inferno of Pearl Harbor ... massive and precise research which goes beyond any other publication hitherto produced in a book available to the public'.

Also by John Costello in Pan Books

D-Day (with Warren Tute)
The Pacific War

JOHN COSTELLO

LOVE SEX AND WAR

Changing Values
1939-45

Pan Books
in association with Collins

First published 1985 by William Collins Sons and Co Ltd
This edition published 1986 by Pan Books Ltd
Cavaye Place, London SW10 9PG
in association with Collins
9 8 7 6 5 4 3 2 1
© John Costello 1985
ISBN 0 330 29270 6

Permission to reprint copyright material
is gratefully acknowledged as follows:
Jocelyn Brooke, 'A Soldier's Song', the estate
of the late Jocelyn Brooke;
Charles Causley, from 'A Ballad for Katherine
of Aragon', The Woburn Press, London;
extract from 'Jane', Mirror Group Newspapers Ltd;
John Hammond Moore, 'Oversexed Overpaid
and Overhere', University of Queensland Press;
Alun Lewis, 'All Day it Rained',
from *Raiders Dawn*, Allen & Unwin, London;
'White Cliffs of Dover' and 'Lili Marlene'
EMI Music Publishing Ltd, London;
'Rosie the Riveter', Famous Chappell.
Illingworth and the *Daily Mail*
for the carton reproduced on page oo

Printed and bound in Great Britain by
Richard Clay (The Chaucer Press) Ltd,
Bungay, Suffolk

CONTENTS

ILLUSTRATIONS

FILLING THE GAP

(National Achives refers to U S National Achives, Washington DC.)

INTRODUCTION

The mutual relations between the two sexes seems
to us to be at least as important as the mutual
relations of any two governments in the world.

Thomas Babington Macaulay,
Historian and British Secretary
of State for War 1840

Sex and war have always been inextricably linked. Two thousand years
ago, the Roman poet Horace pointed out that long before the fall of Troy
lust had been the cause of grievous war. The Greek campaign against the
legendary city of Asia Minor probably owed more to the ancient Greeks'
passion for commerce than the Trojan king's passion for the fabled
Helen. Yet even if economics rather than sex has precipitated wars from
time immemorial, the relaxation of moral restraint endemic to war has
also had a profound impact on sexual relationships and the relationships
between sexes throughout history.

To the men and women who lived and fought through the greatest
conflict in human history, World War II was the pivotal emotional
experience in their lives. Individual testimony indicates that *what* people
were fighting for had less to do with abstract notions of freedom or
patriotism than with individual emotional values represented by sweethearts, wives and families. Sex and sexuality in all its guises and com-
plexities played an extensive role in the war experience.

Love, Sex and War is an examination of the sexual aspect of World War
II. In putting the experience in a social perspective, it does not set out to
tackle the larger issue of why men and women did what they did, or how
the social and psychological forces released by war worked dramatic
historical changes. Forty years later the mechanism of these processes is
still being hotly debated by academic historians and social scientists. This
study is a broad documentary review of wartime sexual activity and
attitudes among the Americans and the British. It is intended as a set of
signposts, rather than a road-map, to the complex social topography that
is the collective and often anomalous wartime experience of sex.

Any account of the sexual aspect of World War II is complicated by the conflict of conviction, the confusions of personal memory and the imprecision of psychological interpretation. Nevertheless it is possible to argue that, by enhancing intimacy and the expression of love, and thus liberating many people from traditional inhibitions, the effects of the war on individuals were in some ways beneficial. It is also possible to establish, from the broad cross-section of documented record and individual recollection, that the war did make a very significant contribution to the economic liberation of women and the sexual liberation of both men and women. Even if this liberation was 'for the duration only', its impact on people's lives proved to be so pervasive that it became a powerful acccelerator of social change.

The trend toward liberalization of moral attitudes and the coincident 'liberation' of the female population was not unique to World War II. The postwar trend towards liberalization of moral attitudes and the coincident 'liberation' of the female population was accelerated rather than set in motion by World War II – wars have always been powerful catalysts of social change. The Carthaginian Wars brought the first recorded campaign for women's liberation in 215 BC, when the Roman senate repealed the discriminatory Oppian tax law – despite Cato the Elder's warning that 'what women want is complete freedom – or, to put it bluntly, complete licence.' The Hundred Years' War saw the patriarchal authority of the church challenged by Joan of Arc when she led the French troops to victory over an English army at Orléans. She was condemned for daring to dress as a man, 'in violation of canon law, abominable to God and man'. Yet three centuries later, American women were increasingly drawn into the active prosecution of war after the Union recruited them to take over the clerical and factory jobs of male conscripts in the Civil War. World War I mobilized industrial and human resources on such a scale that Winston Churchill was moved to write, 'All the horrors of the ages were brought together, and not only armies, but whole populations were thrust into the midst of them.'

The sexual undercurrents stirred by World War I inspired Sigmund Freud to write his *Reflections on War and Death* (1917). In Freud's analysis, the connection between violence and eroticism was evident in the tendency of a society in wartime to throw off the repressions which civilization has imposed on the human sex drive. Existing taboos are not cast aside completely, but in a society at war the mechanism of sexual suppression operates at a lower level. According to Freud the atavistic horde instinct essential to mass killing inevitably inflames the sex drive because the urge to kill and the urge to procreate are both subconsciously related as extremes of the human experience.

'War aphrodisia', as it has been called, had been traditionally ascribed to men in battle. In 'total war', however, a related hedonistic impulse reaches many other segments of society. The forces liberated by this process in World War I accelerated the process of social change by redefining the relationship between the sexes. Many women who had been brought up to look to a man as supporter, breadwinner and head of the family, became 'emancipated' when their men were conscripted for military service. Thousands of women left their homes to do jobs that had been filled by men, and many donned military uniforms for the first time.

As a result of the dramatic improvements World War I brought to their social and economic status, many women began to expect equality in other areas as well. After the war enfranchisement was no longer the controversial political issue that it had been in 1914. In most Western countries, except France, the female population received the right to vote. Women celebrated their new freedom with liberated fashions and liberal behaviour. They bobbed their hair, donned short skirts, smoked in public and wore the heavy make-up which had formerly been the attribute of a harlot.

Nowhere was the new liberation more visible than in the United States, where a buoyant stock market, bootleg gin, and the racy novels of Scott Fitzgerald fuelled the frenetic pace of the social revolution. The emerging American movie industry packaged eroticism for the mass audience, promoting the sex appeal of stars like Clara Bow or the sultry masculinity of Rudolf Valentino. Audiences flocked to films such as *Alimony*, which promised 'brilliant men, beautiful jazz babies, champagne baths, midnight revels, petting parties in the purple dawn, all ending in one terrifying climax that makes you gasp'.

Hollywood films were also rewriting the romantic dictionary across the Atlantic, but Britain's postwar prosperity lasted only long enough to effect a mild moral thaw before the rigours of the Depression restored some of the frigidity of the Victorian social climate. Nevertheless, some social changes could not be reversed. Government issue of contraceptives to protect troops from the wartime veneral disease epidemic had fostered a wider social acceptance of birth control methods, although 'mechanical devices' continued to be condemned by the Church as a sinful interference with God's command to procreate and as a wicked incentive to promiscuity.

Legislative reform had made family planning available, but 'sex' was still a word that most people preferred to avoid. On neither side of the Atlantic was sex education considered a suitable subject to be taught in school. The Depression also ensured that the thirties were a decade of moral, as well as economic retrenchment. Divorce rates had plunged with the collapse of the stock market. Significantly they reached a postwar low – 40 per cent below the 1928 level – in 1933, the year that the dole queues were longest. The number of weddings also fell as hard times caused many couples to postpone marriage.

'Sex is one of the things Middletown has long been taught to fear,' noted the authors of the classic thirties' US survey of Muncie, Indiana. Its citizens wanted to 'keep the subject out of sight and out of mind as much as possible'. The town newspaper advised that 'a girl should never kiss a boy unless they are engaged' and the local librarian, when asked for books on sex education, snapped, 'Not here!' The same attitude prevailed in Britain, where it was still not considered respectable for women to go to pubs unescorted and 'halter-neck' bathing dresses were regarded as immodest by many church-going people. In 1937 British newspaper proprietors refused to publish a series of Ministry of Health advertisements warning the public about the dangers of venereal disease.

Teenage girls might dream of a career outside the home, but only one in five single women in America and one in eight in Britain were in paid employment. The very idea of married women working from choice, rather than of necessity, was fiercely resisted by employers and frowned on by society. Those women who were at work were usually single, subject to discriminatory pay, and restricted in their choice of job by an unofficial code that determined what was suitable 'woman's work'.

The mobilization of the female population in the United States and Britain to fight a 'total war' shattered resistance to the employment of married women and the old notions of 'woman's work'. The mobilization, disruption and excitement of so many lives was not only a catalyst of social change, but it also sowed the seeds of a far-reaching shift in private and public sexual attitudes. 'Moral taboos had not been banished, but their pride of place was gone', observed a veteran of World War II in the sixties. 'The sex code by which this later generation lived was a permissive one, allowing chastity or promiscuity, frowning only on prudery and prurience.'

To a far greater extent than World War I, the century's second global conflict was to prove the truth of the assertion made by A. L. Rowse: 'There is a wide-ranging association of war with sexuality, complex, intricate, intimate and at every level.'

"I SUPPOSE YOU TWO REALIZE THAT THIS UNION HOLDS GOOD EVEN AFTER CESSATION OF HOSTILITIES."
—Cpl. Ralph Newman

Love, Sex and War

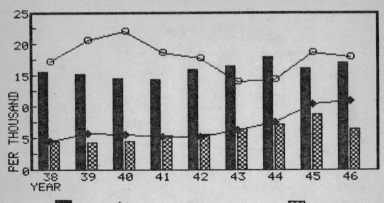

UK MARRIAGES, DIVORCES & BIRTHS

	Births	Divorces	Marriages	Illegitimate Births %
1938	15.56	4.50	17.20	4.50
1939	15.20	5.75	20.60	4.40
1940	14.60	5.70	22.10	4.60
1941	14.40	5.20	18.60	5.50
1942	15.90	5.35	17.70	5.60
1943	16.60	6.25	14.10	6.50
1944	17.90	7.65	14.30	7.30
1945	16.20	10.50	18.60	8.90
1946	17	11	18	6.50

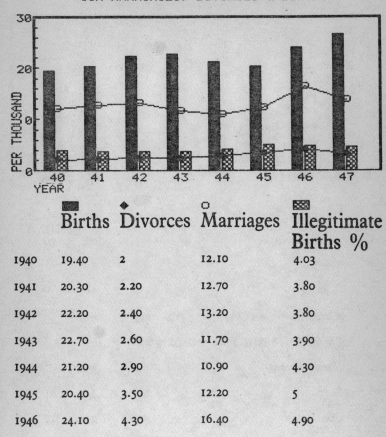

USA MARRIAGES, DIVORCES & BIRTHS

	Births	**Divorces**	**Marriages**	**Illegitimate Births %**
1940	19.40	2	12.10	4.03
1941	20.30	2.20	12.70	3.80
1942	22.20	2.40	13.20	3.80
1943	22.70	2.60	11.70	3.90
1944	21.20	2.90	10.90	4.30
1945	20.40	3.50	12.20	5
1946	24.10	4.30	16.40	4.90
1947	26.60	3.40	13.90	4.60

Love, Sex and War

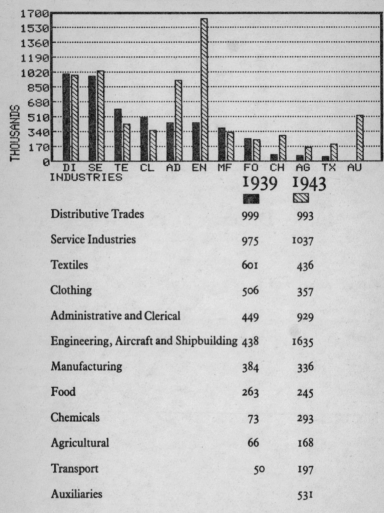

BRITISH WOMEN IN INDUSTRY

	1939	1943
Distributive Trades	999	993
Service Industries	975	1037
Textiles	601	436
Clothing	506	357
Administrative and Clerical	449	929
Engineering, Aircraft and Shipbuilding	438	1635
Manufacturing	384	336
Food	263	245
Chemicals	73	293
Agricultural	66	168
Transport	50	197
Auxiliaries		531

Illingworth for the *London Daily Mail*

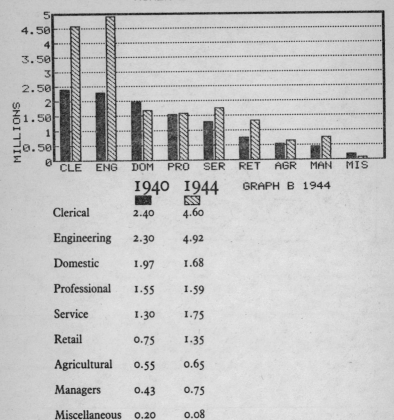

WOMEN BY OCCUPATION US

GRAPH B 1944

	1940	1944
Clerical	2.40	4.60
Engineering	2.30	4.92
Domestic	1.97	1.68
Professional	1.55	1.59
Service	1.30	1.75
Retail	0.75	1.35
Agricultural	0.55	0.65
Managers	0.43	0.75
Miscellaneous	0.20	0.08

I

MAKING LOVE
AND WAR

O war is a casual mistress
And the world is her double bed
She has few charms in her mechanised arms
But you wake up and find yourself dead

Charles Causley, RN

SINCE LOVE AND WAR represent the extremes of human experience, it is no surprise to find that a 'total war' had profound
emotional and sexual consequences for many of its participants.
'We were not really immoral, there was a war on,' was how one
British housewife explained her behaviour during World War II.
So pervasive was this attitude that it seemed that sexual restraint
had been suspended for the duration, as the traditional licence of
the battlefield invaded the home front. 'By most people's standards we were immoral,' admitted an American soldier, 'but we
were young and could die tomorrow.'

The urgency and excitement of wartime soon eroded moral
restraints, and life on many home fronts appeared as cheap and
short as life on the battle front. Soldiers had always claimed fear
of death on the battlefield as an excuse for sexual licence. 'In war a
man has to love, if only to reassert that he's very much alive in the
face of destruction,' explained a US army sergeant. 'Whoever has
loved in wartime takes part in a passionate reaffirmation of his life.'

In the same way, many British women attributed their wartime immorality to aid raids. Statistically the chances of survival in World War II were often worse for noncombatants. Sixty thousand civilians perished in the Blitz in the winter of 1941, a figure that far exceeded the death-rate in the armed forces during the same period.

'It is difficult to write about relationships which occurred during that period without giving the impression that we were having it easy,' explained a newly-married British woman. 'Personal relationships were formed between men and women out of sheer loneliness and the need to be loved. I lived a mile away from the heavily bombed city of Newcastle, so I think you can say I was in the front line.'

The same hedonistic sense of excitement was generated in the United States by the impact of mobilization. Americans married at the phenomenal rate of a thousand a day in the weeks after Pearl Harbor. This twenty per cent leap in the national rate in the first month of 1942 was responsible for the autumn surge in the birthrate. Many war brides were rushed into marriage by soldiers desperate for emotional security before they were posted overseas. This was evident from the attitude of one American girl who was talked into matrimony by her flyer boyfriend:

> I don't love him. I've told him I don't love him. But he's an aviator and says I should marry him and give him a little happiness. He says he'll be dead in a year, he hasn't any real chance of living through the war. But if he should still be alive when the war is over, and I still feel the same way, he says I can divorce him and it will be all right.

Not that everyone got married. 'There was never a shortage of young, healthy bucks,' recalled an Illinois girl who admitted to 'having a ball' in Chicago. 'We weren't as casual about sex as people are now. You held your breath and prayed. It was tough when you didn't want to get pregnant . . . There wasn't anything foolproof except abstinence, and who needed that? I'd already tried that and didn't think much of it.'

Death and separation were the twin spectres that haunted wartime love affairs and provided a powerful incentive for couples to snatch at every opportunity for love. Even the most fleeting wartime affair took on a special intensity because of the shared apprehension that it might be each partner's last chance to discover affection in sexual solace. No-one appreciated this better than a girl in the WAAF who dated the pilots who fought in the Battle of Britain:

It was here today and gone tomorrow, so I did not build up any long-standing relationships. The war encouraged flirtations, although not all were 'dirty weekends' because we girls were well aware of the stigma that went with pregnancy and being an unmarried mother. This encouraged more quickly-arranged marriages.

Inevitably, chastity was an early casualty as lovers were forced to abandon the traditional drawn-out period of courtship. The 'weekend affair', snatched on a forty-eight-hour pass, that preceded many wartime weddings, often substituted for a honeymoon. But a formal ceremony, with as many trimmings as ration books permitted, was still regarded as *de rigueur* for solemnizing matrimony. Barbara Cartland, the best-selling romantic novelist, brightened many a WAAF's special day with wedding gowns borrowed from her society friends. She observed:

> Theirs was a quick, rush wedding of wartime, the snatched honeymoon of sometimes only forty-eight hours, a happiness overshadowed by the inevitable separation from their husbands, a problematical future, with always the fear that THEY would be widows almost before THEY were wives. Yet they had their happiness; however quick, however fleeting, it was theirs. They were loved and beloved, and by this stage in the war love was about the only thing left unrationed.

Like wartime weddings, the course of love during World War II seldom ran smoothly, even for those couples who accepted transient emotional relationships. The passion of affairs in wartime was heightened by the need to make the most of every hour, and the sadness of frequent partings was intensified by the uncertainty of whether the partners would survive to meet again.

It was a time of great personal emotional stress and also of adventure. 'My war memories are some of horror, but also of an immense amount of good times,' remembered one woman. 'It really was the happiest time of my life. People were friendly and we were all in it together.'

For many people, especially soldiers in the front line, the fear of imminent death intensified the yearning for emotional relationships that might give some transient reassurance in an uncertain future. The sentiments of a German infantryman on the eve of Hitler's attack in Europe were to be echoed in millions of wartime letters to loved ones:

My darling Henny! I don't know how long it'll last. I want to tell you something lovely: you were the only woman I've ever loved . . . I don't ask anything from you. Only that you should think of me often, and know that in my life, I've only done my duty, nothing but my duty. And stay happy, even in the misfortune of my death.

Everywhere, men and women turned to each other for affirmation of life amidst death and destruction. A young Polish sculptress wrote of her ecstasy at finding herself in love with a resistance fighter who was killed in the 1944 Warsaw uprising: 'Life has suddenly taken on a special meaning. Has the world changed, or is it that I have changed? . . . How frightfully selfish we are. This sudden wave of personal happiness has managed to separate us completely from all the atrocities of the times in which we live.'

Total war subjected whole civilian populations to extremes of violence and disruption. This stimulated the urge to love and be loved, and led to a rapid increase in extramarital sexual activity. Along with the rise in juvenile sexual delinquency, the statistical barometer indicates the extent to which men, women, and adolescents were eventually to run to sex as one of the few freely available wartime pleasures.

'The most wonderful days of my life,' recalled a British woman. 'Those days were dreams, every day exciting whether it was good or bad excitement,' remembered another. 'Despite the danger and the suffering, the war days were exciting days in many ways,' was how a wartime housewife put it. 'I had some wonderful, memorable and sometimes sad times, but I would not have missed my experiences during the war.'

The rush and contrast of wartime emotions ignited many a romantic flame, but the frequent dislocations of people's lives often made it difficult to keep those flames alive. Jean Taber's a typical wartime romance which began in an Aldersdot public house in the summer of 1942:

Carl was serving with the Canadian Army and I was seventeen and in the ATS. We spent the next two years meeting each other whenever we could get a pass because we were always being posted to different camps. We knew after a few months that we wanted to get married but had to wait for his application to be processed by the Canadian authorities. It came through just before D-Day. A wedding was out of the question then as I had not told my parents because I was afraid they would not want me to go and live in Canada. We managed to get a pass to see each other and, as military personnel were not supposed then to travel more than fifteen miles from their camps, I wore civilian clothes. It was the first time Carl had seen me in a dress. When we parted I knew that he was going into hell. I never thought I would see him again. I assumed the worst when I did not hear from him in France.

It was not until Christmas 1944 that I learnt he was still alive. The news came in letters from people who had heard Lord Haw Haw's German radio broadcasts when he read a message addressed to me which said, 'I am a prisoner of war in Germany. Let all my folks know – all my love. I love you, Carl. "You'll never know."' I knew it really was my Canadian soldier because that was our 'special' song. It was the best Christmas present I ever had. But it was not until the following May that I saw Carl again. I hardly recognized him. He was thin and ill and his teeth had been knocked out by a guard at his Stalag VIII B prison camp. But we decided that nothing was going to stop us marrying this time. We both went Absent Without Leave and arrived at my parents' home at 11 a.m. on 4 June 1945. Carl was a complete stranger to my parents and they were shocked when we said we were getting married. We had five shillings between us, but we got a special licence at 1.30 p.m., and the local vicar promised to marry us the same afternoon.

I felt very lovely at the time, but now I realize I couldn't have done in my ATS uniform, with my hair tied up with a shoe lace. We had no civilian clothes so it was a khaki wedding with carrot-tops and pinks from the garden as buttonholes. We invited people from the local pub to a reception in the bar which consisted of spam sandwiches and a wedding cake 'borrowed' from my nephew, whose first birthday it happened to be that day.

My wedding very nearly didn't happen at all. As I was going out of the door to the church, two military policemen arrived to take us back to camp. But after we gave our word, they joined the party and allowed us to spend a few hours alone together that evening. Our 'wedding night' was a disaster because of Carl's health – and a week later he was taken in handcuffs aboard the *Queen Mary* to return home. It was almost a year before we could get together again in Halifax, Nova Scotia, when I became Mrs Taber for real!

Many wartime love affairs caused or were the result of emotionally shattering experiences. Martha was seventeen when her Viennese mother managed to get her on the last trainload of Jewish refugee children to be allowed out of Vienna before war broke out in 1939. Her fear did not end with her arrival in England and Martha recalled arming herself with a sixpenny Woolworth toy revolver because she was 'frightened out of her wits' of German parachutists. She was in the ATS when she suffered the deep emotional shock of learning that the Germans had transported her mother to a concentration camp:

> My standards of morality went to the seven winds and I felt very dejected when I finally realized that my mother had been deported to the camps and I would probably never see her again. This prompted my search for love and affection. I had affairs, including a very serious one in 1943 with a Yugoslavian naval officer which left me expecting his baby. There was never any question of my marrying him since he was so much older. I was twenty-one and he was forty-nine, but he was a fantastically handsome man who looked just like my father. It was my great wartime romance. In the end I did not have the baby adopted and at the end of the war married a former German prisoner of war. It was a strange choice for a Jewish refugee girl, but he was one of the kindest people I met and not a Nazi, but a soldier who was only doing his duty and who did not want to be repatriated. Although he willingly adopted my son as his own, it was one of those things that happened in war. I suppose I never should have married him and it eventually broke up.

The emotional turbulence of war left a lasting impact on many marriages. Traditionally wives had waved their husbands off to war on the assumption that strict fidelity was incompatible with soldiering, but such was total war that even on the home front many wives were confronted by new choices and opportunities. One English woman who confessed she had 'enjoyed herself' conceded that the old dual standard of feminine fidelity was no longer acceptable to wives.

There was plenty of 'sleeping around'. In the services it was an accepted fact of war, although there were many innocent attachments with no sex involved. Even the most loving of husbands had, at the very least, friendships with the other girls when they were away from their wives. Some marriages came to grief in such circumstances, but plenty survived, probably because the husband sensibly didn't tell his wife – and the wife may well have not realized.

'Personal relationships were formed between young men and women out of loneliness and the need to be loved,' one British wife recalled of her own wartime affairs. As a twenty-four-year-old mother of an eighteen-month child, 'sheer terror' overtook her life when her husband was called up into the RAF and she was left alone to face the bombing raids on Manchester. One night she heard a German parachute landmine sweep over her roof and demolish nine houses in the next road as she huddled with her baby under the staircase. Like many others, 'Mary' is convinced that it was this brush with death that led her into an affair which she looks back on with few regrets and little guilt:

We lived in a world of uncertainty, wondering if we were going to survive from day to day. My husband was away in the RAF as an airgunner, and I'd conditioned myself to the fact that his lifespan was also limited and that our short, happy married life together was over. I lived in a vacuum of loneliness and fright as service in the army, navy, and air force claimed five of our personal friends whom I mourned as if they were my own family. When 1942 came in with the hit-and-run air raids, I began to despair that the war was ever going to end. It was in this frame of mind that fate took a hand in my affairs.

The Yanks arrived and set up camps near Manchester, bringing a wave of glamour, romance, and excitement that has never been experienced before or since. They were not welcomed by the British men, but to the English girls they were wonderful. All I knew about Americans was what I'd seen on the films, but Fields Hotel, within walking distance from my home, became the meeting place where GIs danced under soft lights. Eating in secluded corners with their girlfriends, the GIs were able to forget the war for a few hours. There I was introduced to an American army captain. He was tall with blonde hair and blue eyes. I thought at the time what a marvellous German officer he would make on the films. I felt rather embarrassed at his flattering remarks about my long hair and attractive appearance. I felt even more embarrassed when we danced the American way, cheek-to-cheek. Outside in the blackout, Rick took my hand, clicked his heels together and bowed to me, saying how much he'd enjoyed my company, then he walked down the path towards the waiting jeep. If I was expecting a goodnight kiss, I was surprised and a little disappointed. 'And they say the English are a cold race,' I thought, and I didn't think I would see Rick again.

One weekend, as I prepared myself for another lonely sit-in, an unexpected phone call from Rick made my heart jump with pleasure. He came around about dusk in a jeep carrying a holdall and bounced it on the kitchen table. 'There,' he said, 'take a peek.' It was full of tinned goods, butter, sugar, sweets, coffee, sheer nylons, and make-up – not forgetting cartons of cigarettes. He had also thoughtfully brought two bucket-loads of coal.

So began another part of my life on the home front – I shared my extra food with my neighbours and friends. If they wondered where it all came from, they tactfully never asked. It took a couple of weeks before Rick got around to kissing me good night. He asked me a lot of questions about my husband and married life, which I had to admit was a very happy one. I did, however, write and tell my husband about Rick. He was delighted that I'd found someone to give me a break and that Rick seemed a really decent chap.

With my mind free of guilt, I began to come alive again. It would be foolish of me to say that physical attraction never entered our lives: it did. With Rick, I knew it was love, but for me it was attraction and the need to hold on to someone. So it happened that we finally made love.

There was nothing cheap about our affair, and if Rick had my body, my heart was with my husband and somehow I didn't feel that I was doing anything wrong. Rick being a single man had fallen in love with a happily married woman, but he knew it was hopeless as far as I was concerned. I loved my husband too much to consider leaving him. Yet Rick and I were together for two years during the final stages of the war, until the evening when he was silent and withdrawn after he received orders to leave for Rome.

We said our goodbyes at the garden gate on 31 May 1945. As I looked at Rick's sad face, I asked myself whether the good times were over because I had fallen in love and lost him. One last kiss and he was gone. Then my husband returned home and we tried to resume our old way of life.

This particular couple succeeded, where many marriages failed, in reconciling themselves to wartime infidelities. With her husband's blessing Mary made a post-war visit to America, but when Rick embraced her on the New York dockside before she sailed for hom she suddenly knew that her great affair was over. 'How does one say goodbye to one so dear? Emotions shrink to a pinpoint and the impact hits you a few days later,' she remembered. 'I think we both knew that this was the final goodbye. As the *Queen Mary* moved off into the darkness, I stood on deck for what seemed like hours as New York disappeared from view. My war romance had reached its finale.'

Not all wartime love affairs proved so painless in their aftermath, as another British war bride pointed out:

During the war my husband committed bigamy and never again provided us with a home. It's very easy for some women to say, 'I didn't let the war destroy my marriage.' I tried not to let it destroy mine, but it takes two to make a marriage and if a man's responsibilities are taken from him, he soon finds it easy to let 'out of sight' be 'out of mind'.

The constancy of wives and sweethearts became a preoccupation for all servicemen and a gnawing anxiety for front-line soldiers in World War II anxiously awaiting every letter from home. For many newly-wed soldiers, the army itself became a sort of surrogate wife, as the GI cartoonist Bill Maudlin observed:

> There's the young guy who got married two weeks before shipping out, has been overseas for two years, and is desperately homesick. Some other guy will say to him, 'You wanna go home? Hell, you found a home in the army. You got your first pair of shoes and your first square meal in the army. You're living a clean, healthy, outdoor life, and you want to go back and get henpecked?'

Wartime separation of husbands and wives made it inevitable that the institution of marriage took the hardest blows. Even if the 'war bride' had been left pregnant, the foundations of these relationships were often too fragile to sustain the emotional needs of either partner through years of separation under conditions of danger and loneliness. How well the bonds of a wartime marriage stood up to the strain depended more on mutual affection and respect than on a solemn nuptial oath. 'Through all these troubled times, our love grew stronger,' asserted a housewife from Bristol who believed that 'those six and a half years apart strengthened what we felt for one another.'

Separation left wives in constant dread of news that their spouses had been killed in action. It added a heavy load to the burden of loneliness of wartime women. 'Suspended thus between the joy of living and the thought of dying, there were moments when a sombre mood descended upon our little group,' wrote a German girl before she heard her Luftwaffe fiancé had been shot down over France in 1940. 'All of a sudden life collapsed into a heap. Then slowly I was invaded by the image of a very tall man with straight blonde hair falling on to his forehead, who for all his charm and light-hearted bantering had always seemed perturbed by questions to which there were no answers.'

'A perfect marriage' was Mrs Dee Rueckert's inspiration to continue according to *Ladies Home Journal*, which featured her as the typical American war widow at the beginning of 1945. During their two-month separation she and her pilot husband had exchanged more than a hundred letters, with Dee posting three a day until he was killed on a pre-D-Day bombing mission. She refused to accept the fact of his death until, like many war widows struggling to raise a family on her £50 monthly pension, economic necessity forced her to take a job.

'At first nothing made sense; that you wre dead, that I was alive – I couldn't figure it out,' wrote the grief-stricken young wife of another American flyer in a love letter to her dead husband. 'When a boy like you dies there's always a tormenting "Why?" left in the hearts of those who loved him . . . By clinging to the past I've found a refuge from the future.'

Many romances which began in the frenzy of wartime left the couples waiting years for that longed-for wedding day. When Lieutenant Donald F. Sebald arrived in Britain with an American Liberator squadron late in 1942, he met and fell deeply in love with a WAAF nurse. 'She was very pretty, very vivacious, and very married. Her husband was an infantry officer in the British army serving in Burma. Our relationship was very enjoyable, but she kept it purely platonic. (It did happen that way at times despite the war.)' Not until 1952, when he returned to England as a reporter on assignment, did he succeed in tracking down his wartime WAAF. He eventually married her after a further courtship: 'Over the next five years I convinced her I was serious, honourable and lacking the more heinous of the masculine vices.'

Not all star-crossed wartime lovers managed to live happily ever after. One of the many romances that perished was that of Susan, who joined the WAAF after her brother was killed in Sicily in 1943. She recalled that her passionate romance with a New Zealander in the RAF lasted until he was posted to the Middle East shortly after they had become engaged, when he jilted her. 'The whole episode broke my heart and in my desperation I had an affair with a young Polish sailor. He begged me to marry him after I was expecting a baby. But I could not bear to do anything of the sort, even though he warned me that such a decision might ruin my life.'

Many British women, through loneliness and circumstance, broke social conventions and their husbands' hearts following the 'friendly invasion' of American troops in the year before D-Day. 'Our own servicemen were set aside for the Americans, who appeared more glamorous in every way because of the movies and their generosity with money,' recalled one British woman. 'There were fights between them and our men over girls. I knew of two young wives that left and divorced chaps they seemed to have been devoted to.'

Next to an enemy bullet or mortar shell, the receipt of a 'Dear John' letter from home confessing marital infidelity or desertion was the worst blow that could hit an infrantryman in a front line foxhole. A group of GIs in North Africa had organized a 'Brush-Off Club' whose admission qualification was to have been jilted. Most American girls interviewed in a December 1944 newspaper survey agreed, 'to jilt a soldier is a serious offence'; but one of the more forthright interviewees insisted, 'those guys over there aren't just shy-eyed sheep in a jeep'.

The war had also exposed many servicemen to romantic encounters with women of a different country and culture. One GI writer speculated that their experiences would probably have a profound impact on the post-war attitude to romantic love:

> In America, remember, a tension exists between the sexes. Human love is a disease for the isolation ward, not at all nice. Thus love in America is divided into the classifications of Having Sex and Getting Married. Neither has much to do with love. It was Having Sex which began to strike us in Naples as being so cold-blooded.

Soldiers were especially prone to yearnings for loved ones on the eve of battle, and the war endowed many men who fought in it with a clear perception both of their need and the meaning of love. Even in the most brutal of circumstances, there were times amidst the carnage and destruction when many men and women discovered affection at its intimate, tender, and romantic.

For many soldiers the emotional support came from the memory of the girl they left behind, whose battered photo they wore next to their heart as talisman. This linke to a loved one became especially important when the battle was going badly. Crouching in a trench behind the crumbling defences of the Third Reich, a German soldier poured his despair into a letter to his girlfriend:

> Dearest Liesl,
> I cannot describe to you how it all affects me. I have been looking at your picture and the tears began streaming from my eyes, I feared that my heart would break ... If I should be shot, Liesl darling, and I certainly hope that does not happen, all I can say is that I am sure that you will find another man who loves you as much as I do.

Not every soldier could count on the spiritual comfort of the girl he was fighting to get home for. 'I haven't got what you call a real girlfriend and on a night like this, it sure hurts,' confessed one GI to his parents in a letter before he embarked for the D-Day invasion. 'A guy gets lonely out here and should have somebody to want to come back to and share building a wonderful life together, hand in hand. And that means a girl you'd want to marry and have for the mother of your kids, and who would wait and pray for you on a night like this.'

'It is my contention,' reflected one GI, 'that when a man loves a woman, she always remains a vivid memory.' This particular staff sergeant's 'sensual nymph, with brown eyes and red-black hair', had been a tap-dancer from Spokane, whose memory haunted him before he went into action. 'Now that I may soon die on the battlefield nine years later, I realize more forcibly than ever that I am still in love with her.'

Even when they had found true love, servicemen had to battle against censorship and the often irregular military mails to sustain it. But just how eloquently this spiritual communion at a distance could be supported was shown by the letters written by men who sensed they would not return. 'Our love will never die. It shall be part of your life and mine, that will live on, no matter what may happen,' wrote an American fighter pilot to his wife before he took off on a secret mission over France in 1944. 'That love shall return to you some day, in some way, and you will perhaps not know it, but you will have a strange feeling of having known it before . . . I love you more than anything in life. I have loved you always and it was only a matter of time until fate brought us together. A million kisses, darling, I'll see you again – sometime, somewhere.'

The extensive personal testimony to the emotional impact of the War suggests that what men and women were fighting for had less to do with abstract notions of freedom or patriotism than with the need to protect the personal values represented by sweethearts, wives, and families. Sex, therefore, played an extensive role in the war experience. Whether it was pin-ups of Hollywood stars, well-thumbed pictures of 'the girl back home', 'Rosie the Riveter', the archetypal female factory workers, or women pilots, World War II acquired an undeniable feminine aspect.

2

CINDERELLA LEGIONS

When the barrage opens up to greet the raiding Huns,
Don't forget the girls out there, the girls behind the guns . . .

ATS 'Gunners' song

The position of women in the Services today is a
significant measure of changes both in status
and public opinion which have come about
during recent years. History has many records of
valour and endurance shown by individual
women in military operations. But these were
heroines of romance, whose activities were
regarded as wholly remote from a women's
recognized path.

British Parliamentary Committee, 1942

AT 11 A.M. ON THE FATEFUL SUNDAY of 3 September 1939, it was a female army auxiliary telegraphist who transmitted the British Government's formal declaration of war to the German Foreign Ministry in Berlin. Five years earlier, the Emergency Service formed by the Women's Legion had launched a campaign that paved the way for the conscription of women into uniformed service in a total war.

Long before Joan of Arc's military exploits had made her the most celebrated female figure of medieval Europe, wars had inspired some women to disguise themselves as men to participate in the quintessentially masculine world of soldiering. The American Revolutionary War made a heroine of Deborah Sampson, who successfully disguised herself as a man to fight the British redcoats until she was wounded. General George Washington unwittingly struck a blow for female as well as American liberation when the Continental army recruited hundreds of female water-carriers, whose collective *nom de guerre* of 'Molly Pitcher' was immortalized by Margaret Corbin's command of her husband's gun after he was killed during the battle at Fort Washington on 16 November 1776. Another celebrated eighteenth-century female warrior was Anne Talbot, 'a damsel that followed the drum', who as John Taylor served as both a footsoldier and a sailor in the Napoleonic War.

The Crimean War in 1851 brought the first grudging recognition of women's military role when the single-minded determination of Florence Nightingale broke down male prejudice against female nursing auxiliaries – but only after the public had been reassured that the men 'never forgot the respect due to our sex and position'. A decade later, during the American Civil War, an estimated three thousand two hundred women volunteered as nurses with the Union and Confederate armies despite fierce resistance by some military surgeons who objected to the very idea of 'a delicate refined woman assisting a rough soldier to the close stool, or supplying him with a bed-pan or adjusting the knots in a T-bandage'.

Artillery warfare brought a vast increase in the numbers of wounded and established female nursing auxiliaries as an essential part of the military establishment. By 1914, British veteran volunteer nurses of the Boer War, the First Aid Nursing Yeomanry (FANYS), were the first women to cross to France to help run the ambulance and hospital services. By 1918, eleven thousand British women were serving long hours, often under arduous conditions, in the uniforms of Queen Alexandra's Imperial Military Nursing Service, The British Red Cross, and St John's Ambulance Brigade. But throughout World War I the army staff still resisted anything that smacked of 'petticoat soldiering', although women's voluntary organizations supplied the kitchen staff for army canteens.

It was not until 1917, however, that the War Office reluctantly conceded the army had a place for female auxiliaries. Even then, there was considerable bureaucratic soul-searching among its senior officers as to whether breast pockets on women's uniforms would inflame male passions and encourage public speculation about the lax morality of the corps. Primness won the day, and those girls who 'did their bit' for King and Country in the final year of the war paraded in jackets with no breast pockets and khaki skirts that decently concealed female ankles.

The fourteen cooks and a waitress who crossed the Channel to France early in 1917 were volunteers in Queen Mary's Army Auxiliary Corps. A year later it had grown into a fifty-seven thousand-strong force of telephonists and drivers as well as canteen staff, a fully-fledged military force that proudly marched in the 1918 Victory Parades under the WAAC banner of the Women's Army Auxiliary Corps. Although initially resistant to these females in uniform performing anything other than traditional kitchen and nursing duties, within months the army had been sufficiently impressed to assign women to administrative and communications roles, thereby releasing an estimated twelve thousand more men for the front line. The Women's Royal Navy Service had also been formed and by the end of the war it and the Women's Royal Air Force had each recruited five thousand females into their ranks.

The WAAC volunteers remained with the British Army for two years after the war to assist with the Allied occupation of Germany, but by 1920 they had all been paid off. The politicians paid their debts and expressed the nation's gratitude for the service given by the female auxiliaries by extending the franchise to women over thirty. Most of the veterans, who were in their twenties, were excluded from the promised reward. Many women wanted to continue some military role but were shut out because the generals and admirals subscribed to the popular myth that now the 'war to end all wars' had been fought, the nation would never have to mobilize again.

Some British women were more alert than the politicians to the military threat of Hitler's rise to power, and in 1934 the World War I female veterans in women's branches of the British Legion began voluntarily organizing what they called the Voluntary Emergency Service. The War Office and Air Ministry provided encouragement and instructors for summer training camps. In the aftermath of the national emergency precipitated by the 1938 Czechoslovak crisis, when war clouds were gathering over the Continent, the Government formally recognized their potential contribution by establishing the female volunteers as the Auxiliary Territorial Service. In the spring of 1939, as the ATS began recruiting in earnest, the Admiralty revived the WRNS and the RAF formed its Women's Auxiliary Air Force, so when Germany invaded Poland in September, twenty thousand trained and drilled female auxiliaries stood ready to play their part in 'manning' the nation's sea, land, and air defence systems.

An original volunteer member of this 'very select group' of women, who considered themselves already 'at arms' when war broke out – even though King's Regulations strictly forbade the ATS carrying guns – was ATS Private Oxley. While training she had endured summer downpours under canvas with 'girl-guide-like' enthusiasm, although many units like hers still had not been issued with their battledress.

> The first uniforms did not arrive until six months later, just one hour before our first ceremonial parade. We did not know which was whose, so we quickly used safety pins to make them fit. There was no time to clean the brass and we had to wear our shirts tucked into the most unbecoming, unfeminine KHAKI BLOOMERS, which we called 'The Biggest Bloomer of All Time'. But we made that first parade, even though our feet bled after two hours of marching in the heavy shoes.

Women's khaki uniforms in World War II were equipped with the breast pockets that were considered too risqué in 1917, but they were designed by army supply tailors who made few concessions to the anatomial demands of the female figure. They proved uncomfortable and very unfeminine – externally and internally. Two years later, when some 65,000 recruits had been issued with 195,000 pairs of dreary khaki bloomers, the image and the reputation of the ATS was falling when compared with the dashing elegance of the WAAF and the smart navy blue uniforms of the more exclusive Wrens.

Amy, a young British girl, volunteered for the Auxiliary Terri- torial Service in December 1941, was dismayed by how shocked her parents, staunch Christians with the London City Missionary Society, were when she announced she had joined up. The ATS had a 'bad reputation' because of the popular belief in their loose behaviour with the lads in the army. Like thousands of other young British women who volunteered for military service during the Blitz, Amy nonetheless defied her parents and gave up her well paid job as a secretary. She was determined to hit back at Hitler for the death of her boyfriend at Dunkirk. Although she admitted to 'being a bit of a rebel', Amy was totally unprepared, like most girls from sheltered homes, for her first taste of army life in draughty barracks on the edge of the Yorkshire moors:

> I can remember the shock we had when they came around with the – drink? Washing-up water?? – No, army soup!! That really turned our stomachs. Was this because the camp was still being run by men, we wondered? We were awakened at 6 a.m. next day and lined up outside to be marched off to breakfast across the barrack square. We then had to go and fetch our uniforms. What confusion. The stores were once again manned by men! The first counter we walked past had a sergeant standing by sizing us up – literally. Small, medium, or large were the only categories and we received a kit bag full of goodies according to the size he had given. When we went back to our barrack room to sort them, what a laugh! We first tried on everything as issued: bra, suspender belt – both in old fashioned pink cotton and very coarse. Vests, khaki 'silk' locknit knickers with long elasticated legs – we jokingly called them our 'Man Catchers'. The shirts came with separate collars and we also were issued with blue striped flanelette pyjamas. Then an orgy of swapping started in an endeavour to get a reasonable fit.

The first weeks of basic military training proved a far tougher ordeal for women than men. In bleak, ill-heated barracks they shared the tearful miseries of homesickness and nursed feet swollen from marching and legs aching from drilling in heavy shoes. The army regarded discipline and drill as the prerequisite for all soldiers, regardless of their sex. Long sessions of physical education and games were considered the necessary antidote to 'lecture-room staleness'. The instructions the girls were given covered such subjects as how to survive a gas attack, social – the euphemism for sexual – hygiene, security, and service procedures – hardly subjects calculated to inspire the female imagination.

After a month of parade-ground drill and lectures, the women were considered sufficiently conditioned in service routine to be passed-out as fit to serve on bases as clerical assistants and carrying out traditional 'women's work' as cooks and telephonists. Those taking up specialized technical trades, soon to include motor transport, welding, radar maintenance, or radio and electrical service, were sent on after their passing-out parade to special schools for a further course of training.

Officer candidates were selected from the ranks for a three-month training course – a policy that gave the ATS in particular a cohesion quite different from the class-bound caste of the regular British army. The ranks of the women's auxiliary services were to prove levellers of the traditional British social system, even though most of those who became officers tended to be firmly middle class. A WAAF officer candidate, a former journalist from the BBC, commented:

> There was a Cambridge girl, an elementary school teacher, an art student, two Harrods shop assistants, a child of eighteen fresh from finishing school and presentation at court, and an amusing collar-and-tie type who'd created records on the motorcycle, could take automobiles to pieces and held a pilot's licence. The general atmosphere inclined to heartiness, especially when the flyer was about.

To the surprise of most men, many of their female comrades in arms found the endless drilling a great stimulation – perhaps because it was one area of military life where women were on equal terms with men. 'I was very proud when chosen to be the marker in church parades,' recalled one ATS corporal, 'as the only female to walk out on the square with the men.' Other recruits found the mind-numbing discipline made life unbearable: barking army sergeant majors showed little understanding for the disoriented and apprehensive girls who, as one recalled, had 'to be made into what you were not in a very short time'. Yet the close comradeship fostered by the harsh disciplines of army life helped many women to band together in the face of an alien world and share the problems and privations of barrack life.

One officer recruit found the military to be a 'cross between boarding school and prison' where orders were 'given with an air of God, from a burning cloud, and however impossible and preposterous, they had to be carried out.' This independent-minded WAAF engineered her discharge after a bossy officer with 'large bosom and behind, in a tight uniform that made her look like overblown balloons' had ordered a particularly pointless exercise:

> We were made to march over the innocent English countryside like young Prussians, and when we got rather out of rhythm negotiating a twisting downhill loose stony bit of lane with hedges entwined with blackberry brambles overhanging just at the height of our faces, we were loudly abused by the Senior Section Leader and commanded to whistle 'Hang Out the Washing on the Siegfried Line' to keep in step. The clockwork performance of this same SS leader was such that you simply didn't dare look at her face for fear of having hysterics.

But the majority of women recruits were sufficiently fired by patriotism and the determination to prove they could be as good as the next man to keep going. The evacuation from France, the Battle of Britain, and the Blitz provided the female population with an opportunity to prove their fighting mettle. They drew their inspiration from the shining courage of the 1300 army nurses who had endured the ordeal of the Dunkirk evacuation alongside the men of the British Expeditionary Force in May 1940. A wounded soldier paid this tribute to their bravery and devotion under fire:

> Out on that dreadful beach, with the sun pouring down on them, the German planes continually overhead and shells bursting all the time, they have worked without stopping for days past. If they have slept, they have done so on their feet, attacked by German planes and even tanks, with machine-gun bullets whistling all around. I have seen them crawling into the open and dragging wounded men to shelter beneath sand dunes. I saw one party of them dressing wounded who were just lying out in the open. A plane began bombing. They just lay down over their patients and continued bandaging. They have fetched food and water to assist the men. Angels is the only word you

can use to describe them. I have seen some of them killed as they have gone about their work. We have asked them to go back to the rescue ships, but they have refused. Each of them has said, 'We shall go when we have finished this job – there's plenty of time, so don't worry about us.'

The same coolness under fire was displayed by the women of the ATS transport detachments and signals corps during the evacuation of the British Expeditionary Force from France. One unit of bilingual switchboard operators continued manning the army's Paris exchange until the final hours before the Germans marched into the French capital. The fall of France marked the beginning of the Battle of Britain, when WAAF plotters joined with the female spotters of the Royal Observer Corps serving in lonely hill-top outposts to provide the vital links which enabled RAF Fighter Command to deploy its slender resources to meet the might of the Luftwaffe.

Cool heads were essential for the WAAF fighter controllers and plotters who homed the pilots by radio on to the German bombers. 'We were often too tired to eat after those shifts of plotting, where any mistake in the precise movement of the enemy would have meant disaster,' was how one of them recalled the fast-changing aerial dogfights that she tracked on the board from the messages flooding into her headphones.

These were the girls who were brought face to face with sudden death when their circuit went dead, indicating that another young fighter pilot had been 'killed in action'. Leading Aircraft Woman Ruth F. Martin summed up her emotions in a touching piece of wartime verse called 'HELLO 226 – THIS IS FLYING CONTROL, DO YOU READ ME?' dedicated to one of the RAF's Rhodesian squadrons:

We grew to know those boys so well as we spoke over the intercom,
Scanning the skies for their return, notching the landings, one by one.

In August 1940, WAAF communications personnel found themselves in the firing line after Reichsmarshal Hermann Goering had ordered his Luftwaffe to turn the full weight of its assault on the RAF fighter bases. Many were to be decorated for bravery after they stayed at their posts to continue relaying vital information despite the falling bombs. After Corporal Joan Avis-

Hearn's plotting hut was blown apart by a near-miss she continued to send reports, the first of which was, 'The course of the enemy bombers is only too apparent to me because the bombs are almost dropping on my head.'

The Luftwaffe's failure to secure air superiority for an invasion of Britain forced Goering to switch targets again, and in September German bombers unleashed an attack on Britain's cities. The ATS and WAAF units who helped man the barrage balloons that were sent aloft to snag low-flying enemy dive-bombers now found themselves in the front-line of the unrelenting German assault as they heaved on the ropes and strained to lift the 120lb ballast blocks that controlled the whale-like silver blimps. 'You can't hit back at 'em. You've just got to take it,' was how one member of a balloon unit described downing a German plane:

> 'Christ,' says one of our airmen. 'He's going to machine-gun us.' 'He isn't,' says I. 'He's going to hit the cable.' And he did. He went smack into it. There was a crash and the cable went through the wing just like a grocer's wire goes through cheese. We celebrated our first Jerry with a nice cup of tea. Then of course we realized we'd have to put up another in place of *Annie*.

Britain's air defences relied heavily throughout the Blitz on female bravery and co-ordination. ATS units were assigned to plotting and maintenance roles on the radar units, searchlights, and anti-aircraft gun batteries that sprouted up in the winter of 1940–41 around major cities, ports, and military installations. 'We do not, as many people think, man the guns,' explained a member of one of these batteries in a wartime press release:

> The gun teams are all men, and always will be, for the simple reason that women have not the physical strength to load and unload the heavy shells. The part played by the ATS is to man the instruments which enable the guns to notify the battery of the approach of an aircraft, and to plot their position as they approach.

The British Government still feared an adverse public reaction if it was known that women were involved too directly in the action, though a bureaucrat acknowledged that a fit woman can fire a rifle better than an unhealthy man, and what could be more military than managing the ack-ack guns?' Official policy began to change after the commanding officer of the first mixed 'ack-ack' battery reported unhesitatingly, 'The girls cannot be beaten in action, and in my opinion they are definitely better than the men on the instruments . . . and although they are not supposed to learn to use the rifle, they are as keen as anything to do so.'

'In the beginning, the idea of mixed units was viewed with great suspicion, but as time went on attitudes mellowed,' recalled Joyce Peters, a member of that first unit, whose guns were set up near Richmond and which included 'girls from leading public schools working well with ex-factory lasses to beat the Germans'. She recalled that 'we must have been worthy of note' because Churchill himself paid the unit a visit in January 1941 during an air raid. Suitably impressed, he conceded that to foster *esprit de corps* in the ATS, all such units could take the coveted title of 'Gunners'. Their 'immense importance' was acknowledged with the Prime Minister's subsequent decision to step up female recruiting for 'maintenance of a large number of batteries with the smallest number of men'.

Early in 1941, a contingent of fifty-four ATS girls had completed secret training as operators of the giant searchlights used in conjunction with the anti-aircraft batteries to pinpoint enemy bombers. The dangers of becoming targets for German fighters during the frenzied activity of an enemy raid did not deter women from volunteering for the 'Searchlight Battalions', where they proved highly effective at differentiating enemy from friendly aircraft. According to offical reports, 'the standard reached was higher than most men'. The female telephonists who transcribed the Morse code from the central gun control had to be particularly diligent because 'if one miscounts the pips it means a wrong plot being made and perhaps a target being missed.'

The ATS girls who proudly wore the 'Gunners' and 'Searchlight' shoulder flashes were the elite of Britain's female forces, their morale sustained by plenty of action during the Blitz which they cheerfully described as 'hard work and great fun'. Another member of a mixed ack-ack crew remembered 'rushing across the field in the early hours, dressing as we ran and falling face down in a cow pat. We plotted a hundred or more enemy aircraft, not smelling of violets. But luck was with us that morning because we brought down a German bomber.'

'We had to stay at the site until it was in working order again, often all night, working by the light of a small torch,' remembered a WAAF electrician of the nights when 'A bomber's moon' heralded a certain German raid. One WAAF mechanic recalled the hectic drives between sites along twisted country lanes in a van affectionately known as a 'Tilly'. They were responsible for maintaining the radar on the batteries that were strung out between Bournemouth and Poole. 'Conditions at those gun-sites were often primitive, still all-male, and many problems were caused to us girls as regards toilet facilities. Often we had to go "picking blackberries".' But even primitive toilet facilities on winter nights could not chill the *esprit de corps* of the girls on the ack-ack batteries. Steaming mugs of tea warmed the bitter winter nights, and while they waited for the next wave of bombers they celebrated their victories with the final refrain of their battle song:

> When you hear the boom of fire, and see the sky alight,
> Remember the ATS on duty in the front line of the fight.

The ack-ack barrage, however, hindered rather than prevented most of the German bombers getting through to rain death and destruction on Britain's cities. During the 'Baedeker Raids' in the spring of 1941, few centres of population of any size escaped the attention of the Luftwaffe. Then women in the Civil Defence Corps and the Women's Volunteer Service joined with those in the fire services to defy the bombs, douse the conflagrations, and dig the injured from the rubble.

At the height of the Blitz, a sixteen-year-old girl despatch rider on a pedal bicycle who was a member of the Air Raid Precaution Service became the youngest female recipient of the George Medal. Many women auxiliaries were decorated for their bravery during the German air assault on the British home front. Wren Third Officer Pamela McGeorge was among those who received the British Empire Medal for the cool courage she had shown in delivering her despatches to the commander-in-chief, running through a stick of bursting bombs after an explosion had blown her motorcycle from under her during a heavy raid on Plymouth dockyard.

Yet traditional military chauvinism denied women the Victoria Cross, awarded only for acts of 'conspicuous gallantry' in the face of the enemy, which was interpreted to mean on the field of battle. The George Cross, the civilian equivalent of the VC, was awarded to just four women during the whole war – including, exceptionally, one servicewoman, Corporal Joan Daphne Mary

Pearson. She was a WAAF administrative officer who in May 1940 had shielded a crashed RAF pilot from a 120lb bomb that exploded thirty yards away, saving his life.

The contribution made by Britain's uniformed women had become so vital to the national defence that in April 1941 the Government introduced parliamentary legislation to give female auxiliaries full military status as members of the armed forces of the Crown. A year later the problem of war manpower was to become so acute that Churchill's War Cabinet decided to make Britain the first country ever to order a general female conscription, which gave women the choice of enlisting in auxiliary services or the Women's Land Army, or accepting direction into Government-approved jobs.

If the Blitz put British servicewomen on the home front into the firing line and earned them full military status, the German invasion of the Soviet Union thrust Russian women into military combat. The Russians had set a precedent during World War I when a woman officer in the Don Cossacks became celebrated as 'Yellow Martha' because of her blonde locks. When the British suffragette leader Mrs Pankhurst inspected a female battalion in July 1917, she called it, 'the greatest event in the world's history'. But although some of the women saw action, it was not official Russian policy to put women into battle until it became a dire necessity during World War II.

In the six months after 21 July 1941, when Hitler unleashed Operation Barbarossa, three million Soviet soldiers had been taken prisoner. Leningrad had been circled in the steel grip of the Wehrmacht, and German tanks were pounding their way towards Moscow. Russian women had inevitably been caught up in military operations during the disastrous retreat, and millions had been mobilized into the industrial plants which had hurriedly been relocated east of the Urals. Thousands of Soviet wives and mothers volunteered to become transport drivers, while others joined the air-raid militia and many became nurses.

The Red Air Force was in desperate straits: most of its aircraft and pilots had been shot out of the sky by the Luftwaffe. Female aviators had already been called up to help train fresh pilots when the Soviet High Command, facing a desperate struggle for survival, decided in October 1941 to begin training women pilots for combat. Marina Raskova, Russia's Amelia Earhart and a Hero of the Soviet Union for her pre-war record-breaking flights, broadcast an appeal on Radio Moscow for experienced women flyers to volunteer for action. Two thousand applications were received, and three air regiments of three squadrons of ten aircraft each were planned, in which all the personnel – pilots, bombardiers, navigators, fitters, and mechanics – would be female.

A thousand eager recruits arrived in Moscow to begin training in November 1941. As one of these volunteers recounted in Bruce Myles' book *Night Witches*, they were confronted by Major Raskova, 'her blue eyes fiercely selective'. She offered each a last chance to withdraw, after reminding each of them of the unprecedented demands and dangers they would face in aerial combat missions:

> The girls I do choose must understand beyond any doubt whatsoever that they will be fighting against men, and they must themselves fight like men. If you're chosen you may not be killed – you may be burned so your own mother would not recognize you. You may be blinded. You may lose a hand, a leg. You will lose your friends. You may be captured by the Germans. Do you really want to go through with this?

Not a single girl withdrew, but the fact that the Red Air Force was making no concessions to their femininity was confirmed the next day when they reported to Moscow's Zhukovsky Academy to pick up their uniforms. 'We didn't know whether to laugh or cry,' recalled one of these recruits as they picked through bundles of surplus boots, worn tunics, trousers, and coats. 'Like all young girls we were pretty fashion conscious, even though there was a war on. Most of us had slim waists and, though we didn't expect uniforms tailored for us by a Paris couturier, we hoped that they had made some little concessions to the fact that we were a different shape from most soldiers.' After working all night cutting and stitching, the would-be fighter and bomber crews left for their training base at Engles on the Volga feeling like 'clowns at the Moscow State Circus. God knows what the Germans would have thought.'

The Germans would discover to their cost that women at the controls of a warplane were every bit as deadly as men. Many of these fiercely determined women had lost their homes and families in the enemy advance, and their fighting spirit was roused by a burning desire for revenge. A unique camaraderie grew up between them, recalled a survivor, with 'surprisingly little bitchiness of the sort you might expect when girls are flung together like that'.

> The girls learned to become real soldiers through the experiences they had in combat. That was the real character builder. I know discipline is important in any military force. But really there was never any serious problem of that sort in the girls' regiments. There was so much mutual respect that people just tended to get on with the job without having to be ordered. Of course you need people in command and we had that. But a group of really motivated females does not, I think, need quite the same sort of rigid discipline that men do.

After the melting snows of the spring of 1942 led the Germans to resume the fierce offensive that threatened to rout the Red Army, training was completed and the female aircrews were assigned to their regiments – a third to fighters and the remainder to bombers. They determined to fight and kill like men, yet as one of them recalled, 'none of us wanted to act like men or look like men when we left our aircraft'. Repeatedly they found it necessary to remind themselves 'all the time that we were girls'.

Many of the female aircrew clung to their femininity by defying regulations to cut their hair short. They dyed their white silk under-helmets pastel shades and put on light make-up and pale lipstick before taking off for combat. Their fighter and bomber planes had to be modified because they could not reach the rudder pedals without special blocks, and seat cushions had to be raised to allow them to have all-round vision in the cockpit. Just manipulating the cumbersome and obsolescent YAK bombers proved hard work, often requiring the combined leverage of both pilot and co-pilot just to yank back the control stick to take-off.

When it came to actual combat, most of the female pilots lost any initial fear in the intense concentration and exhilaration demanded by battle. One pilot admitted 'retching as I taxied out for take-off. I felt like switching off and getting out . . . But it was strange – the moment the aircraft left the ground and I raised that undercarriage, all my nerves disappeared'. Another recalled, 'There really wasn't much to think about,' the first time she took off for combat and flew straight into a stream of enemy bombers:

> I flicked the guard off the gun button and pushed the nose straight down. I started firing right away and, keeping the power full on, just

charged straight through the middle of the formation. It was terrifying. I passed very close to one of them as I dived through, then I pulled the stick back and zoomed up above them again, and did the same thing again.

One of the Russian women bombardiers recalled her 'fantastic sense of achievement' in making her first raid on the German advance headquarters at Voroshilovgrad. The YAK PO-2 biplanes crewed by the women of the 588th Night Bomber Regiment were so antiquated they could not have survived daytime raids. Even at night their noisy engines had to be cut and the bombing run made in a shallow gliding dive so as not to alert the German mobile flak batteries. This technique required cool nerve and teamwork between the pilots and their bombardiers:

> I could clearly see the buildings and I knew that if I hit the target, Luba, behind me, would be able to aim at my fires that I started. The Germans hadn't seen me coming because of the gliding approach, but now the searchlights came on and the flak started coming up. I realized, as I got more experienced, that this was indeed light opposition, but on that first night it seemed pretty terrifying to me. I didn't want to spoil my aim so I just flew straight on through the explosions until I was right over the target. The airplane bucked in the blast from some explosions, but we kept on flying. Then I yanked the release wire and dived away from the searchlights and steered for home. I saw flames coming from one of the buildings and thought that Luba would have a beacon to aim at.

When two of their bombers failed to return from that first mission the excitement that they were 'really going to show the men what we were made of' was lost in general grief at the death of the crews. But battle-reaction soon hardened the girls to the dangers of combat and cemented the comradeship in the bombing group. Flying up to ten sorties a night back and forth across the front lines during the desperate climactic months of the battles around Stalingrad in the autumn of 1943, the Germans soon came to respect the courage and skill of the Russian women they dubbed 'The Night Witches'.

The Soviet women's contribution to their country's all-out battle for survival was heavily embellished by Stalin's propaganda machine, with the intention of both rallying the Russian people and persuading his British and American allies to open a second front in Europe. A celebrated girl-sniper, who had reportedly shot no fewer than 309 German soldiers while fighting with the Red Army on the Dnieper Front, was sent on a well-publicized tour of the United States.

Throughout the summer of 1943, American newspapers and magazines featured the heroic exploits of other Soviet military heroines, giving the impression that women and men were fighting alongside one another all along the eastern front. The reality was less spectacular, if no less heroic, for those individual women were not officially in front-line Red Army units but were guerillas operating behind the German lines. Nor, as the testimony of some of the veteran female pilots reveals, had the Soviet military come to terms with the female warriors in its midst.

'We were to have equality in every possible sense, though in reality we had to struggle for that in some cases when we got to the front,' recalled one of the woman pilots. None of them faced a greater initial resistance than a stunning blonde with grey eyes and winning smile called Lily Litvak. The commanding officer of the unit to which she was initially posted near Stalingrad in August 1943 refused to let her fly with his men and ordered her to seek an immediate transfer. But Lieutenant Litvak used her considerable charm to plead for just one chance to prove her combat skill. The sceptical Red Air Force commander could not resist, and Lily was given a plane to show what she could do. After a dogfight in which she skilfully out-manoeuvred a German to share the 'kill' of a Messerschmitt 109, Lieutenant Litvak removed all doubts about a woman's ability to fight in combat. She was welcomed to a permanent place in the squadron.

Her male comrades, however, were probably behind one practical joke which terrified Lily's female wing-mate. While on patrol, ten thousand feet above the river Don, she discovered a mouse. 'I know it sounds crazy – a fighter pilot frightened by a mouse – but I'd always had this fear of mice,' Olga Yemshokova recalled years later. 'And particularly now it was sitting on my lap looking up at me, in that tiny cockpit.' She admitted she 'could feel her flesh creeping' as she opened the cockpit and flung the little furry creature out into the slipstream.

During the next ten months, Lily Litvak led a charmed life as she out-flew and out-fought German pilots over the eastern front to become a Soviet fighter 'ace' as well as the focus of romantic rivalry between many of the men who flew with her. But Lily left no-one in any doubt that she had fallen in love with the handsome Lieutenant Alexi Salomaten, with whom she had flown 'tail' in her first combat mission. Such personal relationships were strictly discouraged in the mixed Red Air Force regiments. Women were deliberately quartered in a distant part of the airfield, even if this meant they had to live in converted cowsheds. But no regulations could prevent many of the female aircrew from forming emotional attachments with the men with whom they shared the dangers of battle.

'Lily told me that it was agony up there sometimes when Alexi was being attacked. But of course it gave each of them an incentive to fight really well,' remembered her mechanic, Ina Pasportnikova. 'Far from their love for each other affecting their concentration, I think it helped. Lily had always shown the sort of aggression you need to be a good fighter pilot. But her love for Alexi was the thing that turned her into a killer.'

Lily Litvak survived a burst of German cannon fire in which she sustained serious leg wounds. The encounter left her with a limp and sharpened her killer instinct, which hardened into a driving obsession after Alexi Salomaten died in a crash. Shortly afterwards she claimed her tenth victim, a famous German 'ace'. He had the misfortune to survive to be confronted with the pilot who had ended his career. The Luftwaffe hero refused to believe he had been out-fought by a woman until Lily icily explained the manoeuvres in the action that had brought him down. 'The German's whole attitude, even his physical appearance, changed,' reported an eyewitness to the confrontation. 'He was forced to concede in the end that no-one except the pilot who had beaten him could possibly have known, move by move, exactly how the fight had gone. There was no question of saluting the victor. He could not meet her eye. To have been shot down by a woman was more than he could bear.'

Only two more victories remained for the legendary 'Rose of Stalingrad'. Lieutenant Litvak was herself shot down and failed to bale out when her fighter, decorated with its white rose emblems, invited a mass attack by a swarm of German Messerschmitt 109s. Her final letter to her mother in Moscow provides a chilling insight into the psychological strain that a woman fighter faced at World War II's sharpest end: 'Battle life has swallowed me completely. I can't seem to think of anything but the fighting'. Combat hardened feminine sensibilities.

Galia Boordina also felt the brutalizing effect of killing. She took part in the titanic aerial actions of 1943 over the Kursk battlefield, in which some four thousand aircraft were locked in the fiercest air-to-air combat of the whole war:

> The sky was so full of aircraft in such a small area of airspace that it was terrifying. German and Soviet fighters were whirling and diving everywhere. You would be involved in a fight with another aircraft and a couple of dogfights would be taking place in between yours, it seemed. The risks of collision were enormous – even with your own side. It was a complete melée, and most of the aircraft were flying at very high speed. I broke out of the fight briefly to gain height and look for a target. I dived down and pulled up underneath a Messerschmitt 109 and raked it with machine-gun and cannon fire. It fell away immediately, burning. I had shot down other Germans before that – a bomber and a transport – but that was my first fighter. I didn't feel any pity for the man I killed. When it's kill or be killed, you don't feel that sort of thing. I preferred not to see the faces of an enemy. Once when I was attacking a bomber I got close enough to see the features of a gunner, and I remembered that it was other human beings we were firing our guns at.

For the first time, the mechanization of fighting weapons had made it possible for women to engage men in combat on more or less equal terms. At the controls of a plane, female pilots proved by their battle records to have mastered the mental discipline of battle as well as the flying skills necessary to overwhelm their male opponents. Soviet female aircrews were credited with taking part in over four thousand operational sorties and a hundred and twenty-five aerial combats that accounted for thirty-eight kills.

Russian women also played an important role in the Red Army. There was female conscription, but not to combat regiments. But so total was the conflict in the Soviet Union that the women who played a leading role in army communications, transport regiments, and medical duties often found themselves swept up in front-line action. This was the case for Assistant Surgeon Pavlova, who assumed command of a convoy of food and medical supplies when it was attacked by the Germans. With a detachment of Red Army soldiers she led a surprise attack that wiped out a German infantry regiment.

Some women engaged in combat in the Soviet armoured regiments, which had suffered very high casualties during the German assault. Female truck and tractor drivers were recruited from the collective farms for duty behind the front test-driving and delivering tanks. It was therefore a short step to the 1943 decision to alleviate the acute shortage of trained male tank drivers by calling on these experienced women to volunteer for front-line duty. In the final year of the war some of them were being promoted to commanders.

The most celebrated of these female 'tankers' was Sergeant Maria Oktyabr'skaya, a resilient Ukranian who was thirty-nine years old when her husband was killed in 1941. She volunteered as a driver behind the battlefront and saw her first combat in October 1943 as the driver of a T-34 tank on the Vitebsk sector of the front, when she knocked out a German anti-tank gun by crushing it under her machine's tracks. A year of almost continuous combat was ended when she was blown up while navigating her tank through a minefield. Oktyabr'skaya was hauled out of the burning tank but later died. She was elevated into a national hero after being posthumously awarded the Order of Lenin.

The Germans made propaganda out of the photographs of the dead bodies of these doughty female fighters, slanted to portray the Soviets as so desperate that they had to force women into the front line – yet another example of the shockingly barbaric face of the inhuman Bolshevist regime. This mirrored Hitler's oft-repeated injunction, 'no woman to bear arms', which right up until the final year of the war denied German women any direct military role, except as civilian adminstrative 'helpers', the *Helferinnen*.

The Fuehrer's determination to keep women out of an effective service role was a paradox in such a highly militarized state as Nazi Germany. Nevertheless, even before war broke out the *Helferinnen* had become an indispensable component of the growing administrative arm of the Wehrmacht. They were, however, denied military status and rank despite wearing uniforms patterned on the style and colour of the armed force to which they were attached. They came under military orders but were designated officially as 'noncombatants' under the Hague Convention. A directive of July 1942 defined the role of the *Helferinnen* organizations as little more than to provide uniformed female clerical assistants and switchboard operators, limited to the support roles that British women had carried out in World War I:

> In numbers women who are trained for office work, telephonists, etc.
> are needed especially in the areas outside the Reich to replace soldiers
> who are urgently required for active service at the fronts. It is the will
> of the Fuehrer that all German women who will be far from their
> homeland, helping the German armed forces, will be given every care
> and protection to make their tasks easier to accomplish . . . On no
> account will they be involved in any type of military operation. A
> woman soldier does not belong to our National-Socialistic ideal of
> womanhood.

As World War II progressed and the Allies advanced to liberate German-occupied territory, the Wehrmacht found it increasingly difficult to adhere to the 'National-Socialistic ideal' for protecting its '*Blitzmadchen*', as the *Helferinnen* were popularly known from their lightning-flash sleeve insignia. An OKW directive issued in November 1944 which called for the repatriation of all *Helferinnen* to the relative security of the fatherland could not be obeyed because an 'indeterminable' number were reported as missing in France, having ignored 'timely orders to retreat'.

Hitler's belated decision at the end of 1943 to mobilize all resources for 'total war' brought demands from the High Command for a relaxation of the strict rules that prevented women taking part in military activities so as to release more soldiers for duty at the front. The Luftwaffe responded to the heavy Allied air raids on the Reich by establishing the *Flakwaffenhelferinnenin* (Women's Anti-Aircraft Service) to assist with the operation of the radar detection and fighter control centres of their expanding air defensive system.

The *Luftwaffenhelferinnen* (Women's Air Force Auxiliary) was expanded to reach a peak strength of a hundred and thirty thousand. As the air assault on the Reich built up, an increasing proportion of the female population were recruited into the RAD (*Reicharbeidodienst* – Reichs Labour Service) and the *Luftwaffenensatz* for duty in the radar stations, fighter control network, and anti-aircraft batteries. By the end of 1944, the raids became so severe that Hitler was persuaded to authorize a limited conscription of German women to take over entire responsibility for manning the searchlight defence system.

The army's *Stabshelferinninen* (Staff Assistants) and *Nachricht-*

enhelferinnen (Communications Assistants) already made up a body of office workers and telephone personnel a quarter of a million strong. Over a hundred thousand uniformed women were serving *Luftwaffenhelferinnen*, in the *Flugmeldienst* (Air Warning Service); *Fernsprechen und Fernschriebbetriebsdienst* (Telephone and Teletype Service) and the *Flakwaffhelferinnen* (Anti-Aircraft Auxiliary). In addition, the *Kriegsmarine* and the *Waffen-SS* had parallel *Helferinnen* organizations for administrative and office duties.

The Nazi policy towards the role of women in total war had taken a dramatic shift. Six months earlier the Fuehrer, severely shaken by the success of the Allied invasion and by the bomb explosion that nearly cost him his life, authorized Dr Goebbels to announce the formation of a *Wermachtshilferinnenkorps* (Women's Military Corps). This umbrella organization was intended to amalgamate the quasi-civilian *Helferinnen* attached to the separate Wehrmacht branches into a unified female auxiliary service along the lines that the British had employed since the beginning of the war.

The attempt to mobilize German women into uniform came too late. Not until March 1945, when the final *Götterdämmerung* threatened the 'Thousand Year Reich', did Hitler rescind his decree banning women from carrying arms, allowing the formation of an all-female army battalion which was to serve as a propaganda inspiration and rally Germans for a last stand against the invaders. Yet so repugnant was the idea that the Fuehrer had second thoughts, and a week later a directive from Wehrmacht Headquarters cancelled the general order. Only those women at flak batteries and guarding vital communications installations would be permitted to carry guns. Not all German women obeyed. Some took up rifles and machine guns to fire on Allied troops during the final weeks of resistance, but their lack of practice made them ineffective snipers.

By contrast, the final six months of the war brought thousands of British female soldiers over to Europe, and they helped man the anti-aircraft batteries that defended liberated Brussels from German bombers. Those women who were killed in the 1945 raids brought to nearly four hundred the ATS casualties during World War II. Britain's female servicewomen had been operating behind the front lines ever since 1940, when transport and signal detachments had been sent to France. Their performance had so impressed the service chiefs that by 1941 the first contingent of the ATS volunteers was on its way to the Middle East, where they helped keep communications and supplies flowing to the front during the North African campaign that defeated Rommel. A pioneer Wren unit was also posted overseas in the summer of 1941, to assist with wireless and telegraphic duties in Singapore. They were evacuated to India before the Japanese invasion, and many of them were to become part of the uniformed female staff at Lord Mountbatten's Southeast Asia Command.

In England as well as at the overseas headquarters, servicewomen played a vital role in securing the Allies' supremacy in wartime codebreaking. Britain's intelligence nerve centre was the so-called Government Code and Cipher School at Bletchley Park. Here, under conditions of great secrecy and security, hundreds of Wrens, WAAF, and ATS telegraphic staff fed the primitive computers with the intercepted enemy cipher messages which had been picked up by listening stations. Many of these stations relied on carefully trained female ears which scanned the radio-waves round the clock, tuning in to the enemy's coded morse transmissions to provide the raw material for the Allied victory in the secret war.

The invasion of Europe in June 1944 was the biggest Allied military operation of World War II. Thousands of women, from the highly-skilled photo-reconnaissance interpreters to the plotters and communications staff, played a vital part in its success. Wren Chief Officer Dorothy Faith Parker made a special contribution to the successful landing of a million Allied troops. As Assistant Staff Officer for Escorts she was instrumental in ensuring the smooth function of the assault and was the only woman to witness the actual Channel crossing from the bridge of a destroyer.

Even if they did not see front-line action, like their Russian allies, British servicewomen established a proud wartime record alongside their menfolk. When eighteen-year-old Princess Elizabeth joined the ATS Transport Corps in 1943, it marked a symbolic endorsement of the fact that military service was now socially acceptable. For the future queen, in common with thousands of other British girls, it was a powerful educative and liberating experience to be thrust into what had always been an exclusively male military environment. A typical female veteran felt that its most important effect was that she 'grew up'. Her one reservation was that, 'Being in the WAAF may have been good for me. But living amongst men for five years made me think like one. It made me much more sociable, but in those days one would probably have said "more common".'

Service in the armed forces inevitably cost women some of their traditional femininity. While many saw it as another demonstration of the legitimacy of their claim to equality with men, many more British women were left in doubt about how to translate their experience into political and economic benefits in what was still a very patriarchal society. It was this indecision that persuaded the majority to return with cheerful resignation to post-war duty with home and family. In Britain to a greater extent than the United States, the liberation that many women had found in wearing military uniforms was seen as time out for the duration.

Even in the Soviet Union, where sexual inequality was supposedly swept away with the class system in the Revolution, veteran female warriors were left with doubts. 'Sometimes, on a dark night, the wind tugging at my hair,' reflected Nadia Popova, one of the decorated Soviet wartime pilots, 'I stare into the blackness and I close my eyes and I imagine myself once more a young girl, up there in my little bomber. And I ask myself, Nadia – how did you do it?'

3

'You're in the Army now, Miss Jones!'

Women made, in my opinion, the best soldiers
in the War.

General Ira C. Eaker, USAAF, 1945

We want to help make the world free – and get
a thrill out of doing it.

WAC Private, 1943

The military services are so conspicuously a
man's world that the appearance of women therein
was startling. Women who joined to do a job
found themselves objects of great curiosity.
Suddenly they were representatives of
'womanhood'. . . . The surprise of men at the
accomplishment of women was not flattering, but
it was fun.

Captain Mildred MacAffee Horton, US WAVES

LONG BEFORE THE JAPANESE ATTACK on Pearl Harbor, the fascination of Americans with the role women were playing in the war in Europe was evident from popular magazines like *Life* and *Saturday Evening Post*, which found Russian female fighters and British girls in tin helmets operating searchlights, dousing blitzed buildings, and marching with snappy precision – irresistible subjects for photo spreads and articles. Yet surprisingly, for a nation where women already played a more prominent role than in any European society, it was to take nearly five months of intensive public debate and lobbying by the administration on Capitol Hill before the House of Representatives and Senate passed the bill that allowed American women to serve their country in uniforms.

A similar uneasiness over the establishment of a female militia had surfaced in America during World War I. In 1917, the Secretary of War had refused a petition from the 'New York Women's Self-Defence League Auxiliary' to be sent to France after they had diligently drilled at the 66th Street Armoury with puttees and rifles. With the same finality he rejected a proposal from the chiefs of staff for congressional approval of a women's army auxiliary that would parade in 'soft brown' uniforms – 'no furs shall be worn' – because 'the action provided for in this bill is not only unwise, but exceedingly ill-advised'.

The War Department held firm to its policy even after receiving repeated requests from the Commander in Chief of the American Expeditionary Force in France for five thousand female auxiliaries. General John – Black Jack – Pershing had been so impressed with the WAAC telephonists that he had arranged to 'borrow' a hundred for his headquarters. But a contingent of American volunteer civilian telegraphists he was sent never matched the efficiency of the British army auxiliaries because they were not subject to military discipline.

The Navy Department, however, had already enlisted twelve and a half thousand female clerical assistants as 'Yeoman F' – popularly known as 'yeomanettes' – bypassing the need to obtain the necessary approval of Congress by ingeniously assigning them as crew of surplus navy tugs that lay on the bottom of the Potomac River. The Marine Corps had also appointed three hundred 'marinettes': the original estimate had been that three women could replace two marines engaged in clerical duties, but in practice the reverse proved to be true.

The American generals proved to have a far greater aversion to women in uniform than the admirals. Not until 1917 were female civilians permitted to be employed in military camps, and then only under 'careful supervision' to prevent 'moral injury either to themselves or to the soldiers'. Proposals for a women's auxiliary were still being shuffled around the War Department when the end of the war enabled the Secretary of War to shelve the controversial plans. The yeomanettes and marinettes left off their uniforms and were re-hired back at their old jobs.

During the inter-war years, the US army's plans for a female auxiliary service were intermittently dusted off and revised by ranking officers who did not share the traditional antipathy to the idea of women in uniform. But it was not until Hitler went to war on the other side of the Atlantic that the patriotic fervour of women's organizations in the United States once again penetrated the offices of the War Department.

The indefinite extension of the Selective Service Act for men following President Roosevelt's declaration of a National Emergency in 1941 prompted groups like the Women's League of Defence to enrol seventeen thousand members 'who can do anything helpful to replace a man in the event of a war'. From Los Angeles to Pittsburgh and Washington to Toledo the War Department was bombarded with pleas from similar groups 'to include women in the national defence plan in some capacity'. In May 1941, Congresswoman Edith Nourse Rogers, who had herself served in France as one of Pershing's civilian auxiliaries during World War I, launched a bill in the House that would establish a twenty-five thousand-strong noncombatant Women's Auxiliary Army Corps.

The majority of the US army staff were still nursing their World War I distaste for anything that smacked of 'a petticoat army'. With little encouragement from the War Department, the Rogers bill quickly sank under the weight of male Congressional opposition. Only in the crisis weeks of November 1941, when it became clear in Washington that the United States was sliding towards war with Germany and Japan, did the army change its tune. An aide to the US Army Chief of Staff, who had been one of the few supporters of the idea of a female auxiliary, remembered how 'General Marshall shook his finger at me and said, "I want a women's corps right away and I don't want any excuses!" At that, I displayed considerable energy.'

More energy and considerably greater initiative was to be shown by a handful of enterprising American women who set out to enlist in the British armed forces as soon as the Japanese attack on Pearl Harbor on 7 December 1941 had plunged the United States into the global war. One of them was Maria Elizabeth Ferguson, who showed her bravery soon after sailing from New York when her ship, the ill-fated *Avila Star*, was torpedoed in a U-boat attack. The nineteen-year-old girl was awarded the British Empire Medal for 'magnificent' courage during the gruelling twenty-one days she spent in an open boat nursing twenty-seven male survivors, eleven of whom perished before rescue finally came. Another, who risked the U-boat-infested Atlantic and reached the shores of England safely early in 1942, was Emily Chapin, a secretary and spare-time pilot from New Jersey who joined the select band of women flyers in Britain's Air Transport Auxiliary, ferrying fighters and bombers to RAF bases.

American women wearing British uniforms were already helping to defeat Hitler when Congress was debating the pros and cons of authorizing the US army to set up its own female auxiliary. Congresswoman Rogers had by now won official War Department and White House backing for a relatively small female auxiliary force of twenty-five thousand, but the arguments continued to delay the passage of her bill through Congress. In Britain, by contrast, there was little opposition when, at the end of April 1942, Parliament approved the conscription of all able-bodied women between the ages of nineteen and twenty-five not already in essential work. The only exceptions were mothers of children under twelve.

Like the British Government, military authorities in the United States insisted women must never be allowed actually to fire guns or engage in combat. Opponents of the bill for establishing a female army auxiliary argued that this violated the historic right of men to fight in defence of their womenfolk and homes. The traditionally conservative military mind also subconsciously resisted the idea of women in uniform because it directly challenged an exclusive male preserve. If women were once allowed to bear arms and female generals conduct battles, it would undermine the central male rationale for war. 'I think it is a reflection upon the courageous manhood of the country to pass a law inviting women to join the armed forces in order to win a battle,' thundered one Senator. 'Take the women into the armed services, who will then do the cooking, the washing, the mending, the humble homey tasks to which every woman has devoted herself. Think of the humiliation! What has become of the manhood of America?'

The belief that women in uniform were an insult to the machismo of the American male was a theme repeated in many of the letters that flooded in from soldiers already locked in battle with the Japanese enemy in the Pacific. Typical of them was the GI who protested that 'we would throw away our own self respect – our right to pledge in earnestness to "Love, Honour, and Protect" the girls we want to marry when we get back.'

That this was not a view shared by the majority of women was evident from the even greater volume of mail that the War Department received from the wives and relations of draftees who begged to be given the chance to serve their country in uniform. At last, on 14 May 1942, the 'WAAC Bill', establishing the Women's Auxiliary Army Corps, was squeezed out of the Senate by an insubstantial margin of just eleven votes. The Navy, which had calculatedly resisted all efforts to win its support for a joint bill, had already initiated its own separate legislative authority – but only after Mrs Roosevelt had interceded with the President to obtain the Secretary's support. The Navy Bill was passed by Congress ten weeks later, establishing a women's auxiliary which would become known as the WAVES, a contrived acronym for 'Women Appointed for Voluntary Emergency Service' that was soon jokingly reinterpreted as 'Women Are Very Essential Sometimes'.

The Navy Bill also authorized a Women's Reserve for the Marines. Its Commandant, in the best tradition of the Corps, refused to make any sexual distinction between male or females – they were all called 'Marines'. The members of the Corps out in the Pacific took a somewhat jaundiced view of this egalitarianism: 'Female Marines? They'll be sending us dogs next!' spat one hardened old leatherneck. The US Coast Guard, which had also come under direct navy control at the outbreak of war, decided to call its female Corps the SPARS, in a contraction of its motto '*Semper Paratus*', 'Always Prepared'.

The final passage of the WAAC Bill had been assisted by the increasing sense of national emergency fostered by the grim news of Allied defeat and reverses on every battlefront. In the week before the crucial Senate vote, Japan had stormed the fortress island of Corregidor in the Philippines, the British army in Burma was retreating towards the Indian frontier, and the Japanese fleet was threatening Australia from the Coral Sea. German panzer divisions in Russia were pounding their way towards Stalingrad and advancing unchecked in the Crimea. In North Africa, Rommel's Afrika Korps appeared poised to drive through Egypt and on to the Middle East. With fewer than two million American men under arms, the female auxiliaries offered the opportunity for a quick increase in the front-line strength of the army if the nightmare of final Axis victory in Russia, the Mediterranean, and Far East became a reality.

Even as Mrs Oveta Culp Hobby was being sworn in by General Marshall as the first WAAC and the new Corps' 'director', the War Department doubled its intended strength to fifty thousand. Mrs Hobby was well qualified for this formidable task. An ex-newspaper executive, a lawyer and thirty-seven-year-old mother of two children, she was married to a former Governor of Texas and had worked in the War Department liaison office long enough to have learned how to cut through bureaucratic tangles in Washington with a determination that earned her the accolade 'Spark-Plugs'.

The sparks nearly ignited her first press conference when questions focussed on such burning issues as whether WAACs would be permitted to wear make-up, whether they would be allowed to date enlisted men, and what would happen to them if they became pregnant? The next day her careful answers were sensationalized under headlines such as 'Doughgirl Generalissimo' and 'Petticoat Army' which suggested that opposition to the whole idea of women auxiliaries was not yet dead. The press proved unable or unwilling to resist the temptation to run pictures under captions labelled 'Whackies', 'Powder Magazines', and 'Fort Lipstick'. One columnist compared the WAACS with 'the naked Amazons . . . and the queer damozels of the Isle of Lesbos'. Another demanded, with ill-concealed prejudice, 'Give the rejected 4F men a chance to be in the Army and give the girls a chance to be mothers.'

The US Army's determination to make no concessions to 'feminine vanity and civilian frippery' soon resulted in a wrangle over women's uniforms. Director Hobby argued for a stylish martial cut that was patterned on those of regular soldiers. Army brass, determined to put as much distance as possible between men and women, argued for blue uniforms – and in the end agreed to olive drab only because the use of existing army cloth was an economy measure. The final design was a committee compromise: the skimped, unpleated skirt with belted jacket and kepi-style cap had none of the smartness or practicality achieved by the Navy, which had commissioned its ensemble from the New York fashion house of Mainbocher, the couturier patronized by the Duchess of Windsor and Hollywood stars.

The US Army was also to deny its female auxiliary the coveted eagle badge: WAAC officers wore a hybrid in their caps that some said was a buzzard. Director Hobby rejected the proposed 'Busy Bee' shoulder insignia because it looked like a 'bug'. The head of Pallas Athene, the Greek goddess of battles, was finally deemed appropriate because of her mythic wisdom and female virtue.

'It will be no picnic for glamour girls,' was how the camp commandant welcomed the press, inquisitive to see over Fort Des Moines in the heart of Iowa, where the first four hundred white and forty black WAAC recruits, selected from thirty thousand applicants, were due to arrive for basic training in August 1942. Female reporters were shocked by the spartan conditions of an old cavalry barracks, which lacked even partitioned showers and toilets. The first intake of WAACs, however, saved their loudest shrieks of dismay for the disconcerting mud-brown slips and foundation garments.

'You're in the Army now, Miss Jones,' was the popular female version of the previous year's hit song about the rigours facing male recruits. Army life made more demands on the girls, who knew they were entering hostile territory when they faced the wolf-whistles of the draftees at the army recruiting offices. 'The recruiting station was the dirtiest place I ever saw,' complained one recruit. 'It was in the post office next to the men's toilets,' recalled another. Many would-be WAACs had second thoughts, including one girl to whom a captain bawled out, 'Are you one of them Wackies?'

Much of the male enlistees' ill-concealed resentment arose because women could choose whether to volunteer for military service, whereas men were drafted. The female intake was also of a much higher standard. Nine out of ten were college graduates, and the others were chosen because they had made successful civilian careers before stepping forward to serve their country 'for the duration plus six months'.

'You have just made the change from peacetime pursuits to wartime tasks – from the individualism of civilian life to the anonymity of military life,' said Director Hobby, addressing the first intake. 'You have taken off silk and put on khaki. All for essentially the same reason – you have a debt and a date. A debt to democracy, a date with destiny.' Most of them were already earmarked for the first officer class and most surprised their male instructors – just as the British ATS had done – by their aptitude and affection for precision drill routines. 'They learn more in a day than my squads of men used to learn in a week,' a sergeant confessed. But on the eve of the parade three weeks later, when they were due to pass out as fully-fledged WAACs, it was found that the young male instructors had given the highest marks to the youngest and prettiest WAACs. The average age of the female intake was significantly higher than the men who trained them, and to the ex-college soldiers of nineteen, any woman over thirty was already an antique. Although some of the younger girls were unfairly upgraded, the mature judgement and stability of the adult women volunteers was soon to prove one of the Corps' most valuable assets.

'You are soldiers and belong to America,' Director Hobby proudly assured the passing-out parade on 29 August. 'This is only the beginning of a magnificent war service by the women of America,' declared US Army Chief of Staff General Marshall, a fervent supporter of employing women to release men for active duty. He encouraged the War Department to increase the planned strength of the WAACs after initial surveys showed that women might eventually replace two out of three men in clerical and administrative jobs, in motor transport and the supply corps as well as in radio communications. The only duties now considered 'improper for women' were those that might expose them to enemy fire – or supervisory positions in which they could decide which men went into combat!

Accordingly, it was decided that by recruiting one and a half million women an equivalent number of men could be released for front-line duty. On paper, a women's auxiliary on this scale translated into a hundred infantry divisions at the front. This was on the bold assumption that the WAACs could recruit nearly ten per cent of the estimated thirteen million American women of service age. Director Hobby appealed for caution, since her advisers were strongly of the opinion that even reaching the new targetted strength for the corps of a hundred and fifty thousand in little over two years would not be practical without British-style conscription. Soundings taken on Capitol Hill, however, quickly revealed that the chances of getting Congress to pass a female draft act were nil. Moreover, as American production geared up, the War Manpower Directorate argued that industry must be given priority for the recruitment of able-bodied women who, they insisted, would make a more effective contribution to the so-called Victory Plan in the shipyards and factories than by unproductive drilling in military uniform.

The services could not offer the same economic incentives as the production line, and a powerful disincentive to military service was what WAVE director Mildred MacAffee Horton termed 'a threat to their individuality'. Moreover, since the WAACs, like the WAVES, were volunteers, nothing could be done to keep those women who grew unhappy with military routine and discipline. After a year, military service had lost much of its glamour for many of the original enlistees. Desertion and AWOL rates began rising sharply after two sisters established a unique military precedent when they ordered their own discharge in a cable to their commanding officer:

HAVE BEEN IN WAACS 3½ MONTHS, NOW AT HOME ON EMERGENCY FURLOUGH. HAVE NO INTENTION TO RETURN, CANNOT TAKE BEING IN CORPS. NERVOUS WRECK AND WILL LOSE OUR MIND IF NOT RELEASED. MA NEEDS US BOTH AT HOME AND CANNOT UNDER ANY CIRCUMSTANCES RETURN. PLEASE TAKE IMMEDIATE ACTION AND REPLY.

New recruits vented their frustrations in songs that nevertheless expressed a touching 'grin and bear it' determination, like one of the many choruses that became popular at the Des Moines training camp in 1943:

> Hats and shoes and skirts don't fit,
> Your girdle bunches when you sit,
> Come on, rookie, you can't quit –
> Just heave a sigh, and be GI.

To check desertions, while boosting the prestige and flagging recruitment drive, the War Department asked Congress to pass legislation changing the status of the Corps from an auxiliary to an integral part of the US Army – a step which the British Government had taken a year earlier with the ATS. After months of renewed political wrangling over the desirability of having women in uniform at all, the WAAC became the WAC (Women's Army Corps) by a stroke of President Roosevelt's pen on 1 July 1943.

Women who elected to stay in the Corps could now enjoy full military status, insurance and pension rights. But they were also to be subject to army discipline – and through the summer almost half the strength of some WAC units melted away as those women who decided not to sign on for a more military career opted for honourable discharge. 'Feel I can do more good in war industry' . . . 'Cannot accustom myself to military life' . . . 'Unable to concentrate since my husband reported missing,' were among the excuses given by some of the fifteen thousand who left by the September deadline. 'Overstatements and unfulfillable promises by recruiting officers,' were other contributory factors according to an official analysis which suggested that the main cause was the public attitude that 'the war is all but won'.

The WAC was less than fifty thousand strong, and hopes were abandoned of a rapid further half million increase in 1943 which would have avoided the necessity of extending the 1943 draft to fathers of young families. With the army planners now calling for two million more men in anticipation of opening the Second Front in Europe in 1944, General Marshall reluctantly passed to the White House the order extending Selective Service.

Army life had become tarnished. Too many girls had suffered from homesickness during basic training; there was mounting public concern at the press coverage given to charges of immorality of servicewomen; and better pay without military discipline was offered by the war industries. A company commander claimed also that male soldiers were becoming increasingly resentful and disparaging of the WACs: 'now every man assumed that their uniforms gave him the right to insult them'. Surveys confirmed that forty per cent of servicemen gave negative answers to the questions, 'If you had a sister twenty-one years old or older, would you like to see her join the WAC or not?'

An ill-judged recruiting campaign on the theme, 'Release a Man for Combat' inadvertently drew attention to the fact that if wives and girlfriends enlisted they might be sending their own or some-one else's loved one to risk death at the battlefront. WAC recruit-ment was never fully to recover from this advertising or the brash posters that followed. These oversold the glamour of military life with the cheery hype of slogans proclaiming, 'We're the Luckiest Girls in the World – And We Know It' . . . 'I Joined to Serve My Country, And I'm Having The Time of My Life' . . . 'I Felt Pretty Important When that Tailor Fitted My Swank New Uniform To Me'. These were greeted with derision by new recruits, and veteran WACs angrily protested at the harm that would be done by painting such an over-rosy and false image of the Corps.

The campaign to restore the appeal of the WAC reached its nadir in Cleveland in the summer of 1943, when an all-out advertis-ing and recruiting drive culminating in the personal canvass of seventy-three thousand families produced only a hundred and sixty-eight new recruits. At that abysmal rate enlistment officials calculated that there were not enough families in the United States to enable the Corps to reach even its modest hundred thousand target strength. The Army therefore decided, against the advice of Mrs Hobby – who now ranked as a full colonel – to drop the mini-mum educational requirements previously required for entry to the WAC and WAVES. This did not markedly increase the inflow of recruits, and furthermore gave the unfortunate public impression that the WAC was desperately scraping the bottom of the barrel.

The public's image of the WAC was further harmed with the discharge of alcoholics, prostitutes, or psychiatrics who had been signed up by recruiting officers desperate to meet their targets. These unfortunate cases attracted the headlines of a press that was always looking to justify the widely-held belief in the immorality of female soldiers.

Nine days after her induction, one new WAC claimed to be the Duchess of Windsor; another woman had joined up after her parents removed her from an asylum. Drunkards and prostitutes who had evaded screening procedures did irreparable damage to the reputation of some units. 'Well I thought it would get her off our hands,' said one police chief who later admitted concealing a woman's criminal records. At another base potential recruits had been scared away by an army psychiatrist, who insisted on testing the emotional balance of potential enlistees by asking the girls to strip before asking, 'How often during the past month have you had intercourse with a soldier or sailor?'

At Colonel Hobby's insistence, standards were raised again at the end of 1943 and recruiting began to improve. Although the Corps was never to achieve its intended strength, it did reach a wartime peak of just over a hundred thousand and made a significant contribution to the American war effort, not just because it released the equivalent of seven army divisions of men for active duty, but because women proved effective and diligent workers.

Inevitably some commanding officers regarded WACs as merely substitute clerical staff, but others were encouraged to apply their talents to a variety of military tasks. The precedent was set by General Eisenhower, who had been impressed by the part British servicewomen were playing in their country's war effort during his mission to London with General Marshall in the spring of 1942. When Eisenhower was appointed Commander in Chief of the Allied landings in North Africa in the autumn of that year, he made female auxiliaries an integral part of his campaign head-quarter's staff. The first five officers were hand-picked WAACs who reached Algiers only five days after the American invasion troops had waded ashore. Their arrival was an occasion of high drama rather than military smartness, although Eisenhower had sent his top aide to provide a welcome: five very bedraggled and grimy WAACs wearing borrowed men's trousers stepped on to the dockside from a Royal Navy destroyer which had fished them out of the Atlantic after a U-boat had torpedoed their transport.

A month later the first company of WAAC enlistees arrived less dramatically but more safely in what a newspaper correspondent called 'the first American women's expeditional force in history'. Their first experience of soldiering behind the lines was being trucked daily between headquarters and the convent where they were housed. Nightly bombing raids, combined with long work hours and the loss of all their typewriters and supplies were overcome with cheerful improvization that won high praise from the military staff, as they performed complicated cypher duties as well as routine clerical and logistical operations.

WAC strength in North Africa had increased to nearly two thousand within a year which saw the Sicilian and Italian campaigns. An advance contingent had joined the Fifth Army headquarters on the mainland by November 1943, bivouacking with General Mark Clark's headquarter's staff in the rough terrain twenty miles behind the front line.

In Italy, despite initial reservations, the WACs appeared to thrive on the hardships and danger. One American WAC corporal wrote to her mother, 'I greatly doubt that I shall ever be inspired to put such wholehearted energy and effort into anything which my life after the war will demand of me.' Like the US army nurses, the WACs were ready to give their all. Some of the nurses did. In January 1944, when the American troops came ashore at Anzio in a bid to leapfrog the German forces which were blocking the advance north to Rome, the ferocity of a concerted counter-attack by tanks and air support almost drove the invasion back into the sea. It killed some of the nurses who were tending the wounded in open slit-trenches.

During the build-up and planning of the D-Day operations in Britain, Eisenhower's headquarters were populated with WACs who, along with their British women counterparts from the navy, army and air force, took on a considerable measure of the administrative and communication burden for the largest amphibious operation in military history. General Ira Eaker singled out the contribution women had made to the crucial pre-invasion bombing campaign: 'They were the best photo-interpreters . . . keener and more intelligent than men in this line of work.'

Amongst the first of the Allied women to set foot on the Normandy beachhead was Frances Sandstrom, a flight nurse from the 9th US army troop-carrier base, whose transport aircraft flew in to pick up the critically wounded only nine days after D-Day:

We were the first plane to land on the first steel-mat strip put down by our advance engineers. They had just finished the job when our C-47 came in. Wrecked gliders were scattered all over the countryside. The troops were fighting only three miles away, and we could hear land mines exploding all around us. I was told to stay in the plane, since all German snipers had not been cleared and were taking occasional shots at the landing mat. The loading teams brought my patients aboard. Many of them were badly wounded. They were dirty, right out of foxholes. Many of them were suffering, but I heard not one murmur of complaint from any of them. It was hot and dusty, but they were calm and asked for nothing except water. Each time I gave a man a drink he smiled, or tried to, and thanked me as if I had done something very heroic and wonderful.

Three weeks later, on 10 July 1944, the first permanent contingent of US army nurses in steel helmets and combat fatigues arrived. As they splashed ashore from a landing craft they were greeted by wildly cheering GIs. The military nurses were soon followed by a volunteer WAC unit which was attached to the forward communication echelon, and by October there were over three thousand American female soldiers in France carrying the myriad communications and clerical duties that a modern army even in the field trails behind it. The WACs took no part in the fighting, but were often close enough to the front to hear the battles and endure the sporadic Luftwaffe attacks.

The WAC girls spiritedly roughed it with the front-line troops, living in tents and cellars and bathing from their helmets. Behind the battlefield some of the more enterprising managed the occasional hair-do. As a reporter who kept up with them recorded, this involved a great deal of improvization:

> Beauty parlours in Normandy had become war casualties along with the pillboxes and enemy strongholds. We set up operations in our tents. There was no privacy from passing cows, nurses, doctors, GIs or German prisoners. Such is the price of vanity. My hair troubles were something the French understood. The French women fought the invasion with fashion. 'If French women had not remained chic, *les Boches* would have known they had broken their spirit,' one of them said.

The reports that appeared in the American press brought a rush of would-be recruits in the final months of the war from girls wanting to join the adventure overseas. When Germany surrendered in 1945, there were eight thousand WACs on the Continent. This was the largest contingent in any foreign theatre, although it was still only half the sixteen thousand Eisenhower had originally planned. The Supreme Commander Allied Force Europe was to hand America's female soldiers a fulsome tribute: 'During the time I have had the WACs under my command they have met every test and task assigned to them . . . Their contributions in efficiency, skill, spirit, and determination are immeasurable.'

On the other side of the world WACs in the Pacific theatre had to share with GIs the rigours of a tropical campaign, including malaria, dysentery, and mosquitoes. In the Philippines they were repeatedly threatened by Tokyo Rose and came under heavy air attacks during the recapture of Leyte. They learned how to survive on K rations and avoid jungle latrines that had been made lethal by Japanese booby traps. General Douglas MacArthur was unstinting in his praise of their fortitude, calling them 'my best soldiers'. He confided that his WACs worked harder than men, complained less, and were better disciplined. This did not prevent some of his die-hard subordinate commanders reporting that women had no business in the south-west Pacific because the 'hardships, isolation, and privation of jungle theatres are jobs for men'.

The WACs who were shipped out to join MacArthur's advance headquarters staff during the New Guinea campaign in 1943 faced not only the perils of the jungle but the humiliation of having to be locked up in barbed wire compounds and given armed escorts because of the fear that GIs, many of whom had not seen a white woman for a year and a half, would be inflamed to sexual assault. Single couple dates were strictly forbidden, and those WACs assigned to mail censorship became demoralized because much of what the men wrote home to wives and girlfriends was sexually explicit. When MacArthur's forces recaptured Manila early in 1945, this military chaperonage had been eased, but the WACs then found themselves deluged with demands for dates and dances.

On Hollandia, during the final stages of General MacArthur's New Guinea campaign, the local regulation required all WACs to wear trousers, not just as protection against mosquitoes but against the husky men of the naval Construction Battalion (nicknamed Seabee). The women in the army air force devised a way to circumvent regulations until, as one of the Seabees recalled, their sister soldiers extracted an uncomfortable revenge:

> At the big Seabee dances, the WACs would appear in their inevitable pants. Then the few flying WACs would come sashaying in, also wearing pants, but carrying overnight valises. The flying WACs would step into the 'head' and appear shortly thereafter *sans* pants and *sans* valises. They'd be wearing trim skirts, and the wolf lines would form on the right. Of course the pants-wearing WACs weren't going to take

it long. After the dance one night, when the flying WACs went back to the head to change their pants, they found that liberal quantities of beer had been poured into their valises: their clothes were saturated! After that the flying WACs never dared shed their pants at the dance hall. Everybody kept her pants on.

The underlying prejudice in the military flared up again during the final weeks of the war when *Yank*, the semi-official magazine of the US armed forces, published a scornful letter from a Sergeant Bob Bowie belittling the contribution that uniformed women had made to winning the war:

> Why we GIs over here in the Pacific have to read such tripe and drivel about WACs beats me. Who the hell cares about these dimpled GIs who are supposed to be soldiers? All I have ever heard of them doing is peeling spuds, clerking in the office, driving a truck or a tractor or puttering around in the photo lab. Yet all the stories written about our dears tell how overworked they are. I correspond regularly with a close friend of mine who is a WAC, and all she ever writes about is the dances, picnics, swimming parties, and bars she has attended. Are these Janes in the army for the same reason that we are, or just to see how many dates they can get? We would like them a hell of a lot better, and respect them more, if they did their part in some defence plant, or at home, where they belong. So please let up on the cock-and-bull and feminine propaganda. It's sickening to read about some doll who has made the supreme sacrifice of giving up her lace-trimmed undies for ODs.

The counter-barrage of protest from outraged servicewomen which crashed on to the editor's desk included a well-aimed salvo at male prejudice by Private Jane Nugent: 'Thanks for the bouquets boys. Go right on sticking the knife in our backs . . . When it's all over we'll go back to our lace-trimmed undies and to the kind of men who used their anger on something beside the WACs!'

Victory was awarded to the women in khaki by an official US army historian, who wrote: 'Perhaps the greatest achievement of the WACs was their triumph over the prejudices of the male military mind. The half-amused, half-scornful attitude of some officers in responsible positions was not justified by the perform-ance of the WACs.'

Women questioned by wartime surveys, however, did not see themselves as the shock troops in a war of liberation. Most preferred to acknowledge more prosaic motivations for joining up.

In-depth interviews conducted during a 1943 survey by the US army among a cross section of typical WACs revealed that over forty per cent of the female enlistees were motivated by a desire to escape from unhappy homes or boring jobs, or by a desire for adventure; twenty-five per cent wanted to improve their economic or social status – and less than twenty per cent were genuinely motivated by patriotism. Typical comments included 'I was sick and tired of that typewriter, I couldn't stand it any more,' . . . 'I wasn't getting anywhere,' . . . 'We wanted to help make the world free and get a thrill out of doing it,' . . . 'I never realized what women could do' . . . 'I guess it is like the soldiers – after so much routine you want to get out and fight,' . . . 'I wanted to see something of the world before the War ended,' . . . 'I think the Army needs me and I need the Army'. Altogether, military service had a powerful liberating effect on many American women which was summed up by one WAC who told the researchers, 'I feel competent for the first time, and independent. It is a good feeling to be able to take care of yourself.'

'Nothing could be more conducive to the emergence of the individual girl, for the first time separated from the setting with which she is normally identified. Wealth, social position, ancestry, professional experience – all vanished upon entrance into the service; and everyone started again to become identified as a person in this new relationship,' asserted Captain Mildred MacAffee Horton. The former principal of Wellesley College, Horton had run the women's arm of the US Navy throughout the war and was therefore in a better position than most to judge the personal and collective impact of uniformed service. She observed in 1946 that, 'If military service individualized women, it also made them more conspicuously women than they had been before.'

Whether women's new-found identity and purpose would produce an immediate wave of post-war feminine liberation was doubted by Captain Horton, who made this prescient forecast:

> It is my impression that women are not likely to demand rights for themselves as veterans on the score of meriting a nation's gratitude. By and large, they know they risked relatively little, compared to their combatant brothers. Their changed estimate of themselves may make problems for themselves and their communities, but I prophesy that they will be the problems of individuals rather than of women veterans as a group.

4

THE KHAKI ISSUE

Vague and discreditable allegations about the
conduct of women in the Forces have caused
considerable distress and anxiety not only to
friends and relations at home but to men
fighting overseas.

British Parliamentary Report, 1942

Men have for centuries used slander against
morals as a weapon to keep women out of
public life.

US WAC Officer

'SHE'LL BE WEARING KHAKI ISSUE when she comes,' was the ribald wartime version of the old American refrain 'She'll be coming round the mountain . . .' Loaded with lasciviousness, it was one of the British soldiers' favourite ways of welcoming the first ATS units in the early years of World War II. But soon the playful joking was to be replaced by a malicious groundswell of male resentment in which servicemen spread tales about the alleged promiscuity of the ATS.

'Virtue has no gossip value,' as one British parliamentarian rightly observed, and the wartime climate of censorship and secrecy was fertile ground for the rapid growth of rumours. The women in the army and air force were considered 'fair game'. The ATS attracted the disparaging epithet 'Officer's Groundsheets', and the WAAF were referred to as 'Pilot's Cockpits' in coarse humour.

'I don't think air-force men went out with WAAFs particularly. In fact, just the opposite,' observed one RAF flight sergeant. 'They tended to shy away from women in their own uniform and go for women in the Wrens and Land Army.' The Wrens escaped such derogatory labels. This may have been because its ranks were drawn largely from middle-class girls or, as wartime Royal Navy officer Nicholas Monsarrat observed, because 'there seems to be a special affection in the Navy for Wrens – by which I mean that they are looked on, not as fair game, but as part of the Service and thus to be protected and preserved from outsiders.'

'There was the attitude about girls in uniform, that they were easy, but they weren't any different from other girls,' insisted one WAAF, who admitted she used to change into civilian clothes at wartime dances to stop men getting too fresh with her. Women who joined the services quickly learned to ignore the wolf-whistles and frequent sexual overtures from soldiers. One sixteen-year-old girl who had added a year and a half to her age to qualify for the WAAF took seriously the adage 'forewarned is forearmed' when attending her army camp cinema:

> An airman got very fresh and several of us younger girls had armed ourselves with hatpins for protection because we could hide them in

the lapels of our uniforms. I had occasion to use mine. The lights came on when the airman screamed and clutched his bottom. Everyone stared at me. After that I was known as 'the pin-up girl'.

Rifles rather than hatpins had to be deployed to defend the honour of the army girls based near Yeovil from marauding male troops in nearby transit camps recalled another WAAF girl:

While on duty at nights, these soldiers often tried to rape us. Several girls had scars and black eyes after they had been caught coming from the ablutions which were at a distance from our barracks. This stopped us from going to use the latrines at night. After we complained, two airmen were sent to guard us. They had guns and orders to shoot anyone found unofficially on our site at night. At another site near where Polish airmen were stationed, many girls had their nipples bitten off by the very passionate ones, so of course we learned another lesson.

Learning to defend themselves against the unwelcome attentions of soldiers who regarded women in khaki as fair game was not part of the formal basic training course, but something most girls had to come to terms with. One new WAAF recruit recalled her embarrassment at 'doing physical education on the beach at Morecambe in the middle of winter in large navy-blue knickers while RAF rookies cheered us on'. Another Scottish ATS girl recalls nearly fainting when she was detailed to assist a quarter-master re-kitting male troops: 'He just gave me a brief talk and showed me how to fill in the clothing forms. But when the soldiers came in and he ordered "Easy and drop 'em!" I was quite shocked as I'd never seen a man without trousers before.'

Confronting the naked reality of masculine army life matured many girls in a manner which, in retrospect, they found more amusing than shocking:

The incident I recall was after one regular monthly medical inspection which took place in a long Nissen hut with changing benches along one wall. We women were allowed to change in the privacy of the doctor's office, but on one occasion we emerged straight into a line of men, absolutely starkers. We fled, but were ragged about it afterwards. In those days we were fairly innocent, the word SEX hadn't entered our vocabulary.

Sex-education lectures were embarrassing, and frequently delivered by unsympathetic army doctors who were also responsible for the regulation medical inspections which, according to one ATS recruit, did more to frighten than inform:

> We were examined for venereal infections when we joined the army, and every month at the medical inspection. Great moral emphasis was laid on not having affairs with men, which sort of filtered through – although nobody paid much attention. Yet at the same time girls in the army became obsessed with the whole VD thing during the war, as it was drummed into you so much. Most of us had never heard of VD or knew what it was, but like many others I developed a discharge out of pure psychosomatic terror.

Medical examinations were not only perfunctory, but were usually performed by orderlies with little or no gynaecological training, according to one ATS private who vividly recalled the morning PT parade was abandoned when a member of her unit unexpectedly gave birth: 'There were men present, but we were even more surprised because, although she looked pregnant, girls who had come in with her swore that she had always been that size.'

Wartime censorship prevented such incidents appearing in the British press, but by the second year of the war the Government's monitoring survey reported increasing public concern about allegations of immorality in the ATS. One woman in York believed there was a local 'maternity home for ATS babies'. Another told her doctor, 'I'd like to join the ATS. He said, "Don't you dare!"' Mothers said they 'would not recommend any girl joining', and one girl confided, 'Oh, I could not join the ATS. All my friends would think I was one of "those".' Such views were so widespread that the conclusion was that the 'morality of the ATS is attacked universally, but this condemnation appears to originate almost wholly with members of the Forces . . . inspired by the men's preoccupation with their own or comrades' lack of morals.' The survey found that the ATS was generally considered to be an "unglamorous" service, the legion of Cinderellas, domestic workers of low degree among whom one expected, and got, a low degree of morality.'

Wild rumours about an epidemic of pregnancies and VD in the auxiliary services in 1941 generated a flood of protests from worried parents; churchmen preached against wartime morals from the pulpit, and questions were tabled in Parliament. So vociferous had the outcry become that, on 2 November 1941, at

the height of the Blitz, Churchill's Cabinet, which was concerned
about its plans for female conscription, announced that a parliamentary committee would investigate 'amenities and welfare conditions in the three women's services'.

The investigating commission was set up under the chairmanship of the distinguished lawyer Miss Violet Markham, and its
leading spokesman became Dr Edith Summerskill, the forthright
Labour member and founder of the Women's Home Defence
Unit. While the Luftwaffe did its best to bomb Britain to its knees
during the winter of 1941, the Markham Committee braved the
disruptions of the railway system to tour a hundred and twenty-
three military camps and interview thousands of servicewomen.

After six months of exhaustive investigations, its report advised
Parliament that there was 'no justification for the vague but
sweeping charges of immorality which have disturbed public
opinion . . . one or two cases which, in the course of gossip, have
been multiplied many times over'. The report acknowledged the
'emotional stresses due to the war which lead to extramarital
relationships', but pointed out that the disciplines of service life
were 'corrective rather than an incitement to bad conduct'. This
was confirmed by the statistics that showed that both illegitimacy
and VD rates for the ATS and other women's services were lower,
and in some cases half that of the comparable age and sex group
in the civilian population. 'In civilian life cases of immorality are
spread over a wide area,' the Markham Committee noted, while
'in the Services they occur in small compact communities and are
at once concentrated and conspicuous'.

Nor did the report find any evidence that Nazi sympathizers
were trying to undermine the national war effort by rumour-
mongering. Instead it blamed the psychological sexism exhibited
by the men of the armed forces towards women in uniform.

> The British, though they fight when called upon to do so with
> unfaltering courage and determination, are not a military race. They
> cherish a deep-rooted prejudice against uniforms; consequently a
> woman in uniform may rouse a special sense of hostility, conscious or
> subconscious, among certain people who would never give two
> thoughts to her conduct as a private citizen. The woman in uniform
> becomes an easy target for gossip and careless talk. To be seen drinking
> a glass of beer in a public house is to provide a text for fluent remarks
> about the low standards of the Services. Further, though the service

rendered to their country by women is generally recognized, there are exceptions and critics within and without the Forces. Strictures, in particular from soldiers, sailors, and airmen, small minority though they be, carry weight out of proportion to their numbers, and may be repeated often with exaggerations, since no story loses in the telling.

The British parliamentary commission noted that similar 'mischievous and false' sexual obloquy had been generated when women donned uniform in World War I. The government commission that had been sent over to France in 1918 to investigate 'wild and fantastic tales' of immorality in the female auxiliaries had also concluded that 'a vast superstructure of slander had been raised on a small foundation of fact'.

The overseas postings of women in uniform had evoked the same response in the Germany army. In 1942, the Wehrmacht issued a directive that 'female army assistants' were to be protected from 'enemy propaganda'. It appealed to the traditional 'chivalry' of 'every German soldier to defend the honour of these girls. If a German soldier humorously refers to the women as *Blitzmadchen* – blitzgirls – there is nothing wrong with that; but if offensive remarks are passed, it is hoped that a more respectful comrade will object strongly.' Despite initial hopes by the WAAC and WAVE directors that GIs, in the best of American tradition, would be more respectful of their female auxiliaries, the same sexual smears circulated. By 1943 'The Slander Campaign', as the phenomenon was labelled by the WAAC directorate, was in full swing.

In the United States the anti-Roosevelt press played on this public impression by inflating stories to headline proportions, as in the classic *Washington Times-Herald* headline, 'STORK PAYS VISIT TO WAAC NINE DAYS AFTER ENLISTMENT'. Army newsheets as well as civilian newspapers delighted in cartoons that made fun of women in uniform. Khaki brassieres, empty or otherwise, were a constant source of comic inspiration to cartoonists, who paid little attention to making fun of male undergarments of the same military colour.

Crank letters condemning the sinfulness of women in uniform were ammunition for radio evangelists who railed against the lasciviousness of army medical inspections that supposedly paraded lines of nude females. Temperance campaigners denounced the increase in wartime drunkenness that encouraged promiscuity between the ranks on mixed military bases, although statistics showed that WAACs contracted venereal infection at a fraction of the male soldiers' rate, and pregnancies in the Corps were a fifth the level of a comparable group of female civilians.

The flames of speculation about sexual laxity in the female army spread with brush-fire rapidity across the United States during the spring of 1943. From New York came the rumour that shiploads of pregnant WAACs were being sent back from England and North Africa under armed guard to prevent them jumping overboard rather than disgrace their families. At Camp Lee, Virginia, soldiers believed that anyone seen dating a WAAC had to report for medical treatment. At Hampton Roads, a major port of embarkation, GIs going overseas were convinced that ninety per cent of the WAACs were prostitutes and that forty-five per cent of the Corps were discharged for pregnancy. In Florida there were stories of WAACs openly soliciting soldiers, and it was said that physicians examining female recruits had been ordered to reject all virgins. There was even a bizarre report from the foxholes of New Guinea that GIs were thumbing through copies of an army sex-hygiene pamphlet illustrated with pornographic photos of WAAC girls.

Such accusations contained about as much truth as other raunchy barrack gossip. Moreover, as an official pointed out, WAACs had not been leading cloistered lives, but were from a cross section of society that had its share of sexual misfits and misadventures. A December 1942 report on pending disciplinary cases from the Fort Des Moines training centre reveals that of the WAACs then under investigation for dishonourable discharge, three were charged with alleged 'homosexual tendencies'; five with what was described as 'fornication' and 'moral looseness'; and one with engaging 'in the activities of a common prostitute'.

In June 1943, the slander campaign reached a peak after the *Washington Times-Herald* leaked a sensational story that Mrs Roosevelt and 'the New Deal Ladies' were behind a super-secret agreement that 'Contraceptives and prophylactic equipment will be furnished to members of the WAAC'. It referred to a pamphlet that the War Department described as a 'wholesome manual' on 'sex hygiene' intended for briefing WAAC officers. The booklet in fact dealt with the various aspects of personal feminine hygiene with a modesty calculated not to upset 'a girl unaccustomed to attributing precise meanings to words'. The sensitive issue of contraception was side-stepped by stressing the need for continence.

The War Department, unwisely as it turned out, decided that it was beneath its dignity to release the inoffensive pamphlet. Nor were official denials issued rapidly enough to destroy the damaging nationwide press story blazing with headlines that suggested the army was condoning and encouraging promiscuity among its troops by issuing free contraceptives to female, as well as male soldiers.

'Long distance calls from parents began to come in, telling the girls to come home,' reported a WAAC camp commander. 'The younger girls all came in crying, asking if this disgrace was what they had been asked to join the army for.' One WAAC sergeant 'went home on leave to tell my family it wasn't true.'

> When I went through the streets, I held up my head because I imagined everybody was talking about me, but when I was at last inside our front door, I couldn't say a word to them, I was so humiliated – I just burst out crying, and my people ran and put their arms around me and cried with me.

Director Hobby, normally a most composed woman, broke down at an emergency staff meeting which decided to launch an official counterattack. The President himself went on record to condemn what he called this 'deliberate newspaper job' which he blamed on 'orders from the top' of the anti-administration *Chicago Herald Tribune* without actually naming his old foe Colonel McCormick. Mrs Roosevelt believed that Hitler and home-grown Nazis might be behind a sinister plot because 'Americans fall for Axis-inspired propaganda like children'. Secretary of War Henry Stimson also saw a Nazi plot, because any drop in WAAC recruiting would 'interfere with the increase in the combat strength of our Army'. Congresswoman Edith Nourse Rogers, the 'midwife' of the WAAC bill, agreed that 'nothing would please Hitler more', and that 'Loose talk concerning our women in the armed services cannot be less than Nazi-inspired.'

A nationwide investigation was ordered. But the combined resources of Military Intelligence and the FBI were unable to bring to light the slightest shred of evidence to suggest the Germans were involved. The unpalatable truth was that rumours of WAAC immorality were not Nazi inspired, but were the product of 'Army personnel, Navy personnel, Coast Guard personnel, businessmen, women, factory workers and others. Most . . . have completely American backgrounds.' Those responsible were believed to be 'Male military personnel who are sometimes inclined to resent usurpation of their long established monopoly' and 'soldiers who had never dated WAACs' or who had 'trouble getting dates'. The investigators discovered that gossip was spread by 'officers' wives over bridge tables' and 'local girls and women who resent having the WAACs around', and encouraged by male fanatics 'who cannot get used to women being in any place except the home'.

Some individual cases of alleged drunkenness and loose behaviour were attributable to uniformed civilian women such as the WOWs – War Ordnance Workers – or to the 'Victory Girl' prostitutes who paraded in home-made uniforms to attract servicemen. Complaints were received from GIs in North Africa who claimed to have seen army girls openly soliciting in Algiers. On investigation these turned out to be native auxiliaries who had been fitted out in some of the five thousand surplus WAAC uniforms lend-leased to the French!

That the biggest perpetrators of slander were servicemen was confirmed by reports from military censors that V-mail letters from GIs were spiced with disparaging references such as, 'You join the WAVES or WAAC and you are automatically a prostitute in my opinion' . . . 'I told my Sis if she ever joined I would put her out of the house, and I really mean it. So if you ever join, I will be finished with you too' . . . 'Get a damn divorce. I don't want no damn WAAC for a wife' . . . 'The service is no place for a woman. A woman's place is in the home' . . . 'About joining the WAACs: the answer is still NO. If they really need servicewomen let them draft some of the pigs that are running loose around town.'

In the summer of 1943 the War Department launched a major counteroffensive to restore the image of the Corps. This coincided with its election to full military status: WAACs were now officially WACs. Statistics were released to show that women in uniform were more moral and cleaner living than the men, and a plane-load of prominent religious leaders and politicians took off on a tour of major WAC training bases. Their joint press statement reported that 'parents concerned about the moral and spiritual welfare of their daughters can be reassured'. But no amount of publicity about the number of servicewomen who dutifully attended mass, or statements by Congressional committees that rumour-mongering was a 'cowardly, contemptible, despicable course' in which 'no self-respecting patriotic American would indulge' could undo all the harm. 'Men have for centuries used slander against morals as a weapon to keep women out of public life', a WAC liaison officer observed, noting how successful the old technique had proved again when the WAC directorate resigned itself to the fact that it would never reach its ambitious recruiting target of over a million.

The slander campaign had a much more drastic effect on American enlistment, which was voluntary, than on the British figures, where women were subject to conscription. The British parliamentary committee, while conceding that gossip about the moral standards of the female auxiliaries was wildly exaggerated, nevertheless agreed that 'a certain bravado in much talk that takes place between young people about sex questions' might have encouraged many stories because 'standards of sexual behaviour have changed greatly in the last generation and some people today conduct their lives on principles remote from those termed Victorian.'

The frank recollections of an ATS corporal suggest that this wartime sexual 'bravado' was by no means restricted to male barrack-room life:

> While in mixed company women were submissive and accepted the role men expected them to play, in our barracks we were something completely different. We played dangerously and talked dirty. Men were an alien element, yet everything that we women desired. Getting enough sex was all part of the dare that the war represented for us women, because it allowed us to express our liberty and rebelliousness from the male-set archetypes of loving wife and mother that they had always tried to tie us to. This naturally brought women together, and, apart from the prim or religious ones – of which there were quite a few – it enabled women to talk together about men.
>
> Yet at the same time, because men were scarce, there was a good deal of competition between us, although we would talk freely about the men we had had. There was one particular working-class girl in our barrack room who always seemed to get as much as she wanted. We regarded her as a little prim, but she was always seen in company with a hulking man who must have weighed at least twenty stone, with such a huge behind that we used to call him 'Elephant Arse'. After she had been going with him regularly for quite a while, the rest

of us became increasingly curious as to why she should stick with such a fat-arse! So one night we got her in the barrack room after she had seen him and asked her what was so special about this giant. She replied in her broad northern accent, 'Ooh, ah! you know it takes a big hammer to drive a big nail!'

The Markham Report had cautioned against using wartime pregnancy figures to measure the level of promiscuous conduct amongst women, since the 'use of contraceptives of recent years has spread through all classes of society and sexual intercourse may be common without pregnancy resulting'. Male service personnel were in fact issued with free condoms even if the servicewomen were not, and such was the stigma of getting 'PWP' – Pregnant Without Permission' – that it was assumed that many servicewomen would ensure their partner took the necessary precautions. But some girls were not always willing – or informed enough – to insist on this. In WAAF barracks a ditty about 'Sleeping Out Passes' was sung to the popular wartime tune of 'Jealousy':

> Twas all over my SOP,
> That settled how my fate was to be,
> For He was an officer in the RAF
> And I was a poor little innocent WAAF.
>
> He gave all his kisses to me,
> And now all too late I can see,
> I'll have to tell mother,
> There's goin' to be another,
> Twas all over my SOP

Pregnancy was grounds for automatic discharge from the women's services in both Britain and the United States, though there was no financial penalty or dishonourable stigma regardless of marital status. After female conscription was introduced in England some girls found that having a baby was their only escape from compulsory military service. 'You could get two months' pregnancy allowance,' explained one former member of the ATS. 'Many women would get pregnant deliberately to get out and then go and have a back-street abortion. The risk was well worth taking for those who had had enough of army life, because you could not be called up again.'

British regulations required expectant mothers to resign by the fifth month, and while unmarried mothers were prohibited from re-enlisting, a married woman was eligible for reinstatement if her child was cared for. The US Army adopted the same practice, but while neither country penalized women getting pregnant, both military establishments concentrated a great deal of effort on preaching continence to their servicewomen because of fears about the public reaction to VD.

A secret conference on the sensitive subject of the 'Prevention of Venereal Disease in Female Personnel' was held in Washington in July 1942, a month before the first women were inducted. It accepted that both the army and navy were ill-equipped with instructional films and pamphlets suitable for women. A survey showed that only a quarter of unmarried GIs were continent whereas twenty-five per cent regularly engaged in sexual intercourse, and the other fifty per cent did so 'sporadically'. The equivalent proportions for unmarried WAACs showed that forty per cent were continent, five per cent were promiscuous and fifty-five per cent had sexual experiences from time to time. 'The forty per cent are taken care of, the five per cent can never be helped particularly,' agreed the Chairman of the National Research Council's Committee on Venereal Disease, who pointed out that the Committee could not evade its 'duty' to give proper prophylactic advice to over half the female intake, who might reasonably be expected to be sexually active. The Committee therefore agreed to study the report of observers who had been sent to England to learn how the ATS dealt with problems of social hygiene.

Britain's Royal Army Medical Corps had been reluctant to release any statistics to the American observers on either VD or pregnancy rates in female service personnel – perhaps to conceal that there had been a rise in the ATS rates that year. But what the American fact-finding team discovered gave it cause for concern. Sex-education lectures were 'entirely inadequate' because they 'skate around sex and briefly mention syphilis and gonorrhoea as venereal diseases'. Checking the spread of these 'social diseases' had been complicated by the thousands of Free-French, Polish, and other exiled soldiers who had taken refuge in England, and it was generally recognized that 'lack of VD control in the Women's Services has created a problem of major proportions'.

A visit to the main VD treatment centre at the British army's Shenley military hospital by an American venereologist had revealed that an anticipated maximum of six beds a night for treating female VD cases had been expanded to fifty. The weekly trainload of female VD cases were 'completely ostracized' by the staff, who appeared to believe that part of the treatment was to deal with the women as 'moral lepers'. This contributed to psychiatric problems and attempts to hide infections while girls sought unauthorized treatment through friendly medical orderlies at their own bases who had access to the new sulfonamide therapeutics: 'If the boyfriend is infected and received treatment he tells her to take the drug too.'

When the committee's recommendations reached Director Hobby, she rejected as potentially explosive the idea of making contraceptive advice and prophylactic stations available for female as well as male soldiers. As a result of protests to General Marshall, the US Army Surgeon General laid down that social hygiene lectures 'should be presented in a dignified and wholly acceptable manner, in line with the common practice in outstanding colleges for women in this country'. It was clearly not the army's wish, or role, to 'promote social reform in time of war'.

Mrs Hobby remained unshaken in her conviction that given 'the character of the women who will likely be accepted in the WAAC, it is anticipated that venereal disease and pregnancy will not offer a problem of major importance'. While the Director was prepared to believe that the etiquette of a ladies seminary could somehow be made compatible with army life, other advisers cautioned against 'efforts to impose boarding school types of discipline on adult female personnel of the WAAC'. But Mrs Hobby was firmly convinced that, 'Taboos and punitive measures do have a deterrent effect on large numbers of people,' and that to provide contraceptive and prophylactic advice would 'reflect an attitude towards sexual promiscuity that, whatever the practice, is not held by the majority of Americans. The Army, I repeat, is no place to propagandize new social attitudes.'

It was inevitable that the herding together of so many women in such close contact would generate a nexus of sexual liberation for WAACs. Army life had already had this effect on the girls in Britain's ATS, according to one of its recruits, who frankly admitted that her sex life began when she joined the army at eighteen:

Quite apart from the free barrack room talk about sex, there was a universal language that we all picked up from the graffiti on toilet walls. We discovered that the men for sure used this as a way of communication with each other about the women in our camp. They would write, 'Try Shirley, she's easy,' and so on. It was particularly useful to those who were in transit and needed quick information as to who was a good lay so that they could get one before moving on. But we women would use it also. I remember that a certain Colonel Jones was always up there on the wall for having thirteen inches but not being very good. There were many others and information as to which lesbian to watch out for, or which officers were particularly to be avoided, and where to go for an abortion. This graffiti was a useful guide for the new recruits; toilet information was a useful 'sexual noticeboard' through which girls could tell each other anonymously what they had learnt. This was one of the ways in which the army really did help educate us about sex, yet because of the competition there was never really any way to be sure how many men anybody really had or with whom – except for the virgins and nymphos – because everyone was eager to be having as much sex as possible.

Confidential US Army records recently declassified now show that WAC bases were certainly not on a moral par with 'ladies' seminaries'. In November 1943, the army's VD Control Inspectors were rushed to a WAC camp in Florida after alarming reports that one in five of the hundred and twenty-five enlisted WACs and their fifteen officers were apparently suffering from gonococcal infections. Colonel Hobby ordered all the offenders to be transferred.

Military nurses came in for more than their fair share of alleged immorality in World War II. Hospitals, in contrast to the home and workplace, had always reversed customary definitions as the 'weaker sex' dealt with helpless male patients. It was not therefore unusual to find that many romance, as well as transient sexual encounters, resulted from the contact between convalescing soldiers and nurses whose emotions were already raw from exposure to the human toll taken by war.

Soldiers who recovered at military hospitals in World War II considered it their duty to flirt outrageously with nurses in the hopes of obtaining personal comfort. A GI wrote of an army nurse from the US military hospital in Casablanca with particular affection:

She told us to call her Butch. She was from Dorchester and she was the biggest gal I'd ever seen. When she bent over to take my temperature, I thought from her wide breasts and budding belly that a witty and motherly cow was ministering to me. We loved the lieutenant for her laugh that was cynical and rich. She specialized in making the appendix patients laugh until they all but burst their stitches. There was a smell of cologne and soap about her. One night she had a baby on the stairs of the nurses' quarters. The colonel had to deliver her himself. It was the first time he'd practised obstetrics in thirty years. He was so mad at her for waking him out of a sound sleep that he shipped her and her baby back from Casablanca to the States.

The military nursing services' immorality was often exaggerated by enlisted men who saw officers monopolizing the company of nurses. A typical incident occurred during a band concert at a Pacific staging base in New Caledonia, when a GI recalled what was observed through the mosquito screen of his tent by the whole battalion:

The captain and three officers could be dimly seen through the mosquito screen, alternately sitting and dancing with four fat, homely army nurses, probably hired for the celebration of the captain's third year in the army. Alcohol was passed repeatedly and often. A pause in the playing by the band and the Master of Ceremonies inquired, 'Any requests?' whereupon the door of El Captain's tent opened slightly to allow a flushed feminine face to appear. The face moved and spake, 'Play "The Waltz You Saved For Me".' The MC responded courteously with, 'We have had a request. The next selection shall be . . . "Take It and Give"!'

The nurses themselves became hardened to the gossip, particularly in the Pacific hospitals where they learned to cope with sex-starved patients and the rigorous life. As Second Lieutenant Elizabeth Itzen summed it up in a verse she entitled 'Personal Report':

> My life consists of bully beef
> Soggy clothes and wiggly teeth
> Gunshot wounds and jungle rot
> And days that are so bloomin' hot
> That even hell compared to this
> Would seem a simple life of bliss

Nurses had been a uniformed army auxiliary since the turn of the century however, and the War Department in Washington was more concerned with countering the bad publicity their sisters in uniform were attracting in the United States. In early 1943, a tighter control was ordered by the WAAC directorate on overnight passes following complaints from hotels near army camps that female enlistees were checking into rooms with soldiers: 'Occupants of some of the rooms were not fully dressed.' But after women were granted equal military status as WACs in September the Judge Advocate General's office pointed out in a review of a hotel incident in July:

> The women who make up the WAC are to be treated as enlisted and commissioned personnel of the Army rather than inmates of some well-chaperoned young ladies' seminary . . . While it might be readily surmised that this young woman and young man, after a certain amount of convivial imbibing, might have withdrawn to a bedroom of the suite to indulge in more intimate relationships, and while it might be conjectured that two people of opposite sexes that were discovered to be alone in a bedroom with the articles that were discovered to be present were there for other purposes than to repeat their Paternosters, yet the law requires more conclusive proof of an evil act before it will sustain a conviction.

In the summer of 1945, WACs being posted to Europe received an illustrated booklet entitled *For Women Going Overseas* which was a frank adaptation of the sort of sex information that had been provided for male soldiers since the beginning of the war. Women were cautioned that 'different moral standards' applied in war-torn Europe, where 'medical facilities have been so disrupted that VD has been able to spread almost unchecked'.

When the WAC established women as full members of the US army it also liberated them from being penalized for their personal off-base activities. Homosexual activity was not considered as disgraceful when practised by women in uniform as by men. Although it posed the same inherent threat to military discipline it did not attract the same penalties, a reflection of the dual standard applied by civilian laws. Queen Victoria's refusal to believe that such women existed excluded lesbians from the harsh criminal penalties of Britain's Sexual Offences Act, and while the so-called sodomy statutes applied to 'all persons' without distinction, they had never been successfully invoked against any American woman.

The WAAC selection boards attempted to screen out the women

with homosexual tendencies who, it had been anticipated, would be attracted to the segregated army life for other than patriotic motives. Many lesbians did, however, serve in the uniform of their country's auxiliaries. Since the percentage female population with exclusive homosexual tendencies was found by the Kinsey Report to be only a fifth of the estimated ten per cent incidence of male homosexuality, they did not pose the same problem for the military authorities. The identification of homosexuality in the female services was complicated because demonstrations of affection such as kissing and embracing were considered socially acceptable amongst women. Army psychologists also advised that the development of close comradeship was an important element in the building of *esprit de corps*.

Nevertheless the 'potential problem which may be expected when a large number of people of the same sex are in constant association' was tactfully dealt with in the Sex Hygiene Course pamphlet prepared in 1943. 'Homosexuality is of interest to you as WAAC officers only so far as its manifestations undermine the efficiency of the individuals concerned and the stability of the group . . . Every person is born with a bisexual nature,' the pamphlet cautioned, urging officers to be 'generous in your outlook' when it came to dealing with 'fine and generous friendships'. Distinction was to be made between the 'active homosexual' who should be 'discharged as promptly as possible' and the female soldier 'who has gravitated towards homosexual practices' because of the new close association with women, loneliness, or 'hero worship'. This type 'can be influenced away from homosexuality by sympathetic guidance'. Transfers, shifting barrack rooms, and the advice of the post surgeon were recommended remedies. Court martials were to be a last resort because of the difficulty of proving that an offence had been committed against army regulations. The guidelines warned that, 'Any officer bringing an unjust or unprovable charge against a woman in this regard will be severely reprimanded.'

The difficulty of obtaining enough evidence to warrant any court martials allowed the official US Army historian to affirm, 'the problem of homosexuality occurred . . . rarely in the WAC'. Even so, early in 1944, the threat of a public scandal forced the army to take action against a lesbian ring at one of the largest WAC establishments in the eastern United States. The Secretary of War received a letter 'to inform you of some of the things at Fort Oglethorpe that are a disgrace to the US Army.' The complaint came from the mother of a twenty-year-old WAC from Wisconsin 'who I know was clean of heart and mind when she joined up . . . It is no wonder women are afraid to enlist. It is full of homosexuals and sex maniacs . . . Unless this vice is cleaned out I am going to reveal that scandal to the world,' wrote Mrs C., giving the names of a lieutenant and sergeant who were among 'many others practising this terrible vice' with her daughter. She explained how the shocking discovery had been made from 'disgusting' letters that had recently arrived for her daughter, who was on sick leave suffering from measles.

Since the WACs had still not recovered from a bad press the previous year in the 'Slander Campaign' it did not take Colonel Hobby long to act to prevent headlines being made of correspondence, on USO notepaper, which contained such phrases as, 'Lover baby, I knew I was going to miss you terribly, but I didn't realize how very, very much' . . . 'How is my little blueberry tart?' . . . 'Oh darling How I wished for you all nite' . . . 'I guess I'll have to either play with myself or go get ★★★★★★.'

Two of the most senior WAC lieutenant colonels and legal advisers of the Advocate General of the Army were flown down to Fort Oglethorpe and began an exhaustive three-week investigation, during which they closely cross-examined the 'named persons' and others who admitted associating with the lesbian circle at the base. The transcript of these hearings, which were constituted to avoid the necessity for an official court martial and inevitable publicity, opened the eyes of the WAC directorate to the nature and extent of lesbian activity, as well as to the difficulty of identifying and dealing with homosexual offenders in a female service.

Under cross-examination, one of the sergeants involved maintained that her affections for the corporal did not constitute unnatural behaviour, and that she had 'engaged in love-making in the manner and type that normally a woman engages in with man'. The pretty young corporal proved on questioning to be neither as innocent nor as unwilling as her mother had charged:

Q What is a 'dike'?
A Well it is a person of Rosemary's type.

Q Is that term applied to a woman or man, or both?

A It is a woman.

Q You mean to a woman of Rosemary's type, a woman who 'goes down' on other women?

A Yes, sir.

Q What Colonel Holt wants is: Did she play with you, love you up, fondle you, or just what did she do to you?

A Well, while we were layng on the bed, yes, she had pulled my skirt off. She was kissing me and then she got down in front of the bed on her knees and she started kissing me on the privates. Is that what you want sir?

Q Beg your pardon?

A Is that what you want sir?

Q Did she inject her tongue into your privates?

A Yes sir.

Q Was that pleasurable to you as well as her?

A Yes sir.

The lieutenant who emerged as the ringleader of the lesbian circle at Fort Oglethorpe was a worldly, divorced lawyer in her early thirties. In an off-the-record session she successfully traded her way out of a general court martial in return for dishonourable discharge, because she admitted 'her guilt and assumed the entire blame and responsibility'. The camp commandant indicated in her testimony that most WAC officers preferred to turn a blind eye to the issue.

> In talking about any of these subjects: sex, venereal disease, homosexuality – with women who have no experience, but after all, these are grown women supposedly. Most of them have at least heard dirty jokes about it . . . I think we have had very few cases of overt homosexuality, of emotional bias. I think we have gotten most of them.

A leading male psychiatrist in the US army confirmed the official view that homosexuality was not considered a major threat to good military order in the WACs:

> I think it is a sort of mutual masturbation, if you ask me. I think it is very frank and haven't said it publicly, but I think they are away from home; they are somewhat lonely; they are away from their mothers, sisters, and so on, and I think it amounts to practically that. I don't think it is anything that they can't be, with any guidance, gotten out of. I would treat the matter exactly as we treat, for example, venereal

disease. We have finally dragged the general subject of venereal disease out into the open to fight it rather than burrowing under ground.

The WAC directorate, however, was certainly not going to let the Fort Oglethorpe affair come out into the open. An officer was sent to Wisconsin to assure the corporal's worried mother that a full investigation had indeed 'cleaned out' the culprits. Mrs C. then agreed she 'would never say anything that would harm the Army . . . I wrote it when I was angry and should have waited, but it hurt me so badly, I have never had anything hit me like that.' This allowed the investigation to wrap up its report on the reassuring note that, while 'homosexual addicts have gained admittance to the WAC', Fort Oglethorpe was not 'full of homosexuals and sex maniacs'. The lieutenant and the sergeant were permitted to resign and the enlisted women involved caught up in lesbian entanglements were transferred to alternate bases. The whole affair was confined to a confidential administrative file that remained stamped 'Top Secret' for nearly forty years.

Among the many lesbians who were never discovered and who found both sexual opportunity and a surprising degree of tolerance in the WACs during World War II was a West Coast writer who recorded her astonishment at the welcome she received the first day she arrived at her basic training camp:

> As I walked in with my suitcase, I heard a woman from one of the barracks windows saying. 'Good God, Elizabeth, here comes another one!' Everybody was going with someone or had a crush on someone. Always the straight women I ran into tended to ignore us, tended to say, 'Who cares? It leaves all the men for us.'

Lesbian activity was by no means restricted to the army: the recollections of a WAVE recruit from Iowa reveal how she discovered her own sexual preference after joining up:

> I was sitting in the barracks in Florida with this one woman I admired greatly. We were sitting next to each other with our feet propped up on the table, and she started stroking my leg, and I thought, 'Wow! What's all this?' Eventually we got into bed together. She said that she had never related to a woman before. We didn't talk about what we were doing; we just did it and felt good about it. I just thought, 'Well, this is the way its going to be forever.'

While most women did not become lesbians as a result of their wartime encounters, many acquired a tolerance of and understanding for such tendencies in others that contributed to a relaxation of their prejudices in post-war life. Just as the vast majority of women who donned uniform in World War II were not whores, so even fewer were lesbians – but it was a sad fact of service life that the charges were repeatedly made as a result of the reaction of men in the armed services to what many regarded as an unwarranted female invasion into the traditionally exclusively male military preserve.

5

SENTIMENTAL BULLETS

I was reminding the boys what they were really
fighting for, the precious personal things rather
than ideologies and theories.

Vera Lynn – 'The Forces' Sweetheart

There'll be love and laughter and peace ever after,
Tomorrow, when the world is free.

'The White Cliffs of Dover'

'WE WANT TO GIVE HITLER a more audible razzing than we've been doing,' announced the chairman of the United States 'Office of War Information' Music Committee in October 1942. The sentimental bullets being turned out by American songsmiths lacked the verve of World War I hits like 'Over There'. He complained that Tin Pan Alley was letting down the war effort with 'just love songs with a once-over-lightly war background' – 'boy meets girl stuff'. The 'Arsenal of Democracy' needed more aggressive songs like 'Der Fuehrer's Face' which contained a rude chorus considered so offensive that radio stations refused to give it air time because of the vulgar 'raspberries' blown at each mention of Hitler. Even so, this sort of number rallied the aggressive spirit, according to the OWI spokesman who told *Variety* that they wanted more 'freedom songs' like 'Praise the Lord and Pass the Ammunition'.

Popular composer Frank Loesser, who had written America's first wartime hit, claimed that there was no incentive to repeat its success because the advertising sponsors of radio shows believed that housewives in World War II were put off by music that sounded overtly martial.

> You stay in the middle sort of. You give her hope without facts; glory without blood. You give her a legend with the rough edges neatly trimmed . . . If you want to sell a housewife Jell-o you don't tell her, 'Madam, it is highly probable that your son is coming home a basket case, or at least totally blind, but cheer up, tonight choose one of the six delicious flavours and be happy with America's finest dessert.'

Radio undoubtedly played a role in denying 'Tin Pan Alley Patriots' the chance to repeat the foot-stamping successes of World War I, most of which were written for marching or dancing to. During World War II swing was all the rage in the wartime dancehalls, and sentimental love ballads dominated the radio. The short-lived success of the flag-wavers such as 'This is Worth Fighting For' or 'Let's Put a New Glory in Old Glory' soon gave way to a revival of pre-war songs with strong nostalgic themes like 'You'd Be So Nice To Come Home To', and 'You Made Me Love

You' that reminded servicemen and their girls of each other.

Patriotism had given way to sentiment two years earlier in Britain. 'We're Going to Hang Out the Washing on the Siegfried Line' epitomized the brash optimism of 1939. But as the British Expeditionary Force retreated to Dunkirk and the nation braced itself for the military storm that was about to hurl itself across the Channel, 'Roll out the barrel, we'll have a barrel of fun' expressed the collective 'we're all in it together' mood. Throughout the critical summer of the Battle of Britain the BBC musical broadcasts provided a reassuring diet of nostalgia and saccharine sentiment as a counterpoint to the ringing Churchillian rhetoric promising 'blood, toil, sweat and tears'.

During what the Prime Minister called the nation's 'finest hour', references to the 'thumbs-up' optimism of young RAF fighter pilots 'braving the angry skies' endowed the 'White Cliffs of Dover' with a painful topicality. It was of little significance that bluebirds were not native to Dover, nor anywhere else in the British Isles, but they symbolized romantic togetherness in an England safe from enemy bombs, when 'Jimmy will go to sleep in his own little room again.'

That this most unashamedly sentimental and patriotic of all the British wartime songs went on to become a favourite in the United States was in no small measure due to Vera Lynn. The evocative vocal style of 'the plumber's daughter from East Ham' endowed romantic wartime songs with a personal sincerity that only Bing Crosby could match. She pitched her songs precisely on the fine edge that divides sentimentality from mawkishness and endowed their often trite lyrics with a meaning that inspired millions of men and women. It made her voice an unforgettable part of World War II.

By 1940, Vera Lynn was the nation's most popular vocalist, and her records were being played by the BBC more often than those of America's top singers of sentimental ballads, Bing Crosby and Deanna Durbin. Songs like 'Yours', 'Faithful For Ever', 'Somewhere in France With You', and 'There's a Boy Coming Home On Leave' expressed the yearnings of lovers who were parted by war. When the *Daily Express* of 17 April 1940 announced 'British Girl Wins BEF Radio Vote' in a poll conducted by the BBC Forces Network, Vera Lynn acquired her enduring title of 'The Forces' Sweetheart'.

'We'll Meet Again', which had done more than any of her songs to make her so popular with the service audience, had first been recorded in the autumn of 1939. Vera Lynn attributed its immediate success to the fact that it was a 'greeting-card song' which expressed the things that ordinary people parted by war needed to say to each other, but did not find it easy to express. It was perhaps *the* World War II song which, better than any other, typified the desperate optimism felt by millions of separated couples who were enjoined to 'keep smiling through' until 'the blue skies drive the dark clouds far away'.

There was a measure of truth in the flippant observation made by one post-war critic that, 'During the war years, Vera Lynn had history working for her as an agent.' Her instinctive judgement, as she recorded in her memoir *Vocal Refrain*, proved her a better judge of the national wartime mood than the army chiefs and parliamentarians who felt, like the US Office of War Information, that too much sentiment made for poor fighting morale:

> Certain belligerent MPs and high military officers – none of whom was actually doing any of the fighting – jumped to the conclusion that a sentimental song produced sentimental soldiers, who would become homesick and desert at the first catch of a crooner's voice. What the boys were supposed to need was more martial stuff, a view that completely overlooked the experience of the previous world war, which, as it got grimmer, produced steadily more wistful songs. As I saw it, I was reminding the boys of what they were *really* fighting for, the precious personal things, rather than ideologies and theories.

Many of the early hits like 'Yours' gave expression to a pledge of constancy 'till the stars lose their glory' for couples separated by the military call-up. But devotion 'to the end of life's story', after two years of war, had to come to terms with the snatched love-affairs which by then had become the staple reality of wartime romance. Anne Shelton, a blonde vocalist with Ted Heath's band, scored her greatest success with 'That Lovely Weekend'. Its haunting melody underscored gently suggestive lyrics that told of the romantic but all-too fleeting intimacies of 'Those two days in heaven you helped me to spend.'

World War II may have cut short long love affairs, but for many British girls the wartime craze for dancing provided the opportunity for meeting new boyfriends. Like the cinemas, theatres, and most other forms of entertainment except the radio, the nation's dance-halls had been shut down by government decree on the outbreak of war, because of exaggerated fears of enemy bombing raids. But by early 1940, many places of public entertainment were permitted to re-open. People flocked to them as never before. The attitude of those in search of companionship and fun was that, 'If Hitler was going to drop a bomb on you, he might as well catch you enjoying yourself as huddled under the stairs.'

London's Hammersmith Palais – later to become a favourite with GIs – and the Paramount in Tottenham Court Road, staged jitterbug marathons and swing contests. Their significance was not lost on one newspaper which noted, 'this noisy exhibition of abandoned convulsions was all in keeping with a mad world in which madmen are conflicting to dominate the continent'. To satisfy the wartime preference for dance bands rather than grand opera, the management of Covent Garden installed a dance floor over the stalls of the historic theatre in Drury Lane. Dancing was the most popular social antidote to anxiety and loneliness because it brought people together to enjoy themselves as well as offering the chance of amorous adventures. Chain-dances like the 'Lambeth Walk' and 'Hokey-Cokey' gave the wartime dance-halls a party-spirit – and men the excuse to hold any pretty girl on the floor. Foxtrots and slow-waltzing enjoyed a wartime revival, accompanied by the classic romantic love-songs such as the lilting melodies of 'Let There Be Love', 'You Made Me Love You', and 'You'll Never Know (just how much I love you)', which encouraged clinches.

A short-lived 'Lambeth Walk' variant was called 'The Blackout Stroll'. Its lyrics urged couples to take advantage of wartime sexual opportunities for cuddling and petting in the blackout. Despite the ordeal of the Blitz, the scantily-clad chorus girls at London's Windmill Theatre kept on dancing all through the air-raids and earned the defiant banner message for the Windmill 'We Never Close'. The Coliseum re-opened early in 1941 with the revue 'Strike Up The Band', and the even more exotic vaudeville 'Nineteen Naughty One' was on at the Prince of Wales Theatre.

Sexual titillation became an established feature of London's wartime entertainment. Although the almost-but-not-quite nude Windmill Girl had to remain statically posed by decree of the Lord Chamberlain, there was more than enough female flesh exposed to arouse the passions of the uniformed men in the audience.

While the moralists protested at this public display of depravity, the Windmill Girls were a regular feature of the popular magazines like *Picture Post* and others such as *Reveille*, *Blighty*, and *Tit-Bits* that were popular with the troops.

While sex became a more overt ingredient in wartime entertainment on stage, radio remained remarkably chaste, and programmes like Vera Lynn's 'Sincerely Yours' broadcast servicemen's requests for songs that were laced with nostalgia and romantic sentiment. These sentimental bullets provided musical talismans and fortified the spirits of the men fighting their way across the world's jungles and deserts. They provided the inspiration for the songwriters who kept the ammunition lockers of Allied morale replenished with ballads like 'Always in My Heart', 'A Little On the Lonely Side', 'I'll Walk Alone (because to tell you the truth I'll be lonely)', 'Silver Wings in the Moonlight', 'I'll Keep the Love Lights Burning', 'My Devotion (is endless and deep as the ocean)', 'Paper Doll', and 'When the Lights Go On Again All Over the World'.

American lyricists churned out ballads such as 'Rosie the Riveter' which celebrated the women in the factories who were 'making history working for victory'. But these songs never featured in the forces radio request programme from the men fighting overseas. They needed reassurance that their girls were waiting for them and not abandoning cosy homes to rivet bombers and weld Liberty ships.

It was not a wife labouring at a lathe but the comforting image of her back home which accounted for the immediate success of Irving Berlin's 'White Christmas'. Soon after it was featured in the 1942 film *Holiday Inn*, it became one of the most widely sung, hummed, and whistled tunes of World War II. Its immense popularity was in no small measure due to crooner Bing Crosby, whose talent for delivering every song as though it was the greatest number in the world endowed 'White Christmas' with an immortality that made it one of the most popular hits ever written. Although its Yuletide nostalgia for snow, carol singers, and sleighbells guaranteed its seasonal success as a chart topper on both sides of the Atlantic for half a generation, its evocation of family, friends, and home ensured that it reached the top of the wartime hit parade no fewer than nine times. 'It came out at a time we were at war and it became a peace song, nothing I ever intended,' Berlin was later to confess.

But it was a German marching song that was destined to become the undisputed favourite of soldiers in every army by the end of World War II. 'Lili Marlene' was a haunting song about a German soldier's girl who crossed the front line in North Africa in 1942 to be adopted by the Allied troops. Her popularity surpassed that of World War I's 'Mademoiselle from Armentières' and the lyrics which told of a girl waiting in the lamplight by the barrack gate were to be bawdified by military versifiers – and bowdlerized by the civilian songsmiths of half-a-dozen nations. The Italians added a verse that began, 'Give me a rose, and press it to my heart', The French gave it an explicit sexuality with the line, 'And in the shadows our bodies entwine.' British troops of General Montgomery's Eighth Army, who had first picked up the song from Afrika Korps radio request broadcasts and soldiers captured from Rommel's desert army, added sexually explicit stanzas and their own refrain, 'We're off to Bomb Benghazi, we're off to bomb BG.'

The United States Office of War Information at first tried to have the song banned from American radio – on the grounds that it was enemy propaganda that would harm GI morale. British WAAFs were ordered not to whistle or sing it within earshot of German prisoners of war because it might lead to fraternization. The BBC, concerned about the salacious unofficial translations as much as by the infectious popularity of a German song, commissioned 'official' English words. Their evocative romance and the simple marching melody made it inevitable that recordings by Vera Lynn, Bing Crosby, and later Marlene Dietrich became big hits:

> Underneath the lantern
> By the barrack gate
> Darling I remember
> The way you used to wait:
> 'Twas there that you whispered tenderly,
> That you loved me,
> You'd always be
> My Lili of the lamplight
> My own Lili Marlene.

The secret of Lili Marlene's phenomenal success was the universality of its theme of a soldier parting with his sweetheart. Lili's remarkable international career began, according to her creator, World War I soldier-poet Hans Leip, as a 'private little love song' about the two girls he became involved with on an officers' course in Berlin in 1917. Lili – real name Betty – was a green-grocer's daughter at his billet. Marleen was a part-time nurse and doctor's daughter whom he encountered in an art gallery. Dreaming of Lili while on guard-duty one rainy evening, with the lamplight flickering in the puddles, Marleen passed by waving her feather boa. Then, while lying on the guardroom's iron cot, Fusilier Leip composed his sentimental poem. 'Their names could no longer be coupled together with an "and". They melted into one, not too shapely, as a single pleasure and pain.'

The poem expressed the sadness of a soldier's last farewell, with its final stanza anticipating his death in action and his ghost returning to meet his girl again under the lamplight. Norbert Schultze, a struggling composer in Berlin, set the words to a wistful march. The song was first recorded by Swedish cabaret artist Lale Andersen after it had proved popular on her Radio Cologne broadcasts in the year war broke out. But its downbeat theme was not considered inspiring enough to celebrate Germany's victorious conquest of Western Europe – and Lale Andersen's records were dispatched to the basement store-rooms of the Reich radio networks in 1940.

A year later an army corporal, dispatched to Vienna in 1941 to collect a consignment of records to be played in Belgrade Radio's nightly broadcasts to German troops in North Africa, included it in his selection. An officer, hearing its bugle-call introduction, decided that it would make ideal signing-off music – and that was how Lili Marlene received its first new airing on 18 August 1941. Within a week, the station was flooded with thousands of requests, and it was thenceforth played on the Belgrade station every night at 9.55 p.m. for three years. The only day it was not heard was when Hitler banned all entertainment the day after the fall of Stalingrad.

Although Dr Goebbels was initially afraid that the song might depress rather than boost morale, German stations were soon spinning the record up to thirty times a day, and in the course of the war Lale Andersen received over a million fan letters from German soldiers. What she was to call 'my fateful song' saved her from the Gestapo after she failed to make good her attempt to join her long-standing Jewish boyfriend in Zurich while on a 1942 concert tour of German army camps in Italy. The security police who arrested her told her that it was the end of her career: 'But a BBC broadcast saved me,' she was to write. 'The BBC put out a report that I'd been taken to a concentration camp and died. Goebbels saw it as a golden opportunity to prove that the English radio told lies. He needed me alive.'

British troops who fought in the Western Desert never forgot the important psychological contribution that the symbolic 'capture' of their opponent's marching song made to their victory in the battle of El Alamein. 'Look here, this is our song! This is the song we hear on our radios in the tanks in the North African desert,' an 8th Army officer claimed shortly after El Alamein. 'Mouth organs strike up "Lili" at night. We sing it in day charges against the Germans. "Lili Marlene" gets us right in our guts. "Lili Marlene" is the theme of the Desert War and get that straight!'

Lili marched with the British Army to Italy, where she also became a favourite with the soldiers of American 5th Army, who added new verses that they derived from the more sentimental Italian version:

> When we are marching in the mud and cold,
> And when my pack seems more than I can hold,
> My love for you renews my might,
> I'm warm again, my pack is light.
> It's you, Lili Marlene, it's you Lili Marlene.

GIs 'fell victim' to the 'captured' German ballad because, as the soldier cartoonist with the 5th Army Bill Maudlin explained, 'Our musical geniuses back home never did get round to a good, honest, acceptable war song, and so they forced us to share Lili Marlene with the enemy. Even if we did get it from the Krauts it's a beautiful song, and the only redeeming thing is the rumour kicking around that "Lili" is an ancient French song, stolen by the Germans. It may not be true, but we like to believe it.' General Eisenhower did not subscribe to this commonly held belief. In 1945, he credited Leip with being 'the only German who has given pleasure to the world during the war'. A reporter for the army newspaper *Stars and Stripes* succinctly summed up that it had done 'something that all Tin Pan Alley has failed to do' by giving the GIs a song that was 'good for marching, cafe singing, and humming to oneself on lonely outposts'.

It was not for the want of effort that British and American songwriters failed to deliver a song to match it. The initial war years produced songs of yearning for absent sweethearts like 'You are Always in My Heart', 'I'll Wait For You Always', 'I'm in Love with the Girl I left Behind Me', and 'I'm Thinking Tonight of My Blue Eyes (and wondering whether she thinks of me?)'. These all reflected the perennial concern of soldiers with the constancy of their girls back home. 'Stick to your Knittin, Kitten', and 'Be Brave, My Beloved' became the US armed forces' favourites as the war dragged and men overseas began to doubt whether the little lady really was waiting for her Johnny to come marching home.

'Somebody Else Is Taking My Place', was too direct an expression of this fear to compete with the enormous success of the Andrews Sisters' vibrant revival of the World War I song 'Don't Sit Under the Apple Tree (with anyone else but me!)' Whatever comfort was afforded the overseas GI in 1943 by 'They're Either Too Young or Too Old' and 'What's Good Is In The Army' was undone by 'You Can't Say No To a Soldier' and Sophie Tucker's gently wicked 'The Bigger the Army and Navy (the better the loving will be)'. It was not so much new Stateside recruits that worried GIs, but 'draft-dodgers' and those young men who enjoyed the benefit of a reserved occupation to stay out of uniform who, they thought, might seduce their girls.

In 1944, thirty thousand bobby-soxers rioted in New York's Times Square before a Frank Sinatra concert. The 4-F classication that kept the skinny young man with the quiff out of uniform increased the resentment many servicemen felt about the sex-appeal of the young crooner with the intense blue eyes and heart-breakingly appealing voice. Although Sinatra was already married with a child, a Columbia University psychologist surmised that 'this little fella represents some kind of an idealized hero, much like the story of Prince Charming' to explain the new phenomenon of 'mass hysteria' among his teenage female fans. When Frank Sinatra finally made his much publicized and often delayed overseas concert tour for the USO in 1945, he was greeted with derisory yells until he melted the GIs' hostility with his talents as a balladeer.

In the final year of World War II the hit songs anticipated

the need to heal the wounds of separation with the passions of homecoming reunions. 'It's Been a Long, Long Time' was followed by Perry Como's overtly suggestive rendition of 'I'm Going to Love that Gal (like she's never been loved before)'. And in Britain, 'I'm Gonna Get Lit Up (when the lights go up in London)' looked forward to a national binge on the 'day we finally exterminate the Huns', when, the singer promised, 'we'll all be drunk for months and months'.

If popular songs were the sentimental bullets in the morale war, the dance band orchestras were its heavy artillery. They provided a sustained romantic musical barrage throughout World War II which an RAF serviceman evocatively recalled:

> A smoke-hazed aeroplane hangar 'somewhere in England', the floor crowded to capacity with uniformed boys and girls swaying gently or 'jiving' wildly according to the dictates of that essential commodity, the dance band, the vocalist, his (or her) face almost obscured by an enormous microphone, singing of love not war . . . The dance was on and all we were conscious of was the music (and what music it was) the exhilarating rhythm and of course, the girl in our arms. She may have been a little WAAF cook, or an ATS orderly, but as the orchestra wove its spell, she was Alice Faye, Betty Grable, Rita Hayworth or whoever our 'pin-up' of that particular week may have been.

No bandleader excelled Glenn Miller at capturing the urgently romantic wartime mood in a sensual but mutedly brassy appeal that could shift effortlessly from the upbeat tempo of 'American Patrol' to the dreamy sentiment of his orchestra's 'Moonlight Serenade' theme music. The tragic disappearance of Colonel Miller when his plane crashed in 1944 added a heroic dimension to the mystique of the music of a band that was more imitated than any other. Glenn Miller was the sound of World War II for many people, but there were plenty of other popular bands that laid claim to the title, including those of clarinettist Benny Goodman – 'The King of Swing' – and Tommy Dorsey, and Harry James in the United States. In Britain the BBC made millions familiar with the piano tessitura of Victor Sylvester and the Geraldo Orchestra's lush strings. In the dance-hall, many preferred the brasher tones of the Joe Loss Orchestra's silver trumpets, or the sweeping syncopations of the RAF musicians who played the popular 'Squadronnaires'.

The wartime tours of military camps by famous bands were just a part of what, by the end of the war, had become a massive logistical campaign that sent popular singers and entertainers to the most distant battle theatres to raise the morale of troops thousands of miles from home. The American USO (United Services Organization) and Britain's ENSA sponsored and organized regiments of singers, dancers, comedians, and musicians who had volunteered to undertake these gruelling overseas tours. On improvized open-air stages, in bombed-out theatres, or sometimes in the backs of army trucks, Allied entertainers endured dust-storms, tropical downpours, the mud of the European front – and in some cases the distant rumble of front-line guns – to ensure that the show went on.

'Munitions and movies are just about equally vital to American fighting men', proclaimed Paramount's leading sex symbol Paulette Goddard after her thirty-eight thousand-mile tour of the China–Burma–India theatre in 1944. Hollywood vied with Broadway in these USO show tours, which made the more limited British ENSA concert parties seem like amateur theatricals. 'Four Jills in Jeep' was a film compiled from sequences shot during a five-month USO tour of North Africa, Italy, and England by Carole Landis, Martha Raye, Kaye Francis and Mitzi Mayfair, who gave up to five GI shows a day.

The leading light behind the mobilization of American show-business talent overseas was comedian Bob Hope. After a dozen overseas tours that took him to every major theatre, accompanied by a bevy of stars and entertainers who played before an estimated seven million troops, he was named the United States number one 'Soldier in greasepaint'. His machine-gun delivery of gags that were a good deal more risqué than he dared use on his radio show never failed to appeal to soldiers. But the loudest roars of approval in these makeshift troop shows were always reserved for the sex goddesses of the silver screen, who braved the weather and the wolf whistles no matter what time of day to bring glamour to what they called the foxhole circuit.

'Carole Landis and the girls dressed to the hilt in evening gowns, although the rain came down in sheets almost constantly,' recalled Jack Benny admiringly after a tour of the Pacific. 'They never covered themselves with coats – after all the boys wanted reminders of the girls back home.' Female stars knew better than anyone what the men really wanted. 'Miss Legs', as Marlene Dietrich was affectionately called by GIs, always made good her reputation by wearing her famous sequinned sheath dress on concert tours and during her many hospital visits. 'I may have seemed slightly incongruous walking into hospital wards in long slim gowns,' Dietrich was to recall, 'but the look in the men's eyes when they saw me made up for the inconvenience of trying to pretend I was just strolling on to a Hollywood movie set.'

The GIs wolf-whistled their delight, but prudish churchmen in America roared with anger that Marlene Dietrich's act constituted 'indecent and sexually exciting entertainment' after the legendary gams that had been bared before a thousand American soldiers appeared in a *Life* photo-spread. 'Miss Dietrich's legs, as you know, have been publicized for many years,' replied the Executive Vice-President of USO Camp Shows Inc:

> This leads me to the conclusion that if Miss Dietrich makes a personal appearance she will be asked to show her legs, and the question arises then as to: 1. Whether or not her granting this request is indecent and 2. If it is not, whether her manner of exposing her leg to the knee is indecent.

It was agreed to leave the final decision on this vital issue to the Senior Chaplain of the European Theatre of Operation. Whether he was a fan of Miss Dietrich is not recorded in the official correspondence, but the legendary Marlene continued to show a leg for victory!

In similar vein another chaplain filed a formal protest at 'the most vile, obscene thing I have ever heard'. After another female USO performer delivered a number he wrote to complain:

> In seductive language she, in her song, is describing why she wants to get married. At the close the mistress of ceremonies yells through the mike, 'Men, you could all get twenty years for what you are thinking!' – and then lets out a vulgar laugh. If what I hear as I sit here trying to write this letter is a fair example of modern cinema, society is truly in a pitiable state.

The USO directorate clearly had to tread a very delicate line in balancing the sensibilities of the military chaplaincy with Hollywood's enthusiasm for satisfying the GI sense of humour, which was a good deal more profane than would have pleased the Hays' office film censors. 'We had two roosters that got caught in the rain; one made a run for the barn, and the other made a duck under the porch', and 'Jack and Jill went up the hill, each with one dollar and a quarter; Jill came down with two dollars and fifty cents. You can't tell me she went for water!' were so mildly blue that they could not have brought the faintest blush to the cheeks of any soldier accustomed to the racy talk of the barrackroom. But after one USO show they sent a chaplain rushing for his typewriter to protest to Washington.

Even Jack Benny and Carole Landis came in for criticism over their suggestive jokes during a 1944 Pacific tour. Miss Landis was censured by one chaplain because 'of the large number of men she promiscuously kissed'. He was not included, which was perhaps why he felt so bitterly that she had failed in her duty to remind the men of 'the finer qualities of their own womenfolk back home'. Although two comedians were discharged from their USO contracts for 'indecent language', sexual titillation and saucy humour remained an indispensable part of the 'foxhole' circuit entertainer's kit bag – although the increasing number of protests from field chaplains forced the theatrical officers of the USO to approve the contents of every script.

The demand for shows was so great that even the USO, which tapped the combined resources of Hollywood and Broadway, could not keep pace by 1945, when the curtain was going up on a performance somewhere in the world round the clock. The Special Services Division of the Army therefore arranged for the distribution of a 'Do-it-yourself-manual' for soldiers to put on their own shows. 'Hi Yank!' was based on the famous GI cartoon strip 'Sad Sack' – the 'army's unluckiest guy'. With music by Broadway songwriter Frank Loesser, it was billed as a 'lusty fast-moving show' by the *New York Times*. It came with complete instructions for crepe paper skirts for the all-male chorus, for outfitting Carmen Miranda look-alikes, and with choreography sketches for the all-male chorus line. Its supposedly 'actor proof, audience proof script' included a sexually suggestive chorus, calculated to bring hoots of delight from the GI audience, in which Sack laments:

I had so much romance in me I thought I would burst;
I hurried off to see my gal, my line was all rehearsed;
I rang the bell – she said, 'So sorry, the Marines have landed first!'
With full equipment ——!

Even without entertainment manuals, music, and crepe-paper costumes, some front-line units contrived to put on variety shows. In Bayreuth, which was captured in the final weeks of the war by Patton's troops, the '4th Armoured Follies' took over Wagner's hallowed Festspielhaus for a revue billed as 'All the pretty ladies in the world'. Hitler's favourite composer 'definitely turned in his grave' according to a member of the audience:

> Actually there were far too few females. Instead, we were treated to half the noncoms in the 4th Armoured (myself definitely excluded) in drag, kicking up hairy legs and intoning 'See What the Boys in the Backroom Will Have' and lecherous verses to 'Lili Marlene'.

6

PLASTER SAINTS

A soldier's the sort
For rape and slaughter
Not fit to escort a patriot's daughter

Sgt Grant. A. Sanders, US Army

The Army does not officially condone profanity;
unofficially, it knows it can do little to stop it.
The society of soldiers is not polite. It is a society
of men, frequently unwashed, who have been
dedicated to the rugged task of killing other men,
and whose training has emphasized that a certain
reversion to the primitive is not undesirable.

US Infantry Journal, 1943

THE MAKING OF THE 'CIVILIAN' SOLDIER during World War II involved the dramatic personal transformation of a large cross-section of male civilian society. According to the US *Infantry Journal* war was to be compared with the 'tussle over a mate' between animals of the same species, or the aggressive defence of their young and habitat:

> Men, being two-legged animals, may fight for any and all of these reasons. But because they have minds capable of being moved by abstract ideas such as honour, glory, freedom, sympathy, justice, and patriotism, men fight also for what they believe to be right.

In another article, 'Psychology For the Fighting Man', it was suggested that civilians could be transformed into effective fighters by a diet which was high in disciplined subordination and red meat – to ensure plenty of thiamin, the so-called morale vitamin. Neither food nor patriotism, however, was enough to make an enlisted man endure the physical privations of soldiering and give him the spiritual motivation for self-sacrifice. The mass citizen armies demanded by total war had to be produced by a rapid and brutal conditioning process designed to overcome the individual instinct for self-preservation and make people capable of killing or dying on command.

Men in the armed forces learned that although they might be called upon to give their lives to defend civilized society, they were expected to abandon its most cherished principles for the duration. The transformation in attitude this demanded was vividly summed up by American author James Jones, who himself went through the process to become a GI:

> He must make a compact with himself or with Fate that he is lost. Only then can he function as he ought to function under fire. He knows and accepts beforehand that he's dead, although he may still be walking around for a while. That soldier you have walking around there with this awareness in him is the final end production of the EVOLUTION OF A SOLDIER.

An essential part of this evolutionary process was intensive lessons in 'the science of slaughter' which were set down in the diary of Sergeant Myles Babcock of the 37th US Infantry Division. They included propaganda 'combined with physical and mental hatred' that hardened soldiers and stripped away their inhibitions:

> The psychological effect of lessons in hand-to-hand killing proved brutalizing. Lack of feminine companionship encouraged vulgarity, almost completely stilled courtesy. The individual civilians poured into the crucible of hate, brutality, and organized murder undergo a subtle change. True, they retain their identity and personality, but all bear the imprint of a common mould. The formula utilized in making a soldier is visualized to be an intangible called 'discipline'. No matter how forceful or unusual the personality, eventually it succumbs to habit, discipline, propaganda, and mass psychosis. He becomes a soldier with salient characteristics and reactions. He embodies myriad vices, virtues, and traits including profanity, vulgarity, chronic complaining, scepticism, irritability, brutality, respect for rights of colleagues, disrespect and envy of civilians, loneliness, hatred of monotony, a type of fatalism, despair, animalism, stamina, a Spartan reaction to pain, and a burning hope that destiny dictates the return to the States.

European conscripts accepted this 'crucible of hate' more readily than Americans, since war and military service had long been a part of the established British, French, German, Japanese, and Russian social order. In the United States it was significant that soldiers became tagged as 'Government Issue' – GI was an appropriate label for the expendable human elements in the mass-produced machinery of twentieth-century warfare. They were distinguished only by the number on the dog tags that hung around their necks. Indeed, military publications officially approved the title 'GI JOE': draftees were told to be 'proud' of 'the wonderful phrase that completely expresses the utter anonymity of the private soldier'.

'Who in uniform would want it otherwise?' asked the US *Infantry Journal* – and many agreed. As one wartime draftee explained:

> The soldier liked being a GI. It was comforting to feel, in this radically different kind of life which so often involved fear and danger, that his own self was submerged in the anonymity of the mass. The role of GI made no undue demands on individual virtue or responsibility. Even

if he continually bungled and became a 'sad sack', his fellows looked upon him with a kind of joking affection.'

James Jones provided a graphic insight into the conditioning process that stripped away civilian privileges in order to make a man a GI:

> Living in herds and schools like steers or fish, where men (suddenly missing deeply the wives or girlfriends they left so adventurously two weeks before) literally could not find the privacy to masturbate even in the latrines. Being laughed at, insulted, upbraided, held up to ridicule, and fed like pigs at a trough with absolutely no recourse or rights to uphold their treasured individuality before any parent, lover, teacher, or tribune. Harassed to rise at five in the morning, harassed to be in bed at nine-thirty at night.

Many enlistees found particularly embarrassing and painful the denial of privacy, especially for personal bodily functions:

> Toilet taboos were suspended for the duration. Fifty of us shared one latrine and took turns at cleaning it, in a symphony of grunts and smells and flushing noises. There were no doors on the booths, nor privacy at the urinal. Answering nature's call meant subjecting yourself to loud and detailed criticism – perceptive and merciless descriptions of your sex organs, ranging from glowing admiration; brilliant critiques of your style of defecation, with learned footnotes on gas-passing. Expert discussions gave new meaning to your technique of urination – which hand, how many, or no hands at all – or how nonchalant you managed to look. We soon learned to flaunt our genitals and brag about our toilet mannerisms. Anyone who was modest about these was immediately and forever labelled a homosexual.

The military environment was oppressively masculine to emphasize the break from the feminine and 'civilizing' influences of civilian life. The operation of aircraft, tanks, and the other technological advances in weapons of mass destruction required sophisticated training in the techniques of slaughter, but when it came down to the actual business of fighting, the conditioning needed to turn the World War II civilian into an aggressive soldier was a brutalizing process that often triggered the release of sexual aggression.

The precise relationship between sexuality and violence has been keenly debated ever since Freud's contention, in his 1915 essay *Reflections on War and Death*, that resort to fighting 'strips us of the later accretions of civilization, and lays bare the primal man in each of us'. Throughout human history the primitive psyche has re-asserted itself through the violence of armed conflict. The sex drive is the most intractable of human instincts. Normally repressed by religious taboos and social convention, it bursts these restraints when social life is disrupted by war and the demands of armed combat. The notion that a sexually aggressive man makes the best fighter has been universal throughout history and in all cultures, as a ranking medical officer in the US navy observed in a 1941 review of the essential qualities to be instilled in the draftee for the armed services:

> The men in a successfully trained army or navy are stamped into a mould. Their barrack-talk becomes typical, for soldiers are taught in a harsh and brutal school. They cannot, they must not, be mollycoddled, and this very education befits nature, induces sexual aggression, and makes them the stern, dynamic type we associate with men of the armed forces. This sexual aggressiveness cannot be stifled. Recently, I read an article by a man who bewailed the effect army life would have on his son. Imagine, if you can, an army of impotent men. This very sexual drive is amplified because of fresh air, good food, and exercise, and exaggerated by the salacious barracks talk. It cannot be sublimated by hard work or the soft whinings of Victorian minds. How important this libido was considered historically can be gathered from the words of Gian Maria, Duke of Milan, who after his defeat stated, 'My men had ceased to speak of women, I knew I was beaten.' The Mongol hordes, who conquered all Asia and most of Europe, recognized this fact too: 'He who is not virile is not a soldier. He who lacks virility is timid, and what rabbit ever slew a wolf.'

Soldiers in a world of ritualized masculinity both consciously and subconsciously came to regard their weapons as extensions of their virility. They were encouraged in this view by instruction manuals such as one which informed the US army infantrymen, 'Your rifle, like your girlfriend, has habits for which you must allow.' Military discipline also produced, as a by-product of its emphasis on obedience and masculinity, profane language and rebelliousness in off-duty pursuits. Hard-drinking – a manifestation of virility – was a common feature of army life, providing an escape from boredom and a method of self-assertion outside the confines of the barracks. Coarse language was a mark of masculine aggressiveness; barrack-room talk was – and is – punctuated with sexual expletives intended to convey male assertiveness and a general contempt for women.

Crude expressions for sexual and excretory acts were common parlance in barrack and bivouac and scorned normal social restraints. 'And, furthermore, by pronouncing those "dirty words" which he never dared utter in the presence of "Mom" or his old-maid schoolteachers, the GI symbolically throws off the shackles of the matriarchy in which he grew up,' was the inference a sociologist drew from his wartime experience as an enlisted man:

> The profane term that most clearly expresses this swaggering masculinity and revengeful, contemptuous (and defensive) attitude towards women is doubtless the most commonly used word (as noun, verb, adjective, adverb, and expletive) in the United States and British armies. In Anglo-Saxon popular culture, moulded by Puritanism, this term suggests that the sexual act can only be 'dirty' and animalistic; and, in keeping with a more nearly universal conception, it suggests that, whereas these qualities do not reflect ill on the male by virtue of his dominant and casual role, they ineradicably contaminate and degrade the human female.

The aggressive sexuality towards women that was enshrined in the military vernacular was evident in the bawdy verses of the chant to which the British Expeditionary Force marched to the French frontier in 1939:

> I don't want a bayonet up my arsehole
> I don't want my bollocks shot away,
> I'd rather live in England,
> In merry, merry, England
> And fornicate my fucking life away.

GI argot also developed a rich scatological and sexual slang that had its roots in an infantile defiance of childhood toilet training. Conversation became 'shooting the shit'; abuse of authority was 'chicken shit'; bawling out was 'ass-chewing', and a downtrodden GI was 'a sad sack of shit' — the origin of the famous American army newspaper cartoon character called 'Sad Sack'. The US army's slang expression for a bungle was 'situation normal all fucked up' or 'Snafu'. Many of these expressions were so universally used that by the end of the war they had been purged of their obscenity and passed into common parlance, like Snafu — politely listed as an acronym for 'Situation Normal All *Fouled* Up!'

'Aside from the richness of the language, army conversation has a beautiful simplicity and directness. It is all on one solid, everlasting subject . . . Women, Women, Women,' wrote American author Irwin Shaw from his wartime experience as a soldier:

> This makes it different from the talk about women and baseball. Occasionally a soldier will deviate a little and his control will leave him, like a pitcher tiring in the late innings, and he will talk about frivolous things like what he thinks ought to be done with Germany after the war. But very soon he will catch himself and start talking about the blonde girl he knew back at Purdue who measured thirty-seven and three quarter inches around the chest, so help him God.

After a tour of Pacific bases, one senator, writing to reassure wives and sweethearts of the American servicemen's moral health, provided a somewhat different emphasis: 'All GI talk revolves around two things – food and home. But their heads don't revolve, they're fixed, right above one spot in the world – the home and the girl they left there.' American writer Charles Allen Smart observed from his vantage point as an enlistee in the navy:

> Of course a boring amount of their talk was about sex, and their language was on the whole repetitious and dull, but some of this talk amused me. For example, I jotted down this scrap of conversation for Peggy (his wife): 'So he got to playing with her titties, and she says, "Mac, you like them titties, don't you? Well they're yours." And by Jesus, she takes them off and hands them to him. They was all rubber! She didn't have no more titties than you or me. Boy, did we give him the bird!'

The reason why sex became the principal subject of conversation of troops everywhere was summed up by James Jones in his post-war literary interpretation of the wartime GI experience: 'When the presence of death or extinction is always just around the corner or next cloud, the comfort of women takes on a great importance.' This suggests one reason why women went to war by proxy, as the pin-ups which were so ubiquitous that they gave a female face to World War II. The icons of female film stars, along with the photos of wives and girlfriends, provided the individual serviceman with a romantic escape from the horrors of combat. It was common practice for soldiers to vaunt the plainest sweetheart – or the most perfunctory sexual contact – and the most popular barrack-room ballads sang the praises of insatiable whores.

British troops in the Western Desert reworked the 'Foggy, Foggy Dew' into a ribald ditty about a legendary Cairene 'Mata Hari', who specialized in the seduction of high-ranking Allied officers:

> They call me Venal Vera, I'm a lovely from Gezira,
> The Fuehrer pays me well for what I do.
> The order of the battle, I obtained from last night's rattle
> On the golf course with a Brigadier from GHQ.
> I often tarry on the back seat of a gharry,
> It's part of my profession as a spy,
> While his minds on copulation I'm extracting information
> From a senior GSO from GSI.

The German Afrika Korps – and later the Allies, who adopted her – embellished 'Lili Marlene' with endless salacious verses. Another favourite of American GIs during the Tunisian campaign celebrated the dubious attractions of the local whores:

> Dirty Girtie from Bizerte
> Had a mousetrap 'neath her skirtie
> Strapped it on her kneecap purty
> Baited it with 'Fleur de Flirte'
> Made her boyfriends most alerty
> She was voted in Bizerte
> 'Miss Latrine' for nineteen thirty.

In the Pacific the theme was the same, and only the words were changed for 'The US Army Flyer's Lament', which began:

> I wish all girls were like B-24's
> And I were a pilot, I'd make them all whores,
> Oh, roll your leg over, roll your leg over,
> Roll your leg over the man in the moon
> I wish all girls were like chicks in the springtime,
> And I were a cock, I'd screw them in swingtime.

The Marine aviators who played a key role in the gruelling battle for the Solomons had their own sexually aggressive song, which they chanted to the tune of 'On the Road to Mandalay':

> Take me east of Iwojima, where the best ain't like the worst,
> Where there ain't no Doug MacArthur, and a man can drown his
> thirst.

Where the Army takes the medals, and the Navy takes the queens,
And the boys that take the fucking are the United States Marines.

That there was a connection between this bold sexual talk and
the deep-seated fear of death which was part of military service is
suggested in one of the stanzas of the English soldier-poet Jocelyn
Brooke and another from his Welsh comrade in arms, Alun Lewis:

> Browned-off with bints and boozing,
> Sweating on news from home,
> Bomb-happy and scared of losing,
> This tent of flesh and bone . . .

> And we talked of girls, and dropping bombs on Rome,
> And thought of the quiet dead and the loud celebrities
> Exhorting us to slaughter, and the herded refugees.

The thought that death might be round the corner was a powerful
incentive towards promiscuity. In civilian society merely dating a
girl was socially acceptable proof of virility, but men in military
society were under constant pressure from their peers to demon-
strate and brag about intimate details of their sexual conquests.

The extended periods of separation from their womenfolk were
felt most keenly by sailors. They had traditionally boasted 'a girl in
every port', and their wartime behaviour upheld that practice, as
an enlistee in the navy confirmed:

> I may say here that my memories of the sex life of the men I knew in
> the navy, as I heard about it and observed it, fully supported the
> Kinsey Report, especially in its emphasis on the different levels of
> education. The sexual life of these men was crude in the extreme, and
> when they had to be and could be, even most of the married men were
> freely promiscuous, but at the same time their loyalty to their wives
> and their best girls was deep, and I suspected that most of them were
> or would be good husbands and fathers – warmer, more unselfish,
> more playful, and more firm in their own rights and dignity, than
> their bosses in civilian life.

Some senior British and American generals had advocated establishing a system of military brothels similar to the French *maisons
tolerées* that had provided women for their troops during World
War I. The most powerful argument against this was that the Axis
powers had established military brothels and that it was morally
indefensible for the Allies to treat female flesh as military logistics.

Instead, continence was preached, but sexual deprivation weighed heavily, particularly on the American forces in the Pacific. US Army aircrews actually wrote to General Marshall during the Guadalcanal campaign in 1942 saying that to win the long battle for the foetid island what they needed was not more bombs and bullets, but women. Men of the 37th Army Division on Bougainville in the Solomons complained in 1943 that they 'have seen only one white woman in nine months, and that is Lois, the nude on the chest of Private Albert Horton'. The Chief of the US Army replied that while he 'appreciated' the need, it was beyond the supply capability of War Department. John H. Burns revealed in his insightful account of GI life, *The Gallery*, how good military logistics clashed with the hypocrisy of Anglo-Saxon moral attitudes:

> Sooner or later every man's thoughts start centring around his middle. The cold and scientific solution would have been to have brothels attached to all our armies overseas, as other nations of the world have always done. But the American people wouldn't have stood for that. I mean the American people back home – too many purity lobbies from old ladies who have nothing else to do but form pressure groups to guard other people's morals.

Individual commanders made unofficial efforts to provide brothel facilities for Allied troops, but the political penalties for doing so became apparent to the British Government as soon as the British Expeditionary Forces had been dispatched to France in 1939. Prime Minister Neville Chamberlain was soon being bombarded with protests from religious groups and organizations such as the Association for Moral Hygiene and demands for 'action to protect the men of the Home and British Empire Forces by insisting that, in France and any other country where the system of licensed brothels still exists, these houses shall be immediately declared "Out of Bounds".'

The War Office advised that putting the *maison tolerées* out of bounds 'might reasonably be interpreted as an insult to the French authorities', whose licensed brothels helped prevent 'the spread of VD in the present abnormal circumstances . . . 'Presumably the houses are not advertised to the troops, and to put them out of bounds because prophylactic precautions are taken in them seems to be no more justifiable than to put out of bounds cantonment bazaars in India because of the *chaklas* (native whore-houses).'

The War Office confidentially accepted that what had failed in peacetime India was not going to keep British soldiers continent in wartime France – the 'moral inducements to chastity' or the 'fear which every right-minded lad and man and women ought to entertain of the terrible consequences of impulsive sexual inter-course.' At the time of the 1938 Munich Crisis, Ministry of Health officials started contingency war-planning to expand venereal dis-ease treatment centres. It was foreseen that the proliferation of RAF and army bases in rural areas would require a fleet of mobile VD units to make weekly inspection tours, but the Treasury refused to grant funds for staffing and equipping the proposed fleet of twenty motor vans.

On the outbreak of hostilities with Germany on 3 September 1939, a Ministry of Health circular alerted local health authorities, 'It is well known that a statement of war favours the spread of VD in the population.' The repercussions of the 'lack of self control' and 'excitement of war conditions' were causing alarm by June 1940, as 'definite signs of the expected wartime increase' in VD rates were seen. This was blamed on the Treasury's penny-pinching refusal to fund the VD vans. As the battle for Britain's health was waged in Whitehall committees that fateful summer, the RAF Spitfires and Hurricanes fought their more famous battle for the supremacy of the skies over England. The Luftwaffe was beaten by mid-September, but it took another month for the Ministry of Health to win its mobile VD units. A major factor in this victory was that the return of the defeated British Expedition-ary Force from Dunkirk placed the burden of dealing with the consequences of wartime military promiscuity on the local health authorities.

Urgent meetings took place at Scotland Yard to discuss ways of controlling the sudden explosion of prostitution in London's West End. The police agreed to investigate whether 'big criminal inter-ests', as vociferous moral campaigners believed, were behind the 'new type of prostitute', dubbed 'Piccadilly Warriors', who were roaming the blacked-out squares of central London. The increase in the numbers of prostitutes was blamed on what the National Vigilance Association termed 'nasty young men' amongst the influx of foreign troops from France and Poland.

The numbers of women who plied the ancient trade in the streets of London and around the main army bases and in British ports in World War II rose in direct proportion to the numbers of men conscripted – an indication that a certain section of the female population was volunteering to meet the sexual demands of the armed forces. Any effort at controlling them was hampered in Britain because while a brothel – or 'disorderly house' as it was quaintly defined by the law – was, and still is, illegal, no action could be taken against street-walking prostitutes unless they actually accosted the man they were soliciting. Only then could they be charged and arrested for 'obstruction' under an arcane bye-law. This encouraged the 'amateur' whore and 'goodtime girl' to take to blacked-out streets which encouraged opportunities for hurried intimacies. Venereal infections spread apace through the military and civilian populations. By mid-1941, the national VD statistics had increased by seventy per cent since the beginning of the war. In London and the seaports the rise was more dramatic, with Liverpool's health authorities reporting an alarming four-fold increase in syphilis cases, with the rate 'still rising'.

So many merchant seamen were reported infected in Britain's main ports that a sinister Nazi plot to aid the U-boats in the Battle of the Atlantic was suspected. 'There is good reason to believe that in at least one neutral port, Lisbon, the enemy has a scheme for infecting British and Allied seamen through diseased prostitutes,' reported a worried British Shipping Federation. Although no conclusive evidence was ever unearthed to show Hitler had enlisted the aid of the nefarious spirochaete in Germany's bid to cut the Atlantic supply line, a special issue of prophylactic kits was rushed to Liverpool for distribution to the crews of cargo ships bound for neutral ports.

The arrival of the first American troops on British soil in the spring of 1942 sent venereal disease rates to almost epidemic proportions. But it was not until October that year, after a series of parliamentary debates, that the Ministry of Health launched a radio and poster campaign to educate the public and emergency powers for compulsory medical examinations of those infected were introduced.

The medical officers of the US army were dismayed by the prevailing ignorance and lack of effective laws to combat venereal infection in the UK. Sex-hygiene, as it was termed in America,

had been a major part of the New Deal health education programme since the mid-thirties, with annual 'Social Hygiene Days'
proclaimed by President Roosevelt. When sixty thousand of the
first million American draftees were found to be venereally infected, public and congressional pressure mounted a crack-down
on the booming 'red-light' districts that sprouted up alongside the
expanding military training camps.

'Pay-day for soldiers, sailors, and marines is looked to with
anticipation by practically everyone in the racket,' stated a 1941
report by the American Social Hygiene Association, which was to
play an instrumental part in the wartime 'Blitz on the Brothels'
in the United States. 'On the last day of each month, and usually
for two or three succeeding days, long lines of "soldier boys"
waited their turn to gain admittance. The "old timers" in the
game admitted, one at a time, only as many prospective customers
as could be accommodated, and Military Police prevented those
who were waiting from gate-crashing.' Red-light district hotels
advertised 'Rooms equipped with every human convenience', and
bellboys and porters at legitimate hotels as well as taxi drivers
were cut in on the racket. A national survey revealed that it was
not just the commercialized vice-rings, but also a burgeoning army
of freelance hookers who operated out of their own cars or taxis.
The more sophisticated girls had trailers, called 'chippie wagons'
by the GIs, which could be towed away from camps and city limits
when police tried to crack-down on prostitution.

A bill passed in July 1941 gave commanders of military bases
the power to summon the FBI to close down local whorehouses.
But many commanding officers preferred to 'wink at prostitution'
and ignore the official army policy directing a 'vigorous repression'
of prostitution. One camp colonel filed an official protest quoting
Kipling's pertinent observation that, 'Single men in barracks do
not grow into plaster saints.' But public moral outrage reached
fever-pitch that month, following publication of a book by the
two ranking members of the US Public Health Service which
charged that VD was the 'No. 1 Saboteur of Our Defence'.

The *New York Times* reviewer found its sensational exposure 'as
fascinating as it is sinister'. It charged that so-called panzer-
prostitutes, well-dressed women in smart automobiles, patrolled
roads around army camps giving soldiers a lift – to houses of ill
repute. There were reports of 'brothels on wheels' and a trailer

camp, near Fort Knox, populated by elderly 'parents', each with a surprisingly large family of dubious daughters available for hire by the hour.

On the eve of the Pearl Harbor attack, US army chief General George C. Marshall issued an official army directive on the need to repress prostitution. Enlistees were to be given sex hygiene brochures and shown anti-VD films regularly. 'Unless extenuating circumstances exist, a high incidence of venereal disease in a command shall be regarded as indicating a lack of efficiency on the part of the commander concerned,' the War Department circular warned. 'The guiding principle shall continue to be that continence and self-control not only develop character but are the only completely satisfactory methods of preventing venereal disease,' directed War Department Circular No. 249.

'Control' was interpreted as necessitating free contraceptives and the establishing of a defensive chain of prophylactic stations around naval and military bases. Education was to be achieved by posters, pamphlets, films, and regular lectures on the perils of prostitution and VD. The campaign was launched shortly after Pearl Harbor by former boxing champion Gene Tunney, then a naval commander, who urged American servicemen to pin what he called the 'Bright Shield of Continence' on their uniforms and display 'moral bravery when confronted by the rouged challenge' of 'motorized brothels' and 'diseased harlots'. His homily, which was reprinted in *The Readers Digest* and other popular magazines, cautioned:

> Tally cards seized as evidence showed how much these prostitutes had earned in one day; three cards showed forty-nine, thirty-seven, and twenty-eight customers . . . Can you imagine what happened to the hundred and fourteen servicemen who visited them that day? . . . Can our sailors and soldiers, as champions of democracy, afford to indulge in sexual promiscuities scorned by most prize fighters? Dare they forget that in the First World War, seven million days of service were lost to the US Army as a result of venereal infections?

The appeal to continence was a failure, as Tunney admitted: 'Men don't get medals for practising it.' It was another failure in the long line of attempts made by generals and religious leaders throughout history to protect the health of their armies from the diseases that resulted from the sexual excesses endemic in warfare.

Xenophon recorded that Greek warriors ignored warnings on

'the issue of the flesh', Julius Caesar had soldiers with symptoms of gonorrhoea flogged – and Richard III had soldiers with the 'pox', as it was known, hanged! It was the promiscuity of French soldiers campaigning under Louis XIII in Italy at the beginning of the sixteenth century that spread a sinister new venereal infection across Europe. Originally called *Il morbo Gallico* – (the 'French Evil'), when it was discovered to be no respecter of nationality it was renamed 'syphilis', after the hapless Greek shepherd who was inflicted with a new plague for defying the god Apollo. The sinister scourge of syphilis had been a consequence of wars ever since. Although the long and painful 'salvarsan' treatment had been introduced before World War I to offer a cure for the long-term ravages of syphilis, the disease produced high casualty rates during the war and an extensive outbreak of congenital infection in infants following 1918.

As one GI put it, 'A man is going to have sexual intercourse regardless of the price or danger to his health.' Allied military commanders could therefore do little more in World War II than resort to lectures and disciplinary measures which resulted in enlisted men losing rank and forfeiting pay. General Frank M. Richardson, one of the British Army's senior wartime medical experts, vividly recalled his own first lecture on the required 'short arm' inspection just before World War II.

> I rejected the advice of the experienced captain and waded into sex, masturbation, the lot; subjects then seldom voiced in public. I could feel the temperature falling to sub-Arctic, except above my collar where it was feverish. When I huskily announced that I was finished . . . into the dead silence burst the roar of a bull-voiced and popular subaltern, one year older than myself. 'Well, doctor – you've certainly taken a load off my mind.' The laughter raised the roof.

In the US, men were subjected to the 'short arm' inspection and lecture every six months. 'There was a colonel who scratched his pants crotch frantically as he warned us that we must never touch a woman,' remembered one enlisted man, 'but that if we did, we should jump right out of bed and run to the nearest Pro Station. Then there were close-ups of male genitals undergoing an excruciatingly painful treatment. Have you ever seen genitals wince?'

Some chaplains devised a more up-to-date approach than St

Paul's traditional homily 'whatsoever a man soweth, that shall he reap'. 'Follow the red line to the shuttle train,' was one original approach which sought to compare the 'moral red line for human conduct' to the directions in the New York subway. The military chaplain's lot was not a particularly comfortable one. As a rabbi in the US Army confessed, 'I have been asked if chaplains considered themselves as the guardians of men's morals. If we saw ourselves in that role, what an unhappy lot was ours. Advocating that the soldiers' language be laundered, that drunkenness be discouraged, that an army-operated brothel be abolished, was an invitation to unpopularity and transfer.'

A sex survey conducted by the US Army in the final year of the war revealed that only a tiny minority abstained from intercourse out of religious conviction. 'Sure I am just as tempted as the next fellow and just as human,' explained one of the less than one per cent of GIs who claimed to have remained continent in Italy in 1945, 'but praying for strength to overcome temptation, I find it easy through Jesus.' The overwhelming majority – more than seventy-five per cent of American soldiers overseas – were restrained neither by prayer nor fear of disease.

Writer John Steinbeck, who observed US servicemen at close quarters, criticized the hypocrisy of public opinion which obliged the army to subscribe to the fiction that 'five million perfectly normal, young energetic and concupiscent men and boys had for the period of the war effort put aside their habitual preoccupation, girls. The fact that they carried pictures of nude girls, called pin-ups, did not occur to anyone as a paradox. The convention was the law. When Army supply ordered millions of rubber contraceptive and disease-preventing items, it had to be explained that they were used to keep moisture out of machine-gun barrels – and perhaps they did.'

For one GI at least, membership of an all male society was what brought out his aggressive sexual virility:

We had been part of the great Second World War, and had proven ourselves in that war. In this fact lay the sense of dignity and self-possession which lent ease to our relations. From it came the glamour which we knew we had for many of the women, and for the youngsters who had not seen service. In it was a strong bond of brotherhood, a feeling of unity, the same deep masculine appeal which I had discovered most notably with the outfit in Italy.

JAGGED GLASS

Present-day Europe is full of respectable,
petty-bourgeois women who have, at least once in
their lives, flung back their legs for the price of
a loaf of bread.

                                        US infantryman

Army life overseas wrecks these old emotional
ties when it takes a man away from his wife or
sweetheart, and leaves him with a set of
memories.

                              US Army Sex Survey, 1945

'WHAT ARE WE FIGHTING FOR?' was the question posed to a cross section of US Army combat veterans. The characteristic response was, 'Ask any dogface in the line, you're fighting for your skin on the line.' Very few of the hastily trained citizen soldiers of World War II, even those whose countries were under attack, were fired by the Roman poet Horace's assertion that '*dulce et decorum est pro patria mori*'. That it really was 'lovely and honourable to die for one's country' was especially difficult for an American to accept, since the GI was called upon to defend not his country, but a vague notion of freedom. 'It is wholly to the credit of the American soldier,' observed one war correspondent, 'that, as the son of a bewildered age, gun-shy of propaganda, with only tardy education under the impact of war, he is still able to fight bravely and die in cool blood for something he conceives to be his duty.'

The sheer size and technical sophistication of the World War II armies was such that two thirds of all troops were in support roles and were consequently never exposed to enemy fire at the front. But the licence to kill implicit in military service transgresses humanity's most sacred social taboo. It forced those at the 'sharp end' of war to come to terms not only with ritualized murder but also with the possibility of their own extinction. Primitive societies had developed elaborate atonement rituals for murders committed in warfare before their warriors were permitted to resume relationships with women. But, as Freud pointed out in *Reflections on War and Death*, Western civilization, despite its frequent resort to war over the centuries, had abandoned such social remedies for releasing the extreme psychological tensions induced in fighting men.

Just how this pent-up guilt contributed to what was called 'combat stress' was not to be fully appreciated until extensive wartime research revealed 'battle fatigue' to be one of the critical factors in cases of mental breakdown. The startling discovery was then made that only one American soldier in six could be consistently relied on to open fire on the enemy – whatever the provocation. 'Fear of killing, rather than fear of being killed, was the most common cause of battle fatigue in the individual, and the fear of failure ran a close second,' was the conclusion of Brigadier General S. L. A. Marshall. *Men Under Fire* was based on the analysis of his interviews of combat veterans and the study of thousands of US Army action reports:

> The Army cannot unmake [Western man] . . . It must reckon with the fact that he comes from a civilization in which aggression, connected with the taking of life, is prohibited and unacceptable. The teaching and ideals of that civilization are against killing, against taking advantage. The fear of aggression has been expressed to him so strongly and absorbed by him so deeply and pervadingly – practically with his mother's milk – that it is a part of the normal man's emotional make-up. This is his greatest handicap when he enters combat. It stays his trigger-finger though he is hardly conscious that it is a restraint in him.

'I remember myself as potentially expendable according to the Rules of Land Warfare, trapped in a war which (I said) was none of my making,' was how one GI rationalized this conflict. Many soldiers steeled themselves emotionally before combat with the thought of home and the wife or sweetheart in whose memory, or offspring, they would have some hope of immortality if their own flesh was shattered by high explosive.

Most soldiers were unwilling or unable to contain their sexual starvation with thoughts of the women back home that they might not survive to embrace. 'In the war a man gets lonely, a kind of loneliness which nothing can drive away except women – real ones and ones you can dream about waiting for you back home,' a GI wrote to his father. 'And it doesn't matter much if they aren't there when you come back. The important thing is to have this dream when you're lying in a dirty ditch with bullets whistling all about you.'

That living with the prospect of death generated a high sex drive in the men most frequently in action was evident from the high VD rates suffered by Allied bomber crews. Unlike the infantryman, who had few channels for sexual release at the battlefront, aircrews had plenty of women around their bases. Lieutenant Ted Binder, one of the 9937 American airmen who perished in the great Allied bomber offensives over Germany, discovered when his turn came as mail censor just how promiscuous aircrews were. He was shocked at their boasts in letters to their pals of sexual adventures with English girls, while their letters to their wives or sweethearts back in the States contained assurances that they were their only loves.

> I have found fifty sets of letters of this nature: one is to the wife or steady girlfriend back home. English girls, Joe says, are a mighty poor substitute for females. But of course even if they were Hollywood glamour girls, he wouldn't be interested, 'cause he can't think of anything but his little Mabel back home. Letter No. 2 is to some girl Joe has met in England, who may or may not know of his previous connections, and who may herself have a husband in the 8th Army. 'Darling,' says Joe, 'I never knew what life was till I met you. I live for those hours we have together on my leaves. You're the luckiest thing that ever happened to me.' And the third letter Joe put in the mail box that night is to his buddy working at Willow Run. 'Pete,' he says with enthusiasm, 'you don't know what you're missing. These English broads really go crazy when they see a Yank. I've got a really nice little date lined up, and believe it or not, it's all free.'

'You went to war for six hours,' was the way one RAF bomb aimer explained it, 'and you came back to clean sheets and when you did an operation you got ham and eggs. Nobody else did.' Extra food was not the only compensation for Bomber Command's suffering the highest continuous losses of all the Allied forces (its average wartime casualty rate of over twenty per cent was exceeded only by the German U-boat crews). The high risks they ran on bombing missions acted as subconscious aphrodisiacs for aircrew. Many became adept at exploiting the relatively poor chance of survival to seduce women, according to the tail-gunner of a Lancaster bomber:

> While girls had a much stricter upbringing, they were sorely tempted when they knew what little chance their loved one had of returning unscathed. There was no doubt that wartime did make more opportunities, and caution was often not exercised under such stress. Equally quite a lot of us chaps would play on a girl's emotions by stressing the possibility of death, even though we as aircrew never believed it would be us who got the 'chop'.

The 'chop' was something all men in the armed forces tried to put at the back of their mind, but could never completely ignore. Yet the 'reality of love and sex amid the conflagration' as one GI explained it, so often became 'jagged glass' for a soldier seeking an outlet for sexual frustration intensified by combat:

The typical soldier gives himself up for dead before he ever sees combat. And then the combat experience itself merely reinforces this sense of doom. So every woman might be his last. This is a cliché, but a truthful and powerful one – particularly if you can imagine what it's like to make love while assuming that tomorrow you'll be dead. You are no more violent in bed than usual. In fact, you're not even necessarily more loving. But perhaps you clutch the girl's shoulders a little more firmly than you normally would.

The girl, meanwhile, even as she's dreaming of her real lover, knows what you're thinking. She herself is torn; while pretending you're someone else, she's simultaneously relating to the actual and awful fact that she's in bed with a man who knows he may die. So watch her face; she alternately opens and closes her eyes, sometimes in ecstasy, more often in a desperate attempt to grasp this essentially ungraspable situation. And she stares up at you with the slightest hint of guilt in her eyes, or is that knitted brow simply knowledge, flowing into her mind like you into her body, of what she herself must mean to you, a man whose name she'll not remember?

Just how traumatic this kind of sexual encounter could be was related by a GI who lost his virginity after a drunken spree with two French whores:

After a while things began to go pretty blotty. Before I knew it, one of the girls got on my lap and was kissing me and whispering all sorts of things to me, and all of a sudden I started to cry, tears rolling down my cheeks, and she was trying to wipe them off, and it was so damned silly but I couldn't stop. I felt so sad and lonely. Then there was another girl trying to stop me from crying, and she was so sympathetic that she cried herself, and that made me even sadder. She gave me a glass of wine, and that was my end, because all of a sudden there was a blackout . . . and when I opened my eyes everything was dark. I looked around without seeing anything, and then I felt somebody's arm on me, and I groped in the dark and felt a girl lying next to me under the blanket. Well, that was a new experience and I got terribly excited. She must have wakened up because she pressed her body to mine, and it was so warm, and she kissed me, and before I knew it, it was all over. And when it was all over, I felt terribly ashamed and disgusted, and I was getting physically sick too, my stomach was turning and choking me, and I knew I had to get out.

Such experiences, combined with the mental ordeal of combat, induced in some soldiers temporary impotence which appeared to have been precipitated by the psychic retreat of the ego in response to overwhelming destructive power witnessed in action. In other combatants, the violence of warfare released the physical and emotional reactions akin to sexual aggression. Pilots appear to have derived a particular sexual catharsis from aerial combat that was characterized by an American flyer's observation, 'the most fun you can have with your pants on'. A World War II combat infantryman confirmed that the 'proximity of danger finds a man obsessed with a wild exhilaration, almost sensual. He feels impervious to missiles of a deadly nature, yet underneath this sense of power . . . gnawing like a rat in a sepulchre . . . is the knowledge that his fellows feel the same, yet some will die.'

Procreation and death are after all the extreme parameters of human existence. They are brought into sharp conjunction by war. Hallucinations of an overtly sensual nature were not uncommon at the front, according to author and ex-marine William Manchester, who has recorded in *Goodbye To Darkness* a vivid account of how a female apparition appeared before him at the height of a fierce engagement with the Japanese which wiped out his comrades. 'Rasped obscenities' were uttered by his 'Whore of Death' who 'hoisted her skirt to her hips and spread her legs', arousing in him 'overwhelming' sexual cravings:

> For the first and only time in my life I understood rape. I have never been more ready. Then from her sultry muttering, I learned her fee. I couldn't mount her here. She gestured towards the Japanese lines. I shrank back, shaking my head and whispering, 'No, no, I won't, no, no, NO.' Just then a random shell rustled over and landed a few yards away. In the flash she disappeared. But my yearning for sexual release remained. I unfastened my dungarees and touched myself. I came in less than five seconds. I was that close.

The subconscious consummation precipitated by a combat soldier's close calls with death were indicative of the manner in which extreme violence produced sexual arousal in individuals whose training involved humiliation and persecution by drill sergeants and officers in the expectation that this would induce aggressive behaviour directed towards the enemy. The psychological regression induced by such conditioning, according to one British infantryman, ensured 'that this killing is quite impartial; it has the cold indifference of a great organization, it is an impersonal routine, a job . . . Fear becomes commonplace – like death, an accepted everyday, ever-present condition. War is no longer entirely freakish and uniquely barbaric. It becomes normal, with the deep reality of a nightmare.'

The concept of the trained soldier as a robot killer has to be reconciled with post-war American research which found that only sixteen per cent of the army's combat troops could be relied on to act, according to the observation of one GI, 'like cells in a military organism, doing what is expected because it is automatic'. Survival in action was often a function of how successfully the individual soldier overcame his human inhibitions and how effectively he handled his weapons. The nihilistic de-humanization appropriate for mechanized warfare was summed up by a German veteran of 1918, who wrote, 'We are soldiers, and the weapon is the tool with which we proceed to shape ourselves. Our work is killing, and it is our duty to do this well and completely.'

This identification of man with his weapons and its association with an individual soldier's sexual aggression has been a celebrated theme in heroic literature from Homer to Hemingway. But in World War II virility became identified with weapons whose potency was far greater than anything previously experienced. It is therefore not surprising to find that this produced a psychological confusion in men such as the American tank commander who wrote of his armoured vehicle as an extension of his own sexuality:

> The tank. It is ceaseless destruction, unstoppable except by another, even more infernal machine. It protrudes shafts of cold metal with which to fuck a landscape and, by fucking, raze it . . . After the tank came Hiroshima and the bomb – a cock so huge we can't even use it. I'm an old man, but sometimes I feel like the last stud left on the face of the earth.

Servicemen in World War II succumbed to the traditional peer pressure to prove their virility on the battlefield and in bed. Sex for front-line troops was usually mechanical. Like the war itself, it was devoid of romance or affection and satisfied only the urgent hunger for immediate physical gratification. Rape, as throughout the history of warfare, was the sadistic consequence of the aggressive virility fostered in soldiers by the brutalization of civilized values and the stresses of military life. The extreme example was the notorious sexual sadism exhibited by Japanese soldiers indoctrinated with the Bushido code, which set human life lower than military virtue. Yet even in Western armies, which paid lip-service to the rules of so-called civilized warfare, acts of sadistic cruelty and rape were far more commonplace than officially admitted.

While the Wehrmacht's iron discipline had maintained restraint during the Blitzkrieg takeover of western Europe, the German march of conquest to the east was a different matter. Nazi racial policy classed the Slavs as sub-human, and although Hitler had decreed that local female populations were unworthy partners for Aryan soldiers, the crusaders who set out to save the world from Bolshevism had taken a savage sexual toll of Russian women. So when the Red Army finally turned the tide of battle, their advance into the heartland of the Third Reich brought a vicious reprisal against Germany's females in the east.

'Many German women somehow assumed that, "it was now the Russians' turn," and it was no good resisting,' wrote a Soviet major, who insisted that it 'was usually very simple. Any of our chaps simply had to say: "Frau komm," and she knew what was expected of her.' In the aftermath of the Russian troops' entry into Vienna in April 1945 it was said that not even the female dogs were safe from sexual assault. The once-mighty Nazi propaganda machine summoned its dying gasps to use the rape of the Austrian capital to galvanize the Volksturm citizen militia into desperate resistance.

Ruined Berlin was peopled largely by old men and women who were unable to resist the medieval ferocity unleashed upon them by Red Army troops. Passions fired by the heat of victory, vengeance, and vodka paid no heed to the screams of terrified girls, *'Aber ich bin noch ein Kind*, 'But I'm only a child'. Soviet historians later conceded that their troops were not 'one hundred per cent gentlemen'. 'War was war', and the Red Army 'did nothing in comparison with what the Germans did in Russia'. Stalin's reaction was characteristically callous: 'Can't you understand it if a soldier who has crossed thousands of kilometres through blood and fire has fun with a woman or takes a trifle?'

Rape at gunpoint by a succession of drunken soldiers may have been sport for Russian soldiers, but it was terror for those women who endured it. A middle-aged Berlin mother left a graphic record of a trauma she shared with thousands of her neighbours:

> I scream, scream . . . Behind me the cellar door closes with a soft
> thud. One man seizes me by the wrists and drags me along the

corridor. Now the other one also pulls, at the same time gripping my throat with one hand so that I can no longer scream. As a matter of fact I have no desire to scream, for fear of being throttled. I'm already on the ground, my head lying on the lowest cellar stair. I can feel the coldness of the tiles against my back. Something falls from my coat with a tinkling sound. Must be my house keys, my bunch of keys. One man stands guard at the door upstairs while the other claws at my underwear, tears my garter belt to shreds and violently, ruthlessly has his way . . . When it's all over and, reeling, I try to get up, the other man hurls himself upon me and with his fists and knees forces me back to the floor. Now the first man is standing guard, whispering, 'Hurry, hurry . . .' Suddenly I hear loud Russian voices. Someone has opened the door at the top of the staircase, letting in the light. Three Russians come in, one is a woman in uniform. They look at me and laugh.

Rape was by no means the monopoly of the armies of the totalitarian powers – nor were German women its only victims. Shortly after the Allied armies landed in Normandy, memoranda of complaints were being discussed by General de Gaulle's military cabinet:

> In the regions occupied by the Americans, women no longer dare go to milk cows without being accompanied by a man. Even the presence of a man does not protect them. In the Manche a priest has been killed trying to protect two young girls attacked by American soldiers. These young girls were raped. In the Seine Inférieur a woman was raped and killed after her husband had been assassinated.

The minister urged that strong representations be made to General Eisenhower: 'If the Americans cannot bring American women for the needs of their men, at least let them respect French women.'

Many cases of the rape of French womenfolk were confirmed by Allied military investigations. On 11 September 1944, shortly after the Allied armies had crossed the Marne, a forty-three-year-old dressmaker called Maria Guerre lodged a deposition at local headquarters describing how she had been brutally raped in front of her husband and family by three GIs:

> Yesterday, the 10th instant, towards 8:00 p.m. in the evening, my ten-year-old son, Gui, came home, bringing with him three American negro soldiers. After drinking a bottle of champagne these soldiers would not leave the house. At a given moment, during which my

husband and children were restrained by one of these soldiers, the two others flung themselves on me and took off my knickers and raped me. An infirmity of my left leg caused one of them to have difficulty in achieving this object, so he struck me all over, wherever he could. These soldiers raped me, one after the other, and repeated this three times in succession . . . During this whole incident, which took place in the bed in my kitchen, I saw my husband, who was guarded by a soldier who held a dagger above him.

American military authorities immediately took steps to locate the men responsible and prosecute them under the 93rd Article of War. A week later, at an identity parade of the 3263th Quartermaster Service Company, the woman's husband picked out a private he identified as one of the three assailants. The unfortunate GI shot himself thirty minutes later, but his accomplices were never brought to trial.

SHAEF headquarters imposed censorship on French newspapers reporting a rash of rapes and assaults on small girls. Many of the horror stories were undoubtedly exaggerations, but enough were confirmed for General Eisenhower's headquarters to announce its 'grave concern' in a December 1944 directive to all US Army and Air Force commanders. Offenders were to be brought to speedy justice and punished with 'appropriate severity' to contain the 'large incidence of crimes such as rape, murder, assault and robbery, housebreaking' to deter 'others of a like mind'.

Despite the denials of Allied propaganda, a double standard was applied in Germany during the spring of 1945 when it came to punishing the sexual excesses that disgraced some of the warriors of democracy. When three GIs were arrested for the gunpoint rape of a group of German women, a political storm was raised in Washington by Congressmen who were unwilling to concede that the levelling morality of the battlefield could turn decent American boys into rapists. One of those arrested under a crackdown ordered by General Slack had written to Senator Green of Rhode Island, who pressed the matter with the Under Secretary of War. A SECRET URGENT cable from General Marshall was sent to General Eisenhower's headquarters:

THE UNDER SECRETARY OF WAR JUDGE PATTERSON HAS JUST RECEIVED FROM SENATOR GREEN OF RHODE ISLAND A LETTER FROM PFC ——— 204 FIELD ARTILLERY BATTALION, APPEALING FOR ASSISTANCE BECAUSE HE

IS NOW 'BEING HELD ON FRATERNIZATION CHARGES ALONG WITH 7 OTHERS, 3 OF WHOM ARE CHARGED WITH RAPE. THE CHARGES ARE BEING PRESSED BY BRIGADIER GENERAL SLACK, XX CORPS'. HE STATES SLACK DIRECTLY ACCUSED HIM AND 4 OTHERS OF WATCHING 3 MEN TAKE 2 GERMAN WOMEN IN THE HOUSE INVOLVED AND COMMIT RAPE. HE STATES THAT WITH THE OTHER MEN HE WAS TAKEN BACK TO HEADQUARTERS OF HIS BATTALION WHERE GENERAL SLACK 'DIRECTLY CALLED US A BUNCH OF DIRTY BASTARDS 2 OR 3 TIMES. HE TOLD THE 3 MEN ACCUSED OF RAPE THAT HE WOULD PERSONALLY SEE THAT THEY WERE HUNG AND UNDERGROUND IN 30 DAYS. HE ALSO SAID THAT HIS JUDGE ADVOCATE, WHO WAS PRESENT AT THE TIME, HAD NEVER LOST A CASE AND WOULD NOT LOSE THIS ONE. THIS TALK WAS GIVEN BEFORE 5 OFFICERS, 1 SERGEANT AND THE ACCUSED ENLISTED MEN.'

Judge Patterson has also received from Justice Douglas of the supreme court a letter written by another soldier in the 20th Field Artillery Battalion, giving a similar account of the alleged speech by general Slack made 'before any trial had been held, and while the men involved were asserting their innocence.' THIS SOLDIER FURTHER ASSERTS THAT GERMAN WOMEN ARE CREATING THE FEELING OF UTTER INSECURITY AMONG OUR SOLDIERS BY UNTRUE CHARGES OF RAPE AND THAT THESE TACTICS MAY BE PART OF A PLAN BY THE GERMANS.

Those who observed the Allied troops in Germany at first hand knew that rape was not a sinister sexual plot by female Nazi saboteurs. 'The behaviour of the troops, I regret to say, was nothing to brag about, particularly after they came upon cases of cognac and barrels of wine,' was the chastening report of one US Army intelligence officer who witnessed the occupation of the German city of Krefeld. 'There is a tendency among the naive or the malicious to think that only Russians loot and rape. After battle, soldiers of every country are pretty much the same, and the warriors of Democracy were no more virtuous than the troops of Communism were reported to be.'

The virtue of the local female population, whether foe or ally, commanded little respect from conquering front-line troops of any nation. One GI was surprised to find that the women whose towns and villages had been overrun appeared to resign themselves to the sexual advances of their conquerors:

She's very accommodating, too. She'll do anything for you – for you as her distant lover, and for the real you as well, the stranger who may die tomorrow. If you're a decent fellow, you demand a lot of love and you get it. If you're a pig, the girl is unlucky but can't say no anyway.

Heroines of the Soviet Union

1 Lily Litvak, the Soviet fighter pilot who claimed a famous German 'ace' among her many victims.

2 During the desperate battles around Stalingrad the Germans soon came to respect the courage and skill of the Russian women flyers they dubbed 'The Night Witches'.

3 One of the celebrated girl-snipers, Sergeant Roza Shanina.

Joining Up

4 Women's khaki uniform made few concessions to the anatomical demands of the female figure and the image of the ATS was falling in comparison to the dashing elegance of the WAAF (5) but by 1943 the haphazard distribution of uniforms had been replaced by a more measured approach (6).

7 Recruitment poster, 1941.

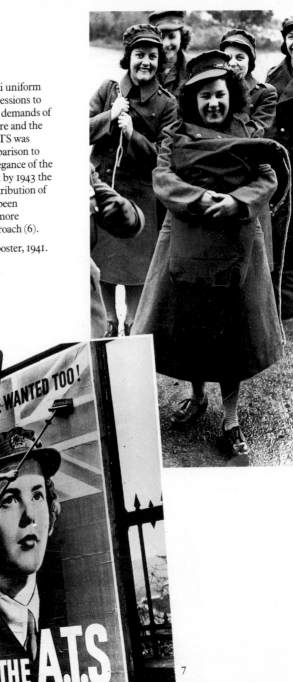

7

9

8

Training

8 The Army regarded discipline and drill as the prerequisite for all soldiers, regardless of their sex. ATS girls underwent three weeks of intensive training before being sent to their posts.

9/10 Lessons in aircraft recognition were equally important for both the Fleet Air Arm and the ATS whatever the sex of the instructors.

11 Although at first they were not supposed to learn the use of the rifle, girls of the ATS 'were as keen as anything to do so'.

12 The US Women's Marine Corps celebrating their second anniversary. To begin with nine out of ten of the female intake to the US services were college graduates.

11

10

Proving Their Worth

The majority of women recruits were fired by patriotism and the determination to prove they could be as good as the next man.

13 WAAF units were in charge of the whale-like silver blimps that were sent aloft to snag low-flying enemy dive-bombers.

14/15 WRNS were equally competent at handling either signals or torpedoes.

16/17 The ATS girls who proudly wore the 'Searchlight' and 'Gunners' shoulder flashes were the elite of Britain's female forces.

18 US Marine privates fixing depth bombs to the undercarriage of aircraft.

14

13

15

17

16

18

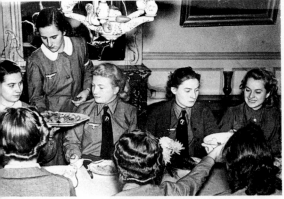

19

The Backroom Girls

19   Although the Fuehrer was determined to keep women out of an effective service role, the 'Helferinnen' became an indispensable component of the growing administrative arm of the Wehrmacht.

20/21   The invasion of Europe in June 1944 depended on thousands of women, from highly skilled photo-reconnaissance interpreters to the plotters and communication staff.

20

21

Separation

2 The sadness of frequent
   partings during World
   War II was intensified by
   the uncertainty of whether
   either partner would
   survive to meet again.
   Picture Post cover, 1942.

3 The lives of millions of
   couples were disrupted,
   not just for weeks or
   months, but in many cases
   for four to five years, a
   theme adopted by government agencies in their
   promotion of war bonds to
   speed the end of hostilities.

Boy meets Girl

'Personal relations were formed between men and women out of sheer loneliness and the need to be loved.' Death and separation were the twin spectres that haunted wartime love affairs and provided a powerful incentive for couples to snatch at every opportunity for love that presented itself.

24 RAF personnel meeting show girls. The stage door attracted servicemen and servicemen attracted the girls.

25 A GI and friend in the famous Rainbow Club in London.

24

25

The average GI found very little difficulty in satisfying the soldier's perennial hunger for female companionship.

26 US service personnel in London.

27 Inside the Rainbow Club.

26

27

VD and Prostitution

'The state of war favours the spread of VD' warned the Ministry of Health in 1939. By 1941 in some places in Britain the disease had increased fourfold and the arrival of the first American troops in the spring of 1942 sent it up to almost epidemic proportions.

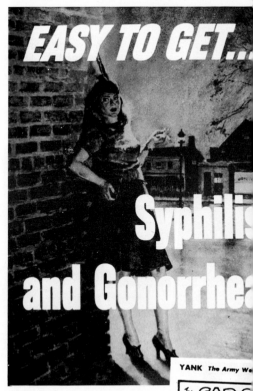

EASY TO GET...

Syphili

and Gonorrhea

YANK *The Army We...*

"Are we good? I ask you, how the blazes could we be otherwise in all this clobber?"

THE SAD S

28 A campaign of posters, films and regular lectures on the perils of prostitution and VD was introduced.

29 Government surveys, contrary to anticipation, revealed that there was no squeamishness to the anti-VD campaign which, by the end of the war had made the public thoroughly familiar with the disease through artfully explicit posters.

30/31 The lighter side of a dark picture.

32

While you are away,

the *Yanks* are "lease-lending" your women. Their pockets full of cash and no work to do, the boys from overseas are having the time of their live in Merry Old England.

And what young woman, single or married, could resist such "handsome brute from the wide open spaces" to have dinner with, a cocktail at some night-club, and afterwards.......

Anyway, so numerous have become the scandal that all England is talking about them now.

Most of you are convinced that

the war will be over in four months

Too bad if it should hit you in the last minute

34

TICKET TO ARMISTICE

USE THIS TICKET, SAVE YOUR LIFE
YOU WILL BE KINDLY TREATED

Follow These instructions:

1. Come towards our lines waving a white flag.
2. Strap your gun over your left shoulder muzzle down and pointed behind you.
3. Show this ticket to the sentry.
4. Any number of you may surrender with this one ticket.

JAPANESE ARMY HEADQUARTERS

投　降　票

此ノ票ヲ持ツモノハ投降者ナリ
投降者ヲ殺害スルヲ厳禁ス

大日本軍司令官

Sing your way to Peace pray for Peace

Tommy, your next leave!

Sex as Propaganda

32/33 Sexually loaded propaganda appears to have had little influence on the course of World War II other than providing amusement. Far from undermining the morale of allied forces in Europe and the Pacific, pornographic propaganda which bombarded the troops was regarded as comic relief from the rigours of warfare.

34 The sexy full-frontal nudes which appeared on the reverse side of a card explaining how US marines could surrender, joined the pin-up parade that decorated the foxholes on Guadalcanal.

35 The British Government, perhaps recalling the legendary *femme-fatale* of World War I, instituted a series of security posters.

35 Keep mum she's not so dumb! CARELESS TALK COSTS

The Special Relationship

To British women the arrival of the American GI was a bright flash of excitement after nearly three years of blackouts and blitz. It seemed to many that these strapping, well fed and confident young men had stepped straight out of a Hollywood movie.

36 'The Americans were so very trusting of us, wanting to be liked and be our guests.'

37 The excitement of wartime had prompted those stationed in Britain to take over 60,000 English girls as brides. A transit camp had to be set up in the South of England to process the migration which the War Department called 'Operation War Bride' and which got under way early in 1946 when the first 600 sailed for the United States.

36

37

I knew some soldiers who procured some pretty bizarre favours from women. In a situation like this the woman doesn't even feel decent saying no to the Marquis de Sade.

But whatever she does, it's not enough for you. It can't be. Women are only human, after all, and war is something more. So you stare down at this German soldier's wife, and, for all you've been through and will go through, she seems unreal. Unreal like a whore seems unreal. But she's not a whore. And you've got to remember that she's not a whore. If her husband survives, he'll come back to pick up their lives again. He'll silently assume she's slept with someone, probably with an American, but if he's any kind of man, he'll never ask.

Unlike the French, German women had no grounds for making the kind of complaint that was delivered to General Eisenhower in April 1945 in which a mother pleaded with him to 'render proper justice' to a sergeant in the US military police who 'took advantage of my absence to abuse my daughter, Madeline, who will now become the mother of a baby in two months'.

If Eisenhower had granted this mother's request for child maintenance, all the offspring from the 'liberation' of Europe would have imposed a costly burden on the American and British treasuries. Instead, in preparation for the advance into Germany in the spring of 1945, Supreme Headquarters Allied Expeditionary Force issued the directive, 'No social intercourse of any kind with Germans will take place.'

Allied military planners who persuaded General Eisenhower to adopt this strict non-fraternization policy had neglected to take into account the sexual hunger of either their troops or German women. This became apparent after Cologne had fallen in mid-March with a disturbing report that was received from an officer of SHAEF headquarters intelligence staff who had been amazed to hear the shouts of, 'Ve haf vaited fife years for you!' across shattered streets still littered with the bodies of civilians killed during the fighting: 'Girls put on their most seductive smiles . . . and the girls in the recently occupied territory don't seem to make any bones about the fact that the lack of young men in Germany left them in a rather receptive mood.'

SHAEF tried to cool the ardour of this reception by issuing an edict that, 'Such women can hardly be considered as the suitable mates for the defenders of democracy,' a promulgation that was more suited to the defeated Nazi regime than sexual reality.

'Women were told that it was right and patriotic to bear children for any soldier desiring the same,' pointed out another report on the failure of the non-fraternization policy. 'Many soldiers of the invading Armies found this situation very much to their liking and have done nothing to change it.'

Heavy mandatory fines also failed to curb the American soldier's appetite for liaisons with willing frauleins. Enlisted men defied the stiff financial penalties, claiming, 'Sixty-five bucks is dirt cheap, it was worth it!' Medical officers protested that such punitive measures only made it more difficult to check the spread of venereal infection, and officers who ignored the orders they were supposed to enforce did not provide a good example to their men. When the non-fraternization policy began to pose a real threat to good order and military discipline, confidential SHAEF memoranda reveal that Eisenhower's staff gave 'very serious consideration that licensed houses should be provided under Army supervision', to be staffed by German whores passed as morally and medically free of contagion.

Germany was particularly vulnerable to 'moral chaos' because the war had not only reduced the cities and economy to ruins but had shattered the rigid dictates of the Nazi moral and marriage laws. In a flourishing blackmarket for the basic necessities of life, sex became a passport to survival for many German women.

'Two things our soldiers can't resist – kids and a glimpse of married family life,' reported the New York *Herald Tribune* from Cologne in a piece about the 'Sixty-five dollar question . . . the fine stipulated for enlisted men convicted of intimate association with enemy civilians.' 'The biological aspects of boy-meets-girl can be rigidly controlled. But the kids here look like the youngsters back home, and the old folks seem harmless and their houses are nice and clean and they appear to live about the same as we do.'

The magnitude of the sexual problems confronting an Allied army of occupation had been foreshadowed in Italy. The 'liberation' of Paris and Brussels brought another leap in VD rates, as sex-hungry Allied soldiers filled the already bulging purses of the madams who ran the *maisons tolerées* in those cities. On the other side of the world, General Douglas MacArthur's army had driven the Japanese out of Manila in the spring of 1945 – only to lose the battle against venereal disease to an estimated eight thousand-strong prostitute army of 'native females wandering through military encampments and intimately associating with military personnel'.

The introduction of the 'wonder-drug' penicillin a year earlier had removed another restraint on the sexual activities of the Allied troops who set out on the crusade to 'liberate' Europe. The rapid upward leap in the VD charts kept by every regiment indicated that even the most cautious of soldiers were tempted to abandon 'the bright shield of continence' now they knew that health and honour could be restored by the 'magic bullets' of penicillin.

'When VE day finally arrived, the rates for venereal disease soared,' reported the US Army medical inspector. 'Those of May were greater than April, and June saw the highest rate in the history of the theatre, with every indication that the end was not yet in sight and that the army of occupation would have an experience with those communicable diseases greatly exceeding that of the period of wartime operations.' Contributory factors, also blamed by the report, were a lack of shipping space that delayed the arrival of seventy thousand VD posters and consignments of rubber contraceptives, which meant they had to be rationed to four per man per month – a rate that medical officers considered entirely inadequate!

An extensive survey revealed that the level of promiscuity among the troops was far higher than officially admitted, and rates rose in direct proportion to the amount of time the men had spent overseas. More than eight out of ten soldiers who had been away from the United States for over two years admitted in the anonymous survey to having had regular sexual intercourse with the women they met 'over there'.

The all-Negro regiments, which made up sixteen per cent of the theatre strength, proved to be the most sexually active with ninety-six per cent of black troops admitting to intercourse, compared to eighty-two per cent of white soldiers. Consequently VD rates amongst black soldiers averaged five times the rate for white ones, and in some units infections were being contracted by every second man. 'Just why the Negro has more sexual intercourse is a matter of speculation,' noted the survey, but other statistics collected by the army during the war showed that black GIs admitted to earlier and more frequent sexual activity as adolescents. When overseas, most of these troops were in supply and quartermaster regiments behind the front lines – so they had more opportunity for sexual activity. Although black troops were more likely to use a condom and take prophylactic measures than whites (sixty-two per cent compared to forty-three per cent), their far higher VD rates, the report pointed out, was because 'women to whom they have access are much more likely to be diseased on the average than the white enlisted male contact'.

The survey uncovered the deep resentment of the sexual consequences of ingrained racialism in a segregated army. One man complained that, 'Our fellow "white" soldiers have so influenced the better group of civilians that nothing is left but the poor diseased Italian trash and all men will indulge in sexual affairs regardless'. Another reminded the army that, 'Our white brother, who in turn calls himself an American and fought this war to preserve the term democracy or its sacred meaning, should refrain from telling the Italian people that the Negro is no good.' Yet another put his resentment more bluntly: 'Personally I haven't seen a monkey tail on any human and it really hurt to hear those damned Italians ask "Where is it?" This is the reason why we have such a high VD rate. You figure it out.'

The extent and detail of the US Army survey left no doubt that after more than a year abroad, whether they were black or white, married or single, most American soldiers had thrown restraint to the winds. 'Sex patterns of males are established relatively early in life, and the matter of being in the army had little influence upon the individual's willingness to expose himself to VD,' the report announced. Three out of four men were having intercourse with Italian women, on average once or twice a month. Of these, seventy-two per cent paid for their favours in cash, twenty-seven per cent paid nothing or gave gifts of rationed food, and less than one per cent said they paid with cigarettes or clothing.

Nearly a third of all the enlisted men who filled in the anonymous report-forms admitted to having wives at home, while almost half indicated they intended marrying their girlfriend in the States. That over three quarters of all men with such stated attachments did not consider the 'girls they left behind' a bar to sexual adventure overseas was a measure of the war's dramatic impact on the average soldier's morality. Typical of the responses was one from a soldier who had been married for six years, who confessed:

Until nine months ago, when I came overseas, I had never had intercourse with any woman other than my wife since I married her. When an older married man is in the same tent with a bunch of unmarried boys that are out most of the time, it puts him in a bad frame of mind.

Still more significant was the discovery that fewer than half the men who anticipated returning to marry the girls they had left behind believed that they had 'stayed loyal' to them! One respondent insightfully noted, 'The army gives us plenty of beautiful posters and interesting movies on sex and how to avoid diseases and why we should not indulge in sexual intercourse – NOW – How about producing some really good shorts on the same stuff to show our wives and sweethearts back in the United States?'

'There is a new set of accepted rights and wrongs in this overseas situation,' concluded a senior US Army officer in his review of the sex survey from the Mediterranean theatre. 'It is right to have intercourse with any available women, it is not wrong to get VD unless one fails to go on sick call, it is wrong to punish a man for VD – even for repeated offences.'

This is the apparent situation with regard to sexual intercourse among those overseas men. The normal (in the case of civilian) disapproval of intercourse is missing except as one is reminded by memories or by letter. It has been shown, for instance, that having a *loyal* sweetheart somewhere else is *not* a powerful deterrent for all the men overseas, although it is for a minority. Under normal conditions this is one of the most powerful sanctions, leading to abstinence with other women.

The survey concluded that there was 'no evidence that frequent VD talks or movies cut down the exposure of men to VD overseas'. Not only did the troops repeatedly ignore advice by chaplains and medical officers to 'keep it in your pants', but fewer than half of the respondents used sheaths or prophylactics because, as one soldier put it, 'most GI rubbers are so damn thick you can't enjoy yourself' and another explained, 'GI condoms are no good. Half of them bust anyway. Try one sometime.'

One factor that persuaded many enlisted men to ignore the repeated lectures on continence and prophylaxis was that the officers who gave it failed to practise what they preached. The widespread habit of officers persuading WACs and native girls to share the privileges of rank in a 'shack-up' relationship was bitterly resented:

> What's sauce for the goose is sauce for the gander. We should not be handicapped *because of rank* in our search for clean women or in our ability to entertain them. And this means using government vehicles too.
>
> As for the officers having all the WACs, I believe there is an Army regulation out which states that an officer is not to associate with an enlisted WAC. Why isn't this adhered to? Give the enlisted men a chance to be with and talk to a few American WACs and also have a dance with them.

It therefore came as no surprise to the officers who analysed the questionnaires to find that one out of five respondents also favoured 'GI whorehouses'. They wanted the US Army to do 'as most other armies do, put up government-sanctioned and inspected houses' to reduce the dangers of disease and to 'keep their price down'. Another soldier suggested that 'five to a company' would be adequate – 'Of course this would have to be kept from the press.'

The US Army sex-survey of 1945 that provided such a frank and detailed insight into the sexual impact of World War II on American troops was to be kept a classified secret for nearly forty years, because it reflected on the public image of the GI as a clean-living crusader for democracy. While no such detailed research into military sexual habits appears to have been conducted by British forces, their very similar VD statistics suggest that soldiers in both armies shared the same sexual habits.

The most revealing aspect of the US Army sex-survey was that it exploded once and for all the traditional belief that if a man *knows* a girl is waiting for him somewhere he will be true to her; he will not seek outlets with other women. 'When it is an activity which is approved of by the group as a whole, not only by a man for himself but for the other fellow too, this powerful social sanction makes the activity almost uncontrollable.' The American survey concluded with an observation that was appropriate to the sex lives of all soldiers in all the armies who fought in World War II:

> However, the man in this study is *not* having an unusual amount of intercourse at all for men of his average age (twenty-six years). Any man of age twenty-six, and certainly any married man in the theatre

(thirty-two per cent) can rightfully feel that he is being cheated sexually by this overseas situation which is not of his making. The steady rise in the frequency of intercourse with time overseas gives credence to this notion of being cheated of the sex life which society taught him was his as soon as he became a man. Furthermore, only ten per cent of all those men are having intercourse at least once a week, which is certainly not an indication of anything like abnormal sexual activity. The average frequency of once to twice a month is certainly not high, if we hazard guesses as to the probable frequency of intercourse for this group if they were in normal civilian life . . . the Army would make a mistake in either charging these men with sexual abnormality or threatening them as such.

8

COMRADES IN ARMS

Sodomy is specifically denounced as an offence under the provisions of the 93rd article of war. Administrative discharge in lieu of trial in cases of this character is not only contrary to the War Department policy, but to the express intention of Congress.

US Army policy circular, 1941

Sex was not really an issue on the *Dido*. There was much the same atmosphere as at a fairly easy-going public school.

Seaman George Melly, RN

'WHAT AIN'T WE GOT? We ain't got dames!' was the Broadway show-stopper that made a musical sensation out of the sex-starvation endured by American servicemen who fought against the Japanese during World War II. In real life on a 'No women atoll' like Eniewetok, GIs had chanted less elegant choruses which advocated the so-called Pacific Prescription:

> Masturbation is the fashion
> For your unrequited passion
> If the girls can do it, why can't we?
> But out here in the Pacific,
> Purely as a soporific,
> Nothing equals simple self-abuse!

What US Navy white-hats referred to as 'the sordid imitation' was so widespread amongst servicemen that one British army doctor 'had no hesitation' in advising the men in his unit that masturbation 'was perhaps the easiest and safest way of obtaining relief, there being no reason why they should not embellish this experience with some fantasy of their loved ones at home'. But Victorian taboos died hard, even in the army. Another officer in the medical corps admitted he was 'shocked to learn how openly, even boastfully, masturbation was performed in some barrack rooms'. Drill sergeants frequently made it a term of verbal abuse when bawling out a weedy recruit: 'You couldn't knock the skin off a rice pudding. You want to keep your hands outside the blankets!'

'Formerly my wife was my right hand,' a World War I soldier had quipped, 'in the army my right hand became my wife.' In World War II many servicemen resorted to the same substitute to satisfy their sex hunger, although 'masturbation guilt' was still considered a medical disorder in the psychiatric textbooks of the period. But as long as men in the armed forces kept their hands to themselves, no military regulations were broken.

If their comrades, however, provided the stimulation, they risked a court martial, imprisonment, and in the case of German SS officers after 1942, the firing squad! Yet the military segregated millions of young men at the height of their potency, forcing them to adopt a life of close comradeship devoid of female companionship, and exposed many men to what was called 'emergency homosexuality'.

Unlike the ancient Greek armies, which had not only tolerated but had exploited the amorous bonds that developed between comrades in arms, modern military organizations had long proscribed homosexual activity. It offended basic Christian sexual taboos and was perceived as a threat to the essential aggressive 'manliness' of soldiers. But above all, homosexual relationships were 'prejudicial to good conduct and discipline' because they broke down the divisions between military ranks.

Deprivation homosexuality had long been recognized as a problem by navies. Historically it had been dealt with either by tolerating it and enforcing a complex pecking order for sex, as in the galleons of the Spanish Armada, or it had been made a capital offence, as in the Royal Navy, when as late as Nelson's time, officers had been hung from the yardarm for sodomy. 'Ashore it's wine, women and song, aboard it's rum, bum, and concertina,' ran the nineteenth-century sea shanty that doubtless prompted Winston Churchill's salty aside during World War II, 'Don't talk to me about naval tradition. It's nothing but rum, sodomy, and the lash.'

In World War I military leaders had constantly been concerned that the close-packed trenches of the Western Front would lead to an epidemic of homosexual behaviour. The German Army High Command, which had been touched by pre-war scandal, was especially sensitive to the issue and had launched periodic witch-hunts in regiments where excessive numbers of requests for front-line duty suggested that homosexual partners might be attempting to emulate the Spartan military tradition of fighting alongside male lovers. The war also offered many confirmed homosexuals, or urnings as they were then called, not only the opportunity for male camaraderie but also the chance to prove their masculinity and defy social stigma by performing acts of bravery which brought decorations.

In World War II the scant military data that has been made available together with the statistics on sexual preferences suggest that homosexuality in the armed forces was more widespread than in society as a whole. According to Professor Kinsey's wartime surveys, one in ten American males between the ages of sixteen and fifty-five were more or less exclusively homosexual, three out of ten admitted to some adult sexual experience with other men and one in five was bisexual. He therefore concluded that, 'nearly forty per cent of all males could be arrested at some time in their lives for similar activity, and that twenty to thirty per cent of unmarried males could have been arrested for homosexual activity that had taken place that same year'. The official records, however, reveal that the American Selective Service Boards had rejected only one per cent of draftees as homosexuals unfit for military service and that less than a half a per cent of the men in the military were subsequently discharged for homosexuality.

'History paints lurid pictures of abnormal sexual practices which become associated with men at sea,' Captain Joel T. Boone of the US Navy medical service proclaimed in 1941. 'We have no place in the service for the homosexual, the panderer, or the pederast. He is – as soon as discovered – and this happens with amazing speed – taken to one of the naval psychiatric institutions for treatment.' Yet for all the 'amazing' efficiency of the navy's ability to purge itself of homosexuals, the 1941 records of new admissions to the two main naval prisons, at Portsmouth, New Hampshire and Mare Island, San Francisco, disclose that a quarter were committed as a result of homosexual charges. That only thirteen navy and seven marines were committed that year showed either that the number of homosexuals in the navy was far below that in the population, or that shipmates and commanding officers were turning a Nelsonian blind-eye to the old 'naval tradition'.

This appears to be confirmed by the degree to which homosexual activity was tolerated aboard Royal Navy warships, provided relationships did not cross the disciplinary divide between lower and upper decks. In his memoir, appropriately titled *Rum, Bum, and Concertina*, author and jazz singer George Melly describes the relatively relaxed attitudes he found as a seaman aboard one of His Majesty's cruisers shortly after the war:

> Sex on the *Dido* was comparatively low key, but uncensorious. There were a few obvious homosexuals, the doe-eyed writer for one, many total heterosexuals, and a fair number of those who would, on a casual basis, relieve sexual pressure with their own sex. It was accepted, for instance, on my mess deck, that on our Saturday 'make seven mends' (half days off) anyone who fancied some mutual masturbation would

crush down in the coat locker, a structure of closely-meshed wire like a medium-sized cage. As an open part-time invert, I was often solicited on these occasions and usually accepted. Sometimes my masculine role both surprised and disappointed those who had misread my predilections. Mostly, however, it was no problem and there was as relaxed and tolerant an atmosphere as any I've ever encountered. I had a sometime affair with a corporal of the marines who shared my watch on the quarterdeck, but this was only in the middle watch and, mostly, from his point of view, to allay boredom.

Although stern penalties were laid down by navy regulations, captains dealt with homosexual cases aboard their vessels with a latitude that derived from their sole authority. The more liberally minded dealt with offenders in a manner which caused the least disturbance to the functioning of their ship as an efficient fighting unit. Army commanders, however, had neither the same degree of control nor the same problems with sexual offences, since troops were not usually devoid of contact with women for such long spells.

'Many conscious homosexuals have found their way into the army, and of these only a certain number have come to the psychiatrist, either at their own request or because their odd behaviour has brought attention to them,' reported a British Army psychiatrist in a study of 'conscious and unconscious homosexual responses to warfare'. His conclusion was that four per cent of all military psychiatric cases admitted for 'war neuroses' were 'conscious inverts'. 'Sexual inversion does not necessarily imply a corollary of military uselessness', the study pointed out, citing both the 'acceptable homosexual warrior of warfare in classical times' and that many of the men under examination had been mentioned in dispatches. Nor were offenders unpopular with the other men, and he cited as an example the guardsman who worked out his masochistic homosexual fantasies polishing boots: this particular trooper's commanding officer made 'urgent representations' for the soldier's speedy return to his battalion.

'There is frequently a homosexual bond between the leaders and the led,' noted British military historian Brigadier Shelford Bidwell:

> This may be entirely free from actual homosexual relations (although these do occur, for quite different reasons, in most young, virile, all-male societies), but there is a natural tendency for leaders to collect

a sub-group of able and brave young men around them to act as their champions, aides, favourites, and even jesters, who are permitted to take liberties that even the leader's senior lieutenants would not dare take.

Homosexual charisma undoubtedly contributed to the success of such famous military leaders as Alexander the Great, Richard Coeur de Lion, Prince Eugene of Savoy, Charles XII of Sweden, Frederick the Great, General George Gordon, and Lawrence of Arabia. The popular conception of homosexuals as weak and effeminate men does not square with the courage and manliness demanded of such commanders on the battlefield. Their valour has never been in question. Nor has history questioned the bravery of the three hundred-strong Sacred Band of Thebes, 'every man the sworn lover of another', who died to a man at the Battle of Chaeronea in 338 BC. Indeed the very success of the classic Greek 'phalanx' depended on the front-rank and rear-rank men who called each other 'comrades in arms'. As one British general observed, 'Being what they were, they were probably found in one another's arms more often than would accord with modern ideas of military discipline.'

The percentage of World War II servicemen who ended up in each other's arms – either by inclination, or out of 'deprivation homosexuality' – is a matter for speculation. It was the opinion of wartime army psychiatrist Colonel Harry Pozner that:

> Those military personnel suffering from sexual disorders and voluntarily reporting on this account to their service doctors are comparatively few, and in general only seek advice from some ulterior motive or when threatened by disciplinary action or indiscreet sexual behaviour. That they represent only a small section of sexual deviates in the services is confirmed by police reports, sociological surveys, and semi-documentary modern novels indicating the active participation of service men of all ranks and social status in the homosexual underground of every large port and city.

The experience of prisoners of war and concentration camp inmates confirms that 'deprivation homosexuality' was not an uncommon practice among men of otherwise heterosexual inclination. A married Belgian officer, for example, wrote about his awareness of homosexual feelings watching a blonde strip-dancer after three years' sexual starvation in a German Stalag:

This innocuous display occasioned palpable discomfort among the audience, and the actors were much less enthusiastically applauded than the members of our POW troupe, who usually collect generous plaudits. I myself was as shocked as a fifteen-year-old. Our compulsory chastity must have turned us into Puritans. My first response was actually, 'God, how ugly the female body is! Most of the boys I see in the showers are more pleasant to look at.' I was disturbed at discovering this tendency '*à la Gide*'.

The same phenomenon was noted by a British prisoner in Malaya: 'I had always considered myself the normal male, and it was with a sense of shock that, during the latter months of Pudu and our stay at Changi, I found in myself certain homosexual tendencies.' In the Japanese camps the poor food and heavy work diminished the libido of the fifty thousand womanless young men, and the POWS became 'so debilitated that sex, in deed and in thought, failed to exist'.

Deprivation homosexuality was also to become endemic in the Nazi concentration camps. The men convicted under Article 175 of the German penal code were forced to wear identifying Pink Triangle arm patches. Hoess, the Commandant of Auschwitz, records in his autobiography how at Sachsenhausen an attempt was made to reduce homosexuality by dispersing the Pink Triangles throughout all the huts instead of confining them together in one section. This only increased homosexual activity, and the decision was taken to establish brothels in the camp to check it.

The details of wartime courts martial and investigations remain classified, making it difficult to assess the extent of homosexuality in the British and American armed forces, but comparable data is available from the captured Wehrmacht files. Sexual offenders were harshly persecuted in Germany following the 1934 purge of Major Ernst Roehm and his homosexual leadership of the brownshirted SA 'Storm Troopers'. Yet the Nazi leadership cannot have been unaware that their policy of segregation of adolescents increased the incidence of homosexuality in the Hitler Youth, causing some Germans to refer to it as the 'Homo Youth'. Consignment to a concentration camp was not considered a severe enough penalty for officers of the Nazi elite, according to the Reichsfuehrer SS, Heinrich Himmler.

Himmler's obsession with eugenics had convinced him that the ten per cent of Germany's male population who refused to marry and breed were guilty of national sabotage and deserved to be systematically exterminated before they spread the 'poison of racial suicide'. 'When a man in the Security Service, in the SS, or in the government has homosexual tendencies,' Himmler announced in 1940, 'then he abandons the normal order of things for the perverted world of the homosexual. Such a man drags ten others after him, otherwise he can't survive. We can't permit such a danger to the country: the homosexuals must be entirely eliminated.' After toying with the drowning of sexual deviates in swamps like the ancient German tribes, the Reichsfuehrer SS persuaded Hitler to issue a secret directive in 1941 warning that:

> Any member of the SS or Gestapo who engages in indecent behaviour with another man or permits himself to be abused by him for indecent purposes will, regardless of age, be condemned to death and executed. In less grave cases, a term of not less than six years' penal servitude or imprisonment may be imposed.

Escalating the severity of the punishment for homosexuality, however, made little impact on its prevalence. The German quarterly courts martial statistics indicate that sexual offence cases actually increased by nearly fifty per cent in 1944 over those for 1943 and that sixty-four per cent of the offenders were from the army (the largest component of the Wehrmacht), twenty-four per cent from the Luftwaffe and eleven per cent from the navy. Out of every hundred cases brought to trial, on average four were officers, twenty-eight non-commissioned officers, and sixty-eight other ranks. If Himmler's one in ten of the male population was the approximate incidence of homosexuality – a percentage that was coincident with Kinsey's researches – then there must have been at least a million in the ten-million strong Wehrmacht. The eight thousand men who were actually court martialled for homosexual offences represented less than one in a thousand of those in military service. The vast majority, therefore, managed to escape detection or punishment.

A 1945 study by the US Army confirms that most homosexuals did indeed manage to adapt to the military environment without being exposed. 'Many of those who were caught were normal heterosexuals who were accused of homosexual behaviour on a single occasion, usually while under the influence of alcohol,' observed Lt Colonel Lewis H. Loeser. His study concluded that there had been 'gross inequalities' because the 'true homosexual who admitted to repeated acts of sodomy was brought to trial infrequently, while the infrequent or first time offender was usually court martialled'. The Colonel pointed out that the equivalent in civil life was that 'habitual criminals and repeat offenders are permitted to go free while single first offenders are punished.'

The situation was remarkably similar for the British forces. According to one army doctor's assessment, 'the frequency of men *known* to be suffering from any form of sexual disorder was less than one in a thousand (0.0007%)'. The inference was that the reported cases represented only a very small percentage of the military homosexual community. This was given credence by his assertion in an army medical journal that the 'impression was also gained that there was more sexual disability amongst officers and less amongst other ranks than would seem at first evident from the available official data.'

King's Regulations clearly stated that 'confirmed homosexuals whose rehabilitation is unlikely should be removed from the Army by the most expeditious and appropriate means'. The discrepancy between actual cases and the statistical estimate of the homosexual population was evidently a question of semantics, subterfuge, and tolerance by some commanding officers. A British Army study of sexual offenders concluded that homosexuals 'achieved gratification from those of their comrades who turned towards them as substitutes for women.' The same study also revealed that the active military homosexual often exerted excessive authority 'to dominate the male group, obtain love, respect, and acknowledgement of his prowess. He must lead, cannot be led, and finds it intolerable to be in a passive position of obeying.' Over a third of the cases examined 'had Fascist leanings and were facile exponents of power politics'. The report concluded that homosexuals 'form a foreign body in the social macrocosm' and vindicated the wartime policy of offenders being 'quietly invalided out of the service, with appropriate advice about medical treatment, unless they had to be brought up before courts martial'. Formal charges were usually only instituted in the British armed forces for those sexual transgressors who had committed a flagrant breach of discipline, especially between officers and other ranks, or civilians.

One such case was that of the writer G. F. Green, who had confided to his wartime diary that he had 'chosen a way of life deliberately not the way preferred'. As a wartime army lieutenant in Ceylon he had insisted on pursuing his chosen way and had flaunted his homosexuality to the fury of the mess. He pursued his amorous attachment for native youths despite warnings. He was court martialled, cashiered, and sentenced to two years in a gruelling military detention centre. According to a brother officer, his colonel had no choice but to let the case be tried by a military court because Green was 'found on his bed, all lights on, in the wrong place, at the wrong time, with someone whose company, in the circumstances, could only be regarded as conduct unbecoming, to say the least'.

An example of the lengths some British soldiers went to in concealing their tendencies was that of a forty-two-year-old sergeant. He was a highly-regarded soldier who had repressed his homosexuality to the point of mental instability by leaving letters from a fictitious son lying about the barracks. Fear that he would be exposed had finally resulted in a suicide attempt and, while hospitalized, he demanded to be castrated or imprisoned.

Though some duration-only officers with little or no service experience treated every sexual offender strictly by the book, the professional officer corps, many of whom had seen service in India where homosexual activity, particularly amongst the Sikh regiments, was not uncommon, were prepared to be more lenient. Just before the Battle of El Alamein, one British major recalled how a potentially embarrassing court martial was hushed up:

> A sergeant in our brigade was discovered masturbating with a private in a tent, and they were both put on a charge by the sergeant major. Our colonel, who was himself a homosexual, was absent, and so the case went right up to brigade headquarters. The brigadier, who had been a boy soldier promoted through the ranks and to whom nothing in army life was a surprise, dismissed both men with a reprimand. The colonel was absolutely furious that it had got as far as it did. 'The battalion's been out here for two years, these two youngsters had never had home leave,' he stormed afterwards in the mess. 'Out in India when I was in the ranks, reveille brought every man tumbling out of everyone else's bunks. What the hell do they want the men to do for sexual relief, go down to the brothels in the bazaar, chase Arab women and catch syphilis?'

In wartime such tolerance was practised wherever possible, because the potential loss of one soldier in ten would have left front-line regiments badly under strength. 'When the conservation of manpower was an essential priority,' admitted one army psychiatrist, 'it was often considered practical and realistic to post known homosexuals of good intelligence and proved ability to large towns, where their private indulgences were less likely to be inimical to the best interests of the service.'

Unofficial policy in the US Army was also to avoid courts martial proceedings by resorting to 'administrative discharge'. The 93rd Article of War nonetheless laid down that 'soldiers ascertained to be sodomists' were subject to 'dishonourable discharge, forfeiture of all pay and allowances, and confinement at hard labour in a Federal penitentiary for five years'. Fearing that draft dodgers might feign homosexuality to get out of the service on 'administrative discharges', the War Department in autumn 1941 issued a directive that 'administrative discharge will not be used for summarily ridding the service of undesirable soldiers who, by their misconduct, have rendered themselves liable to trial by court martial.' Six months later, however, when the United States was at war and facing a severe military manpower crisis, the Adjutant General's office relaxed its previously inflexible policy on administrative discharges.

In the months after Pearl Harbor a spate of embarrassing courts martial, and in particular an investigation into allegations of widespread homosexuality at Moffet Field California, resulted in a new policy directive in the US Army that was set out in a report from the Adjutant General's office entitled a 'Study of Sodomy Cases'. Concerned to avoid the 'wholesale discharge of soldiers', the Judge Advocate General of the US Army established the criteria that the 'primary consideration should be the interest of the service of men possessing a salvage value'. It designated three classes of sexual offence. The 'true sodomists', who were to be court martialled; homosexual offenders in 'extenuating circumstances' or where there was insufficient evidence for a conviction, who were to be given an administrative discharge; and 'men who through either alcoholic over-indulgence or curiosity, will submit to unnatural relations', who were to be 'studied carefully by a qualified psychiatrist and if not found to be moral perverts . . . be returned to duty after appropriate disciplinary action.'

Draft boards who were supposed to screen out sexual inverts

and examiners at induction centres, were advised to be on the look-out for 'effeminacy in dress or manner'. In practice it was not difficult for homosexuals to slip through the screening process – often with the sympathetic assistance of members of the board. 'I walked into this office and here was a man who was a screaming belle,' recalled one homosexual New York draftee. 'He was a queen if ever I saw one, and he asked me the standard questions, ending up with, "Did you ever have any homosexual experiences?" Well I looked him right in the eye and I said, "No!" And he looked right back and said, "That's good!" – both of us lying through our teeth.'

Administrative discharge became the preferred method of dealing with those homosexual offenders deemed 'non-reclaimable'. It was intended as neither an honourable nor dishonourable discharge, merely listing the section of US Army regulations which meant the individual was 'not eligible for re-enlistment.' Civilian employers soon recognized that the bearer of a blue discharge form was a homosexual, and the ex-servicemen who received them took to calling themselves 'Blue Angels'.

In the US Navy, officers found guilty of 'Scandalous conduct tending to the destruction of good morals' could be punished with dismissal and a maximum of twelve months' hard labour, but enlisted men faced a dishonourable discharge and ten years' imprisonment. Such are the privileges of rank.

Naval prison records, however, reveal that the most severe penalty handed out for a sodomy conviction in 1941 was only half the maximum, and the small numbers convicted in a year that the navy was rapidly expanding suggests that most homosexual incidents were dealt with as psychiatric cases. By the final year of the war, administrative discharges were approved for self-confessed homosexuals or where there was no proof of offences committed in uniform.

One sailor who escaped a general court martial under the revised wartime policy was 'Roy', a Seaman 2nd class at the Jacksonville Naval Air Station. He was arrested and charged with 'wilfully, knowingly, indecently, and lewdly' permitting an act of oral sodomy with a civilian. Under questioning he admitted to a variety of 'homosexual acts with soldiers, sailors, and civilians in hotels, parks, and restrooms.' Naval investigators also obtained a confession from one of his partners that 'Roy' was 'very gay'. A naval yeoman at the naval air station testified to 'association with members of this gay circle,' a term in use even then. The psychiatrist's diagnosis was 'HOMOSEXUAL' and his verdict that the seaman was 'unsuitable for retention in the naval service'. The accused's naval career came to an end when he signed 'an undesirable discharge for the good of the service and to escape trial by General Court Martial'.

There were many inconsistencies in the application of the revised policy towards homosexuals in the navy. The evidence of two zealous Miami police officers resulted in the discharge of a navy lieutenant for 'scandalous conduct' after they had arrested him for 'kissing and fondling the buttocks' of a sailor. A Seaman First Class was arrested in 1944 for desertion and then compounded his crime by seducing the three inmates of the brig at the US naval base in Texas. 'Bob', a Seaman Second Class in the US Coast Guard from Virginia, was held to have provided all the evidence needed for a general court martial for 'scandalous conduct' in an explicit letter to an army lieutenant which began:

Dear Hal,
Your good letter came today. Also picture, which I'm fond of. Like your nose and ears. Always a good sign of a big piece of meat. No kidding think you are handsome. And I wish you were here now.

There followed a graphic description of what they would do the following weekend when they met in a Fayettesville hotel, concluding 'all soldiers very understanding' – an opinion that was evidently not shared by the one who censored mail at Fort Bragg, North Carolina, who promptly filed a report. When confronted with what the Office of the Inspector General of the War Department described as a 'very obscene' letter, both men 'resigned for the good of the service'.

There was strong opposition to the introduction of a more flexible US Navy wartime policy towards homosexuals, and particularly to the review of those already serving sentences for 'scandalous conduct'. In 1944, a strong protest was made to the Navy Department from the Eighth Naval District near New Orleans, where an investigation of a 'homosexual ring' had resulted in the arrest of seven officers and twenty-three sailors as well as ten officers and seven enlisted army men. 'It is not believed that the present "hush hush" manner of handling homosexuality and perversion is effective,' complained the memorandum from the Commandant and Admiral commanding the Eighth Naval District. They argued that the administrative discharge policy was 'in error' because it granted homosexuals 'complete liberty to pursue their practices at will'. They charged that 'the practice is widespread throughout the naval service'; that it was a 'criminological rather than a medical problem', and that all homosexuals should be court martialled and confined to 'an institution for the insane, to remain there for an indefinite period'. In colourful language the alarmist District's medical officers reported a threat to the navy and nation from the 'dry rot' of 'homosexualists' bent on 'racial suicide'.

Only a very small fraction of the homosexual population of the US armed forces were purged from the service, and the majority certainly served their country no less bravely and efficiently than their heterosexual comrades. According to the only available official study of homosexual soldiers in the US Army during World War II, their performance ratings 'average considerably higher than in the Army as a whole,' although the report concluded that, 'the group is lacking in the temperament and skills necessary to the combat soldier'.

Individual cases that have emerged since the war do not support the contention that homosexuals who served in the military lacked the 'temperament and skills' to distinguish themselves in action. One of the foremost American carrier task force commanders of the Pacific war was avowedly homosexual. When his predilections brought investigators from naval intelligence to question him, he unceremoniously ordered them off his ship. His 'scandalous conduct' was brought to the attention of the Chief of Naval Operations in Washington, but Admiral Ernest J. King, although a staunch disciplinarian, ordered investigations to be dropped in order that this particular officer could continue to play a vital role in defeating Japan.

Such cases do not appear to have caused concern because they challenged the bravery of homosexual officers, or because they raised the possibility of a public scandal. Concern rather stemmed from the risk that a senior officer's homosexual entanglements might distort his military judgement. In at least one case a shipboard romance in the Royal Navy would appear to have cost Britain a capital ship and the lives of many men. The incident is cited by Oxford historian A. L. Rowse in his study *Homosexuals in History*, which contains the following intriguing reference:

> Some of us know of such episodes as that in the Second World War, when the captain of a battleship lost one of his planes at sea and had the great ship put about to search, to be torpedoed by a submarine: the commander was in love with the young flight lieutenant who had not returned.

Most homosexuals in the armed forces were to prove that they were as courageous as their heterosexual comrades. Testimony to their bravery was given by a homosexual who served as an officer in a front-line infantry regiment:

> During the last war I met 'queers' in all ranks from private to general. One of the bravest was a Battle of Britain fighter pilot who won his DFC and Bar shooting down German 'planes over England. Twice he baled out of blazing Spitfires. Once his parachute landed him in a greenhouse. Twice the King congratulated him. Eventually he became a group-captain, although he had started his Royal Air Force career as an aircraftsman. He was a highly emotional man, but he willed himself to do everything his companions did. He shot down more enemy planes than most of them, was a likeable and highly efficient fellow, and he really loved the RAF. So his companions accepted him readily and regarded him with affection. He commanded a squadron of Polish fighters, among the best and most reckless of airmen. Most of the leading pilots who met him suspected or knew that he was homosexual, but no-one minded.

This former British infantry captain discovered to his relief that no-one at British Middle East GHQ in Cairo appeared unduly concerned that the famous Shepheard's Hotel was the rendezvous for a wide circle of the homosexual military elite. At the beginning of 1943, he was a regular at the bar, which he noted was the favourite gathering place for the officers of Colonel Stirling's Long Range Desert Group. One evening a decorated Battle of Britain ace made a pass at him. The Group Captain was then in command of an RAF base in Egypt, and the two men struck up an intimate friendship, socializing with other homosexual officers in parties held in a flat overlooking the Nile which belonged to one of the senior secretaries at the American embassy.

Shepheard's Hotel and its discrete coterie of Allied military and diplomatic officers was largely immune from the periodic efforts made by British Military Police to crack down on the wartime homosexual network in Cairo. Like Algiers, Naples, and later Paris, Cairo and the port of Alexandria were meccas of sexual adventure for servicemen of all proclivities. In back streets Arab boys lurked who were willing to provide for the sexual satisfaction of many a serviceman whose inhibitions about homosexuality were not so great as their fear of catching venereal disease from a Cairene tart. These brief encounters did not turn the average soldier into a confirmed homosexual – any more than did sharing a blanket for warmth in a slit trench at the front.

The thunder of heavy artillery that preceded a major offensive often had a powerful aphrodisiac effect on heterosexual soldiers which their homosexual comrades were able to take advantage of. During the final tense hour of the earthshaking bombardment before the second battle of El Alamein on 24 October 1942, the Major recalled how a young married lieutenant crawled over: 'In a few minutes this boy was groping me and we were kissing passionately. It was a powerful emotional climax for both of us, although I knew that he was married and not a homosexual at all.'

In his personal combat memoir as a US marine in the Pacific, William Manchester describes how a Japanese barrage unhinged his tough veteran sergeant, who was 'macho in ways which, we thought, were the exact opposite of homosexual'. None of his company had apparently taken seriously the heavily muscled six-feet-two sergeant's drunken boast that he intended to write a book called *Famous Cocks I Have Sucked*. Later, he learned that the sergeant major had been court martialled for 'scandalous conduct'.

'There was so much excitement (and apocrypha) about heterosexuality,' Manchester wrote of his wartime sexual experience, 'that we seldom gave it [homosexuality] a second thought.' But the recollections of another Pacific veteran suggest that in the Pacific theatre homosexual activity was far from uncommon. Many of the GIs, he claimed, took advantage of a variety of homosexual substitutes for the 'dames' they sorely lacked:

> Honolulu was memorable for the twenty-four-hour service available at a bamboo fence called the 'Mouths of the Hundred Delights'. There weren't a hundred openings in the fence in a back alley on the outskirts of the town, but behind each one a moist tongue gave sidewalk relief to almost any height of man who stuck his knob through a 'Mouth'.

The fence was well named, delightful as well as convenient.

In the Philippines, a section from one motor pool used to requisition a jeep for 'midnight reconnoitring', stopping at MP guardposts in isolated positions. When the MP leaned down to confirm directions to the area requested, you kissed him full on the mouth. The driver then stepped on the gas, leaving an amazed, sometimes annoyed military policeman in the dust thrown up by spinning tyres. Once when I was in the 'action seat' I gave the MP on solitary duty a big wet smack and waited for the driver to roar off into the darkness. This time the motor failed! To my surprise, the MP put an arm around my neck and kissed me back. My travelling companions were startled, and then jealous when the guard undid his trousers and I complied readily.

On Okinawa, all 'Gooks', both female and male natives, were locked up behind barbed wire at night. A variety of substitutes sprang up to fill the need. The most notorious was one of the company mess sergeants who held 'open tent' after evening chow. A line formed quickly after supper and moved at a lively pace because the sergeant would take two at a time, masturbating one man and fellating another. The other night-time outlet was on an army transport truck shuttle to the Seabees, down the stretch from Naha, to see a film. If you wanted to get blown you tried to sit on the side benches of the canvas-covered truck. Depending on how horny you were and how badly you wanted to see Betty Grable you could ride the trucks until you were satisfied. Daytime sexual relief could be obtained at a spot on the seashore marked by three reddish rocks soaring up like phallic symbols at the beach where many units went bare-ass bathing.

The prevalence of such extensive male-to-male erotic activity indicates that American military authorities adopted a somewhat more tolerant attitude to homosexual behaviour in the Pacific than in Europe or the United States. Only when incidents threatened battlefield discipline was punitive action taken. Manchester recounts the case involving 'a colonel who had been one of the great heroes of Guadalcanal. This exemplar of heroism was caught *in flagrante delicto*, his penis rammed to the hilt in the anus of a corporal. Because of his fame (and perhaps his rank) he was spared imprisonment. He was allowed to resign.'

A remarkably similar case involving a first lieutenant is recorded in the records of the 3rd Marine Division. The charge was that he did 'on 5 January 1944, in a foxhole of the said Company, wilfully and knowingly, and with indecent, lewd, and lascivious intent attempt to insert the penis of him, the said ——— in the rectum of one Charles ———, Private First Class USMC Reserve, for the purpose and intent of enabling him, the said ———, to commit sodomy in and upon the body of the said ———, the United States then being in a state of war.' The lieutenant was actually caught *in flagrante delicto* committing oral sodomy with another private and only admitted to the first offence. Threatening to commit suicide if court martial proceedings were commenced, the lieutenant was evacuated to a base hospital. It was a threat that paid off. His commanding officer was persuaded to accept the psychiatrist's report that the 'acts performed' by the lieutenant 'are merely symptomatic of mental illness' and it was agreed that he should submit his resignation 'for the good of the service'.

Enlisted men were not always so fortunate. The military attempted to pre-empt such problems by offering GIs who admitted 'homosexual tendencies' a passage home and discharge without loss of benefits. 'We were treated as insane people,' recalled one soldier, who reported his 'tendencies' to his medical officer. Half of those who came forward were sent to hospital psychiatric wards and the other half incarcerated behind barbed wire in a 'queer stockade'. When they arrived back in the United States this contingent of homosexuals from the 6th Army were stripped of their campaign medals and given 'blue angel' administrative discharges.

Wartime studies indicated that so-called sexual inverts were less resistant to trauma in their personal lives than heterosexual troops. A British report cited the example of a sergeant, 'an active homosexual who had been an excellent fighting soldier', who had to be invalided out of the army as a psychotic when his long-standing passive partner broke up their relationship to get married. Other such cases included soldiers who had concealed their sexual nature with wartime marriages. One suffered a mental breakdown when his wife was unfaithful and another was hospitalized when the birth of his child was taken as 'signal proof of his partner's femininity'.

Military psychiatrists also identified homosexuals as being especially vulnerable to mental breakdown when their male lovers were killed in action. 'Prolonged mourning tendencies are found in those to whom the loss of a comrade means the loss of a homosexual love-object, and the grief is all the more profound in that its occasion is neither apprehended nor formulated,' advised a British army doctor. Invariably the surviving partner complained, 'the bullet should have got me, not him'.

In one case the survivor had discovered his friend with the top of his skull blown away – and within a few hours developed a hysterical sense of numbness and constriction. Another witnessed the sudden amputation of a comrade's legs and became a hysterical paraplegic when he heard of his lover's death. Not all the patients studied were conscious homosexuals, as in the case of a twenty-five-year-old private who had suffered for two years from intense headaches, battle-dreams, and weeping. He was reluctant to recognize the sexual nature of his attachment to his dead comrade until, as his case notes reveal, he was hypnotized by the doctor treating him:

> Under light hypnosis he expressed a rather odd relationship with his dead comrade. 'He held my hand when I was frightened and gave me confidence. He is the best pal I ever had. We were like a loving couple, like husband and wife. I saw him shot and his neck was covered with blood. I tried to bring him back to life with water but he died while I was holding him up.' In most of the nightmares that beset him, his friend would come back to life together with his bloody injury, and on a few occasions there were emissions during these episodes. Occasionally he dreamed he was dressed in ATS uniform walking arm in arm with his chum, along the streets of his home town. The meaning of these simple wish-fulfilment dreams was very obvious and puzzled no-one save the patient. He was in fact an evident and glaring example of the usually more subtle homosexual mourning reactions.

The 'mourning reaction' of homosexuals in the military was often made all the more intense because the surviving lover was forced to hide the real reason for his grief for fear of exposure. One GI whose long-standing homosexual buddy died in the battle for Manila recalled, 'I went into a three-day period of hysterics. I was treated with such kindness by the guys I worked with, who were all totally unaware why I was hysterical. It wasn't at all because we were being bombed; it was because my "boyfriend" had been killed.'

'No-one asked me if I was gay when they called out "Medic!" and you went out under fire and did what you were expected and trained to do,' observed a homosexual medical corpsman who had enlisted at the age of eighteen. 'Buddies from medical training days were dying like flies and it became lonely. I was wounded at Cherbourg during the Normandy invasion and during the Battle of the Bulge. There were so many gays in the medics and so many of them gave their lives.'

The military experience of homosexuality in World War II chipped away some of the old taboos. Servicemen living in close proximity to one another were made aware that men who chose a sexual relationship with other men were not suffering from a deadly disease, nor were they cowards or effeminates. Many thousands of homosexuals discovered a new consciousness of their collective identity in the sub-culture of bars and camaraderie which expanded to meet the wartime demand.

In the post-war reaction to the liberal morality of wartime, there was an inevitable homo-phobic campaign. But World War II, by the very act of bringing so many homosexuals together, contributed to the evolution of the so-called Gay Liberation movement in the United States twenty years after the war had ended. Ancient taboos, like old soldiers, did not die easily. As William Manchester wrote, 'Had we been told that the practitioners of oral sodomy wanted to live together openly, with the approval of society, and insisted on being called "gay", we would have guffawed. That just wasn't one of the rights we were fighting to protect.'

9

AMMUNITION
FOR THE HEART

We're all in this fight together. Women as well
as men sharing our responsibilities. I want to
be part of you – the part that goes with you into
the battlefield.

'This is the Army', 1943

In trench or camp or ship,
Here's wishing you Good Luck from Jane –
And she hopes you like her strip!

JANE Cartoon, *Daily Mirror*

AFTER GERMAN TROOPS OVER-RAN EUROPE in the summer of 1940, and Churchill defied Hitler to invade Britain, a military draft in the United States was making Americans apprehensive that they might soon be dragged into the fight. Films like the blockbuster *Gone With the Wind* with Clark Gable in romantic pursuit of Vivien Leigh in the American Civil War, had struck a powerful chord of contemporary concern among millions of men and women who were worried about how their lives and loves might be affected by a war.

Vivien Leigh was back on the screen in 1941 playing Lady Hamilton battling against the tides of fortune. Producer Alexander Korda described the film, which starred Laurence Olivier as Nelson, as 'propaganda with a very thick coating of sugar'. But this did not stop American isolationist protests that the film was yet another effort to undermine United States neutrality by regaling the virtues of fighting for one's country.

Prime Minister Winston Churchill pronounced that *Lady Hamilton* was his favourite wartime film. He had every reason to be delighted at the way in which Hollywood was turning public sympathy against Germany while boosting British morale in, for example, Charlie Chaplin's caricature of Hitler in *The Great Dictator*.

Despite the isolationist outcry, American film-goers' attention continued to be directed to Britain's struggle with Vivien Leigh's 1941 remake of *Waterloo Bridge*, which was reset as a melodramatic love affair in the Blitz. Mickey Rooney and Judy Garland, in the teenage musical *Babes in Arms*, sang 'Chin Up, Cheerio, Carry On', which promised to 'turn the Blitz on Fritz!' Meanwhile Hollywood was doing its bit to spur the United States to mobilization. *Sergeant York* retold the saga of the all-American World War I hero, and in *I Wanted Wings* Veronica Lake and Ray Milland managed to combine romance with a recruiting campaign for the US air force. Dorothy Lamour made army life bearable for Bob Hope in *Caught in the Draft*. In *Navy Blues* Ann Sheridan broke into passionate song to convince her sailor boyfriend that it would

be unpatriotic of him to go back to his Iowa farm, and Jimmy
Durante and Phil Silvers in *You're In the Army Now* gave a musical
endorsement of selective service, 'The draft has begun/I'm number
two-eighty-one/I'm glad my number was called.' But it was romance against the backdrop of the war in England that proved to
be the biggest draw of the year. In *A Yank in the RAF*, Tyrone
Power helped save English soldiers stranded on Dunkirk beaches
and found time to marry his dancer sweetheart. This was made
possible after the British Government had intervened to have the
screenplay rewritten so that Betty Grable did not die, as originally
intended, in an air raid on the eve of her marriage.

The formula was perfected in the 1942 Academy Award-winning
film *Mrs Miniver*, which successfully brought to the screen the
drama of war's impact on the lives and loves of a 'typical' British
family. Its distortion of middle-class archetypes prompted one
English critic to disown 'a world which seems to consist of giggling
housemaids with their bucolic young men; doddering servile
stationmasters; glee singers in their feather boas; duchesses and
their granddaughters, blackmailing comic grocers and truculent
ever-leaving cooks.' But the finely judged performances of Greer
Garson and Walter Pidgeon as the British couple coping with their
wartime trials brought tears to audiences on both sides of the
Atlantic.

For all its glossy sentimentality, *Mrs Miniver* presented an
evocative cinematographic tribute to the quiet courage of women
in World War II. Greer Garson was the epitome of that genteel
feminine resolve which triumphed over enemy bombs, her husband and son going off to war, and a ranting German parachutist
invading her kitchen. The emotional demands placed on married
women in wartime were characterized by the manner in which
Mrs Miniver's daughter-in-law confronted the prospect of widow-
hood. 'If I must lose him, there'll be time enough for tears, there'll
be a lifetime for tears,' announced the bride-to-be with stoic
resolve on the eve of her wedding.

In a powerfully emotional finale, Mr and Mrs Miniver consoled
each other at the funeral service of their son's wife, who was killed
by a strafing German fighter while he lived on to fight in the
RAF. As Spitfires roared over the bombed-out church, the rector
defiantly proclaimed Hollywood's inspired epitaph on World War
II:

> This is not only the war of soldiers in uniform, it is a war of the people
> – of all people – and it must be fought not only on the battlefield, but
> in the . . . heart of every man, woman, and child who loves freedom.
> This is the people's war. This is our war.

The film's 1942 release coincided with the United States' entry into the war. Romantic films were no longer purely entertainment, but were ammunition for the heart and inspiration for the men in battle and the women in war production on the home front. In *Mrs Miniver* Hollywood had made good on the promise made in 1941 by the Deputy Director of War Information that, 'the screen can be used to give the people a clear, continuous, amd total pattern of total war'.

Romance, nonetheless, remained the staple ingredient in wartime film production because, as the trailer for a B-movie called *China Girl* succinctly put it, 'An American will fight for only three things – for a woman, for himself, and for a better world.' The studios found it more difficult to sustain the love interest during the first year of the war when most of the top-flight male stars, including Clark Gable, Tyrone Power, William Holden, Alan Ladd, James Stewart, Robert Montgomery, and John Wayne, patriotically joined the armed forces. But the shortage of glamorous male leads and film stock did not stop the romantic glamour factory. In the absence of the top male box-office stars, Hollywood promoted women into major film leads, thus satisfying the servicemen's demand for sexy symbols and flattering the ego of a largely female wartime home audience. They also produced a box-office bonanza.

World War II brought Hollywood its second golden age, as film-going became the main form of wartime entertainment and the English-speaking world flocked into the cinemas. The Hollywood stars became national heroines. They raised millions of dollars in War Bond fund-raising drives and toured the home and overseas fronts entertaining servicemen, yet many still managed to find time between film-making to staff the Stage Door and Hollywood Canteens. January 1942 brought Hollywood its first war casualty, when the lovely Carole Lombard was killed in a plane crash on a bond promotion. Dorothy Lamour stepped forward to complete the tour. She became known as the 'Treasury's Sweetheart' when the cash poured into the federal coffers after her trip around the shipyards and defence plants. The glamorous sex-appeal of such film stars not only spurred American wartime productivity, but also helped to persuade the workers to invest in Government war bonds.

Booming wartime box-office receipts encouraged the American studios to marshal their huge resources into turning out an average of four hundred films a year. Hollywood's war output included propaganda documentaries and patriotic tributes to the American fighting man. Films like *Wake Island*, *Bataan*, *Five Graves to Cairo*, *Thirty Seconds Over Tokyo*, and *Guadalcanal Diary* spurred on the efforts of the war production workers. Keeping the wartime audiences laughing on both sides of the Atlantic were Bob Hope and Bing Crosby, who took *The Road to Morocco*, and the following fabulously successful 'Road' series, with Dorothy Lamour, whose clinging sarong made her a favourite of the GIs. *Swing Shift Maisie* sent the irrepressible blonde Ann Sothern into a war plant, while *Buck Privates* put Abbot and Costello into uniform and the audiences into stitches. In 1942 Humphrey Bogart's enigmatic affair with Ingrid Bergman in *Casablanca* elevated the anti-German espionage film into a romantic art-form. The same year Judy Garland, George Murphy, and Gene Kelly in *For Me And My Girl* started a wartime craze for musicals featuring men and women in uniform.

'Motion pictures are as necessary to the men as rations,' insisted an American general. *Time* magazine was to publish a 1944 poll which indicated, 'GIs like musical comedies best, comedies next best, then adventure films and melodramas'. When General Eisenhower was planning D-Day he demanded, 'Let's have more movies' – and the troops cheered. 'Without movies we'd go nuts,' wrote a GI from the Pacific. Soldiers' favourite films were those which were heavy on sentiment like Rita Hayworth's *My Gal Sal* and Judy Garland and *Meet Me In St Louis*.

Films were uniquely suited to boosting the morale of the armed forces. They could be sent where no live concert party dared to go, and cans of film and projectors reached jungle camps, desert bases, and Nissen huts in Arctic tundra. Testimony to the unique contribution that wartime Hollywood made to boosting Allied morale came in a 1943 letter from a Marine private who had seen six months' action in the Pacific:

I know what it is to be cut off from everything . . . to sit on my bunk with my head in my hands . . . to walk a post in some lonely nowhere . . . to wait and wait for God only knows what. Those hours can stretch into centuries – and would, if it weren't for a movie now and then. Movies that stop us from thinking of ourselves and our surroundings. Movies that remind us that there are such things as pretty girls, gay music, and a civilization worth living for . . .

Of all Hollywood's outpouring of wartime entertainment, the musicals provided the biggest boost to the wartime morale of servicemen and civilians alike. The flimsy boy-meets-girl plots disguised in a lavish package of sexy glamour and cheerful songs offered the tonic of a few hours respite from the grim realities of war. Ironically, while musicals had buoyed American spirits through the Depression, their attraction had faded until the war-time demand for escapist entertainment revived them. No greater contrast to the war could have been concocted than these frothy visual sundaes, whipped up around nubile female chorus lines and topped off with glittering stars such as Betty Grable, Ginger Rogers, Judy Garland, Rita Hayworth, Alice Faye, and Carmen Miranda. Musicals turned their stars into national cheerleaders and at the same time promoted them as erotic symbols for a 'pin-up' parade of the armed forces.

Warner Brothers' enormously popular *Yankee Doodle Dandy* was a timely salute to the flag-waving music of composer George M. Cohan. It won an oscar for James Cagney's rags-to-riches title role and revived the World War I hits 'Over There', 'Give My Regards to Broadway', and 'You're the Grand Old Flag' just in time to rally American spirits after Allied fortunes hit rock bottom as the flood-tide of Japan's military conquest rolled over the Philippines, Malaya, and Burma.

Two years later the same studios produced Irving Berlin's no less red-white-and-blue soldier-boy love story, *This is The Army*, which set the pattern for a spate of parade musicals. This patriotic salute and tribute to the GI with its rousing title song also made a hit of the wistful 'I left my Heart at the Stage Door Canteen'. It managed to tie the knot between patriotism and love, with Ronald Reagan the draftee soldier who is reluctant to wed his sweetheart before he goes off to war. In a symbolic wartime reversal of the traditional roles, it is Joan Leslie who finally persuades *him* to marry her, with lines that doubtless put the seal on many real life wartime romances: 'We're all in this fight together. Women as well as men sharing our responsibilities. I want to be part of you – the part that goes with you on the battlefield. This is a free United States. If we want to get married – let's get married.'

The success of *This is the Army* prompted the other Hollywood studios to adopt the same formula, in which a romantic plot was less important than the number of stars and dance routines that could be mustered on the screen. Not to be outdone, Warner Brothers retaliated with *Hollywood Canteen*, a musical pegged together on the improbable story of a sailor in from the Pacific who finds himself the millionth serviceman to enter the famous Los Angeles Club founded by Bette Davis. For his prize he chooses as his weekend escort the 'as American as apple-pie' Joan Leslie. The Andrews Sisters performed the films calloused title song, which celebrated the Hollywood Canteen where 'GI Joes can forget their woes and boogie with any movie star'. America's most popular wartime female trio then went on to complain in close harmony of the pain they endured from the 'patriotic corns' they developed through jitterbugging with too many GIs.

Thank Your Lucky Stars was Columbia Pictures' entry in the 'musical parade'. It was notable for Bette Davis singing to a huge Victory poster of US soldiers, sailors, and marines, and lamenting that the men who were left were 'either too young or too old' and 'there is no secret lover the draft board didn't discover'. *Star Spangled Rhythm* was Paramount Pictures' contribution. It featured an irrepressible Bob Hope introducing Paulette Goddard, Dorothy Lamour, and Veronica Lake in a slyly sexy ditty: 'A Sweater, A Sarong, and a Peek-A-Boo Bang.' The big chorus routine, 'On the Swing Shift', was a musical salute to the girls in the home front factories in which Betty Hutton saucily sang, 'I'm Doing it For Defence'.

These wartime musicals not only celebrated female talent, but also contributed to the wartime blurring of sex roles by casting men in women's roles for comic situations. *This is The Army* and *Hi Yank* featured dance routines for soldiers dressed up in female costumes. In other wartime comedy films, Danny Kaye had to don a WAC's skirt to date his officer girlfriend and Red Skelton dressed as a ballet dancer to pursue Esther Williams into a posh eastern girl's academy.

Carmen Miranda, the 'Brazilian Bombshell', as she became known after the 1940 release of *Down Argentina Way*, became famous as a Latin American *femme fatale* whose Mickey Mouse mouth, clattering maracas and exotic headpieces made her an outrageous parody of a woman out to get a man. Her most stunning screen performance was in the 1944 musical *The Gang's All Here*, when she sashayed through a tropical fruit salad chorus routine concocted in glorious technicolor by Busby Berkley to sing 'The Lady in the Tutti-frutti Hat' in her unique style. Carmen Miranda, as one critic noted, 'projected about as much sex-appeal as a Christmas tree in July' but she sent up the traditional notion of female allure with rolling eyes, ruby lips, and a suggestive turn of phrase that delighted audiences. By the end of the war she had become its most travestied star, and no improvised vaudeville all-male army show was without a hilarious impersonation of the lady in the tutti-frutti hat!

If Carmen Miranda represented the kind of non-threatening sexual confusion that servicemen could laugh at, GIs found less to joke about in those movies which presented women taking over the customary male role. The 1943 film *Broadway Parade* was intended as Hollywood's musical tribute to the female war workers, and it opened with a masterpiece of choreographic cinematography in which a high-kicking chorus line-up dissolved into a marching battalion of female welders while a soldier sang:

> Once they had so many dates life became a bore,
> Now they're in defence work making bombers by the score.
> They gave up fancy clothes and are happy in navy blue,
> They are wearing cotton hose and are happy in khaki too!

There was not much sex-appeal or glamour for the service audience in such films, as Paramount found when it brought out *Rosie the Riveter*. The tortuous plot of this 1944 musical strained even Hollywood's power of romantic invention. It told the 'inspiring' tale of a pretty girl who delayed her marriage so that she could take a job in an aircraft factory because 'winning the war is more important'. Although it played to packed audiences of female war workers who shared the heroine's belief that they 'typify Miss America today', its interest for GIs was on a par with the large notice over the factory set: 'IF YOUR SWEATER IS TOO

LONG, LOOK OUT FOR MACHINES – IF YOUR SWEATER IS TOO SMALL, LOOK OUT FOR MEN!'

Rosie the Riveter was not a hit with the American male audience, and nor were the other wartime 'women's pictures' in which Hollywood pandered to its large female wartime audience with films that depicted women coping with the war by fulfilling traditional male roles. The novel situations of women in wartime offered Hollywood producers scope for new dramatic plots and situation comedies. *Swing Shift Maisie* was about the trials of Ann Sothern, an aircraft worker, and *Government Girl* featured Olivia de Havilland as a Washington bureaucrat. Lucille Ball played a film star turned defence worker in *Meet the People*. *Keep Your Powder Dry* featured Lana Turner as a pert heiress who joined the WACs only to burst into tears when she was commissioned, and Betty Hutton frolicked in uniform through *Here Comes The Waves*, playing twin sisters.

The wartime 'women are coping' films did not play well to the American male audience, either. This was especially true of movies like *So Proudly We Hail*, which starred Claudette Colbert, Veronica Lake, and Paulette Goddard in a celebration of the courage of a group of army nurses on Bataan, and those that dealt with war-widows, like *Since You Went Away*. It had always been expected that women would manage temporarily when their menfolk were mobilized for military service, but these films showed them surviving in combat zones and reversing the traditional gender-typing in the workplace and armed forces. The images aroused in the American male the fear that World War II might be banishing forever the traditional values of home and hearth that many GIs believed they were fighting for.

Although German bombs demolished one in ten cinemas, attendances in Britain trebled through the Blitz, the total weekly attendance rising to over thirty million. Twice-weekly changes of programme ensured that there were always queues waiting in the blackout at the local cinema, where the principal fare was more likely to be romances or musicals than home-produced Gainsborough films. Plagued by shortages and the Blitz, the British film industry struggled to produce documentary salutes to the 'people's war' such as *London Can Take It* and *One of Our Aircraft is Missing*.

There was a spate of patriotic features made about spies and fifth columnists such as *Night Train to Munich* and *Gestapo*. But the story of a Polish flyer escaping to join the RAF and his love affair with a British girl, *Dangerous Moonlight*, was a box-office success only because of Richard Addinsell's Rachmaninov-like score, with its famous Warsaw Concerto. Three years later his 'Cornish Rhapsody' theme briefly saved *Love Story* from the oblivion to which it was destined by its sentimental plot centred on a concert pianist's romantic obsession with a blinded RAF pilot. The wartime British film industry paid patriotic homage to national heroines. *They Flew Alone* told the story of aviatrix Amy Johnson, and *Nurse Edith Cavell*, starring Anna Neagle, was an anti-German tribute to the World War I heroine for whom 'patriotism was not enough'. Alexander Korda returned to England in 1943 to direct a documentary on the RAF, *The Lion Had Wings*, and then made *The Perfect Stranger* with Robert Donat and Deborah Kerr playing a husband and wife struggling to rebuild their marriage after three years of wartime separation.

Noel Coward and David Lean produced the most memorable British war film, *In Which We Serve*, which won an Academy Award in 1943 and was praised by *Newsweek Magazine* as, 'The finest film to come out of the war.' It celebrated the courage of the men of a Royal Navy destroyer, HMS *Torrin*, and their families, with Coward playing the captain, who was modelled on Lord Louis Mountbatten. It drew a symbolic parallel between the fate of the warship's crew and the fate of the British people: sailors braved torpedoes at sea while their wives and sweethearts faced enemy bombs ashore. Coward's 1944 production, a sentimental celebration of a working-class family in two wars based on his play 'This Happy Breed', was a wild success when it was released at home, but it generated less enthusiasm in the United States.

Across the Channel in occupied Europe, the Minister of Propaganda and Public Enlightenment supervised the German film industry's efforts to boost wartime morale by cranking out romantic films. Dr Goebbels recognized that 'films constitute one of the most modern and scientific means of influencing the masses', but although he condemned Hollywood for 'Jewish subversion' he failed to match it with Aryan 'spiritual sustenance'. The German audience wanted escapist relaxation, but their film diet consisted mainly of historical romances or melodramatic war dramas that glorified the Wehrmacht. *Fighter Squadron Lutzow* only incidentally told the love-story of a pilot who sacrificed his girlfriend and life to save his fellow crewmen. *U-boats Westward* was a Battle of the Atlantic saga in which sailors were constantly reminded of their wives and girlfriends by the shortwave broadcasts.

After flying into a jealous rage at his private screening of *Gone With the Wind*, the Minister of Public Enlightenment assembled producers from the seventeen UFA film studios he controlled to demand they emulate its triumphant success. But Nazi dogma always interfered with romantic plots, resulting in love stories on such disparate themes as *Thrice Wed* which told the story of a Russian prince who tried three times to marry a peasant girl, *Under the Bridges*, about two bargees and a female suicide, and a love melodrama set aboard the *Titanic*.

However operatic their plots, Goebbels had decreed that German films must have an underlying patriotic theme. *Request Concert*, which was the nearest the Nazi cinema came to emulating the success of the American 'parade musicals', was no exception. The need to put duty before love was the message of the 1940 release based on an enormously popular Sunday afternoon Wehrmacht radio request programme. The average film-goer sat through *Request Concert* twice, lapping up the courtship of a handsome Luftwaffe officer and a young girl he met at the 1936 Olympiad. After service in Spain and on the Western Front they were finally reunited as Germany was celebrating her triumph with a special 'Request Concert' at which the Luftwaffe was represented by the hero playing the Olympic fanfare. The nobility of sacrifice was the theme of *Rite of Sacrifice*, in which Katrina Soderbaum portrayed a Nordic beauty at the centre of a tragic love triangle. More sinister was *I Accuse*, which made a persuasive case for euthanasia through the trial of a doctor who was moved by love to poison his paralysed wife. A blatant example of how the Nazi film industry exploited romantic melodrama to reinforce racial hatred was *Jew Suss*, in which a villainous Jew's rape of a virtuous German girl, played by Katrina Soderbaum, drove the distraught heroine to suicide.

Anti-semitism proved a more potent inspiration to Goebbels' producers than the quest for a great Aryan romantic musical. *The Heart of A Queen* was an ill-starred effort at making an anti-English musical out of the tragedy of Mary Queen of Scots. It was followed by another period musical, inauspiciously called *Women Make the*

Best Diplomats. Although it featured Germany's most popular vocal duo – Marika Rokka and Willy Frisch – Goebbels flew into a rage when shown the rough-cut, yelling, 'take this shitty mess out of my screening room and burn it'. He was later persuaded to release a re-edited version. But even Goebbels never had the nerve to let the public see *Symphony of Life*, a romantic epic about a struggling composer whose disastrous neo-Brucknerian score had been written by Norbert Schultz, the man who had given the world the haunting music for 'Lili Marlene'.

The closest that the Nazi film industry came to an American musical film was the 1942 release of *The Great Love* which featured the popular Swedish-born singer Zarah Leander. It told the story of a Luftwaffe officer's infatuation for a celebrated Scandinavian revue artiste. 'I know there'll be a miracle', and 'The world's not going to end because of this' became popular German wartime hits. The Wehrmacht was upset by the alleged immorality of the story-line, and Goebbels' diary recorded how Goering, tongue-in-cheek, relayed a formal protest:

> The Army High Command considers itself morally insulted by this and insists that an air force officer would not do such a thing. Goering rightly objects to this on the grounds that an air force lieutenant who didn't make use of an opportunity like this has no business being an air force lieutenant. Goering makes fun of the High Command for being so prudish, which is absolutely fine for me since the High Command gives me a lot of trouble in my film work.

The German High Command might have been more sympathetic to Goebbels' quest for a particular kind of 'spiritual sustenance' if they had known how successfully the Hollywood musicals were boosting the morale of American and British troops. The skilful blend of sex-appeal and patriotism reminded soldiers at the front of the good things they were fighting for, and the filmstar pin-ups provided inspirational female talismans that were found in every Allied soldier's battle kit – erotic 'ammunition for the heart'.

The pin-ups of World War II originated in the French *cartes postales suggestive*, which appropriately described the 'naughty postcards' featuring artful pictures of semi-nude girls in frilly negligees that had made Paris famous with the Allied troops in World War I. 'Cheesecake' photographs were christened in 1915 after a New York newspaper editor had approvingly exclaimed that such pictures were 'Better than cheeseccake!' By the 1930s, the Hollywood glamour cameramen had streamlined the pin-up. The World War II version showed shapely legs in seamed stockings and a slim figure defined by a skin-tight bathing suit which emphasized the curvaceousness of a full bosom. Only the teasing 'come-on' smile remained unchanged.

Betty Grable, with her 'Million Dollar Legs', was the undisputed leader of the wartime pin-up parade. Her pert blonde looks were the distillation of the sex-appeal of the 'all American girl-next-door'. A unique part of her attraction was that women liked her too, suggesting that her success was based less on eroticism than on a wholesome image of American womanhood, untouched by the war, work, or ambition, an image carefully exploited by Twentieth Century Fox, for whom she was the biggest wartime money-spinner.

The year after the enormously popular *A Yank in the RAF* had taken Elizabeth Ruth Grable to number eight in the box-office ratings, she made a trio of movies: *The Dolly Sisters*, *Sweet Rosie O'Grady*, and *Coney Island*. These were nostalgically sentimental roles which enhanced her girlish exuberance and apple-pie sex-appeal. Her studio lost no opportunity to endorse her image as the American serviceman's favourite. A shot in *Guadalcanal Diary* had William Bendix as the rugged marine hero shaving in front of her famous bathing suit pin-up, appropriately pinned to a palm trunk. Twenty thousand requests a week for the photo made her the serviceman's most popular pin-up.

Daryl Zanuck's fears that Grable's Number One Pin-up status might be harmed by her 1943 marriage to bandleader Harry James proved groundless. It only increased her appeal for many soldiers – and their wives. 'We ought to be mad at you for marrying the sweetheart of our camp, but it couldn't happen to a nicer guy,' was typical of the letters her husband received from GIs who wrote asking for her wedding photo.

Alongside Betty Grable was an array of Hollywood stars whose appeal was more erotic than inspirational. Rita Hayworth was the runner-up to Grable in the wartime pin-up stakes. She was a brunette who had originally been stereotyped as a 'Latin firebrand', an undeniable beauty who exuded the sultry sex-appeal of a mature woman, where Grable relied on her innate, teasing charm. Hayworth leapt into the wartime pin-up stakes in 1941 after *Life* magazine had displayed the star on a bed of satin sheets with a scanty lace bodice clinging to her shapely body: The picture was captioned, not without erotic justification, 'The Goddess of Love of The Twentieth Century'. She secured her position after she sang and danced with Gene Kelly in the 1944 musical *Cover Girl* which included the hit song 'Long Ago and Far Away'.

The prize for the sexiest pin-up photographs of the war went to Jane Russell, a relative unknown whose thirty-eight-inch bosom was shamelessly exploited by Howard Hughes to publicize his RKO production *The Outlaw*, in which she played Rio in an otherwise unmemorable remake of the legend of Billy the Kid. Grable's famous back-to-the-camera come-on was innocent cheekiness compared to Russell's passionate sprawl on the hay with her remarkably 'full figure' held high, wide, and handsome by a brassiere specially engineered by Hughes himself. Photographer Leslie Hurrel was hired to get what Hughes called 'promotion out of Jane's breasts'. Hughes advertised the forthcoming film in 1942 with publicity stills bearing the slogan, 'What are the two great reasons for Jane Russell's rise to stardom?', provoking a furious public discussion and beginning a four-year struggle with the Motion Picture Association to get approval for public release of *The Outlaw*. Hughes lavished $1.5 million on the publicity, most of it spent promoting the sensational physique of its star. The flamboyant sex-appeal of Russell made her pin-ups wildly popular with GIs overseas as they relished reports of the scandal that her full figure was stirring up back home. 'How would you like to tussle with Russell?' made her breasts so celebrated that when a skywriter made two circles with a central dot over San Francisco, everyone knew what was being advertised!

The Hollywood publicity stills that appeared in popular film magazines fell into several categories. There were the 'wholesome' pin-up stars like Joan Leslie and swimmer Esther Williams who imitated Grable's coyness by posing in silk dresses and one-piece bathing costumes. Their muted sex-appeal contrasted with the sultry eroticism typified by Paulette Goddard, Russell, Hayworth, and Ann Sheridan, whose chest profile left no doubt about why she was known by her fans as the 'Oomph Girl'. Other stars whose poses were in the mid-range of eroticism were Veronica Lake, 'the peek-a-boo girl', and Lana Turner, whose full figure did for sweaters what Dorothy Lamour did for sarongs.

While female 'cheesecake' became a wartime staple for most men in the armed forces during World War II – even the Wehrmacht's magazines included glamour shots of popular German actresses and singers – the military authorities in women's auxiliaries took exception to male pin-ups. The female libido was not aroused by the exposure of male muscle according to Hollywood, so most of the publicity photographs of its leading men showed them clothed. Even so, in many ATS barracks in Britain pictures of famous male stars like Tyrone Power, Errol Flynn, and Clark Gable were banned from the women's lockers by female commanding officers who considered them unhealthy and bad for military discipline.

Men in uniform were more fortunate. While some officers had at first adopted a prudish attitude to pin-ups in barrack-room lockers, by the end of the war these cheesecake pictures had become a universal accoutrement of the Allied armies. They were featured in magazines like *Life* and *Look* and encouraged a wartime boom in the publishing of so-called 'girlie' magazines featuring 'pin-up parades', such as *Tid Bits of Beauty* and *Glamorous Models* in the United States and *Tit-Bits*, *Blighty*, and *Reveille* in Britain. Other publications carried more blatantly erotic presentations, keeping the mail censors busy on both sides of the Atlantic because the law banned from the post what was later to be termed 'soft pornography'.

Since before the war, *Esquire Magazine*, like the British *Men Only*, had catered for a middle-class male audience with the artistic eroticism of the diaphanously-clad glamour-girls created by artists George Petty and Albertos Vargas. The Petty or Varga Girl was a fantasy whose airbrushed skin beneath a wispy negligee suggested the colour and texture of a ripe apricot. These luscious full-colour spreads were much sought after by servicemen, a market that *Esquire* was quick to cultivate with the addition of patriotic symbols such as the Stars and Stripes, or a medal dangling enticingly by the Varga or Petty Girl, who had nothing on which to pin them.

Such blatant commercialization of sex directed at GIs grated on the stern Catholic morality of the US Postmaster General, Frank C. Walker. In 1944, he finally cancelled *Esquire*'s mail privileges because of its alleged obscenity. The magazine commenced a lengthy legal battle, and hearings took place on Capitol Hill with clergymen, Harvard professors, and representatives of women's organizations lining up to testify. But until the magazine was acquitted of publishing 'lewd and lascivious' pictures, the American serviceman overseas was deprived of his favourite colour pin-ups. Angry protests flooded into the editorial offices and Capitol Hill. One letter from an army private minced no words about their outrage:

> You won't find one barracks overseas that hasn't got an *Esquire* Pin-Up Girl. I, for one, have close to fifteen of them, and none of them seems to demoralize me in the least. Those pictures are very much on the clean and healthy side and it gives us a good idea of what we're fighting for. What will these ignorant specimens think up next?

'Such pictures are objectionable to all persons of refinement and good taste,' was the official view of the US Army Chaplain General. Others supported the Postmaster General's view, condemning all pin-ups: 'Their suggestiveness does not add to moral practices nor to the production of virtuous thoughts.' That at least one GI agreed was evident from a letter received by a Catholic priest from a soldier who condemned the Army magazine *Yank* for pin-ups and cartoons 'that should make any decent man blush with embarrassment . . . why does the Army always try to play upon a man's sensual appetite . . . I was lonely many, many times. I needed a morale booster; however, these sensual appeals tended to lower my spirits, rather than boost them.'

The War Department found itself in a fine bureaucratic conundrum since the most popular features of the semi-official service publications *Yank* and *Stars and Stripes* were their full-spread pin-up parades. So did the officially approved British service magazine *Reveille* which had carried pictures of girls in bathing suits since the beginning of the war, in recognition of their beneficial effect on the morale of soldiers overseas.

'Bathing suit "art"' and 'pictures of the comparatively undraped female form' presented a moral dilemma to the chaplaincy. It was eventually addressed by the Acting Chief of US Army Chaplains in a 1945 memorandum which concluded:

> It is not one of the primary functions of Army information channels to provide beauty for the adornment of dugout walls . . . However, one cannot refrain from quoting from a lengthy editorial salute by an Army newspaper at an isolated post in Alaska to a New York striptease artist who has posed for special pictures for their small publication. 'You are the bear grease in our lupin-root cakes. You are the seal blubber in our bowl of salmon berries,' is a touching acknowledgement

of the fact that in the life of this isolated garrison, the likeness of the obliging young woman was more warming to the quonset hut than any mere coal fire!

Confirmation, if any was needed, that pin-ups did indeed warm the cockles of many a soldier's heart and therefore made an indispensable contribution to the Allied war effort came in the flood of mail that arrived at *Yank* magazine after it printed a Sergeant O'Hara's complaint about a luscious pin-up picture of starlet Irene Manning: 'I would much rather wake up in the morning and see a picture of a P-51 or 39 hanging above my bed or the picture of my wife.'

'Don't slam our pin-ups. If I had a wife I would make sure her picture was up, but Irene Manning will do until that big day,' was one sailor's reaction. 'Maybe if some of those "panty-waists" had to be stuck some place where there are no white women and few native women for a year and a half, as we were, they would appreciate even a picture of our gals back home,' was the retort from GIs in Alaska. Another letter demanded an apology to Miss Manning: 'I have her picture over my locker and I like it very much. I suggest Sgt O'Hara go out and learn the facts of life from someone who has been around . . . Keep the pictures coming. We like them.'

A sociologist, who served through the war in US Army, concluded from first-hand observation that the sexual significance of the pin-ups was that they 'probably served less for individual enjoyment than as occasions for the social affirmation of virility'. He noted the sexual ambiguity of the cheesecake pictures spawned by the famous Betty Grable pose:

> The pin-up girl, for example, is often distorted to maximize the proportions of the upper torso and lower extremities which are more distinctly feminine and expressive of the passive role. (If her breasts were removed, it would often be difficult to know whether she were a boy or a girl.)

Whether as aids for a soldier's private sexual fantasies, romantic reminders of home, or public statements of masculinity, the pin-up, in all its forms, certainly provided a great quantity of ammunition for the hearts of soldiers in every army. The British, French, German, and even Japanese had their stereotyped ideals who reflected national attitudes and ideals of feminine pulchritude.

But it was the Hollywood pin-up girl who was the most prolific and manufactured with the most artful degree of erotic titillation. It was one of the sexual ironies of World War II that servicemen transferred the most popular female forms to the machines of war. By 1945 there was hardly a tank or a plane in the US military that was not adorned with its own painted icon of femininity as a good-luck talisman. In one US Army bomber squadron based in England the custom grew of pasting the latest Varga girl and pin-up clipped from *Esquire* and *Men Only* on to the centre section of their Flying Fortresses:

> One navigator had most of the film stars, including Gypsy Rose Lee, accompanying him on day trips to Berlin, and in his enthusiasm had pasted pin-ups on both the inside and outside of the Fortress. On each flight down the 'Kraut Run', the navigator's skipper swore that their particular plane was singled out for special attention by the German fighter pilots who 'wondered what all the queer pictures were about'.

The military contribution that the pin-ups made in World War II can never properly be assessed, but there can be no doubt that they contributed to boosting individual servicemen's morale as comforting symbols of what many believed was worth fighting for.

In the Pacific theatre, the pin-up may have played a more direct role in the United States' victory over the Japanese, since included in some of intelligence summaries sent out to the ships were sexy pin-up sketches. The Pacific Fleet intelligence officer calculated that this would ensure that proper attention was paid to his reports. Unfortunately the practice had to be halted after a prudish kill-joy officer sent a message of complaint to headquarters. But no-one protested that under the glass-top desk of Captain Dyer, one of the navy's leading codebreakers at Pearl Harbor, resided one of the finest pin-up collections in the Fleet. What became known as 'Dyer's Desk' was one of the attractions of the subterranean chamber whose occupant contributed to the deciphering of Japanese messages which led to the American victory at the Battle of Midway.

There can, however, be no denying the tremendous success achieved by the *Daily Mirror* strip-cartoon heroine 'Jane'. Her adventures were to be chronicled in *The Stars and Stripes* as 'that girl who picks 'em up and lays 'em down, puts 'em on and takes 'em off!' Jane and her pet dachshund, Fritz, became the Army's girlfriend, the mascot of the Royal Navy and the pet of the RAF.

She began her modest career in a 1932 comic strip about a feckless 'Bright Young Thing'. When war came it seemed quite natural that she should begin shedding her clothes to boost national morale in the dark days of the Blitz. Jane became a special favourite in submarines on long patrols, which were assigned a special newssheet which reprinted her cartoon strips, with a new instalment being passed around to eager hands each day. Only once was this strict rule broken, and that was during a depth-charge attack which had sent one of His Majesty's submarines to the bottom with damaged engines. To relieve the tension a crewman asked, 'What's Jane doing tomorrow?' The coxswain peeled off three weeks' worth of issues and gave them to men who did not expect to live. When the engines were restarted the crew naturally attributed their lucky break to Jane.

It was popularly believed that the morale and effectiveness of RAF bomber crews on their night raids over Germany depended on how much clothing Jane had left off in the *Daily Mirror* that morning. 'I remember at the Admiralty during the war no admiral ever settled down to his day's work until he had looked to see whether the young lady's clothes were on or off,' recalled one member of Churchill's coalition government. 'During periods of bad news the Editor always kept up morale by keeping her clothes off.'

The legend quickly grew up that Jane always stripped for victory. So her dainty figure in skimpy panties and bra became the talisman for scores of Britain's planes and tanks. It was said that the first armoured vehicle ashore on D-Day carried a large representation of Jane naked. True to form, when she finally lost the last vestiges of her modesty by dropping her panties during the Normandy campaign, the word was passed round the front, 'JANE GIVES HER ALL' – and the Allied breakthrough followed a few days later!

10

A WOMAN'S WORK
WAS NEVER DONE

Earlier I buttered bread for him, now I paint
grenades and think this is for him.

> German woman munitions worker

It's no longer a question of what is the most
comfortable arrangement for each family. We
are fighting for our lives – for our freedom and
our future. We are *all* in it together, and what
is already being done by other women, you can
do!

> BBC broadcast, May 1941

The burden of total war falls upon the women of
the country with ruthless impact.

> British Official History

'THE BRITISH GIRL who has taken her place in the War Machine,' wrote a wartime journalist, 'has little in her life now except work and sleep.' This was the lot of the female workforce, which increased by a dramatic forty per cent to bring an additional two million pairs of hands in the United Kingdom and nine million in America to help turn the wheels of the Allied war effort.

After the British Government had taken the step of introducing compulsory female mobilization at the end of 1941, the Ministry of Labour estimated that over eighty per cent of all single women between fourteen and fifty-nine, forty-one per cent of wives and widows, and thirteen per cent of mothers with children under fourteen were at work or in the uniform of the auxiliary forces. Even without the conscription of women in the United States that same marked wartime increase in the employment of wives and mothers was to be reflected in the ten per cent increase in the numbers of married women at work. Making up almost a quarter of the total wartime labour force, married women outnumbered single women in the workplace for the first time.

The involvement of such a large percentage of wives and mothers in the World War II production battle was to accelerate the erosion of the sexual division of labour and the traditional reluctance of mothers to join the industrial workforce. It was as much the redistribution of the jobs they successfully undertook as the overall increase in the numbers of women employed that sowed the seeds of a far-reaching change in attitudes to what constituted 'women's work'. Custom had combined with high unemployment to ensure that more than a third of British women at work during the 1930s were in domestic service. The textile industry, historically the largest employer of female labour, was contracting, but jobs had increased in service, distributive trades, and the tobacco industry – and especially in the expanding electrical and vehicle assembly factories. The accelerating technical revolution of the so-called new industries increased the opportunity for repetitive, unskilled light industrial work which was considered by male-dominated craft unions and employers as particularly appropriate for females.

Yet the majority of working women who entered the pre-World
War II workforce were, in keeping with tradition, unmarried,
under thirty-five, and paid less than half the male rate. Notwithstanding the 1919 Sex Disqualification Removal Act, which in
theory had opened up all the professions except the top grades of
the civil service, women remained concentrated in the lowest
grades and most poorly paid sectors of teaching and the civil
service. In industry, although mining and working in the lead-
paint industry were the only jobs specifically forbidden to women
by law, in practice they were denied entry into much heavy
factory work by parliamentary legislation, which prohibited the
employment of women on night-shifts and on Sundays and prevented them from labouring for more than the statutory maximum
forty-eight-hour week. Many feminists suspected that such regulations, ostensibly passed to protect the female labour force from
an unhealthy and unsuitable working environment, were a subtle
means of depressing the average female industrial wage, since they
excluded women from high-paying 'men's work' in the steel,
engineering, and shipbuilding industries.

Nor did the opening year of the war bring any major shift in
the traditional sexual distribution of Britain's industrial labour
force. Although manpower mobilization began in earnest on 3
September 1939, with all males betwen the ages of eighteen and
forty-one eligible for call-up for military service, no attempts
to redistribute the female workforce were made until Churchill
became Prime Minister in May 1940. Less than a third of a million
additional women were recruited. Only a few opportunities
were opened up to them when the call-up began to remove men
from the retail, food and distributive trades, and the transport
industry.

In the vanguard of what would later become a major wartime
female invasion of the workplace were the bus conductresses who,
by the spring of 1940, had become a familiar part of the British
travel scene. 'To be a good bus condustress, you have to be a dab
hand at figures, juggling and backchat,' reported one journalist
after a week as a 'clippie' plying across Birmingham in a red
double-decker bus. Her first journey on an early-morning run
picking up factory workers coming off night-shift with loud demands to be introduced to the new girlfriend 'was a riot'. The
'top deck passengers got going with a cheerful, if insinuating

song,' and her advice to other women considering becoming a wartime 'clippie' was:

> Whether you'll like a conductress's life (in preference, say to munitions work, nursing or the services) depends on your temperament. This is no job for the cool, aloof, or misanthropic character. It's essentially a jolly job. A human, sociable job, involving perhaps six or seven hundred separate human contacts a day. The life is varied and indepen-dent, and you get plenty of breaks and fresh air. Against this you must set the fact that the hours are long; that you are always on your feet; that passengers can be exasperating and rush hours exhausting.

So many girls were recruited into the transport industry to take over jobs previously done by men that by April 1940 British women won a significant if limited objective on the long road to equal status when the Industrial Court ruled that women over twenty-one were to be paid the male rate after six months on the job. It was an advance towards equal rights that was not reflected in the manufacturing and engineering industries vital to the war effort, where powerful craft unions vigorously resisted what they saw as attempts by employers under government pressure to dilute the skilled and semi-skilled male workforce.

Even in the state-run munitions factories during the first year of the war there was neither equal pay nor much employment offered to the daughters of the women who had packed shells with the cordite powder that stained hands and faces yellow in World War I. Not until the national emergency became acute after Hitler's divisions had over-run Europe and the threat of an in-vasion loomed did the engineering industry, which had one of the lowest proportions of female workers, agree to allow the training of women in some of its skilled trades such as fitting and welding – but they would be permitted to work alongside men as what were termed 'dilutees' (because they diluted the skilled workforce) for the duration only.

After May 1940 there was a major shift in government policy. The 'Dunkirk Spirit' and the ringing rhetoric of Winston Churchill rallied the nation for the fight. The new Prime Minister made the concentration of labour and production into the war effort an integral part of his 'blood, toil, sweat and tears' policy by closing 'inessential' industries for the duration. Many of those factories that ceased to operate or were turned over to war production were the textile, clothing, hosiery, shoe, paper, and pottery works that employed high proportions of women.

In the dire national emergency many women joined the rapidly expanding production lines turning out fighter planes for the RAF and tanks and guns to re-arm Britain's miraculously rescued army, which had abandoned almost all its weapons on the beaches of Dunkirk. Ten, eleven, and even twelve-hour shifts were not uncommon in the factories whose workers laboured to turn out the Spitfire and Hurricane fighter planes for the embattled pilots of the RAF. While young able-bodied men were called up and those over age for military service drilled with pitchforks and improvised anti-tank bombs, the women of Britain turned their hands to unfamiliar and unfeminine work with lathes, heavy presses, and drills that forged the weapons which their menfolk needed if they were to carry out Churchill's call to fight the invaders on the beaches.

The national peril that confronted all British people in 1940 was immediate enough to begin to erode the industrial sex barriers, to forge an emergency alliance in the workplace that was far more extensive than during World War I, when women had been brought into aircraft factories to apply their traditional housework skills to sewing fabric and applying dope to wings and fuselages. Female labour played its part in every aspect of weapons production in World War II – from machining and assembling engines to riveting, wiring, and testing complete aircraft systems. Like the burgeoning wartime electronics industry, the aircraft production lines offered plenty of opportunity for the lighter industrial work for which the female hand and eye was considered well suited.

'At first you think you'll never do it,' a former Blackpool grocery store assistant told a fresh female trainee in the machine shop of a Ministry of Aircraft Production plant building fighter aircraft. 'You drop your tools and everything. But the men are very good. They teach you. To anybody with common sense, it's quite simple. And when you can do it – well it's a real man's job.'

Early in 1941, the government training centres were opened for the first time to females who sought skilled training in the engineering trades – and within two years, four out of ten workers in the British aircraft industry were women, who were performing half of all the production tasks needed for building fighters and bombers. But considerable hostility met this steadily increasing invasion. 'In they came, brunettes and blondes and gingers, quiet women and cheeky ones,' recorded a shop steward at a railway engineering factory in 1941. 'The men watched them with curious eyes, wondering whose jobs they were going to take.'

An opinion poll of steelworkers revealed that while most agreed emphatically, 'It's not women's work here,' their real concern was not the unfeminine environment, but to defend their own jobs against what they considered to be an invasion by a rival labour force. In some plants the men would tamper with the lathes during the night-shift to cause problems for the day-shift women. 'We don't like you to be working on this machine,' one male worker confided. 'Here's one woman doing it – they'll be getting other women in and then we'll be out of jobs and sent into the army.'

Such deep-rooted male hostility came as a shock to women like Rosemary Moonen, who left a hairdressing salon to learn to weld, solder, drill, and rivet at one of the training centres. She felt that her semi-skilled fitter's certificate 'seemed such a waste of effort' when she encountered hostility, reinforced by oaths of the male factory workers:

> I was sent with a group of die-hards (men) to report to a certain foreman. He surveyed us all grimly, gave each one a job to do, with the exception of yours truly. No doubt I looked nervous and scared. He ignored me, and as he turned to walk away, I said, 'What shall I do?' He turned towards me, sneered, 'Oh yes! We've forgotten sunshine here! What shall *you* do? – Here! Take this!' indicating a broom, 'And sod around!' – With that he threw the broom at me and walked off. I was stung to humiliation . . . As time went on I found my niche. They discovered I could work a certain machine and get good results. I was transferred to another department. Many of the men with whom I worked tried to 'date' me, but as most of them were married, their wives and children evacuated, I declined all invitations. Even the foul language began to flow over my head, and the coarse jokes which prevail in factory life, I ignored.

Honor Balfour, perhaps because she was a well-known writer and broadcaster, was more fortunate when she did her spell as a forty-three shillings a week war-worker turning out fighter planes. She found the main vexation was the boredom of repetitive work:

> On the final assembly line, there is interest and variety. The work is light, but you must be agile enough to nip up and down ladders, or haul yourself into unfinished cockpits, over half-made wings or through an

incomplete fuselage. Light is good and the place is airy. On some jobs, you may smoke. On all of them there is a chance to pass a word to your workmates, or rest if you feel tired. At 10.30 a.m. the tea trolley comes round – tea 1d a cup, piece of cake 1d – and at midday you knock off for dinner. Some bring their own food; they can get hot drinks in the canteen. For the rest, there is a variety of snacks or a full-course meal. Food is plentiful, freshly-cooked and quite cheap – soup 3d, meat (more on one plate than I've seen for months!) potatoes and two veg. 9d., jam tart 3d., coffee 2d. Back on the job at 1 o'clock. Tea-trolley at 2.30 p.m. Knock-off at 5.30 p.m. unless you are working overtime.

Food was an important attraction at a time when strict rationing was forcing a national belt-tightening, but the principal incentive for most women to leave their homes was the chance to earn relatively good pay. By the end of 1940 even this was clearly not enough. Veteran civil servant Sir William Beveridge, who had masterminded the mobilization of the labour force in World War I and headed the Manpower Requirements Committee in 1940, estimated that the country was less than halfway to the target of bringing two million additional women into the war industries. Accordingly the Minister of Labour and National Service, Ernest Bevin, told the House of Commons that, 'we shall have to call into service many women who in normal circumstances would not take employment'.

Apprehensive about the public reaction to a general call-up of the female population, the Government decided that this mobilization would have to be achieved without direct compulsion, by inviting women to register at employment exchanges under the wartime regulations which actually gave the Minister of Labour the power 'to direct any person in the United Kingdom to perform such services' as the Ministry might direct. The Women's Consultative Committee, consisting of the two leading female parliamentarians – Dr Edith Summerskill (representing the Labour Party) and Irene Ward (for the Conservatives) – together with representatives of national women's organizations and the unions, was set up in March 1941 under the chairmanship of the Minister of Labour's Parliamentary Secretary, who promised Ernest Bevin, 'presiding over the ladies on your behalf, I think I could resist their charms'.

The Committee met to advise on wartime recruiting 'from the

woman's point of view', and although only consultative, it took the lead in addressing such issues as, 'Should we pay any special regard to the marital status of women? Should a young married woman without any family responsibilities be treated differently from a single woman?' It was also instrumental in shaping the 'voluntary' policy asking all single women aged twenty to twenty-one who were without household responsibilities and full-time employment to register at government employment exchanges as 'mobile' labour – to be directed to filling vacancies in 'essential' war factories.

The concentration of British industrial plants in the Midlands and north-west of the country required the co-ordination of a huge administrative effort to recruit and relocate this 'mobile' female workforce from the outlying areas of England, Scotland, and Wales. Shunting a sizeable part of the female population from one part of the country to another necessitated a major welfare operation. As the population in the wartime towns jumped by between a quarter and a half, the expanding war industries and evacuees returning from the countryside had put a considerable strain on the shrinking housing supply. The demand for living quarters rose as the number of homes destroyed by enemy air attacks increased. With an estimated one in five houses damaged by air-raids, the Government was obliged to set up the National Service Hostels Corporation to provide digs for women working away from home who could not find lodgings in the blitzed industrial cities.

The voluntary scheme for directing the so-called 'mobile' women was not to prove the success that the Women's Consultative Committee had envisaged. A special survey commissioned from Mass Observation discovered that most of the jobs available to females were routine, undemanding, and distinctly unglamorous, as a typical interviewee explained:

> My machine is a drilling one, and I am given a heap of small brass plates to drill holes in . . . It is quite dark when we come out – which strikes one with a curious shock of surprise. For one feels not so much tired, rather as if one has missed the whole day.

The boredom of repetitive factory work was also to explain why the war plants failed to attract even half the female workforce made redundant by the closures of 'inessential' factories in the first twelve months of Churchill's national coalition Government. 'The release of a specified number of women did not add the same number to munitions manufacture,' according to a report made by an observer for the US Department of Labour: 'Some workers thrown out of employment were lost sight of altogether, some remained jobless or drifted into occupations other than munitions, and many eventually filtered back into their original employment.' In October 1941, Lord Beaverbrook, whose Ministry of Supply was struggling to keep the armed services equipped, protested in a memorandum to the Cabinet that it was necessary to 'recall these women for work in the war factories.' Because only half those released had taken jobs in munitions, he called for a drastic change in labour policy: 'There should be more expedition and ruthlessness in combing out women from non-essential occupations. Too many are still allowed to stay in kiosks and the distributive trades generally which still absorb over one million women.'

The stringent food rationing in force hardly made this a credible theory, and the Minister of Labour continued to argue for maintaining the voluntary measures already introduced. Two million had dutifully registered at employment exchanges by August, but of the half million of those interviewed, only eighty-seven thousand had been recruited into the Women's Auxiliary Services or the Government munitions factories. This meagre increase was in spite of a massive Ministry of Labour advertising campaign launched in 1941 to persuade British women to leave the clean comfort of their homes for the production battle. It appealed to patriotism in brightly coloured posters which stressed the heroic nature of factory work with proclamations such as 'WOMEN OF BRITAIN COME INTO THE FACTORIES'. The same theme was reinforced by broadcast appeals by the BBC:

> Today we are calling all women. Every woman in the country is needed to pull her weight to the utmost – to consider where her services would help most and then let nothing stand in the way of rendering such services. Like her, many women have made their sacrifice already and are doing their utmost to help win this war. But to those thousands who have not yet come forward I would say that here and now *every one of us* is needed.

Slogans were hammered home from hoardings, pamphlets, and newspaper advertisements urging Britain's female population to take up the challenge of war work in a variety of jobs that had been the exclusive pre-war preserves of men:

> Did you know that over 10,000 women are doing men's work on one British railway alone, acting as platelayers, and permanent way labourers, helping with maintenance work, clerks, ticket collectors, porters etc?
>
> GO TO IT!
> Want a job to stick to? Then try billposting!
> BRAVO THE WOMEN FLIGHT MECHANICS!
> Ever thought of yourself as an electrician?
> BE A WELDER!
> COME INTO THE FACTORIES!

A series of 'War Work Week' parades staged in November 1941 brought a temporary carnival-like atmosphere to bombed cities like Coventry, with women dressed in overalls and gowns adorned with V-signs riding on tanks followed by lorryloads of girls busily demonstrating filing, riveting, and drilling airplane components. The banners enjoined, 'DON'T QUEUE LIKE SHIRKERS, JOIN THE WOMEN WORKERS,' but the women to whom the slogans were addressed were reluctant to take full-time work. 'We would get war in our homes if we took it,' one potential recruit told the officer who interviewed her at the employment exchange. Surveys soon revealed that for most married women, her primary duty was to her husband and her home.

One woman who gave up her war work explained: 'My husband's on night-shift and I used to get home about six – it wasn't time to cook him his dinner and he was losing sleep doing it himself. Then they wanted us to stay and do overtime till 6.30 or more – I couldn't do that.' Another housewife had considered volunteering, but rejected the idea: 'I feel very guilty sometimes, but there's my husband to think of. I know our homes are not supposed to count any more now, and it's only my husband and myself, but you have to do *something* in a house, or you'd get overrun by rats and mice.'

Many of the menfolk also felt that their contribution to the war effort was at home. As an air-raid warden put it:

> If married women are called up home life will vanish, and it will be very hard to revive it after the war. Men coming home on leave will find that they can only see their wives for an hour or two a day. Men in reserved occupations will come back to cold, untidy houses with

no meal ready. Friction in the home will be greatly increased, and with children evacuated there will be nothing to hold it together.

It was not surprising, therefore, to find that employment exchanges reported by the end of 1941 that women were growing increasingly choosy about leaving their homes to take full-time war jobs which did not bring the glamour, high pay, and excitement they had been led to expect by the posters and broadcasts. Long hours on a factory shift left women little opportunity for shopping and still less time for the domestic chores necessary for looking after a family. One survey-taker arrived to interview a housewife who was struggling to catch up with a pile of dishes at the sink, a bundle of washed but un-ironed clothes, and a table which was a mass of crumbs and dirty crockery. Mrs B. distractedly explained that it was impossible for her to take care of her housework before rushing back to the factory: 'It's no good, I can't keep up with it. I thought I'd like to do a bit and bring in some money, but I can't keep up with it. If I could just have a couple of days to get straight, then it would be all right, you could keep it under, but I just can't manage like this.'

Nearly two years of contributing to the war effort had boosted female membership of British trade unions by a million and a half, but women shop stewards were all too often ignored when they complained that their special problems were being neglected by the male leadership who negotiated working conditions with the employers and the Government.

> We have no objection to working in the factories but we do object to the conditions we have to work under. Women in industry are called upon to bear burdens that are beyond imagination. Many are soldiers' wives who are obliged to go to work to keep their homes together as their allowances are so inadequate . . . Our hours are ordinarily an eight-and-a-half-hour day, but with overtime this is brought up to ten hours. In the morning we feel fresh and do a good amount of work but the ventilation is so bad that by the afternoon we are weary. Then down goes the output.

The burden that war-work and housework put on the shoulders of Britain's women was felt especially by young mothers like twenty-three-year-old Mary, who was discharged from an ATS battery because she 'got herself in the family way'. She described the special strain she endured while she laboured in a Manchester plant making Lancaster bombers with no factory day-care facilities:

> As soon as my son was a year old I found someone to look after him so that I could do my bit for the war effort again. I became a riveter, using a hydraulic gun to seal the rivets holding the metal skin to the frame of the bomb doors. These were made in sections and joined together when they were put in the planes. There were about ten of us girls and we made the doors for a couple of planes each day. We worked from seven thirty in the morning to five in the afternoon, with only a half hour off for lunch. I was up every day at six to get the tram to take my baby boy, half asleep, to his day-time mother. I was too busy and tired to miss my husband much.

The old adage that 'a woman's work is never done' was never truer than in wartime, when they were expected to work the fifty-seven to sixty-hour week reported by the Factory Inspectorate's survey of 5493 war plants. Such long hours made the mundane problems of housekeeping almost insurmountable, the *New Statesman* reported in December 1941:

> In an industrial centre such as Birmingham, a number of shops close at five o'clock or even earlier, which makes it impossible for those employed on a normal working day to do any shopping. In the London area it was found that over half the women shopped on Friday nights, and two thirds of them on Saturday afternoons. Half the women had difficulty in obtaining their meat supplies, whilst it was practically impossible for them to get cooked meats or any of the non-rationed foods because they could not go to the shops in the mornings. The great majority of the women questioned had to do their own shopping, and normally had to queue. As a solution to the shopping problem it is suggested that the shops remain open until late on certain evenings of the week and remain open during the lunch hour. Some firms give weekly morning leave of up to three hours, or a shopping break before the lunch hour, but such schemes inevitably reduce production. And an even greater difficulty than the shopping problem arises if the women have any children. Creches and nursery schools are seldom available, and meals are not obtainable at a considerable proportion of the schools.

Absenteeism was to become a chronic wartime problem for those factories employing large numbers of married women, many of whom could only attend to essential household duties like shopping by taking time off. A 1942 Ministry of Labour study was sympathetic to their plight:

> A married woman with a house, a husband, and children, already has a full-time job which is difficult to carry out these days. Yet thousands of them are working long hours in factories. They are trying to do two full-time jobs. If they can carry on with a mere half-day per week off in ordinary factory hours they are achieving something marvellous.

'While winning the war is the only big consideration,' warned a 1942 Mass Observation report on women at work, 'if the bonds of family and continuity are weakened beyond a certain point, the morale, unity and work effort of the country is weakened.' Yet the provision of adequate time off for shopping or day-care facilities for the children of married workers had not even rated a mention in the 1941 Ministry circular. It was left to a journalist to point out that housekeeping was unpaid, had never been economically rated, and that 'a whole family of five to eight people is looked after entirely by one woman, and if she is sent into full-time work, her jobs have to be taken on by no fewer than six different groups of workers, i.e. for day nursery, shopping, washing, meals for school children, evening meal for husband, care of children after school.'

The Minister of Labour himself admitted he was not 'anxious to increase the employment of women with young children if it were possible to obtain the labour otherwise' – but by the end of 1941 Bevin was obliged to concede that the voracious manpower requirements of total war would oblige the Government to tap every available resource, including young mothers with pre-school children. More day-nurseries and factory-operated creches were needed if mothers of the very young were going to be recruited into the work force, but such facilities, as the Minister himself had admitted the previous year, were 'very much neglected'. At the beginning of 1941 only fourteen Government-sponsored nurseries had been set up, and a survey of a typical industrial town in Lancashire revealed that of 241 mothers of pre-school children interviewed, only 36 were at work, because of the lack of cheap child-care facilities for their infants.

The provision of school meals and nursery education had to be dealt with at a national level. A bureaucratic dispute then ensued between the Ministry of Labour and the Ministry of Health's local officials, who irrationally campaigned against expanding factory-run nurseries because of exaggerated fears of epidemics of infantile disease. The Minister of Labour became the target of a public campaign that he was not making good his promise that 'Every Woman will have work who wants to.' Women took to the streets and staged what the press dubbed 'Baby Riots' – traffic-stopping demonstrations of women wheeling prams daubed with protests such as 'We Want War Work – We Want Nurseries.'

While Britain's wartime government, probably out of fear of the political repercussions of tampering too much with the traditional role of married women in the home, never made adequate provision for a national child-care system to serve the needs of working mothers, it did attempt to improve their working conditions in the factories. Managers were sent a circular offering suggestions on how firms might clean up their shop floors and toilet facilities so as to make industrial work more attractive to women, and employers were advised to give 'reasonable leave of absence' to wives when their husbands got leave from the services. Female welfare officers who the press dubbed 'Bevin's Belles' were sent around to inspect the improvements and advise on the special needs of female workers. One of the more important tasks, according to one of these welfare officers, was 'weeding' – fitting women into the right jobs:

> On the whole we find that the women over thirty-five are more useful on general unskilled work, replacing youths, and our problem is to arrange the work so that it is not too heavy for them. A factory like ours always has a lot of more or less 'childish' jobs that would irk a lively youngster in five minutes, but which we find ideal for the grannies. We have four deaf and dumb women extremely happy on particularly noisy jobs, and we make a point of employing our share of the physically handicapped.

Blacked-out windows increased the gloom and noise level of the older factories. The din and grime of steel and heavy engineering plants made them veritable 'caves of vulcan' where women were often deafened by the din and depressed by the dirt.

> Working in factories is not fun. To be shut in for hours on end without even a window to see daylight was grim. The noise was terrific, and at night when you shut your eyes to sleep all the noise would start again in your head. Night shifts were the worst . . . The work was very often monotonous. I think boredom was the worst enemy.

To lighten the monotony and long hours of wartime labour the BBC had in 1940 introduced the twice-daily programme of lively tunes, 'Music While You Work', which proved so popular that it endured as a national broadcasting fixture for a quarter of a century. When they were not singing along to the music blaring out over loudspeakers, women crowding the long workbenches or hunched over drilling machines struck up their own patriotic war songs. One that achieved wide popularity in the Midlands aircraft factories ran:

> I'm only a wartime working girl.
> The machine shop makes me deaf,
> I have no prospects after the war
> And my young man is in the RAF
> K is for Kitty calling P for Prue
> Bomb Doors Open.
> Over to you!

'Music While You Work' and government 'War Work Weeks' proved insufficient incentives to attract enough women into the factories. After the Minister of Labour had reported to the War Cabinet in November 1941 that the number of women in 'essential' war production was a third lower than planned, Churchill's Cabinet reluctantly decided, in December, to take the momentous step of introducing compulsory female mobilization. The National Service Act No. 2, which was passed by Parliament just ten days after the Japanese attacks on Pearl Harbor had brought the United States into the war, made Britain the first nation in history formally to conscript women. But the Government, still sensitive to possible public hostility, was careful to announce it as a measure of 'direction' rather than compulsion, which gave women the choice of going into the auxiliary services, civil defence, farm work, or the munitions factories.

Churchill and the chiefs of the armed forces had argued that there was a national sentiment 'against *any* compulsion of women', and the Cabinet eventually compromised on the call-up of all single women between the ages of twenty and twenty-one to begin in January 1942. Although married women were specifically exempted, 'they should be allowed to volunteer'. The mobilization was extended in February 1942 with the Employment of Women (Control of Engagement) Order, which directed that women between the ages of twenty and thirty could be hired only through employment exchanges, and this too was extended at the beginning of 1943 to women up to forty. At that point it was announced that the Ministry of Labour had the power to direct them into part-time as well as full-time work. In deference to service opinion, both single and married women with responsibilities for running a home could apply for 'H(ousehold) R(eserve)' status, thereby gaining exemption.

So from January 1942 the British Government effectively instituted a limited but nationwide female mobilization order that affected childless widows as well as single women in the respective age groups, who were by law required to make themselves available for service in 'vital war work' or as auxiliaries to make up the recruiting shortfalls, which had been falling up to thirty thousand behind the monthly targets. The list of occupations defined as 'vital war work' included jobs in munitions factories, Civil Defence, nursing, the Women's Land Army, aircraft manufacture, the NAAFI (Navy Army and Air Force Institute – the civilian outfit which provided catering and recreation facilities to the armed forces), the Royal Observer Corps, the radio industry, tank manufacture, and the transport industry.

Women who refused to register and take Government-approved employment, or who left vital war work, found that 'direction' and compulsion amounted to one and the same thing. They could be fined up to five pounds a day and even imprisoned. The first of several hundred female pacifists to be brought before the courts under Section 5a of the Defence of the Realm Regulations was Constance Bolan, a former housemaid who was sentenced to a month's imprisonment in January 1942 for declining hospital work which she held would indirectly assist the war effort. While in jail she insisted on hewing to her strict pacifist principle by refusing to knit socks for the army.

The vast majority of British women wanted no truck with pacifism, however, and many rallied to the call from the prominent member of Parliament Dr Edith Summerskill, who, angry that women were denied the chance to join the Home Guard militia, formed the Women's Home Defence. This voluntary organization 'gathered size and speed like a snowball'. Its newly-formed units met once a week to learn how to fire rifles, throw hand grenades and deal with German parachutists. The Government encouraged this patriotic display of female militancy, and approved regular army officers and the Home Guard acted as instructors.

By mid-1943 the labour crisis in Britain's factories had become so severe that the Government suspended recruiting for the women's forces for twelve months. Womanpower was directed to the factories rather than the ack-ack batteries as the battle for production reached its peak. The only alternative to factory work for those girls who were called up was to take a job on a farm.

The Women's Land Army had a marching song, 'Back to the land, we must all lend a hand, To the farms and the fields we must go.' Few of the eighty thousand who eventually joined up 'to do their bit with a hoe' regarded it as a soft option. 'The recruiting officer of the Women's Land Army won't quarrel with me if I say quite plainly that it's no rest cure,' wrote Jane Morgan, who was one of those who donned the bottle-green sweater and khaki dungarees which the Government supplied to the girls who chose to work on the land. A forty-eight-hour week brought them just thirty-two shillings in pay and, like most city girls, Jane found wartime work away from the grime and din of the factory healthy, but no country picnic:

> My first job was to help pulling the beetroot. That looked easy. Our gang started on a large field which had been marked out into sections. Row by row, the tractor drove down and lifted the beetroot ready for us to pull out, clean with our hands, twist off the tops, and throw tidily into the line of boxes alongside; row by row we kept pace with the tractor. After two hours I loathed that tractor and its unfailing, inhuman progress up and down the field. The other Land Girls were sympathetic enough to call out inquiries about what they knew would be my breaking back. It was consoling to be told that they all went through it, and that the third day would be the worst. It was. After that the muscles began to do the work intended for them.

'If you think you are going to make ornamental garden gates you can think again,' an employment official informed one British girl who wanted to take her call-up in 'Rural Industry' after her Polish boyfriend was killed in the RAF. She found herself 'pitchforked' into the Land Army and eventually came to enjoy the work and the nickname of 'Buttercup' the farmworkers gave her:

> The life was quite strange at first. Each time I cleaned out the pigs, I

brought up my breakfast! But I soon got over that. I made up my
mind right from the start that I was going to 'make a go' of this Land
Army business, for who was I to grouse? I was lucky to be alive, not
too far from home and with kindly country people. That boy just
killed had been through hell to get here and he had always been
cheerful and never groused. I was not going to let him down. I could
take it – and take it I did.

During my service in the WLA I changed jobs several times between
milking and general farm work on small and large farms. Then I
worked with a gang of four girls going round Wiltshire farms with a
steam engine and threshing tackle. It was hard and dirty work. In the
spring and summer we did field work, hoeing and 'singling' root
croops and spud picking. We were not always treated with respect by
farmers, but we learned how to put up with that and how to throw
back the appropriate remarks along with the piles of dung we had to
spread over the land.

I worked with all kinds of folks, countrymen and women. Some of
the womenfolk thought of the WLA as 'tarts' after their farmer
husbands, but they got used to us in the end. I worked with gypsies
and prisoners of war as well as quite a few younger women who had
got out of Hitler's Europe. One cannot forget any of these men and
women. But for me it started with that young Polish man who taught
me how to stand on my own two feet. Unfortunately he never knew
it, but I have never forgotten him.

The wartime British press ran flattering accounts of the impress-
ive agricultural achievements of Land Girls which reassured the
public that the bucolic tradition of the country was still intact. At
harvest time pictures similar to one showing a line of women
perched on tractors in a mass reaping assault on a four hundred-
acre wheatfield appeared in the papers. 'Land girls are hard at
work in Hertfordshire operating excavators on the heavy wasteland
of the district,' another newspaper reported: 'They can cut ditches
at the rate of twenty yards an hour.'

Although most Land Girls enjoyed better food and conditions
than their sisters in the factories, like the majority of World War
II conscripts they resented their long hours and the hard work.
Their discontent often surfaced in humorous protest songs, like
their version of the famous soldier's complaint from World War I.

> When this silly war is over
> Oh how happy I shall be
> When I get my civvy clothes on

No more Land Army for me
No more digging up potatoes
No more threshing out the corn
We will make that bossy foreman
Regret the day that he was born.

The Government, to its surprise, found that extending the National Service Act to women proved neither as unpopular nor unworkable as Bevin had feared. So in August 1942, registration and 'direction' were extended to women aged up to forty-five, and fire-watching duty was made compulsory unless they were employed for a minimum of fifty-five hours a week. Only women with children under the age of fourteen were exempted – whether married or not.

'Nothing that a woman can do, or can learn to do, should be allowed to absorb a man of military age,' proclaimed Labour Minister Bevin after a 1943 report recommended the extension of the female labour force in the shipyards and heavy industry. The fourth year of the war saw the addition of a million women, many of them married, to the full-time labour-force waging the production battle. Mobile recruiting vans toured towns and cities to draw in another quarter million mothers for part-time work. Women played a direct role in the shipbuilding effort that contributed to the defeat of the U-boats in the hard-fought Battle of the Atlantic, which marked one of World War II's climactic turning points. The wartime peak of seven and a quarter million women in full-time work was reached by the middle of 1943, a figure which, together with those in part-time occupations, represented over half the total female population.

At the National Conference of Women sponsored in 1943 by the Government, Prime Minister Winston Churchill paid tribute to the part that British women were playing towards the achievement of final victory:

This war effort could not have been achieved if the women had not marched forward in millions and undertaken all kinds of tasks and work for which any other generation but our own – unless you go back to the Stone Age – would have considered them unfitted: work in the fields, heavy work in the foundries and in the shops, very refined work on radio and precision instruments, work in the hospitals, responsible clerical work of all kinds, work throughout the munitions factories, work in the mixed batteries.

'When there is, practically speaking, no reserve whatever of labour, you are forced to do things you wouldn't have done without the irresistible urge of absolute necessity,' a member of Britain's Womanpower Committee told a meeting of the War Manpower Commission in the United States in 1944. Fortunately for the Allies, Adolf Hitler did not recognize the 'irresistible urge of absolute necessity', which might have harnessed Germany's female population into the war effort, until it was too late. For too long the Nazis persisted in sticking to the Fuehrer's belief that it was a man's role to fight while, 'There is nothing nobler for a woman than to be a mother of the sons and daughters of the people.' The policy was articulated by Gertrud Scholtz-Klink, who wore her hair braided in the approved Volkish style while she fiercely articulated Hitler's model of the housewife-creator made famous by her 1937 proclamation, 'Though our weapon in this area is only the wooden spoon, its impact will be no less than that of other weapons.'

Yet despite the Fuehrer's dogmatic assertions that a woman's work was in the home, a third of all German women – fourteen and a half million – laboured out of economic necessity, almost half on family farms. These women were urged by the Women's Office of the German Labour Front to 'utilize the feminine and maternal forces within them in the interest of the whole nation' in what was officially designated 'womanly work'. In 1939, single women were supposed to register for a 'duty year' of such activity or, as an alternative, do twelve months in the uniformed Labour Service which drilled them in ideology and agricultural activities. Most girls from well-to-do and middle-class families feigned compliance by nominally working as domestics with family friends.

In 1942, the newly-appointed Armaments Minister, Albert Speer, urged Hitler to consider expanding female factory employment now that Germany was fighting a production and military battle against both the United States and the Soviet Union. But the Fuehrer refused to consider any female mobilization plans for fear that it would damage the health of the 'present and future mothers of our nation'. Instead over six million foreign labourers were shipped in from the conquered European nations. Hitler's failure to appreciate the productive and military potential of the Third Reich's female population was to prove a significant factor in Germany's ultimate collapse.

Not until 1943, when the Wehrmacht's invincibility had been shattered by the defeats in Russia and North Africa and the Reich was being hammered nightly by British and American bombers, did the Fuehrer consider it necessary to begin mobilizing the entire nation for 'total war'. The German economy and labour force at the beginning of 1943 were not geared for an all-out production war, since six million workers were still turning out consumer goods from refrigerators to lipstick cases, in industries which in the United States and Britain had long been turned over to more essential manufacturing.

New laws called for the compulsory registration of all women between the ages of seventeen and forty-five. Only those who already worked a forty-eight-hour week or were pregnant and mothers with one child under six or two under fourteen were exempt from the order. Two and a half million women had registered by the end of March 1943, but very few actually joined the labour force. Nor was any concerted effort made to force them into war work, because this would have shattered the image of the Nazi woman doing her duty at home.

'Womanly work' was redefined in the Nazi ideology to include factory work in heavy industry which was designated *kriegsentscheidend*, or decisive for the war effort. Women now had to consider the whole of the Reich the home: 'Our men at the front do their duty in the face of death – we women at home, with the same unflinching courage, go in whatever direction the Fuehrer indicates,' declared the Reich 'Mother-in-Chief'. 'For every shell and gun that women at home help to produce increases the security of our soldiers and spares our people unnecessary loss,' proclaimed the propaganda posters.

Yet despite the quickening pace of the Allied bombing offensive against Germany's cities and industrial centres, most of the better-off women resisted all efforts to get them into the final scramble of war production, preferring to stick to their traditional role – spreading butter rather than making guns. Nor was there the same economic incentive for the wives of German soldiers to take on war jobs, because the marriage allowances and pensions paid by the Wehrmacht were far better than the allowances made to wives and widows by the British and American services.

In the final year of the war the number of women who responded to a barrage of Dr Goebbels' patriotic propaganda urging them to take a factory job added less than a fraction of one per cent to the Reich's labour force. 'The Russians are fighting a total war, we are fighting an elegant war,' complained a German officer on leave from the Eastern Front in 1944. Hitler's miscalculation of the national effort required to win the war and consequent failure to mobilize the productive potential of Germany's female population was disastrous. There simply weren't enough German women working to meet the requirements of a total war, and the ill-fed and poorly motivated foreign workforce lacked energy and commitment. Hitler's error was to prove critical to the final outcome of World War II.

II

THE GIRLS BEHIND
THE GUYS
BEHIND THE GUNS

Whatever the degree of adjustment, whatever the
outward appearance of harmony, the ancient
doctrine was never wholly abandoned – that the
real and only power of women was the power of
sex, and that their sole possible contribution to
the field of masculine endeavour was one of
negative distraction and disturbance rather than
positive aid.

A 'Rosie the Riveter'

It is our inescapable conclusion that most of these
men have never in all their lives thought of a
woman as anything but something that you go to
bed with.

Josephine von Miklos, precision grinder

AFTER HER 1942 FACT-FINDING TOUR of British wartime factories, Eleanor Roosevelt returned to America mightily impressed by 'the completeness with which the British have disregarded their prejudice against women workers'. Everywhere she found 'women at work, many on highly skilled industrial production jobs that are ordinarily held only by men'. Total war had apparently submerged traditional male resentment towards women who did 'men's work' because of what Mrs Roosevelt termed the 'obligation to produce'. But it did not escape the notice of America's First Lady, who was an ardent campaigner for women's rights, that the 'age-old fight for equal pay is still going on'. She noted, however, that 'the principle is being recognized more and more', which she believed foreshadowed 'a considerable movement toward its fulfilment before the war is over'. She was also struck by the fact that every second person she met in the Ministry of Labour was a woman, which led her to suggest that the 'responsibility of women in these things has made a difference to the position of women'.

A representative of the American War Manpower Administration's 'Women's Advisory Committee' who had accompanied Mrs Roosevelt confirmed that there was 'very little complaint' among the British about the female workforce. 'Women are working at all kinds of jobs – in the navy yards, in the factories, on the land, and even on demolition squads in the bomb-devastated cities.' Mrs Gould advised the American committee, 'One hears much discussion of what will happen after the war and much speculation as to whether women will be willing to go back to their old place when the need for them is over,' and she quoted the British Home Secretary, Herbert Morrison, who although 'very pro women' had remarked, 'You can't help wondering if they are going to be a little bit hoity-toity after the war.'

> The thing that interested us, me particularly, was the fact that there are so many who are older women and women who have family responsibilities which they can't shake off and are still doing these jobs and doing them often ten and eleven hours a day . . . I think the men still can't escape a little surprise, and I think one finds that a

little annoying. You cannot discount the fact that these people went through that terrible experience of Dunkirk and the evacuation; followed by that terrible winter of bombing – it has given them the feeling that people have – if some member of the family has been desperately sick and just pulled through, or the people in the family sort of walk on eggs and are very kind and good to each other; very careful; very thoughtful, and very thankful that they are there at all. They are much more ready to accept certain things than would be comparable in this country.

Britain's female mobilization had been closely studied by the American administration's labour agency as the 'arsenal of democracy' geared up for its own war effort during 1941. The accelerating draft had mopped up much of the male unemployment hanging over from the Depression years, but employers were still very reluctant to hire women outside the traditional areas of retailing and light factory work. For every woman taken on in industry during the latter half of 1941, twenty men were hired by firms which kept eighty-one per cent of their production work closed to females. They protested that women did not have the necessary skills, yet at the same time females occupied fewer than five per cent of the places available in the government-sponsored training schemes – and almost a third of those were in sewing and typing courses.

Yet the mounting enthusiasm of American women to play a part in the National Emergency that President Roosevelt had declared in 1941 was evident in the numbers who volunteered for national defence. 'Give the women something to keep their hands busy as we did in the last war – then maybe they won't bother us,' was the attitude expressed by one government official responsible for channelling this fervour into voluntary civil defence efforts. It was an attitude that was remarkably slow to change even after the United States was actually at war with Germany and Japan.

Many women came forward after the President had put Mrs Roosevelt and New York's feisty mayor, Fiorello H. La Guardia, in charge of co-ordinating the nation's air-raid and blackout precautions in the national hysteria following Pearl Harbor. When the enemy bombers failed to appear, many women, like Josephine von Miklos, grew disenchanted with pointless duty as volunteer wardens. 'Poking with a flashlight into your neighbour's closet in the course of your duties as an air-raid warden didn't seem to me a contribution to the war effort,' she concluded. She decided to trade in her fashion designer's drawing board for an oily lathe in a New England factory turning out shell fuses:

> Working in munitions, as it is turning out, isn't very exciting, if you want the truth. Most of it is filthy and grimy, much of it is a very boring job. I can't say that I love it. I wasn't sure that this kind of life was going to work for me – me, the irrational, the spoiled and the individualistic, the so-called artistic, intellectual kind of person that I am. And I *hated* the grime and filth and getting up at five-fifteen in the morning and using an open latrine for a ladies room. But neither did the men of Bataan like their grime and filth. The Chinese and Russian and Australian soldiers haven't any fun fighting, nor do the men at sea.

Even the disastrous American defeats in the Philippines that marked the lowest ebb of Allied fortunes in the gloomy spring months of 1942 did not generate the sense of national peril that would have allowed the President and his newly-appointed War Manpower Commission to persuade Congress to agree to a conscription of the female population. It was estimated that only twenty-nine per cent of the fifty-two million adult women in the United States were already employed in full-time work so it was decided that the drive to mobilize a large part of the thirty-seven million still tied to their homes was to be effected through advertising and public relations campaigns.

It was left to local state and city authorities to begin 'enrolment drives' with mail and house-to-house canvassing. The first state to launch an enrolment drive was Oregon, and the February 1942 canvas revealed that three hundred and two thousand women were ready and willing to seek war work. Michigan and Connecticut followed suit and so did important manufacturing centres like Akron and Detroit. The factories in America's automobile manufacturing plants were then being rapidly transformed into tank and aircraft production plants. Ford was pouring millions of federal war dollars into the vast Willow Run complex, which would eventually become the largest employer of female labour in the area. Detroit reported that a hundred and eighty thousand women had registered for war work, and female employment was to rocket from forty-four thousand to a hundred and seven thousand by August 1942.

That same month the Women's Bureau of the Department of Labour reported that its latest survey showed that 'the war industries expansion has permitted women to work side by side with men on the same jobs without taking over the jobs held by men.' But Government training centres were providing more women with technical courses, and it was envisaged that the increasing skills of female factory workers would allow them to take over jobs as lathe operators and precision grinders in engineering, for example, when the men were drafted. The biggest expansion had so far been in assembly work on aircraft production lines, where thirty-four thousand females were now employed – a seventeen-fold increase in less than nine months.

Women were also helping to expand technical services as flying instructors and ground mechanics, but the biggest influx of female labour during the first months had been in services related to civilian rather than war needs:

> In large and small places, Women's Bureau agents find women at work as elevator operators in hotels, stores, and office buildings; as telegraph messengers and in other messenger services; as clerks, cashiers, soda-fountain girls, and pharmacists in drug stores. Women are serving as taxi-drivers and filling-station attendants. They are being hired as men are drafted from shoe, electrical-supply, and food plants. They are replacing men as finger-print technicians in laboratories . . . Women are serving at airports as registration supervisors, dieticians, passenger-service superintendents, and dispatch clerks. Women are reported as machine-shop instructors, as mechanics, and mechanics' helpers. They service typewriters, act as bank-tellers and assistants, and are reported at work in brokerage offices, and as stock-exchange floor employees. They are serving as guards in industrial plants, with police power.

Just as in Britain, after an initial rush to do their patriotic duty, American women who put their names on enrolment registers then failed to volunteer. Few women had been employed in the four hundred and sixty jobs in heavy industry that the Labour Department had decreed could be performed by females, because half required 'some re-arrangement' of processes to take account of the limitations of physical strength. There was also the traditional resistance to women performing heavy work, especially if they were married. The general male reaction to their spouses doing any kind of factory work was revealed by a *Ladies Home Journal* poll of wives, which indicated that one in five did *not* have her husband's approval. Fewer than thirty per cent of men answered 'yes' to a 1943 Gallup survey question, 'Would you be willing for your wife to take a full-time job running a machine in a war plant?' Notwithstanding, over half the women questioned in the same poll said they would be willing to take such a job.

That the average American male still rejected the idea of married women working was evident from a typical protest letter published by a Seattle newspaper in the autumn of 1942: 'I never let my wife work, and I know she is a far sweeter woman than many women who have been coarsened by having to get out in the business world. I say, let's keep women out of industry and out of the war.'

The Administration took a different view. The War Manpower Commission estimated that at least two million more women had to be recruited into the workforce in 1943. The shortage of male labour was quickly forcing employers to abandon their traditional attitudes, and the President had set seemingly astronomic targets of thousands of aircraft, hundreds of tanks, and millions of tons of shipping to be produced by the 'arsenal of democracy' during that critical year, when the Allies hoped to turn the tide of battle.

'The Fortresses and the men who fly them – are fighting for you – your home – all the things you hold dear,' was how the Boeing aircraft company launched its recruiting drive in the Seattle area, where women were bluntly asked, 'Are You Doing Your Part?' The press co-operated with stories celebrating the heroic production efforts of individual women war workers who were portrayed as the 'girls behind the guys behind the guns'.

'We do feel that we are doing something for the war effort,' commented a female bus driver. 'Besides that, it's thrilling work, and exciting, and something women have never been allowed to do before.' Job advertisements and newspaper stories emphasized the excitement and opportunities that war work opened for women in heavy industry. Housework was dull and unexciting compared to what had formerly been considered 'man's work', according to a woman working in a navy yard, who told a reporter, 'somehow the kitchen lacks the glamour of a bustling shipyard'.

Yet the excitement of heavy industrial work quickly wore off for those already in the labour force, like Josephine von Miklos:

Maybe they read of so many bombers made each month, or production goals passed by eight per cent or short by fourteen. They are proud if the numbers are great; they get sore when production isn't up to what it should be. But there isn't any glamour in *making* bombers and shells. That is just a job, a job to be done day after day, carefully and deliberately, with every person doing a certain thing, doing it exactly the same way, maybe a hundred thousand times, or five thousand times a day. The average man thinks 'twenty-five thousand time fuses', and it is just a number. But that is the number which an average shift turns out in an average eight-hour day, in just one little department of The Company, day after day.

'In the next twelve months, the American housewife must show that she can keep her head and her temper and roll up her sleeves at one and the same time,' observed one newspaper commentator, who minced no words in spelling out the choice facing the country's womenfolk in the summer of 1942. 'If she can't, the menfolk fighting on distant atolls are likely to get slaughtered in the hot sun for lack of ammunition.'

The Women's Bureau had set the priorities for its recruiting drive to attract two million more workers:

First, women with factory experience who have lost their employment because of priorities in materials and plant adjustments to war production.

Second, other unemployed women who are registered with the Employment Service seeking work.

Next, if necessary, the more than eight hundred thousand girls coming from high schools and colleges.

Last, women caring for their homes, particularly with small children, should not be asked to go into factories and workshops until it is absolutely necessary. They can be much more helpful to the Nation by staying at home and taking care of the children, though it is recognized that in some cases these women find it necessary to work.

The War Manpower Commission then turned to Hollywood, as well as Madison Avenue, to boost its national campaign to attract first-time women workers. The emphasis was placed on patriotism, glamour, and the economic advantages. Not that every appeal was directed to inspiring women to tie up their hair, put on dungarees and march into the war plants. Wives who were also mothers of young children had to be reminded that they were contributing to the war by staying at home. This was the rationale behind *Women at Arms*, which was hastily cranked out by RKO pictures to tell the story of Mrs Larkin – 'just a plain housewife' – who was prevented by her two children from joining the WAACs or going into a factory. 'She's the keeper of the Home, the thing we're all fighting for,' the synopsis explained, 'she's among the strongest, bravest, and most valuable of America's women at arms.'

In contrast to Mrs Larkin, the heroines of *Women on the Warpath* were flag-waving female war workers charged with doing their feminine patriotic duty in a script that steamed with the heady rhetoric of a Hollywood epic:

> Staunchly, have the women of America stood shoulder to shoulder with their men in the pioneering past. Today they take up a new burden as the nation calls for five million . . . a women's army trained and ready to help save the homes it has been their duty to adorn . . . Gone is the day of the remote battlefield, a day when war is strictly a man's job. At hand is the opportunity for women to assume a new responsibility. And so on they come, these home-keeping, home-defending soldiers of America, to put the feminine torch to the fuse of an almighty explosion of tyranny.

'In 1943, America will have to produce more war materials than any country has ever been called upon to produce in the history of the world,' announced a cheery US employment leaflet to support the slogan, 'The More Women at Work the Sooner We'll Win the War.' It listed the jobs a girl was now considered able to perform as part of the Government's bid to raise the national female workforce to eighteen million. 'To win the war, we must meet these tremendous production quotas, we must release able-bodied men for fighting and for heavy industrial jobs . . . This means about two million *more* women working than worked in 1942. Every skill must be put to patriotic use immediately to help save *lives*.'

Financial factors counted more than patriotic sentiments with women, especially servicemen's wives, who received a minimum of fifty dollars a month – twenty-eight provided by the Government and twenty-two from her husband's pay. Economic necessity obliged Mrs Amelia Bondelid, like many GI brides, to take a war job in San Diego, where she first worked in a dime store before joining the tool department of the Convair aircraft factory. There she became a draftsman designing tool jigs for B-34 bomber wings and hulls:

> Women couldn't work overtime beyond six days a week. The only other day I had off in two years was Christmas Day. The pay was better than anything else in town, but naturally women weren't paid as well as men. Other than that, I really liked the work. I took a course that lasted three months in drafting for aircraft, and they took us women and put us in tool design. You should have seen the looks on the men's faces when they saw Jackie and me walk in there. 'The women are taking over,' they said. We were teased a lot, and some asked us for dates or propositioned us. The whole bit . . . Sometimes a group of us women would come out of Convair and we'd see army trucks or navy trucks full of guys in their combat gear going down to the ships, those big grey ships, and the guys would whistle at us and we'd wave back at them. But we knew where they were going and we practically cried for them.

Women workers in the heavy industries, like Mrs Rosair Earley, who became a shipyard coppersmith, discovered that some areas of so-called heavy industrial work were not so very demanding on physical stamina:

> It wasn't heavy work at all, and that is where I found out a little about men's work. I thought men did a lot of heavy work, but I found that they have a pretty soft deal. That was rough on a lot of men after shipyard work because we found out that they didn't have to work so hard after all. But we worked six days a week and got time and a half for Saturday. They treated us pretty well. In fact, there was too much help. People were falling all over each other. So far as I was able to make out, it was the same in all the shipyards. I don't think it was that way in some of the aircraft plants; they worked harder.

'It was interesting how fast these plants converted to an all-female crew, except for men and the older 4F types,' recalled Mary Dandouveris, a student from the University of Wisconsin who spent her summer vacations working in an aircraft assembly plant:

> I worked on the swing shift as a riveter, and I didn't like the shift – 3 p.m. to 11 p.m. – it was cutting into my social life too much, so I asked to be transferred to a later shift, and then I did the filing. It was on the graveyard shift. We were filing the metal for the leading and trailing edge, which is the outer edge of the plane. You had only one-one-thousandth-of-an-inch error, and there were gauges and in-

spectors who came around to make sure that you didn't go beyond that. Women were particularly careful, you see, and light fingered enough, so that, working the files, you didn't make heavy dents or go beyond the minimum tolerance.

Nowhere was the wartime shift of American production to female hands more dramatically evident than in the vast aircraft factories. At Boeing's sprawling plant outside Seattle, over half the workforce was eventually made up of women. The assembly lines ran twenty-four hours a day turning out Flying Fortresses to bomb Germany.

The influx of an army of female war workers forced a minor revolution in production techniques in American factories, as in Britain. Jobs and equipment were modified to accommodate women's muscular capabilities, and pressure for clean canteens, lounges, and toilet facilities resulted in an overall improvement in working conditions.

Cartoonists had a field day. 'This is a lot better than cooking,' a newspaper humourist had one blonde telling another as she poured explosives into shell-cases, 'You just follow the recipe and hear no crack from your husband about it not being like Mother used to make.' In the working environment, sexist humour like this was sharper and more intimidating.

'That American women should take an active part in the man's job of building and repairing ships was almost inconceivable,' pointed out a 1943 Women's Bureau pamphlet on 'Employing Women in Shipyards'. Just two years earlier the most publicized women-employing shipyard had refused to hire female secretaries and their lone female telephone switchboard operator was 'kept under lock and key'. But the two hundred per cent growth in the American shipbuilding industry since 1941 – some shipyards employing forty thousand workers had been marshy flats only eighteen months earlier – could only have been achieved by relying heavily on the input of female labour. There had been tremendous opposition from the unions, and the International Brotherhood of Boilermakers' and Iron Shipbuilders' referendum on women workers brought strong protests that made fun of the whole idea, as typified by the views of one Seattle local:

Some of them want the silliest jobs. At the aircraft factories they use the Buck Rogers' riveter, driving 3/16th rivets. They don't understand that in the yards they'd be using an outfit that drives rivets ten to twenty times bigger. If one of these girls pressed the trigger of the yard rivet guns, she'd be going one way and the rivet the other.

Union protests notwithstanding, the hiring and training of large numbers of women by the shipyard began in the autumn of 1942, as the draft drained men into the armed services. Within the year a third of the workforce in some west coast yards was female, and their welders and riveters became the headline-making heroines of the 'Ships for Victory' programme. A national recruiting campaign flooded the east and west coasts with posters proclaiming that female shipyard workers were 'Soldiers Without Guns', and the press ran accounts of prodigious feats of welding performed by women. The competition to build a Liberty ship in the fastest time reached a climax in November 1942 when the *Robert E. Peary* was launched by Henry Kaiser's Richmond yard in the never-to-be beaten record time of four days, fifteen hours.

'Rosie the Riveter' became the World War II heroine of heavy industry. Radio stations across America blared with a popular recording of the song, celebrating how patriotic Rosie was 'making history working for victory', complete with the sound effects of the production battle:

> Rose – (Brrrr-rrrr) the riveter
> Rosie's got a boyfriend Charlie:
> Charlie, he's a marine.
> Rosie is protecting Charlie
> Working overtime on a riveting machine.

Norman Rockwell immortalized a muscularly defiant Rosie with dungarees and rivet gun on a May 1943 *Saturday Evening Post* cover. But that same month a shipyard foreman stated: 'The clamour was for big, husky women with the accent on youth. Yet slender, deft-handed women of all ages are our best welders and ship-fitters. A Danish woman welder of fifty-three can match the best record of our best man.' There were actually many more 'Wanda the Welders' than 'Rosie the Riveters' labouring in the shipyards and aircraft factories. But 'Wanda' found no artist of Rockwell's calibre to popularize her, although welder's chrome-tanned leather outfits were featured in *Harpers Bazaar*, whose fashion artist designed as 'a thoughtful touch' matching leather spats and a 'tab stitched over the heart to hold identification badge'.

Some women, however, found they just did not have the stature or strength to man-handle heavy rivet guns or welding torches:

> My first job was as an operator of a turret lathe, and I was a little scrawny teenager at the time. I had to brace my feet on the front of the lathe just to open the chuck. It definitely was not women's work, so I quit after three days. Then I went to work at the Liberty Tool and Lathe where they were making bullet dies. I operated drills and reamers to bring the metal up to the shape of a bullet. But after a while they put me in the office, where I stayed all during the war. I was sort of glad to get into the office because I rode the bus to work with a bunch of 'Rosie the Riveter' types, and boy, were they a tough crew. Really tough customers.

Women in shipyards quickly learned that psychological resilience was just as important as brute strength for survival. Many 'Rosies' shared the apprehension that Lili Solomon felt on her first day at the yard:

> Maybe you think it didn't take nerve for a woman to make that first break into the yards . . . I never walked a longer road in my life than to the tool room. The battery of men's eyes that turned on my jittery physique, chorus of, 'Hi, sisters' and 'tsk-tsk' soon had me thinking, 'Maybe I'm wrong. Maybe I'm not just another human. Maybe I am from Mars.'

When she transferred from factory work into an east-coast shipyard, Josephine von Miklos encountered far fiercer resentment from the men, who regarded the female invasion as 'a huge joke' – but one with unpleasant sexual overtones:

> The truth of the matter is that we live among a legion of waterfront Casanovas. Now you'd think that at least some of these ten thousand guys would have seen women before. We have reason to assume that these men were bred by mothers, that they have wives and daughters and sisters and sweethearts. But that's where we evidently are wrong. These fellows, most of them, have not been bred by mothers, they have *no* wives and daughters and sisters and sweethearts. They have, in fact, never before seen or heard or touched or spoken to anything remotely resembling a female. We haven't the faintest idea whether they have ever been told that the world is inhabited by anything but men in shipyards. Nor do they show the slightest sign of knowing that women are people too. Well it is pretty funny. It is funny when a few

of us walk through the yard and they whistle and hoot at us. We have discovered that the only way to stop them is to whistle back at them and hoot louder than they do. It is funny when they yell, half in astonishment, and half derision: 'There's women in the yard!'

Sociologist Katherine Archibald recorded at first hand, in the Moore Dry Dock Company in Oakland, a graphic insight into the sexism that plagued the wartime shipyards:

Sex attitudes made up the tangled background of the male worker's point of view. Sex was his greatest avocational interest. Whether bounded by the proprieties of marriage or unconstrained in the reaches of bachelor fancy, it was the spice of his existence, the principal joy of his social life. The largest part of shipyard conversation, beyond the routine of the day's necessities, was occupied with some aspect of the pleasures or the problems of sex; and shipyard jokes were broad and racy in the extreme . . . The emphasis upon sex, moreover, as it evoked the biological distinctions between men and women, also reinforced the lines of social demarcation. Traditions supposedly governing the proper division of labour between men and women were linked with even more profoundly rooted traditions concerning divisions in the biological function, and change in the structure of the former might seem to imply a threat to the latter's sacrosanct stability.

Women were more often than not denied the opportunity to work together as a team but were divided up in mixed groups. Virginia Wilson, a housewife turned wartime welder, discovered the reason for this the morning her yard foreman assigned a three-girl team to take sole charge of constructing a prefabricated keel section:

For once we had been given responsibility, for once we had been put on our own, for once we had enough to do. 'When we finish we'll hold open house and invite you in to tea,' we told our leadermen. Our enjoyment was such that we did not notice that something was amiss until late in the afternoon. Then we became gradually aware of the hostility of the men. Our woman burner reported they were 'seething with resentment' that women should be given a unit to construct. The women checkers said, 'You should just hear what we hear outside our checking shed, my dears.' This was the first time I had come up against the hostility of one sex towards another and I could not believe it.

The wolf whistles and the lascivious gestures were taken in good humour until they were translated into direct sexual harassment.

But the grabbing and pinching by men of the dungareed female bottoms, although resented, often went unreported by the women 'when, for instance, the man is your boss, and you depend on him and his good will to help you learn about the new machines around you'. This continual pestering was regarded by Josephine von Miklos as a juvenile attempt by males to protect their territory, which extended to silly attempts to make the women's work more difficult:

> They're just like schoolboys who think that bathroom jokes make them sound grown-up. If a guy shows us a job, and tightens the machine just before we take over, the screw or nut or bolt or handle will invariably be so tight that it takes an enormous amount of extra strength to undo it. When we tighten the stuff, the machine works just as well. But they seem to love to see us pull and push and puff, and then, maybe, have to ask for help. We haven't quite decided yet whether they do it to prove to us that we can't do the work, at least not as well as they can, or because they want to exhibit some more of the superior and boundless strength of the male animal.

The management of some war plants banned women from wearing make-up in an attempt to contain the temptation to male sexual harassment. When the Boeing Aircraft Corporation sent home fifty-three girls for wearing tight sweaters, it became a *cause célèbre*. Their union objected that what was considered perfectly moral attire in the office should not be considered immoral on the shop floor. Management brought the National Safety Council into the dispute by claiming that sweaters caught fire, attracted static electricity, and were a dangerous hazard because they might snag in rapidly turning machinery. Ann Sheridan, from the film 'Oomph Girl' entered the fray by declaring that while a small figure in a large sweater might be a threat to safety, a big girl in a tight sweater was only a moral hazard to men.

Controversy also erupted over the much-copied 'peek-a-boo' long hair of Paramount star Veronica Lake, which was held to be a hazard near machinery. Patriotically she sheared off her locks, thereby sending her film career into a decline from which it never recovered.

Bundling their hair into the approved wartime factory turban and concealing their 'oomph' in loose-fitting dungarees or thick welding leathers did not unsex women – or prevent the sparks of sexual attraction taking fire in the most inhospitable of shipyard environments. According to Katherine Archibald, passion always found an opportunity for fulfilment:

> In the shipyards, rumour was continually busy with suspicions and reports of salacious activities in the obscurer parts of ships or in some vaguely identified warehouse. Like evil-smelling breezes, tales of scandal floated from group to group: of a stolen kiss or an amusing infatuation; even of the ultimate sin, with or without price, in the fantastic discomfort of the double bottoms. One persistent report concerned the activities of enterprising professionals, for whom a shipyard job was said merely to provide opportunity for pursuit of a yet more lucrative career. The end result of all such talk, of course, was to deny the possibility of the establishment of businesslike relationships between men and women on the job and to discredit women as effective workers.

The feminine figure in male garb working in an industrial environment had a unique sex-appeal that the advertising industry was not slow to exploit. The wartime sales pitch for everything feminine, from cigarettes to face cream, soft drinks to soap, was given a patriotic slant by featuring glamorous crane operators pouring steel, pretty girls behind ploughs, earnest housewives assembling aircraft. The stereotype 'Rosies' and women welders populated the pages of popular romantic fiction in wartime magazines. Pond's Cold Cream ran a series of ads featuring women in a variety of war jobs with the copy line, 'We like to feel we *look* feminine even if we are doing a man-size job . . . so we tuck flowers and ribbons in our hair and try to keep our faces looking pretty as you please.' Pacquins hand cream reminded women in war plants that 'Hands that do a man's work can still enchant a man'.

It was not just the advertisements that attempted to preserve the socially acceptable feminine image of women war workers. Magazine articles focused the ladies' attention on the need to keep their FQ (Femininity Quotient) high. A *Life* feature on a pretty 'Rosie' from a Boeing bomber factory revealed the secret beauty tips that enabled her to look like a 'Hollywood factory girl':

> Now at day's end, her hands may be brusied, there's grease under her nails, her make-up is smudged and her curls are out of place. When she checks in the next morning at six-thirty a.m. her hands will be smooth, her nails polished, her make-up and curls in order, for Marguerite is neither drudge nor slave but the heroine of a new order.

While women were publicly urged to preserve their femininity in a man's world, their employers showed little patience in meeting their special needs. A Woman's Bureau survey of three thousand female workers in thirteen factories revealed that more than half were married, widowed, or divorced, with the responsibility for running the home as well as their job. But when the high rate of female absenteeism became a major issue during the peak of the war production drive in 1943, women were bombarded by literature and posters accusing them of 'throwing a monkey wrench in the war effort' and being a 'boon and ally to the Axis'.

Women AWOL, as it was called, made newspaper headlines, and the Labour Department proclaimed 'Absenteeism is Sabotage.' 'The workers not producing all they can are denying our men in the South Pacific the right to live, because they are keeping from them materials that they need to live by,' was the blunt, emotive theme in the War Manpower Commission's drive to bring in more female labour for the factories with a recruiting booklet 'This Soldier May Die – Unless You Man This Idle Machine'.

The campaign against 'Women AWOL' was taken to an unpopular extreme by one navy yard manager who had the doors removed from all the women's latrines to deter 'toilet malingerers' who were too long away from their work. Male self-righteousness resulted in women being accused of a lack of patriotism when they took extra days sick – until surveys revealed that the monthly female cycle was often cited as a cause. The Women's Bureau promptly rushed a little pamphlet to the rescue: entitled 'A Modern "Refresher" on Menstruation to Help You Reduce ABSENTEEISM', it provided helpful hints on how to cut down the 'loss of time' during those 'difficult days' which 'among hundreds of thousands of women mounts up to a major headache these days when every minute counts'.

The provision of child-care facilities became a major issue in the United States in 1943, just as it did in Britain, when the labour crisis forced industry to bring in more and more married women with young children. President Roosevelt ordered the Federal Works Administration to build nursery schools, but Congress held up funding in response to the popular belief that it was bad for mothers of infants to be at work. The Federal Works Administration's child-care director protested. 'Whether we like it or not, mothers of young children *are* at work. So we do need day-care centres.' In the end only three thousand nurseries were built during the war to care for a hundred and thirty thousand children, and staffing problems and the relatively high fees charged made even these unpopular with working mothers.

Providing shopping facilities to cut absenteeism was solved by the enterprise of American retailers. The lead was taken by New York's Bloomingdales department store, which set up a pioneering branch at the Sperry plant on Long Island. 'It's no slapdash affair, either,' enthused a press reporter, explaining that the connection between a 'lipstick and a bombing raid over Germany' was that women no longer had to take shopping days off that harmed the war effort. Other large American department stores were quick to recognize the opportunity to sell through their own branches at the major war plants, where American women had exchanged their kitchen sinks for well-paid jobs at the wartime factory bench.

Surveys confirmed that the most interviewees gave 'high pay' as their second reason for working after the more patriotic response, 'to help win the war'. 'They're here to make money,' was the frank assessment of a New England war-plant manager who criticized the amount his machine-shop women spent on clothes: 'When they come to work, before they change to slacks, you'd think they were going to the opera.' In the east, many female office workers deserted their desks to make twenty cents an hour more at the factory bench. The highest rates of pay were earned by women who did 'men's work' for the first time in the shipyards, steel plants, and aircraft factories.

Typical of thousands of high school girls who abandoned further education for the duration was Corinne Aldridge, who worked at the Emerson gun-turret plant outside St Louis. 'I used to earn $15 a month at college baking biscuits. Then I got my first pay cheque here – $32.60 all in one week – I tell you. But somehow when you get working it's more than money. You learn about the war and you feel different about a lot of things.'

American women also learnt during World War II about the importance of organizing to press their demands for equal pay. In 1940, fewer than eight hundred thousand wage-earning women were unionized, representing less than ten per cent of the organized labour force. Four years later, this had more than doubled to three million women, representing twenty-two per cent. The activity and success of union campaigns for the rate for the job for women was in direct proportion to their female representation. Discriminatory pay differentials were eliminated entirely by 1945 by the United Electrical, Radio and Machine Workers, a union in which women represented more than a third of the membership. Similarly the United Rubber Workers, which represented a large number of women, negotiated an equal pay clause for many of its contracts, and the United Auto Workers' union, with over a third of a million female workers, was a powerful voice arguing for maternity leave and other special benefits for women.

However in general, although the Roosevelt adminstration had supported the principle of equal pay for equal work from the outset, the male-dominated unions and management claimed that women had to be paid less because they did not have the men's skills or seniority.

Hundreds of thousands of 'Rosy the Riveters' and 'Wanda the Welders' had stormed the bastions of traditional male dominance, but when it came to such crucial issues as pay and job security, the men still had the political power. Sexual discrimination continued in many wartime workplaces because union leaders and management regarded much of the female workforce as employed for the duration only. Even before the war had been won, American and British industry were preparing to use the principle of 'last in first out' to lay off many women workers.

BLACK PROPAGANDA AND SEXPIONAGE

A lady of doubtful nativity
Had a fanny of great sensitivity
When she sat on the lap
Of a Nazi or Jap
She could detect fifth column activity

> Limerick given to
> Sir William (Intrepid) Stephenson

Greetings, everybody. How are my victims this evening? All ready for a vicious assault on your morale? . . . Now let's have more close harmony work from the New Guinea nightingales and other chapters of the Pacific Orphan Choir. It's dangerous enemy propaganda, so beware!

> 'Tokyo Rose' broadcast

The Land Girls

By mid-1943 the labour crisis in Britain's factories became so severe that the government suspended recruiting for the women's forces for twelve months. The only alternative to factory work was to take a job on a farm.

38

Come and help with the
VICTORY HARVEST

You are needed in the fields!
APPLY TO NEAREST EMPLOYMENT EXCHANGE FOR LEAFLET & ENROLMENT FORM
OR WRITE DIRECT TO THE DEPARTMENT OF AGRICULTURE FOR SCOTLAND
15 GROSVENOR STREET, EDINBURGH.

39

9 Life in Britain's Women's Land Army was healthy but no country picnic and required working a 48-hour week for 32 shillings in pay.

0 In 1943 the shortage of male labour in the US quickly forced employers to abandon their traditional opposition to women workers and by 1944 they were working even as 'lumberjills'.

40

'Rosie the Riveter'

41/42 While young able-bodied men were called up for military service, the women of Britain and America turned their hands to unfamiliar and unfeminine work with lathes, heavy presses and drills that forged the weapons which their menfolk needed.

43 The aircraft production lines offered plenty of opportunity for the lighter industrial work for which the female hand and eye was considered well suited.

44 A stack of '1000 pounders' being checked at a factory in Oklahoma.

45 A Florida grandmother, with two sons in the army, operating industrial cutting gear.

46 A 48-year-old Lancashire widow stoking a large Cornish boiler supplying steam for eighteen workshops.

41

WOMEN OF BRITAIN
COME INTO
THE FACTOR

"ASK AT ANY EMPLOYMENT EXCHANGE FOR ADVICE AN

COVER YOUR HA
FOR SAFETY

42

YOUR RUSSIAN
SISTER DOES !

43

44

45

46

47

48

'A Real Man's Job'

From January 1942 the British government effectively instituted a nationwide female mobilization order for 'vital warwork' followed in 1943 by the proclamation of Ernest Bevin, Minister of Labour: 'Nothing that a woman can do, or can learn to do, should be allowed to absorb a man of military age.'

A US employment leaflet the same year stressed the slogan: 'The more women at work the sooner we'll win the war.'

47 The 200 percent growth in the American shipbuilding industry in two years could only be achieved by relying heavily on the input of female labour.

9/50 Railway maintenance and track laying in America and Britain.

51 Loading beer barrels in Britain.

Civil Defence

The heavily bombed cities of Britain
throughout the war, but particularly during
the 1940 Blitz, were looked upon by many
women as the 'front line'.

52 Loneliness was the universal wartime
epidemic, but its cure was found in the

53

increase in social intercourse. 'People were
friendly and we were all in it together.'

53/54   The Women's Voluntary Service (WVS)
accompanied evacuees and also helped to
sustain the Royal Engineers engaged in
building bridges across bomb craters.

Women! you are needed in

THE NATIONAL
FIRE SERVICE
AS FULL-TIME OR PART-TIME MEMBERS

You can train to be a telephonist, despatch rider,
driver, canteen worker and for many other duties.

APPLY FOR PARTICULARS TO NEAREST FIRE STATION OR EMPLOYMENT EXCHANGE

55/56/57

In August 1942
registration was extended
to women up to age 45 and
firewatching duty was
made compulsory unless
they were employed for a
minimum of 55 hours a
week.

58   Practice and training was
essential for all the
emergency services.

Cleaning up the Debris

59/60 On a fact-finding tour of Britain in 1942, Eleanor Roosevelt's team found women 'working at all kinds of jobs . . . even on demolition squads in the bomb devastated cities'.

59

60

Femininity Preserved

61 The feminine figure in male garb working in an industrial environment had a unique sex appeal that was exploited by the advertising industry. Women workers were publicly urged to preserve their femininity in a man's world with advertisements and magazine articles on the need to keep the 'FQ' (feminine quotient) high.

62 'She does a man's work in the ground crew servicing airplanes but she hasn't lost any of her glamour, sweetness and charm,' ran a *McCalls* headline. The photograph shows a hairstyle known as the Liberty Cut.

63/64 A cosmetic company advertised that the war could not be won on lipstick, 'But it symbolizes one of the reasons why we are fighting . . . the precious right of women to be feminine and lovely.'

Social Gatherings

5 Dancing was the most
popular social antidote to
anxiety and loneliness. Chain-
dances like the 'Lambeth
Walk' gave wartime dance
halls a party spirit and for
many British girls the craze
for dancing provided the
opportunity for making new
boyfriends.

6 Soviet and American forces
celebrate with a dance at the
Elbe in April 1945.

8 The Rainbow Club that
opened for Americans in 1942
in the old Del Monicos on the
corner of Shaftesbury Avenue
promised a taste of home with
its canteens, juke boxes, pool-
tables and regular dances.
'Rainbow Corner' became a
magnet for homesick GIs in
the London blackout.

68

69

71

72

75

74

76

Pin-up Girls

The ubiquitous pin-up of World War II provided a boost to morale and some romantic escape from the horrors of combat. In all its forms it contributed a great quantity of ammunition for the hearts of soldiers in every army, but it was the Hollywood pin-up girl that was the most prolific, and manufactured with the most artful degree of erotic titillation.

69 Lauren Bacall
70 Irene Manning
71 Jane Wyman
72 Jane Russell
73 Unidentified girl
74 Rita Hayworth
75 Ann Sheridan
76 Carole Landis
77 Betty Grable

78/79/80

Servicemen transferred the most popular female forms to their machines of war. By 1945 there was hardly a tank or plane in the US military that was not adorned with its own painted icon of femininity as a good-luck talisman.

81

Entertaining the Troops

ENSA was part of the massive logistical
campaign that sent popular British singers
and entertainers to the most distant battle
areas to raise the morale of troops thousands
of miles from home. The American USO
sponsored regiments of singers, dancers,
comedians and musicians who volunteered
to undertake gruelling overseas tours.

81 A group preparing to leave Drury Lane.

82 Dinah Shore singing to GIs at Versailles.

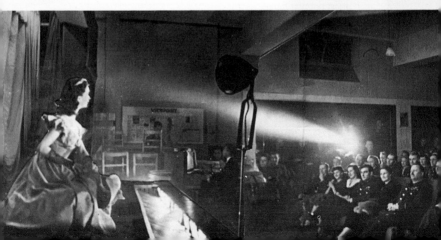

82

85

83

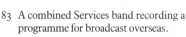

84

86

83 A combined Services band recording a programme for broadcast overseas.

84 Vivien Leigh re-enacting a scene from 'Gone with the Wind' at a bomber station in England.

85 Marlene Dietrich who recorded 'Lili Marlene', and Irving Berlin who composed 'White Christmas', were two of the 'forces favourites'.

86 The Special Services division of the US Army distributed a 'Do-it-Yourself Manual' for soldiers to put on their own shows complete with crepe paper skirts and choreography sketches for the all-male chorus line.

Liberty and Fraternity

87/88 The welcome received by American troops in Paris and British troops in Sicily was more or less what liberators would expect.
The Allied planners, though, tried to adopt – particularly in Germany – a strict non-fraternization policy which neglected to take into account the sexual hunger of their troops.

EVER SINCE RAHAB THE HARLOT harboured Joshua's spies before the capture of Jericho, sex has often played a part in clandestine intelligence operations as a means of extracting, concealing, or disseminating intelligence. World War I produced the legendary *femme fatale* Mata Hari, whose H-21 German code-designation was to expose her in 1917 after French counterintelligence deciphered a cable to Berlin. Less notorious – because she was never caught – was 'Fraulein Doktor'. Dr Annamarie Lesser exploited her powerful sensuality to ensnare high-ranking French officers and stay one jump ahead of discovery while she spun a web of German espionage in wartime Paris that cost France one of her key fortresses.

It was not only spies who used sex in the cause of military and political advantage in World War I. British and French propaganda posters and cartoons luridly dramatized the so-called German rape of Belgium in a way that helped inflame American opinion against the Kaiser's soldiers, who were represented as raping murderers.

Twenty-one years later, the Nazi's regime had transformed propaganda into a sinister art. Dr Joseph Goebbels was able to exploit sexual and racial themes in broadcasts, films, and posters. For an outwardly puritanical regime which banned prostitution, abortion, and contraceptives and banished homosexuals to concentration camps, the German leaders had no private reservations about employing sexual themes in propaganda or using sex as both a weapon and bait in clandestine intelligence-gathering operations.

Although brothels were officially outlawed by the Third Reich, the elite Nazi SS security police had been authorized by Himmler before the war to engage prostitutes in intelligence gathering. The infamous Salon Kitty in Berlin's Giebachstrasse was the brainchild of the Deputy Reichsfuhrer SS, Reinhard Heydrich. The high-class brothel was set up to increase surveillance of foreign diplomats and visitors as well as to gather dossiers on the sexual indiscretions of Nazi party big-wigs and government guests.

Hand-picked girls were specially schooled in the arts of seduction to pry confidential information – as well as high fees – from their clients. Cameras were concealed in hollow walls and the luxuriously ornate bedheads were bugged with microphones that were cunningly placed to convey the most intimate of amorous whispers to the battery of listening posts and recording machines set up in the basement. But Salon Kitty proved an expensive investment whose 'sexpionage' value never lived up to Heydrich's expectations. Its recordings provided a great deal of bawdy entertainment for the SS listeners in the cellar but few significant political or diplomatic indiscretions were picked up by the time the outbreak of war reduced its usefulness.

The German foray into sexual 'black propaganda' in the first year of the war did not bring any greater success, although the Fuehrer himself had predicted it could be decisive. 'The place of artillery preparation will be taken by propaganda before the armies arrive,' Hitler had boasted. 'Mental confusion, indecision, panic, these are the first weapons.'

The first test was made during the lull at the front in the long months of the Phoney War. A concerted effort was made to demoralize the *poilus* manning the Maginot Line by barraging them with leaflets and radio broadcasts in which provocative sexual themes were a vital element. Paul Ferdonnet, a turncoat Frenchman, took to the microphones in Stuttgart to reveal an intimate knowledge of French military personnel and their movements. He was also able accurately to predict which officers were to be joined by their wives and mistresses for weekend reunions in nearby towns while their men remained cooped-up and frustrated in the warren of clammy barrack tunnels. To add to their discomfort, anti-semitic leaflets and jigsaw puzzles were dropped from the air showing a naked British girl, with the *Times* newspaper title reversed to *Semite*. To sow disaffection amongst the Allies and reinforce the message of the pictures depicting perfidious English soldiers walking away laughing from a French soldier who was up to his neck in a pool of blood, pornographic cartoons showed British officers in Paris fondling a naked French girl while her husband stood duty on the Maginot Line. Huge hoardings were erected in sight of France's frontier fortresses bearing messages such as, 'SOLDIERS OF THE NORTHERN PROVINCES, LICENTIOUS BRITISH SOLDIERY ARE SLEEPING WITH YOUR WIVES AND RAPING YOUR DAUGHTERS!' In one section of the line, however, the propaganda backfired: the French men of the French regiment reacted with, 'We don't give a bugger, we're from the south!'

How this attempt at sexual 'black' propaganda affected the resistance of those regiments manning the massive frontier fortress was never tested, because the twin thrusts of the 1940 Wehrmacht offensive side-stepped the 'impenetrable Maginot Line'. But Hitler's propaganda may have contributed to the generally low level of morale in the French army which proved unable to stem the Blitzkrieg advance on Paris.

In other spheres, sexually-loaded propaganda appears to have had little influence on the course of World War II – other than providing amusement to those on its receiving end, as well as those producing it. Far from undermining the morale of Allied forces in the Pacific, the Japanese pornographic propaganda which bombarded the American and Australian troops was regarded as comic relief from the rigours of jungle warfare. Marines battling through the Solomons laughed hysterically over the crudely drawn naked girls cavorting round tombstones with the message, 'We've got oomph and we've got curves/We've got stars and a lot of stripes/We've got passion and we've got breasts/We've got everything 'cept our desire/And only the crosses mark them here.' Rugged Australian troops roared at the graphic portrayal of copulation that was directed to them under the caption 'Australia Screams GIs', which portrayed Americans bedding their girls back home. Cards with sexy full-frontal nudes on the front carrying an explanation in phonetic Japanese of how US marines could surrender on the back joined the pin-up parades that decorated the foxholes on Guadalcanal.

More sophisticated, but just as ineffective, were the daily English broadcasts from Radio Tokyo which began early in the summer of 1942. These featured female announcers who interspersed recordings of popular dance bands and light classical music with exaggerated threats concerning the numbers of GIs about to die in forthcoming operations and frequent reports of the infidelities of their wives and sweethearts back home. In a theatre where long spells of boredom between bouts of fierce fighting were relieved by little entertainment and less sex, the female voices of Japan's sirens of the airwaves and the sweet music that was intended to make the men homesick actually made one particular announcer, who was dubbed 'Tokyo Rose', into a popular 'radio pin-up'.

Although there were about a dozen female announcers, 'Tokyo Rose' became the legend, and the name was applied by GIs to 'at least two lilting feminine voices'. One of these belonged to Iva Toguri d'Aquino, a Los Angeles-born Nisei girl in her mid-twenties who joined Radio Tokyo as a typist after the outbreak of war barred her passage home, and who was persuaded to assist the team preparing 'Zero Hour', the nightly propaganda programme aimed at undermining the morale of American troops. Far from undermining the morale of GIs, 'Tokyo Rose' became a boost to their spirits. 'If a radio popularity poll could be taken out here among American fighting forces,' the *New York Times* reported in March 1944, 'a surprisingly large number of votes would go to Tokyo Rose and other of the programmes beamed from the Land of the Rising Sun.'

For American troops garrisoned in lonely bases in Alaska it was 'Madame Tojo' who brought the same nightly fare of popular music and ineffective invective. And although much was later to be made of the vicious and sinister propaganda intended to make the GIs homesick, 'Your favourite enemy, Annie', as the seductive female announcer like to introduce herself, was awarded a spoof US Navy citation in August 1945:

> Tokyo Rose, ever solicitous of their morale, has persistently entertained them during these long nights in foxholes and on board ship, by bringing them excellent state-side music, laughter, and news about home. These broadcasts have reminded all our men of the things they are fighting for.

Yet despite such testimony to the contribution she made to American morale, the unfortunate Miss d'Aquino, whose US citizenship made her a convenient scapegoat, was tried in 1945 and convicted as a traitor. She was sentenced to ten years in prison and fined ten thousand dollars for the entertainment she had provided to millions of GIs. The same fate was also meted out to another siren of the enemy airwaves, whom the GIs affectionately called 'Axis Sally'. She was an American woman, Mildred E. Gillars, who became the German equivalent of Tokyo Rose in propaganda broadcasts that were beamed to American troops fighting in Europe during the final year of the war.

If the Axis efforts at using seductive female broadcasters to undermine the morale of Allied servicemen backfired completely, post-war evidence was to show that the intensive British and American efforts to turn sexually-loaded propaganda against the enemy met with no greater success.

Britain's 'black propaganda' was sponsored by the Government's Political Warfare Executive, which had been set up to counter Dr Goebbels' skilfully directed radio offensives. Stations were set up which purported to be broadcasting secretly from inside the Reich, run by various anti-Hitler groups. The German authorities' sophisticated direction-finders quickly identified them as an enemy propaganda operation and announced severe penalties for anyone caught listening to these unauthorized broadcasts. To attract an audience British stations often included salacious or pornographic material – a favourite theme was to broadcast the intimate details of the sexual eccentricities of Nazi officials or Hitler Youth Leaders.

The mastermind behind Britain's black sexual propaganda was Sefton Delmer, an Austrian expatriate who invented and played with great relish a tough Prussian character known as 'Der Chef'. Night after night he took to the airwaves to condemn the depravity and corruption of the Nazis. His scripts, a potent brew of patriotism and pornography, apparently attracted quite a following in Germany and Station GS-1, which was his identifying call-sign, was condemned by the German High Command for its 'quite unusually wicked hate propaganda'.

Nor were the Germans the only ones to complain about the diet of sex and sadism with which Der Chef was spicing up his reports of the Reich's administrative corruption and military bungling. A lurid account of an orgy broadcast by GS-1 in the summer of 1942, which supposedly related the graphic sexual acrobatics of a Kriegsmarine admiral, elicited a strong Foreign Office protest after the transmission had been picked up in Moscow. Sir Stafford Cripps, the austere British Ambassador to Russia, raised a bureaucratic storm about the propriety of such broadcasts. Delmer's chief submitted a retort that drew an interesting parallel about the way that the undercover war was being fought:

> If the Secret Service were to be too squeamish, the Secret Service could not operate. We all know that women are used by them for purposes which we would not like our women to be used, but we say nothing. Has any protest ever been made? This is a war with the

gloves off, and when I was asked to deal with black propaganda I did not try to restrain my people more than M. (the Head of the Secret Service) would restrain his, because if you are told to fight you just fight all out. I am not conscious that it has depraved me. I dislike the baser sides of human life as much as Sir Stafford Cripps does, but in this case moral indignation does not seem to be called for.

Delmer, who was described by his boss as 'a rare artist', was instructed to tone down the pornographic element of Der Chef's scripts, but was otherwise encouraged to continue his contribution to the black propaganda radio war with his gloves off. His artful exploitation of sexual themes was to find its way into the broadcasts made by the other 'secret' British wartime radio stations, such as the 'Atlantiksender' station, which beamed its transmissions to U-boat crews, and the various 'Soldatensenders', which broadcast news and music to German troops in Europe. Actual news was peppered with items reporting the scandalous sexual behaviour of Nazi party bosses with the wives of absent Wehrmacht troops; or revealing that Wassermann tests had shown that a large quantity of blood in German army field hospitals was contaminated with syphilis; or announcing the births of children to the wives of U-boat men who had not been on home leave for a year. These stations offered, like Tokyo Rose, plenty of music and a clever concoction of personal information and names of actual people gleaned from captured German sailors, soldiers, and airmen that was intended to upset the morale of the men at the front. They were reinforced by thousands of leaflets like those dropped over the French U-boat bases in 1943. These emphasized the high casualty rates in a captioned picture strip that stressed the awful suffering caused to seamen's widows and families in the fatherland.

Yet for all Delmer's acknowledged genius at inventing credible sexually-loaded propaganda – which was incorporated in the broadcasts made during the European campaign by Eisenhower's SHAEF psychological warfare teams – post-war evidence suggests that such broadcasts had little impact on Germany. As a leading member of Britain's wartime Political Warfare Executive put it: 'I am very dubious whether black propaganda, despite its brilliance in radio work, had any marked effect on the course of the war. It had to be so entertaining that it probably maintained morale!'

What is not disputed is that all the wartime broadcasts and

sexually explicit leaflets had by their very nature initiated changes in Western society's definition of pornography. By exploiting sex as legitimate – and entertaining – content for propaganda, both the Allied and Axis powers may have unwittingly helped to initiate the shift in public attitude that permitted the explicit treatment of sex in post-war novels as well as the reinterpretation of the magazine publishing laws which made popular what came to be known as the 'Playboy Philosophy'.

When it came to exploiting sex for espionage, Hitler's Abwehr military intelligence organization failed to repeat Germany's World War I success with female agents. One reason for this was that each attempted infiltration of Britain was intercepted, and Berlin was fooled until the end of the war into believing that its male as well as female spies were carrying out their assigned missions instead of having been 'turned' into double agents.

Vera de Schallberg was the first female spy to be put ashore on the British Isles by the Germans. She was an elegant blonde cabaret singer in the Mata Hari tradition who had become a practised *femme-fatale* after running away from her Copenhagen home at the age of fifteen to seek an abortion. De Schallberg had attempted to make a career as a Parisian nightclub singer, but an affair took her to Brussels, where she took up with a small-time black-marketeer called Theodore Druecke. Vera then met Hans Dierks, a man whose ugliness had a fascination for some women, including Vera.

Dierks exploited his curious sex-appeal as an undercover Nazi agent and recruiter for Nikolaus Ritter, the chief of the Luftwaffe's espionage operation in Hamburg. The glamorous Vera, Ritter quickly decided, would make an ideal spy. After training at the Luftwaffe's Camp 4 espionage school in Prussia, she joined an espionage team that included Druecke, Dierks, and a Swiss named Werner Heinrich Waelti who had spied for the Germans while he chauffeured the French Consul about pre-war Hamburg.

The disasters that plagued this espionage team first struck after their celebratory 'going-away' party on the eve of departure for England when their car crashed, killing Dierks. Badly shaken up but only slightly injured, the trio of survivors was told by Ritter that their operation was to go ahead as planned, and they were flown to the south of Norway. At Stavanger, in the early hours of 30 September 1940, they were put aboard a twin-engine Heinkel

III floatplane for the bumpy flight across the North Sea to a lonely spot on the Scottish coast in Banffshire. In the pre-dawn darkness, the bicycles which were supposed to transport them inland fell out of the rubber dinghy that carried them ashore. Once on the beach, they cut their boat adrift. Waelti headed east while Druecke and Vera – who had now assumed the passport and unlikely French alias of Madame de Cottani-Chalbur – walked west.

Their search for public transport was to prove their undoing. All placenames and signposts had been removed under British wartime regulations, so when they arrived at the little station at Port Gordon, on the coastal line between Banff and Inverness, shortly after 7.30 a.m. and asked to know where they were before buying two single tickets to Forres, the stationmaster was at once alerted. His suspicions about these early-morning travellers in city clothes were confirmed when he noticed that the man had wet trouser legs and that the woman's shoes and stockings were damp. While his janitor kept the couple talking, stationmaster John Donald telephoned the police.

A few minutes questioning resulted in a search that put an end to the brief career of this would-be successor to Mata Hari. Incongruously, the couple were found to be carrying a Mauser pistol, a flashlight that was 'Made in Bohemia', and a sausage with a German wrapper, evidence that made further protests about where they had come from futile. Vera quickly confessed, and through her description the police were soon able to pick up Waelti, who had managed to get as far south as Edinburgh.

Although her two companions were made of sterner metal, it was obvious to the MI5 interrogators that the blonde Danish woman was prepared to be co-operative. Spared the rope that ended the life of her lover and Waelti, Vera de Schallberg became one of the first recruits into one of Britain's most successful wartime counterintelligence operations, the so-called Double Cross system. It was to succeed beyond all initial expectations in 'turning' captured German spies into British agents who were then used to feed their erstwhile masters with intelligence information that was designed to confuse and mislead the Wehrmacht's military planners.

The efforts of Anna Wolkov to carve a career for herself as an amateur spy were to have more far-reaching consequences than she herself realized when, on 20 May 1940, Scotland Yard's Special

Branch officers came down the steps of the dingy Kensington basement from which she had sallied forth at night to stick up pro-German posters in the blackout. Her arrest and subsequent trial alongside a cypher-clerk of the American Embassy in London was to be MI5's first big counterintelligence coup of the war.

Anna Wolkov was a stocky Russian-born woman in her mid-thirties. She had cast herself in the role of self-styled *aide-de-camp* to Captain Archibald Maule Ramsay. This distinguished ex-Guards officer and World War I military hero had been a founder member of The Link, the Anglo–German fellowship organization which had promoted contacts with the Third Reich throughout the 1930s. When the outbreak of war forced its dissolution, he established the less flagrantly unpatriotic 'Right Club', which continued clandestinely to foster pro-German sympathies amongst its blue-chip establishment secret membership. It included leading aristocrats, bankers, and parliamentary figures who feared the ultimate communist takeover of the West if Britain failed to take advantage of Hitler's repeated peace offers. The Right Club committee used as its clandestine meeting place the cramped quarters above Wolkov's father's 'Russian Tea Room' restaurant, which also happened to be conveniently located near Ramsay's London house and South Kensington underground station.

Anna's ambition to become an important agent was fired by a pre-war pilgrimage to Germany in 1938, when she had briefly met Hitler's deputy, Rudolph Hess. Although she was never actively recruited as a German agent, she became an ardent Nazi 'fifth-columnist' and might have remained a misguided fanatical gadfly to the British security services had not the Russian emigré circle in London brought her into contact with a personable young staffer from the American Embassy called Tyler Kent, who showed her copies of Churchill's top secret cables to President Roosevelt. Anna Wolkov realized that if she could get Kent's collection of documents to Berlin it would establish her reputation as a successful agent. Unfortunately for the conspirators, their plans were uncovered by a team of MI5 agents.

Kent protested that he was an isolationist sympathizer who was merely doing his patriotic duty by collecting proof of Roosevelt's unconstitutional efforts to involve America in the war, evidence that might be used to demolish President Roosevelt's anticipated bid for re-election in 1940. But a select trial nonetheless convicted both him and Wolkov, and although it was assumed at the time that Wolkov's amateur conspiracy was directed to benefit the Germans, post-war FBI documents and British sources indicated that the Soviet Union was the real *éminence grise* in the affair – and that Tyler Kent's long-time affair with a NKVD girl in Moscow indicated his own recruitment as a Russian agent to monitor the traffic passing between London and Washington. In addition, Kent's arrest on an espionage charge embarrassed one isolationist American Ambassador, Joseph P. Kennedy, who was suspected of clandestine approaches to Berlin.

Anna Wolkov was the amateur spy at the centre of a very tangled web of intrigue whose outcome was to have a profound influence on the course of World War II. The Wolkov Conspiracy was used to persuade the War Cabinet to pass the draconian Defence of the Realm regulation in May 1940.

In the United States, official secrecy still protects the sexual machinations of an expatriate Hungarian woman of whom President Roosevelt noted in 1942, 'this is the kind of scandal that calls for immediate and very drastic action'. The Princess Stephanie von Hohenloe was a widow whose affair with Hitler's former commanding officer in World War I, Captain Fritz Widemann, had taken her right into the highest Nazi circles. Wittily vivacious, but no stunning beauty, she was an assertive female whose clever charm and fervent devotion made her a favourite of the Fuehrer's 'court circle'. Although half Jewish, she had been accorded by Himmler the rare distinction of 'Honorary Aryan' for the services she had rendered to the Third Reich. These included her flair for extracting funds and support for the Nazi cause from influential business and newspaper magnates, one of whom was the British press-baron, the late Lord Rothermere.

Princess Stephanie and her lover, the handsome, square-jawed Captain Widemann, became the toast of influential circles on either side of the Atlantic. He was one of the leading agents of the 'Auslander Organization' through which the Nazis channelled support from Germans and German sympathizers abroad. Hitler himself was to credit their public relations effort with smoothing the path for Germany's annexation of Austria and Czechoslovakia – services for which the Fuehrer's 'Nazi Princess' was awarded Leopoldskron Castle near Salzburg, an extensive estate that had been owned by the celebrated Jewish theatrical producer Max Reinhardt.

In the years before the war broke out in Europe, the Princess shuttled between London, Paris, Berlin, Madrid, and Rome. With Fritz Widemann she crossed the Atlantic on the unofficial but highly publicized mission for which Hitler was to make her the personal gift of a diamond-studded swastika brooch. One of her coups as an international go-between with the Nazis was to have been instrumental in arranging the 1938 meeting in London between Widemann and British Foreign Minister Lord Halifax which encouraged Hitler to gamble with certainty that Prime Minister Neville Chamberlain would avoid a war over Czechoslovakia at the time of the Munich Crisis.

The Princess's deft behind-the-scenes manoeuvres amongst the rich and politically influential on both sides of the Atlantic convinced many observers that she was 'one of the most dangerous women in Europe'. The week after the war broke out in September 1939, she was lunching at the Ritz Hotel in London when a group of titled ladies publicly branded her a spy and insisted that the *maitre d'hôtel* asked her to leave the restaurant. Princess Stephanie, with the cool defiance that was to distinguish her wartime intrigues, continued to eat. She also refused to leave England, and pressed on until December 1939 with an unsuccessful law suit against her former patron Lord Rothermere for non-payment of travel expenses on an assignment he had given her.

Meanwhile Fritz Widemann had already arrived in the United States to take up the post of German Consul General in San Francisco – from where he was ideally placed to put the case publicly for supporting Germany while masterminding clandestine operations of Nazi sympathizers on the west coast in their bid to keep America neutral. The arrival of a 'Nazi Princess' in California early in 1940 prompted a whirl of publicity and social engagements through which Stephanie von Hohenloe was able to generate sympathy and attention for Hitler's 'peace offensive'.

FBI Director J. Edgar Hoover was convinced that the Princess and her diplomat lover were dangerous Nazi agents and ordered a twenty-four-hour tail on their movements. FBI agents arranged hidden microphones through which they eavesdropped on a meeting that took place at the Mark Hopkins Hotel on 26 November 1940, when Princess Stephanie von Hohenloe and Widemann discussed possible peace initiatives with Sir William Wiseman, a banker who had been involved in British intelligence operations in America during World War I. Whether Wiseman was actually at the meeting with the official authorization of Sir William (Intrepid) Stephenson, then head of British Security Co-ordination in America, now appears highly unlikely in the light of recently declassified FBI and US Army intelligence files. They indicate that he was then already under suspicion as a pro-German who was busily trying to further Hitler's peace offensive by soliciting American business pressure to force Britain to open negotiations with Berlin.

FBI telephone taps also revealed that the Princess was trying to get Wiseman's help to avoid deportation by getting her visa extended through Stephenson's British Security Co-ordination line to the British Government: and that Widemann was passing on to Berlin information being provided by a high-level sympathizer in the State Department. J. Edgar Hoover, the FBI Director, backed the moves to have the Princess deported, but she was to outmanoeuvre him by taking her new lover the head of the Immigration and Naturalization Service, Major Lemuel Scholfield.

The arrest of Hitler's Princess made headlines, but Schoefield personally squashed press speculation that a Hohenloe deportation was imminent by announcing on 20 May 1940 that proceedings had been dropped against her. 'While in custody the Princess Stephanie has co-operated with the Department of Justice and has furnished information of interest,' he told the press. 'The Department believes her release from custody will not be adverse to the interests and the welfare of this country.' Precisely what this important information was, Major Scholfield declined to reveal, but reporters noted that he was to be seen driving the glamorous princess around San Francisco, and sensed that a spy scandal was about to be uncovered. Columnist Drew Pearson dropped hints in *The Washington Times-Herald* that the Princess had won her freedom with 'some amazing revelations about subversive operations in this country and Britain'. Hoover, who wanted to deport both the Princess and her ex-lover Captain Widemann, could not get the Justice Department to deliver any of these revelations: all he was told was that 'it was being typed up by Lemmy' (Scholfield).

However, Widemann was forced to abandon his operations and

pack his bags when all Axis consulates in the United States were closed in retaliation for Japan's takeover of Indochina in July 1941. By this time Princess Stephanie had moved to Washington's luxury Wardman Park Hotel, where her continuing affair with the chief of the Immigration and Naturalization Service threatened to become a national scandal as she hinted to reporters that she was about to publish a book containing the startling 'secret information' she had given Scholfield.

Finally, in August 1940, Acting Attorney General Francis Biddle instructed Scholfield to get his mistress out of town before she became a public embarrassment to the administration. The FBI was still being denied the information needed to arrest her when, using the alias 'Nancy White', she managed to slip away to Pennsylvania. The press sleuths were soon to uncover what they called a 'love nest', where the FBI was already keeping tabs on the comings and goings of her continuing passionate liaison with Scholfield.

On 8 December 1941, a matter of hours after Roosevelt made his formal declaration of war, Hoover acted on the new powers the FBI had been given by executive order to round up potential enemy spies. The Princess Stephanie von Hohenloe was unceremoniously bundled into an FBI limousine as she stepped out of a Philadelphia theatre, leaving her eighty-nine-year-old mother screaming on the pavement. At the Gloucester immigration station in New Jersey, she was put in solitary confinement. When Hoover finally discovered that the 'confession' Scholfield had announced had never existed, the sparks began to fly within the Justice Department. Even the Attorney General's role in the affair came under suspicion after the Princess's address book was found to contain his private office telephone number.

The report to Hoover made it very clear that she must have enjoyed the protection of someone high in the administration besides the Head of the Immigration Service as there was evidence of 'a very influential friend in the State Department whose mistress she had been'. Just who this mysterious protector was is still blanked out in the sanitized FBI reports. But his influence must have continued after her arrest since, threatened with expulsion from the country, the Princess feigned illness and, with the tacit assistance of her lover, resisted deportation from the Gloucester detention centre. The President himself took a hand in the affair.

He wrote to Attorney General Biddle on 11 July, 'Unless the Immigration Service cleans up once and for all the favouritism shown to that Hohenloe woman, I will have to have an investigation made and the facts may not be very palatable, going all the way back to her first arrest and her intimacy with Scholfield . . .'

Biddle appears – with good reason – to have taken Roosevelt's threat personally, since he decided to transfer the case as far away from Washington as possible. The Princess was dispatched to a Texas detention centre at Seagonville with her mother and Scholfield following with the baggage. While her mother established herself in a suite at a nearby Dallas hotel, the Princess renewed her offer to tell the FBI about her association with Fritz Widemann and the implications of her liaison with Major Scholfield – offering too, in desperation, to include personal information about Goebbels and Hitler if she could be guaranteed her freedom. 'Princess H. is a very clever and, consequently, a very dangerous woman,' noted the FBI memorandum to Hoover which advised, 'she is manoeuvring now to play the Bureau against the Immigration Service so she will get something out of it.'

The Justice Department then closed ranks and nothing came of the Princess's final machination, which was a last ditch letter to Hoover in which she sought to reveal 'matters which I can only relate to the President'. Roosevelt nonetheless personally overruled the board that recommended releasing the Princess from detention in March 1944. Despite a suicide attempt early in 1945 Princess Stephanie von Hohenloe was not set free until just before V-E Day – when she went to live with Major Scholfield, who took her home to his Philadelphia farm.

The tough resilience which had been the cornerstone of an extraordinary career enabled the Princess to make a quick recovery from her long ordeal, and she even triumphed over the stigma that had attached to her during the war to make a comeback of sorts on the New York social scene. Fritz Widemann also secured immunity from prosecution at Nuremberg, having spent the remainder of the war in China after successfully claiming that he had been instrumental in saving Jews and giving encouragement to the plots against Hitler.

A diplomatic wife turned British spy whose cool cunning and audacity made Mata Hari look like a novice became one of the most successful female undercover agents of the war. She was Elizabeth Amy Thorpe, who was born in Minneapolis in 1910. The precocious daughter of a captain of marines, Elizabeth was seduced at fourteen when she fell into a tempestuous affair with 'an old gentleman of twenty-one'. After completing her education in Switzerland and a smart Massachusetts ladies' college, she became an aggressive socialite. Her success was guaranteed by her striking beauty that was crowned by fine auburn hair and eyes 'like a dash of green chartreuse in a pool of limpid brandy', according to one of her admirers. At the age of twenty-one and pregnant, she married Arthur Pack, a second secretary at the British Embassy. Twenty years her senior, Pack had attracted her because his maturity contrasted with the American youths of her own age.

Friends were astonished at the odd match, because Pack's pomposity was combined with physical ill-health caused by old war wounds from 1918. Marriage, however, in no way interfered with Mrs Elizabeth Pack's continued promiscuous dalliances. She found no lack of opportunity for sexual adventures on the diplomatic circuit in Chile and then in Spain during the Civil War, where her remarkable powers of persuasion were employed in getting her Spanish aviator lover released from a Republican jail. And when Arthur Pack was posted to the British Embassy in Warsaw in the summer of 1937, she quickly became a sought-after companion for the young men of the Polish Foreign Office.

A trivial piece of intelligence gleaned during one of these liaisons started the diplomat's wife on her long and successful career as a spy. After being put on the payroll as a part-time spy for British intelligence, Elizabeth Pack soon discovered that the game of espionage added a certain spice to amorous adventures, especially when she was told to strike up a relationship with the confidential aide of Colonel Josef Beck, the Polish Foreign Minister. 'I would have made a dead set at him, even if he had been as ugly as Satan. But happily this wasn't necessary,' she later confessed. Through her affair with him Elizabeth Pack picked up vital clues that led to the unravelling of the German 'Enigma' codes which were to play such a crucial role in the Allies' wartime intelligence effort. Accompanying Beck's aide on his official missions to Prague and Berlin, she was able to obtain information that confirmed the extent to which the Polish Secret Service had successfully penetrated the Wehrmacht's top-secret cypher system.

After her first mission was completed, the Packs were posted back to Chile, where Elizabeth made a name for herself as a freelance journalist with a Santiago newspaper. When war broke out she took it as a cue to desert her ailing husband and moved back to the United States where she worked as a reporter under her maiden name of Elizabeth Thorpe.

Summoned to New York by William (Intrepid) Stephenson, she was recruited as a full-time agent under his control with the code-name 'Cynthia'. In the winter of 1940–1 Stephenson's BSC undercover intelligence operation arranged for her to rent a two-storey house in Washington's select Georgetown district, as a base for her mission of obtaining the Italian naval ciphers. The target she selected for her sexual advances was Admiral Alberto Lais, with whom she was already acquainted and who was therefore no stranger to her persuasive charms. It was not long before the beautiful woman with the green eyes, who claimed she was working for American naval intelligence, had talked him into providing code books, which within a matter of weeks played a part in bringing about the defeat of the Italian battlefleet off Cape Matapan on 28 March 1941.

Lais had also told Cynthia of an Axis plan to sabotage British ships in American ports, so it became easy for Stephenson to effect his removal from the scene by passing the information to the FBI that his diplomatic status was compromised. Then, in May, Stephenson personally briefed Cynthia for her next task: to obtain all the Vichy French cypher systems and code books.

Starting out in New York's Pierre Hotel, which was a favourite of the wartime Vichy diplomats, Cynthia used her cover as a journalist to target the French Embassy's press officer for her initial assault. Captain Charles Brousse, a former fighter pilot with the French Navy, was an officer who took his duty seriously. But he had no special love for the Germans, as Cynthia discovered when he sat in on the interview which she had astutely arranged with his Ambassador for an article on current Vichy policy towards Britain and the United States.

A bouquet of red roses together with a luncheon invitation which arrived next day initiated a passionate affair, and for two months they managed to carry on the liaison under the nose of Brousse's wife. Cynthia and Stephenson anticipated that they would soon have the code books in British hands. Then Brousse announced he would have to accept half pay or be posted back to France as a result of economy measures by the Vichy Government. He asked Cynthia to go to France with him, but she and Stephenson hatched a scheme in which she was to offer to make up his salary by pretending to be working for the still-neutral American Government, who she said would pay handsomely for copies of cables and ciphers.

Brousse, as Cynthia had confidently predicted, fell in with the scheme and soon a regular flow of embassy reports, intelligence traffic and files were passing through the BSC headquarters in New York. Cynthia then moved into the Wardman Park Hotel, where Brousse and his wife were living, to facilitate their contacts and avoid the attention of the FBI, which was becoming concerned at the extent of the BSC undercover operations. Valuable though the information that Brousse provided was, he still could not get his hands on the naval cypher books and codes that the British Admiralty was pressing for. Cynthia managed then to seduce the French Naval Attaché, but failed to persuade him to betray his navy's secrets. His complaints to the Ambassador about her activities were skilfully countered by Brousse's denunciation of his colleague's other scandalous affairs.

In a new scheme to get the naval cypher books out of the safe in the guarded code-room, Brousse began working late at the embassy – while Cynthia was instructed by BSC's lock-picking experts. After two attempts to open the safe failed, they decided to call in a professional Canadian safe-cracker. Brousse managed to get him into the embassy once the lone security guard had been encouraged to beat a discreet retreat after opening the door to see Cynthia and Brousse entwined naked on the floor making love. This time the crucial code books were extracted and passed out of Brousse's office window to be photographed and returned to the safe. The operation succeeded without a hitch, and possession of the Vichy naval cyphers enabled the Anglo–American forces involved in the North African landings in November 1942 to be certain that the French naval units in the Mediterranean did not make any hostile move towards the Algerian invasion beaches.

After these landings the United States ended its neutrality with the Vichy regime and Brousse was interned with the rest of the Embassy staff. Cynthia was posted to the Special Operations Executive in London, but was never given another operational mission. After the war, with news of her husband's suicide, Cynthia married Brousse, who had obtained a divorce from his wife.

The intelligent exploitation of Cynthia's sexual charm and capacity for adventure had certainly rewarded British intelligence with information that directly helped to speed the course of ultimate Allied victory. Indirectly, she provided cover for the much more important 'Ultra' operation, because information about the break-in at the Vichy Embassy was later to be leaked to Berlin to allay German suspicions that their top-secret code 'Enigma' cypher traffic was being read.

Although the Mata Hari label was attributed to all female agents and saboteurs, very few actually resorted to sex as a *modus operandi* – any more than it was exploited by the majority of male agents in the manner that was later to be popularized by Ian Fleming's fictional James Bond. Women, however, had certain advantages as secret undercover operatives in occupied Europe during the war. They did not require the extensive documentation that the German occupation forces issued to every French male who could be challenged about military or labour service, and women could blend more easily into the local population because of a natural lack of suspicion of females.

The British Special Operations Executive deployed no fewer than fifty-three female agents in France during the war. The bravery displayed by women like Odette Sanson and Violette Szabo as Resistance fighers became legendary – as did their courage in resisting their Gestapo torturers. The American OSS also made use of the services of female agents behind German lines to report on the impact of Allied bombing.

The World War II intelligence operations in which sex played an important role were by no means limited to the exploitation of the normal physical attraction between male and female. Homosexuals also became a natural target for espionage. Since it was a proscribed activity, punishable with imprisonment in most belligerent nations, it made those homosexuals who were snared by enemy agents extremely susceptible to blackmail. The enormous expansion in the numbers of men in uniformed service and the prevailing wartime spirit of hedonism opened up many more opportunities for both officers and diplomats with homosexual tendencies to be compromised into becoming valuable providers of intelligence. It was an opportunity that Himmler's SS and the Gestapo could not resist. Germany's first efforts at homosexual espionage commenced when their agents infiltrated a male bordello in Brooklyn, across New York's bustling East River. The house on Pacific Street lay just a stone's throw from the Brooklyn Navy Yard, and it specialized in providing its clients with servicemen, especially sailors.

The nominal proprietor of the bordello was a burly American of German extraction, Gustave Beekman, whose illegal operation was easily taken over by Axis agents who provided plenty of liquor and cash for the impecunious young seamen. They paid particular attention to securing information from the seamen from British warships that frequently put in for repair at the US Navy facility and the scores of merchantmen that loaded up with Lend-Lease supplies in New York harbour before running the gauntlet of the U-boat-infested North Atlantic.

The FBI and Naval Intelligence finally moved in on Beekman in April 1942, when he confessed that the mastermind behind the operation was William Elberfeld, described by the FBI as 'the Nazi's ace spy in the US'. But the most explosive information contained in the affidavit he signed in Brooklyn's Raymond Street jail was his detailed testimony that a prominent Massachusetts' senator had come to the brothel on Sunday afternoons at least ten times between July 1941 and March 1942, and on some of these occasions he had been observed in deep conversation with Elberfeld. The senator he named in his affidavit was none other than David I. Walsh, Chairman of the Senate Naval Affairs Committee.

At first the FBI were inclined to disbelieve Beekman's charges, but investigators soon found a young seaman named Zuber who was able to confirm the brothel-keeper's story by graphically describing precisely where the distinguished senator had 'ripples of fat' and where he did not. When J. Edgar Hoover passed on news of Walsh's involvement with German agents in his daily confidential report to the White House, Roosevelt decided to use the information to neutralize Walsh, one of his main Congressional critics and a leader of the isolationist lobby on Capitol Hill. But someone appears to have tipped off the Senator for Massachusetts before incontrovertible proof could be obtained: in the six weeks the FBI kept the house on Pacific Street under surveillance from a hospital bedroom opposite, not one of the many public figures seen entering the bordello was identified as Walsh.

The President decided that he had enough dirt to defuse the recalcitrant Walsh and it was Roosevelt himself who gave the orders to Hoover that the whole affair was to be hushed up. According to Beekman's attorney, the President got Walsh off the hook in return for his assurances that he would give his wholehearted support to the war effort. Significantly, it was Hoover himself who grilled Beekman and persuaded him to change his testimony, with the promise of a reduced penalty for full co-operation. Although he carried out his end of the deal – the raid led to the arrest of the elusive Elberfeld and three other Axis agents – the trial judge overlooked the bargain struck with the FBI and sentenced Beekman to the maximum twenty-year term when he was convicted on a common sodomy charge.

Walsh himself denounced the 'diabolical lie' that he was in any way implicated in the affair, and on 20 May the majority leader of the House restated J. Edgar Hoover's 'conclusion' before the assembled Congress. 'The Federal Bureau of Investigation has reported that there is not the slightest foundation for the charge that Senator Walsh visited a "house of degradation" in Brooklyn and was seen talking to Nazi agents there.' The *New York Post*, which had offered Beekman a substantial sum to revert to his original testimony, did not agree. Nor did *The Nation*, which strongly supported the *Post*'s demand for a full and public investigation in an editorial that read, 'So summary an attempt to bury an unpleasant affair may involve the side-tracking of a full and open investigation of the house in Pacific Street.'

No further investigation was ever conducted, however, perhaps because the FBI, taking a leaf out of the German sexpionage manual, had decided to open up its own bordello to exploit homosexuals as a source of information. Just how J. Edgar Hoover went about recruiting and training his male Mata Hari agents is still a classified – and no doubt embarrassing – Bureau secret. But it appears that valuable information about Axis blockade runners and commercial agents was obtained from a male brothel that operated for most of the war on MacDougal Street because it was patronized by many foreign seamen whose vessels tied up along the nearby West-side piers.

The American and German male brothel operations represented

a crude attempt to exploit homosexuality to obtain information about shipping, but Soviet intelligence was able to tap the highest Allied councils with a far more sophisticated operation which used the secretiveness of an elite homosexual network to burrow moles into the British and American bureaucracies. This far-reaching intelligence strategy, whose full ramifications were not to become apparent for another quarter century, had commenced shortly after World War I when candidates willing to serve the long-term cause of communism were recruited from the academically gifted sons of the British ruling establishment, studying at Cambridge and Oxford.

These converts to communism, such as the scholarly art historian Anthony Blunt and the wildly promiscuous Guy Burgess, who combined precocious intellects with homosexual inclinations, were suited for the task of burrowing into the British establishment. They were aided by university colleagues like Donald Maclean and Kim Philby, who were not committed homosexuals but were no less dedicated to the Marxist cause. The political delusion of the 1930s was that the rise of Fascism and Nazism appeared to force democratic societies into making a choice between the extreme right and the extreme left. With the encouragement of their Russian control officers, this secret fraternity of politically 'enlightened' young high-flyers kept in touch and furthered each others' careers as they set out to scale the academic and bureaucratic fabric of Britain's 'Establishment', awaiting the call from Moscow when they were in positions of trust and influence.

The Soviet penetration strategy worked so well that by 1941, when Stalin needed to marshal Russia's military production and diplomatic sinews to stave off the German military onslaught in World War II, the Kremlin could rely on a high-level intelligence network that accurately monitored the policy-making decisions of Britain's Foreign Office, the deliberations of the State Department, and the White House itself. Moscow had tapped the 'Ultra' secret from Britain's tightly guarded Bletchley Park code-breaking facility; had monitored the development of the atomic bomb through agents working on the Manhattan project; and, perhaps most seriously, had penetrated MI5 and MI6, the British military intelligence agencies. This astonishing success of Blunt, Philby, and Burgess – and perhaps other 'sleepers' – was achieved not by hiring Mata Haris or sending spies on cloak-and-dagger missions, but by the skilful manipulation of a dedicated network of traitors.

One of the most insidious and successful of these wartime moles was Professor Anthony Blunt, the art historian and 'managing director' of the Cambridge homosexual spies, many of whom he had personally recruited. In 1938 he volunteered his services to the War Office and was posted to the training school for intelligence officers a year later. When it was noticed that he had visited the Soviet Union in 1935, he was easily able to allay suspicions about left-wing sympathies by pointing to his impeccable connections: as a second cousin of the Queen-Mother, and with his advice on paintings sought and valued by the highest in the kingdom, it was impossible to believe that Blunt was a security risk.

After an ill-fated spell with the Field Security Police in France, which almost led to his capture in the German advance on Dunkirk, Major Blunt was posted briefly to MI5's security division. At the instruction of his Soviet controller, 'Henry', he applied for a transfer as personal assistant to the director of the counter-espionage division. His fellow communist conspirators were already rising in Britain's wartime intelligence. Philby was with MI6 counter-intelligence and a place had been found in SOE for Burgess, his chief wartime collaborator, who acted as a link with a Swiss diplomatic informant.

For most of the war Blunt remained in charge of one of the most sensitive of all MI5's operations – the interception of the diplomatic bags of the neutral embassies in London. The pouches were intercepted and collected under Blunt's supervision then carefully slit open: their documents were copied and the stitches reinserted and dyed to match the worn side before the pouches were sent on their way. Blunt, on his own admission, must therefore have passed a great deal of extremely valuable information to Moscow that would have facilitated Stalin's strategy in taking over eastern Europe and making a grab at the Balkans. But Major Blunt's most infamous hour came in the spring and autumn of 1944, when he was transferred to General Eisenhower's SHAEF headquarters to liaise with military intelligence. His involvement with the D-Day deception plans meant that Stalin was almost certainly informed well in advance of the secret that Roosevelt and Churchill were at great pains to keep from the Soviet leader – the time and place of the Normandy invasion. Stalin must have decided that it was not in Russia's military interests to inform Berlin of the vital secret which could have turned D-Day into the Allies' biggest defeat of the war. He needed the opening of the Second Front to draw off German reserves and accelerate the Red Army's advance westwards.

Blunt and his coterie of fellow conspirators were able to feed the Soviets with vital items of military intelligence. They also provided Moscow, throughout the war, with an invaluable stream of political background and policy decisions tapped from the circles in which they moved. If the Germans were the immediate losers in the war of sexpionage and sexually-loaded propaganda which Hitler had launched into with such confidence, despite American and British triumphs, it was the Soviet Union which won the ultimate victory in this arcane form of total warfare.

13

THE GIRLS THEY LEFT BEHIND

Hasty war marriages, on embarkation leave, sometimes between comparative strangers, with a few days or weeks of married life, have left both parties with little sense of responsibility or obligation towards one another.

London probation officer, 1945

From Buffalo to Wichita, it is the children who are suffering most from mass migration, easy money, unaccustomed hours of work, and the fact that mama has become a welder on the graveyard shift.

Washington Post, 1944

TRADITIONALLY, SOLDIERS WENT OFF TO FIGHT leaving their sweethearts, loved ones, and wives to 'keep the home fires burning until the boys came home'. World War II, to a far greater extent than World War I, broke this traditional pattern. The lives of millions of couples were disrupted, not just for weeks or months, but in many cases for four to five years. Many couples who might otherwise have delayed tying the conjugal knot married rather than risk the uncertainties of a long separation. An American was to reveal that even those who did wait had unstable marriages because 'War . . . is a notable breeder of personality and physical changes and many of those engaged couples who had been compatible before the war were so changed physically and psychologically that there was no longer any compatibility. And yet because they felt bound by their previous betrothals they entered into unsatisfactory connubial relationships.'

In the first year of the war it is clear that many young American men married to escape the draft, since fathers with young children had a lower rating under the 1940 Selective Service Act. An official was quoted as estimating that up to December 1941, 'about half the increase in marriages must be traced to barefaced draft evasion'. Other couples cut short traditionally long engagements and moved up their wedding dates to enjoy some married life together before the husband joined the military. Many succumbed to a 'last fling' fever which sociologists blamed for the 1941 epidemic of 'military weddings'. They ran a high risk of their unions ending in wartime divorce, since the American National Conference on Family Relations warned that, 'In every war, the family is the first and greatest casualty.'

A War Department bulletin proposed that, while there was no question of an official moratorium on marriages, drafted men should be discouraged from marrying in haste. Up till then only six per cent of enlisted men had wives. Matrimonial entanglements were not considered good for morale because a worried GI was an inefficient soldier, 'And what boy can help worrying if he is trying to support himself and a family on thirty dollars a month?'

Economics should not be the sole criterion, however, according to Eleanor Roosevelt's 'Ask Me' column in *The Ladies Home Journal* of March 1942. In answer to a reader's request for advice on whether 'young engaged couples should marry or wait until the war is over, if the man is called to active duty?' the First Lady suggested this must be 'a personal question'. But in the urgent atmosphere of war, the heart more often than not ruled a draftee's head. 'It was a very emotional time and so many of them got married on leave to total strangers,' recalled an American woman. 'Some of the guys used the line that it would be their last leave, and then got carried away by it and got married.'

Women were also 'carried away' because they wanted to be sure of their man during a long separation. Some girls who surrendered their virginity under the emotional assault of a new recruit's 'last farewell' then felt they had to legitimize their relationships, like an American college girl who married her soldier on his first leave after basic training:

> We were both emotionally tense after months of separation. I don't know just how it happened, but suddenly I realized that I was no longer virginal. The seven-day furlough was almost over and the pressure to get married was now greater than ever . . . We were married on the sixth day of the furlough. Then I received a letter from him stating that he had found a room for me near the camp and that he had made arrangements with his commanding officer to have his weekends free. I could surely find a job there. So overnight I packed a few belongings and boarded a train for another part of America where I had never been before. One and a half days each week were deliriously happy; five and a half were dismally lonely, like a prisoner in a foreign land . . . Then he received orders to move and I went back to my home community.

In the United States a rash of teenage girls married their high-school boyfriends as they were drafted. Thousands of young brides followed their new spouses to rural towns near army training camps. This put a severe strain on housing and medical facilities. 'When the troops came, right on their trail would come the little war brides, fifteen and sixteen-year-old kids from every corner of the nation,' recalled Dr Thomas J. Taylor, whose small mid-west practice was swamped by young mothers-to-be from the adjoining army transit camp. 'They'd just be dumped off in our little town, and of course every one of them was pregnant and ready to deliver.'

Apart from the obstetric complications, the welfare problems which resulted were enormous:

> I vividly recall when a second-class rooming house was jammed with war brides and babies and I was called there because of a rather severe flu epidemic. I remember walking through that rooming house and each room had three or four mothers with babies, all of them, and they all had the flu. A bathroom down the hall, no money, desperate. I tried to do right and called the Salvation Army. In that particular case they did a heroic job clearing up that mess. This was repeated over and over in staging areas throughout the country until finally, late in the war, the message got through to most of these kids and they didn't follow their husbands out.

In addition to the social problems created by the migration of rootless teenage wives, there were the notorious 'war-brides' called 'Allotment Annies' who hustled departing soldiers into marriage to collect the twenty dollars a month the US Government automatically allotted to servicemen's wives. With a private's pay rising to fifty dollars a month for overseas service, some greedy 'Annies' took on four, five, and even six husbands. These unscrupulous women made bigamy a business, and in return for V-mail letters to GIs overseas they lived very well off the pale blue-green Government cheques. Some, with the financial acumen of actuaries, specialized in airmen, anticipating that their higher mortality rates would increase their chances of collecting the ten thousand dollar jackpot Government insurance cheque issued if their husband was killed in action.

Elvira Taylor achieved national notoriety as the 'Allotment Annie' who operated out of Norfolk Virginia and specialized in sailors. She managed to snare six live ones and was about to hook a seventh when she was arrested as a result of two of her 'husbands' starting a fight in an English pub when they showed each other her picture as their 'wife'. When they had been cooled off by the military police, they joined forces to expose the duplicitous Elvira, who was discovered by checking the navy pay records to have contracted four other bigamous marriages.

While 'Allotment Annies' took care not to become burdened with offspring, the twenty per cent leap in the American marriage rates resulted in a baby boom. A similar celebratory jump became apparent nine months after the navy's tide-turning victory at the Battle of Midway in June 1942, and through to the end of the war the American birth rate continued to peak nine months after every Allied triumph – El Alamein, D-Day, and the fall of Berlin. This natal phenomenon appears to indicate that victory euphoria confirmed many couples' hopes of a stable future.

In Britain, by contrast, the birth rate actually declined between 1939 and 1941 in spite of the record number of marriages recorded in the first two years of the war, doubtless an indication of parental apprehension about the nation's chances of survival. The Allied victories in 1943 and 1944, however, appear to have been celebrated with the same procreative urge as in the United States, as births in those years were pushed up ten and twenty-five per cent over 1939 in anticipation of ultimate Allied victory – and the presence of a million American troops in England in the run-up to the long awaited invasion of France.

The 'friendly invasion' of the Yanks satisfied the sexual hunger of some British women who found the long wartime separation from their husbands unendurable. One of these was a Birmingham nurse who fell in love with a curly-haired American lieutenant:

> We met often and began to like each other a lot. One night, as we were all having a drink, Curly said, 'Let's go on our own tonight.' We did – and landed up in a deserted air-raid shelter where we made love. We did this several nights. Curly said he loved me and I said I loved him. I was worried, as there was one thing I had not told him. I was already married. I used to take my wedding ring off and put it in my purse – then put it back on again when I got back to the hospital. I did this every time I met him. Then one night in 'our' shelter, he asked me to marry him. I did not know what to say, being already married. When I told him, he said his mother would understand. I wanted to say 'yes' so much, but somehow I knew that I had to keep putting him off. When the war came to an end, Curly went back to America. We wrote often to each other and he sent me gifts. But then my husband came home, so I stopped writing to him as I was so afraid that my husband would find his letters. When I had a son, I kept wishing it was Curly's.

Many others remained dutifully faithful, like 'Ivy' of Bristol who kept her love alive for the four years her husband was in the Middle East. She read his farewell letter 'over and over again and cried buckets every time'. To alleviate the long days of wartime waiting and wondering, she took a job in a munitions company making magazines for Spitfire fighters:

When the sirens went off, we were supposed to run to the shelters, but most of us stayed at our workbenches. I told myself that every rivet I hammered home was a nail in Hitler's coffin – and consequently I broke three hammers in one week, much to the amusement of my foreman. Every night after I got home and had done my housework and put my child to bed, I would sit down and write to my husband. I would start a letter one night and finish it off the next night, which meant that he was getting three or four letters a week from me. I never told him worrying things. If either of us was ill, I kept it from him and told him after we had recovered. He had enough to be worried about out there in the thick of the fighting.

In the United States a Vassar graduate provided a moving account of why so many women took a war job:

We must learn to wait. To endure the slow trickle of time from hour to hour, from day to day, for weeks, in anguish and suspense. And wait for some message, a letter from far off – a small scrap that tells something of how he was – some time ago – when it was sent . . . The war work we can do is more than welcome – we work hard to put off the next returning cycle of thought – is he safe, is he well, will I hear from him soon? We learn to crowd a lifetime of living into one week – or a few days – or hours. War brides, married while he was on furlough, we wait for the next leave when he can get back. In those brief days, the joy is desperate, underlain with the knowledge of certain separation again – the clock ticks off numbered moments gone. And the train takes him off again – off to unknown places where our love cannot follow . . .

The strain of separation made even the most devoted serviceman's wife susceptible to the chance of temporary emotional solace with other men. But, as many were to discover, the wagging tongues of neighbours could spread unpleasant rumours to the most distant of battlefronts. Gossip may have been unfounded and malicious, but distance magnified the suspicions of soldiers enormously.

Keeping their minds on their distant partners was difficult for some emotionally starved wives who accepted innocent invitations. One American wife who had no intention of being unfaithful nevertheless found her marriage under considerable strain when she was faced with a dilemma that must have confronted many wartime wives:

One day someone suggested I go on a date – a purely platonic date, of course, with a fraternity brother of my husband. And the date was platonic to the point of brutality . . . Gradually I began to realize that I was falling in love with this man and he with me. And accordingly we broke off the relationship, abruptly. Soon thereafter I discovered I was pregnant – by my husband of course. (The other affair had never gone that far.) When I wrote the news to my husband he was very disturbed. Though solicitous of my welfare he couldn't help revealing the fact that the role of father was incomprehensible to him under the circumstances. I could understand him because I felt the same way. We had never been truly married and both of us knew it. The sum total of our married life was seven weekends . . . I was haunted by my recently discovered relationship with the second man . . . I [have since] learned that my husband has gone overseas. I shall not see him now for the duration at least. The second man, like me, finds it difficult to call our relationship off, even though he knows I am pregnant and I strongly wish to remain loyal to my husband . . . I haven't the slightest idea how it will all turn out, but I must confess, being as rational as I am, that I can see many possible outcomes – but none is satisfactory.

Wartime wives were haunted by fears about how the war would affect their particular marriage. 'I think that as well as the fear of death, one realized that things might never be the same again,' recalled one British wife. 'I remember praying that my husband would never have to kill another man, how could anyone have to face that experience and remain the same person?'

An American girl who had been going steady with a soldier posted overseas in 1943 jilted him after receiving a letter from him telling of the emotional strain of life at the front:

He was sent to Italy where the fighting was very intense for a long time, and he wrote to me whenever he could. Then, in one of those V-mail letters, he told me he cried many nights during the heavy fighting. In my sheltered life with my stereotyped notions of what a man constituted, the thought of his crying turned my stomach. I was convinced I had loved a coward. I never wrote to him again.

There were just as many heartaches at the other end of these V-mail relationships. One GI even resorted to writing to the Secretary of War in 1945 after his wife had refused to answer charges made by a friend back home that she was 'running around' with other people and he had decided he wanted a divorce:

So at this time I am writing to you people and seeing if you can help me out in any way and if you can I would sure be glad if you could. My age is twenty-five years and I think I ought to know what I am doing, anyway before I have to live with my wife I stay in the Army the rest of my life and I come in the Army in Oct 1941. So I close now and I hope you can help me out with getting my divorce.

A GI stationed in Persia in 1943 received what GIs came to know as the 'Dear John' letter asking for a divorce:

The time has come to clear things between us. You will have realized before now, that our marriage was a mistake. I beg of you to put an end to this mistake and get a divorce. I left your house this morning, because I didn't want to saddle you with the role of a betrayed husband. As a matter of fact, I have never been yours, but now I belong to someone else, and this finishes things between us . . . Elaine.

In anger and desperation, this particular soldier passed his wife's brush-off letter to *Yank* magazine, asking if his faithless wife could still go on receiving his monthly allowance. He was advised to apply to a legal assistance officer for a divorce: 'Yours is a classic version of a common problem. All the proof in the world that a soldier's wife is faithless does not change the fact that a family allowance is given to her regularly as long as she remains legally married to the soldier.'

Nor was it only the absent fathers who suffered as a result of their wives carrying on. One wartime child remembered how his playmate was affected:

His mother wasn't a woman of high morals, if you know what I mean. She sort of slept around a lot while her husband was gone, and sometimes when she got the twitch in the middle of the day, she'd bring her boys home with her for a little tumble and send the kid over to see us. We knew when that was going on because he would always arrive crying, or, if he wasn't crying, we'd see him hanging around in our backyard looking like he'd been kicked.

Even stable marriages contracted long before the war could break up under its stress. A welfare counsellor to a large mid-west US army base cited the case of a sergeant with a son of fifteen and a daughter of twelve whose wife dutifully corresponded two or three times a week throughout the war with her husband, who had survived the bitter fighting in the Ardennes. 'Two weeks before he sailed for America and was separated from the service, he received a letter from his wife stating she did not desire to see him and wanted a divorce. She believed that she had managed better without him!'

That war jobs and long periods of separation gave many wartime wives a new sense of independence was indisputable. 'The more money, the less family life, is an established pattern in the United States which war psychology has merely emphasized,' wrote an American sociologist of the new mood of the sixteen million working women – six million of whom were married, worked, *and* continued to rear children under fourteen years of age. Fired by this new sense of financial independence, some women abandoned their husbands and families without even the formality of a divorce. In the cities of the north-east it was not uncommon for school teachers to ask whether the children of deserted fathers were not as eligible for relief as deserted working mothers.

One reason why many wartime marriages did not survive the new-found independence of the wife was that they were contracted on a sexual impulse rather than as a result of enduring affection. 'For most soldiers, the obligations of husband and father are unknown – wives become the dominant members of family during the war . . . and have shown marked reluctance to give up their authority and freedom when the family is to be united again,' wrote the Counsellor of the Separation Centre at the US Army's Fort Leavensworth camp. Men returning home were disillusioned not only because their wives 'wore the trousers', but because they had aged during the years of separation and could not complete with their wartime diet of glamorous Hollywood pin-ups.

Many marriages survived while the war was on because the separated partners needed emotional reassurance and a romantic idealization made divorce unthinkable. Only when the servicemen returned did both discover that the romantic aura was gone and that little remained except personal incompatibility. Inherently unstable unions quickly came apart under the stress of two strangers actually having to live together for the first time.

One out of every three American servicemen were married by the end of the war. There was a doubling of petitions for divorce by 1945 when, for every hundred couples getting married, thirty-one were legally separated. In Britain the comparable figures was five divorces for a hundred marriages, but this was up from the one in a hundred level of 1939.

Under US wartime law if a GI husband overseas refused to consent to proceedings, his wife often found it impossible to obtain a divorce as long as her husband was in uniform, because many American judges regarded it as their sacred duty to try to preserve the sanctity of the family while the war was on. After V-J Day this restraint was removed and the number of divorce petitions shot up.

The wartime divorce phenomenon afflicted British servicemen to the same increasing degree. The number of adultery petitions filed after 1942 rose by a hundred per cent *each year* above the 1939–42 average. The final twelve months of the war also saw a spectacular eightfold jump in the number of husbands who were suing for divorce on the grounds of adultery. By 1945, two out of every three petitions were being filed by men, whereas until 1940 female peitions had been in the majority.

'Separation was intolerable for some wives and sweethearts,' was one British wife's rationalization of the epidemic of wartime adultery. According to her, the pressures that led many wives into extra-marital affairs were compounded because they even achieved a measure of social acceptability.

Wartime matrimonial difficulties were familiar problems for the voluntary welfare officers attached to Britain's women's auxiliaries. Barbara Cartland, who herself acted as a voluntary welfare officer, wrote from first-hand experience in her war-memoir *The Years of Opportunity*:

> Men came home and found their wives had been unfaithful; women who wanted a divorce after a few months of marriage; girls who were pregnant; soldiers who arrived home to their wives ill and no-one to look after the children; children with a bad mother and a father overseas – there was no end to them.

Cartland related how she was able to dissuade one young WAAF bride of six months from divorcing her husband on the grounds of sexual incompatibility with an explanation of how the necessity to 'keep a stiff upper lip' and repress emotion in the face of danger often made a serviceman 'an indifferent lover'. As a wartime counsellor she admitted that it was hard to condemn the girls for succumbing to the temptations of wartime promiscuity:

> It is very easy to say what a woman should do or should not do when she hasn't seen her husband for four years . . . They were young,

their husbands were not fluent letter-writers – they started by not meaning any harm, just desiring a little change from the monotony of looking after their children, queueing for food, and cleaning house with no man to appreciate them or their cooking. Another man would come along – perhaps an American or an RAF pilot. Girls were very scarce in some parts of the country and who could blame a man who is cooped up in a camp all day or risking his life over Germany for smiling at a pretty girl when he's off duty? He is lonely, she is lonely, he smiled at her, she smiles back, and it's an introduction. It is bad luck that she is married, but he means no harm, nor does it cross her mind at first that she could ever be unfaithful to Bill overseas. When human nature takes it course and they fall in love, the home is broken up and maybe another baby is on the way, there are plenty of people ready to say it's disgusting and disgraceful. But they hadn't meant to be like that, they hadn't really.

Miss Cartland adopted a down-to-earth practicality when dealing with husbands who had faced death and danger on the battlefield unflinchingly but who were 'white-faced and shaken' when they returned to find that their wife was expecting another man's child. She counselled them that, but for the war, their worried and lonely spouse might have resisted the temptation of what had probably started as an innocent friendship. 'Sometimes there were tragedies and crimes,' she wrote, noting that she admired those who adjusted to the situation. 'At first they swore that as soon as it was born it would have to be adopted – then sometimes they would say, half-shamefaced at their own generosity, "The poor little devil can't help itself, and after all it's one of hers, isn't it?"'

Of the 5.3 million British infants delivered between 1939 and 1945, over a third were illegitimate – and this wartime phenomenon was not confined to any one section of society. The babies that were born out of wedlock belonged to every age group of mother, concluded one social researcher:

Some were adolescent girls who had drifted away from homes which offered neither guidance nor warmth and security. Still others were women with husbands on war service, who had been unable to bear the loneliness of separation. There were decent and serious, superficial and flighty,' irresponsible and incorrigible girls among them. There were some who had formed serious attachments and hoped to marry. There were others who had a single lapse, often under the influence of drink. There were, too, the 'good-time girls' who thrived on the presence of well-paid servicemen from overseas, and semi-prostitutes with little moral restraint. But for the war many of these girls, whatever their type, would never have had illegitimate children.

Illegitimate births increased from an annual pre-war average of 5.5 per 1000 births to 10.5 per 1000 over the six wartime years, with a 1945 peak of 16.1 per 1000. But analysis of the United Kingdom statistical records indicates that in wartime, at least a third of the 'shotgun weddings' that would have resulted from such 'irregular conceptions' in peace did not take place. This implies that more than a hundred thousand babies would have been born legitimate but for the dislocations that war brought to people's lives.

The upswing in the illegitimacy rate was almost as great in the United States, rising from 7.0 per 1000 births in 1939 to a peak of 10.0 in 1945, which averaged out at a wartime rate of 8.3 illegitimate births per thousand. Some six hundred and fifty thousand wartime babies were officially estimated to have been born out of wedlock in America. Contrary to the expectations of the US Census Bureau, it was the latter part of the war which brought the biggest increase in the illegitimate birth rate. In the period immediately after Pearl Harbor, marriage still preceded pregnancy and, as the 1943 official report stated, 'it is somewhat surprising that the ratio of illegitimate live births to total births has not increased but actually declined in the first year of the war.'

Neither British nor American statistics, which indicate that wartime promiscuity reached its peak in the final stages of the war, take account of the number of irregularly conceived pregnancies that were terminated illegally. Abortionists appear to have been in great demand during the war. One official British estimate suggests that one in five of all pregnancies was ended in this way, and the equivalent rate for the United States indicates that the total number of abortions for the war years could well have been over a million.

These projections are at best merely a hypothetical barometer of World War II's tremendous stimulus to extra-marital sexual activity. The highest recorded rate of illegitimate births was *not* among teenage girls, as might have been expected. Both British and American records indicate that women between twenty and thirty gave birth to nearly double the number of pre-war illegit-

imate children. Since it appears that the more mature women were
the ones most encouraged by the relaxed morals of wartime to
'enjoy' themselves, it may be surmized that considerations of
fidelity were no great restraint on the urge of the older married
woman to participate in the general rise in wartime sexual promiscuity. Babies born to married women in Britain were regarded
as legitimate unless registered otherwise, and therefore children
who were fathered by someone other than the husband were
often not declared illegitimate and did not appear in illegitimacy
statistics. That many British women married to absent servicemen
did bear children is confirmed by the detailed investigation conducted by some of the larger municipal authorities. The records
kept by Birmingham, for example, indicate that almost a third of
all confessed illegitimate births were to married women and that
the pre-war rate had trebled by 1945. Although this level was
pushed up by the large number of American service camps around
the urban area, a similar rise was observed in other large cities.

Illegitimacy rates were highest among the young wives of servicemen, suggesting that their work in war production encouraged
an independence that often snapped the bonds of marital fidelity
already strained by the extended absence of their husbands.

The wartime rise in illegitimacy rates put pressure on the public
welfare authorities in Britain and the United States to assume the
burden of a social problem which wartime conditions had greatly
accelerated. Historically, the unmarried mother had been made
an object of disgrace, to be pilloried in the market place or forced
to stand at the Church door on Sundays shrouded in a white sheet.
In World War II, however, the unmarried mother became a
candidate for social welfare rather than a target for moral outrage.
The demand for female factory workers had encouraged many
young girls to leave rural areas and sheltered homes, and drafting
women into the armed forces exposed them to increased sexual
temptation. The Government, therefore, could hardly turn its
back when some of these girls came to grief.

Before the war, an unmarried mother who was cast out by her
strait-laced parents would probably turn to a religious charity,
making the church, as one authority aptly put it, 'the main driving
force in tackling the problem of illegitimacy and the greatest
obstacle in the way of its solution'. But this was to change as the
number of unmarried mothers outstripped the resources of the

voluntary organizations like the Salvation Army. Many of the wartime unmarried mothers were also wage earners, independent of parent or husband, who resented being branded as sinners and objected to the atmosphere of reproach and moral censure that pervaded the church-run homes, whose austerity was a hangover from the old poor-laws.

The British Government groped towards a solution that would be politically acceptable to conservative religious opinion, which was already alarmed at what it perceived as a national moral decline. But by 1945, guidelines had been set by the Ministry of Health and funding was being made available to local authorities and the voluntary societies for the provision of maternity homes and services. The most significant change was that unmarried mothers were enabled to collect minimal child support and maternity grants. This assisted the increasing number of women who were determined to raise their infants themselves rather than resort to the traditional solution of adoption.

The impact of World War II was to effect quite dramatic shifts in the behaviour and attitude of society. 'Total war is the most catastrophic instigator of social change the world has ever seen, with the possible exception of violent revolution,' was how a leading American sociologist put it. Francis E. Merrill, a professor at Dartmouth College, observed in his 1946 study how wartime duty had transformed the American nation into a 'people doing new things – grimly, protestingly, gladly, semi-hysterically – but all changing the pattern of their lives to some extent under the vast impersonality of total war.'

> Millions of families work out new adjustments, as the wife and mother plays the roles of the absent husband and father. Millions of women go to work for the first time in their lives, often at hard and exacting manual labour in shipyard and aircraft factories. Millions of their children somehow learn to fend for themselves and come home from school to an empty and motherless house. Millions of wives, sweet-hearts, mothers, and fathers are under constant nervous tension with their loved ones in active theatres of operations. Millions of wives learn to live without their husbands, mothers without their sons, children without their fathers, girls without their beaux.

The universal wartime disruption of family life would have its most profound effect on adolescents, who by the final years of World War II were creating a major juvenile delinquency problem

in every warring nation. Arrests of teenagers were up, no matter
whether it was Munich, Manchester or Milwaukee. The files of
the German SD security police, British probation officers, and
juvenile courts across the United States attest that juvenile sex
delinquency was one of the most widespread social problems of
the war.

Britain was the first nation to be afflicted with high wartime
arrest rates for teenage girls. There was a one hundred per cent
increase in the first three years after 1939 and large numbers of
them were judged in 'need of care and attention' – indicating that
they were morally 'at risk'. An East London magistrate stated that
the 'earlier maturity' and the 'jungle rhythms heard by juveniles
from morning until bedtime, and slushy movies are in part responsible for an increase in sex delinquency among youths'. Other
factors were the unsettling experience for city schoolchildren of the
1940 evacuation to the country, and the government's mobilization
of women, which included the mothers of adolescents aged fourteen
years or more.

So many fathers were absent from home in military service that
wartime adolescents were deprived of parental supervision and
discipline at a critical stage in their emotional and sexual development. Girls could leave school at fourteen, and there were plenty
of servicemen to provide excitement as an escape from wartime
deprivations. By 1943, London and the other large cities were
crowded with GIs, Canadians, and other foreign troops. In one
London borough the number of teenage girls judged 'in need of
care and attention' had multiplied sixfold in the year before the
invasion of France. Americans had a special fascination for such
girls, according to a probation officer from London's dockland
area:

> All that seems to be necessary is for the girl to have a desire to please
> . . . Those girls who are misfits at home or at work, or who feel
> inferior for some reason or another, have been very easy victims. Their
> lives were brightened by the attention . . . and they found that they
> had an outlet which was not only a contrast, but was a definite
> compensation for the dullness, poverty, and, sometimes, unhappiness
> of their home life.

An emergency Home Office study commissioned that year left
no doubt that the GIs were a major stimulus of this wave of sexual
delinquency:

To girls brought up on the cinema, who copied the dress, hairstyles, and manners of Hollywood stars, the sudden influx of Americans, speaking like the films, who actually lived in the magic country and who had plenty of money, at once went to the girl's heads. The American attitude to women, their proneness to spoil a girl, to build up, exaggerate, talk big, and to act with generosity and flamboyance, helped to make them the most attractive boyfriends. In addition, they 'picked-up' girls easily, and even a comparatively plain and unattractive girl stood a chance.

If it was the glamour of the GIs' Hollywood image which aroused the erotic passions of British teenage girls, their counter-parts across the Atlantic were stirred by a misguided adolescent patriotism. While their brothers participated in the national war fervour by joining up, thereby assuming the trappings of man-hood, adolescent American girls had no such outlet. Psychologists surmized that the 'Victory Girls' or 'cuddle bunnies', as they were called, saw 'uniform-hunting' at railway stations and bus terminals as their way of sharing in the wartime adventure. When detained by the police they would often claim that they were sexually promiscuous 'Because it's my patriotic duty to comfort the poor boys who may go overseas and get killed.'

An army flyer at a base-training camp in rural Illinois recalled that the adolescent prostitutes in the nearby town would 'pick up guys at a soda fountain or in movie theatres and take them out in daddy's car and go at it. Some of them took on four or five guys a night'. Most of the young servicemen preyed upon by these girls were lonely and naturally not averse to accepting the sexual invitations they were offered. The 'patriotutes' as they were dubbed in the American press often dispensed their favours for a Coca-Cola, a meal, or the price of a movie. As one Boston doctor observed, 'The young soldier on leave with healthy instincts is quite likely to seduce a "good girl" if there is no "bad girl" around or if one is too difficult to find. The "good girl" is handicapped by her emotional attachments, is motivated by patriotism, or is uniform-mad. Usually, she knows little or nothing of prevention . . . The bad girl is usually wise. Her past experiences protect her as well as the boy.'

The V-girls were often branded as semi-prostitutes, but few sought sexual relationships with the cold commercialism of women who made their livelihood in the world's oldest profession. The

American Social Hygiene Association held a conference on the problem in the autumn of 1942, which concluded that this type of girl was involved in 'sexual delinquency of a non-commercial character' and that a 'basic motive in her sex hunger is adventure and sociability, but she does not confine her attention to one or two male friends'. Such teenagers were often the pathetic flotsam of hasty marriages contracted at the last minute by soldiers looking for emotional security before going overseas. One such was a Times Square pick-up in New York who told a *Time Magazine* reporter, 'I've only gone with three or four men a week since I've been here. I didn't take money from any of them. I'm not bad, but a girl who's been married gets lonely. I couldn't go back to a small town after Broadway. It's so quiet at home, no place to go, nothing to do.'

'Good-time girls of high-school age are the army's biggest problem today as a potential source of disease' announced a 1943 report from the base surgeon of large mid-western army airfield. The report concluded, 'While mothers are winning the war in the factories, their daughters are losing it on the streets.' Well over half of all the women arrested for sexual offences in the United States by the end of the war were under twenty-one. FBI statistics show that there had been a seventy per cent increase in teenage prostitutes, and in cities like San Diego, with a large transient service population, the number of girls arrested had increased threefold. According to US Army records, nearly half of the soldiers who contracted VD blamed girls under nineteen years of age.

In a series of reports filed by Agnes Meyer for the *Washington Post* a million American children were estimated to have dropped out of high school to participate in the war effort. In the gypsy-like encampments that had sprung up around the new plane factories in Wichita, Kansas and the unplumbed and overcrowded framehouses for workers from Detroit's massive sixty-seven acre Willow Run bomber factory, she found the disruptive social conditions that bred juvenile delinquency.

> Many of them under crowded living conditions are witnesses of parental immorality . . . In fact, parental behaviour is the cause of much delinquency everywhere. Marital upsets and promiscuity among the workers are increasing. Women who earn money for the first time after a lifetime of being home slaveys acquire a defiant psychology.

From Los Angeles in 1943 came reports of 'Zoot-suit' riots by teenage gangs sporting over-large jackets and pegged pants, and from Washington States the press headlines featured the 'Wolf Packs', hard-drinking urban teenagers who assaulted girls and tore up cinema seats. Former President Herbert Hoover launched into print to remind American mothers who might be failing to provide 'watchful care' over their children that they were losing the battle against immorality on the home front even as their soldiers defeated the Axis powers overseas.

Press and public concern stirred Congress into action and early in 1944, Senator Claude Pepper's Committee on Wartime Health and Education held a five-day hearing into the 'Number One wartime social problem in America.' The hearing concluded that 'absentee parents' and homes upset by the war, along with substandard educational facilities in many of the wartime boom-towns, were to blame. While not disagreeing with the cause, *Time* magazine's comment on the 592-page Pepper Report was that its remedies for the problem were 'a dime a dozen'. Some of the Committee members wanted to set up 'Parent's Courts' to fine and imprison mothers and fathers who could be proved guilty of excessive neglect. Youth centres with chaperoned dances were favoured by many communities. New Jersey passed a law forbidding soldiers from dating girls under sixteen, and New York set up 'Wayward Minors Courts' to deal with the large number of girls arrested not 'properly escorted' after the 10 p.m. curfew in the Times Square area.

The chief of the US Children's Bureau, writing in May 1944, delivered a telling indictment of the lot of the wartime American teenager:

War situations may intensify adolescent unhappiness and insecurity, and lessen the possibilities of satisfaction within normal family and community relationships of the basic need for affection and attention. Earlier feelings of unhappiness and rejection may be intensified by absence of the father from the home; absorption of the mother in gainful employment, voluntary war service, or the difficulties of home-making; deprivation of companionship of elder brothers, sisters and companions . . . Yet the consequences of delinquency press far more heavily upon girls, and intensify their need for social guidance and protection.

The full impact of World War II on adolescent behaviour was not to be fully appreciated until, as parents, they had to deal with their own rebellious and sexually promiscuous adolescents.

14

THE GIRLS THEY MET 'OVER THERE'

The type of woman who approaches you in the street in Italy and says, 'Please give me a cigarette' isn't looking for a smoke.

> GI Handbook, 1943

Lust, bargaining, exploitation, the trading of a *quid pro quo* disguised as a pretence of affection in some transitory relationship – such is sexuality in wartime.

> Willard Waller, 1944

PROSTITUTION AND ARMAMENTS MANUFACTURE share the dubious distinction of being the principal commercial beneficiaries of twentieth-century warfare. In common with the 'merchants of death', the women who pursued 'the lively commerce' discovered that fear generated by war was a potent stimulant to their business. Long lines of soldiers formed outside the French military brothels which catered for the sexual needs of the Allied armies who fought on the Western Front in World War II: according to the dictates of good discipline, officers' whore-houses were indicated by blue lights and other ranks' by red lamps. For those who preferred to risk contracting venereal infection rather than copulate under military supervision, there was always a willing 'mademoiselle' to be found in staging towns like Armentières, where thousands plied the ancient trade that made one of them the subject of the popular war song.

These female 'camp-followers' had always been part of the baggage-train of European armies. In the 1620s, during the Thirty Years' War, it was recorded that one forty thousand-strong army which devastated the Rhineland was accompanied by 'a hundred thousand soldiers' wives, whores, servants, maids, and other camp followers'. The practice spread to the United States during the Civil War, when the regiments of women who followed General Joseph Hooker's Army of the Potomac became known as 'Hooker's girls', coining the popular colloquialism for prostitutes.

Nell Kimball, the celebrated New Orleans 'Madam', ascribed the increased trade that World War I brought her famous whore-house to the epidemic of anxiety that gripped the male population after the United States became a belligerent in the spring of 1917:

> Every man and boy wanted to have one last fling before the real war got him. One shot at it in a real house before he went off and maybe was killed. I've noticed it before, the way the idea of war and dying makes a man raunchy, and wanting to have it as much as he could. It wasn't really pleasure at times, but a kind of nervous breakdown that could only be treated with a girl and a set-to.

The same 'nervous breakdown' in European soldiers brought the 'red-light regiments' out into the streets of Berlin, Paris, and London – leading to the 1917 music hall quip that the American doughboys were 'Over here to make the underworld safe for democracy.' The London whores were considered so numerous by the New Zealand Red Cross that they dispensed six prophylactic kits each to protect the health – if not the morals – of their native sons, whose six shillings-a-day pay made them targets for streetwalkers used to British soldiers who had only their daily sixpence to offer for their pleasure.

Nor was it just the Piccadilly tarts whose avarice was stirred by foreign military uniforms in World War I. A Canadian major was invited by a titled lady to spend the weekend at her country estate. 'You men in the army lead such dangerous lives, and may never return from the next offensive,' announced his hostess over dinner, explaining that her husband had recently been killed in action. 'It is our duty to make your leave enjoyable, so here I am.' It was impossible for the major to resist such an invitation, but he was to be nonplussed when the butler confidentially advised him the next morning, 'Her ladyship has the greatest difficulty maintaining this estate. It would be helpful if you would leave a contribution of a hundred pounds.'

It is a reflection on the social transformation that followed in the wake of World War I that when the Wehrmacht goose-stepped into Paris in June 1940, one of the first acts of the Reich's Military Governor of Paris was to issue a decree making the city's most select brothels in Rue Chabanais and Rue des Moulins 'Lodgings For German Officers In Transit'. What offended the honour of the staff was not the prospect of their conquerors bathing in the copper tub in which Edward VII, as Prince of Wales, had doused the prettiest girls in champagne, but the leaflet which advertised their services and gave the address of the nearest Metro station. For the female staff who were accustomed to receiving only 'carriage trade' clients this was insult enough, but the German leaflet advised all visitors to the two houses to immediately visit the nearest army prophylactic clinic because '99.5% of all venereally infected cases have caught their disease from uncontrolled prostitutes'.

The new military government's proclamation put all but a few of the hundreds of houses of prostitution in France off-limits to

Wehrmacht personnel. To protect German troops from disease, some were taken over and their inmates were medically inspected.

Prostitutes were made synonymous with venereal disease not just by the Germans, but also by the British and United States army commands, who declared war on the women who had been blamed for the million and a half syphilis and gonorrhoea casualties suffered by the Allied armies in World War I. The Wehrmacht applied the lessons learned twenty years earlier when the Kaiser's army strictly regulated the 'sexual logistics' of the troops and thereby cut its VD casualty rate to half that of the French army by 1918. Corpsmen collected the fees at the medically supervised military brothels behind the front lines, imposing a strict ten-minute time-limit per man during the evening 'rush hour' and providing prophylactic treatments as well as keeping a detailed log of the visitor's rank and regiment so that fines could be levied from those who failed to report contracted venereal infections.

In World War I the venereal infection rates of the British army were seven times higher than the Germans, principally because national prudery prevented the British high command from acknowledging that there was any problem at all until 1915, when the Canadian and New Zealand prime ministers forced the chiefs of staff to issue free contraceptives to the troops. The American forces would follow suit, but the controversy over birth control required official statements that the policy was adopted to prevent the spread of disease abroad, rather than to interfere with natural procreation at home. After the war, the British Government's efforts to control the unmentionable 'social diseases' had fallen far short of the Roosevelt administration's 'National Social Hygiene Policy'. So when the Selective Service Act of 1940 drafted millions of young American men into military uniform, Congress was soon being pressed to pass laws to protect the health and morals of its soldiers and sailors from a growing army of female camp followers and the mobsters behind them, who anticipated that the prostitution rackets that sprang up around the new military bases after mobilization would bring a fat profit.

'Blitz the Brothels' became the national war-cry of the 'Eight Point Agreement', the attack on commercialized prostitution in the United States that was launched in 1940 by the armed forces, the US Public Health Service, the Federal Security Agency, and the American Social Health Association, 'For the Control of

Venereal Diseases in Areas Where Armed Forces or National Defence Employees Are Concentrated'. It was given the authority of Federal law by the so-called May Act, which was signed by the President on 11 July 1941 with a call for 'a united effort for total physical fitness'.

The May Act, which restored the provisions of Section 17 of the 1917 Draft Act prohibiting 'prostitution within such reasonable distance of military and/or naval establishments . . . needful to the efficiency, health, and welfare of the army or navy', frightened off many of the would-be brothel racketeers. Its provisions also alarmed some senior American army commanders, who regarded Senator May's political handywork as a potential threat to morale – and many base commanders hesitated to use the powers they had been granted. It was only invoked on two occasions in 1942 before the implicit threat of joint FBI and military action brought about the closure of most overt red-light districts. At the end of the year a survey revealed that commercialized prostitution, while not eliminated, had been dramatically reduced in 526 out of 680 local communities.

Blitzing the brothels might have been successful in checking a possible wartime explosion of organized vice in the United States, but it simultaneously created a new phenomenon, according to Dr John H. Stokes of Philadelphia, who wrote in the American Medical Journal, 'The old-time prostitute in a house or formal prostitute on the street is sinking into second place. The new type is the young girl in her late teens and early twenties . . . who is determined to have one fling or better . . . The carrier and disseminator of venereal disease today is just one of us, so to speak.' The burgeoning of freelance prostitution in the United States was soon providing spicy copy for the press, as lurid reports flooded in from major navy bases and army camps. Cab drivers serving the US Navy's large base on the Virginia Coast were reported to have been threatened with losing their licences for graft they received by ferrying customers to and from illicit whorehouses. Even the staidly moral *Time Magazine* ran a piece on the social problems of the US Navy's principal east-coast port:

> Whereas before Pearl Harbor, the majority of Norfolk's prostitutes were professionals, today probably eighty-five to ninety per cent are amateurs. Many are young girls lured to Norfolk by the promises of big paying jobs. Hundreds of these girls arrive every week. They hang

around bus terminals while phoning for a room somewhere . . . Farm girls and clerks from small towns find it easy to have all the men they want . . . many do not charge for their services.

In San Antonio, Texas, one out of every four 'car-hops' – as the streetwalkers were called – was reportedly infected with VD, causing the 'professional prostitutes' to blame the amateurs: 'they say the young chippies who work for a beer and a sandwich are cramping their style'. In New York State, Canadian girls often crossed the border on evening trips into Plattsburg and tended to leave their infection behind: the local community pleaded for action to seal off the frontier to them. 'We've got the finest beach in the country; the biggest naval air station in the world and the hottest red-light district this side of New Orleans,' was the wartime boast of cab drivers in Pensacola, Florida, whose fares were quoted as, 'A dollar to the beach, half a buck to the Air Station, and a dime to the District!'

At the other side of the country at the nation's notorious 'divorce capital', Reno, the famous old 'Stockade' red-light district was shut at the army's request. However, this sent the prostitutes out on to the streets, as one girl who was then resident in a city college remembered:

When they closed down prostitution, you know what happened. They just spread all over the area. They had guest homes where the divorcees could come and live for their six weeks, and a lot of prostitution was in the guest homes throughout the area. What they accomplished by closing it down was to lose control of it. Some Air Corps guys came into town looking for whores and saw some girls going into our fraternity houses on Greek Row. So two or three of them came to our house and asked one of the girls if they could see the madam. These were freshman girls, and one of them said, 'Oh, you must mean the housemother.' . . . Rather than embarrass the housemother and the boys, one of the seniors said 'Fellas, you've got the wrong house!'

The much-publicized official crackdown on organized prostitution encouraged servicemen to take advantage of the teenage 'Victory girls' who swarmed round military installations chasing men in uniform. By 1943, the army and navy were so concerned about complaints that girls and women were roaming the streets of Miami that a special directive was issued to military police to stop men soliciting these 'women of easy virtue'. But they were soon reporting failure to curb 'soliciting of women in the streets' because 'the females in question often take the initiative in making the acquaintance of a soldier or sailor'. Off-duty servicemen flocked into Miami every night from the large number of navy and army bases at the outskirts of the resort, so the women's search, according to the report, was 'usually crowned with success because of the large number (about fifty thousand) of young and virile soldiers and sailors stationed or visiting that area, a larger number of whom, likewise, appear to be primarily interested when off-duty in seeking the companionship of the opposite sex.'

Colonel Eugene L. Miller and Navy Captain Thomas E. van Metre surveyed the extent of the problem on a Thursday, an average night free of the wilder excesses of Saturday. Cruising around in an unmarked car they visited the bars, dance-halls, and parks and found many 'well dressed, unattached women sitting at bars and tables in saloons and nightclubs' whose obvious intent was 'picking up a soldier or sailor, which they usually succeeded in doing before the saloon or nightclub was closed at midnight'. At the Tatem Hotel, Miami Beach, they stopped at the popular 634 Club and Charlie's, whose burlesque and striptease shows chaplains had accused of immoral excess. Members of the audience were quizzed, 'but no grown person interviewed considered them to be lewd or obscene'.

The Servicemens' Recreation Centre at Pier 42 had closed early, but the Colonel and Captain noted, tactfully, that it was 'well managed but not well patronized'. The Frolic, Bali Night Club, Club 600, Bowery, and The Spur Bar were packed, and in most of the bars it was very noticeable that the female population considerably exceeded the male – and that girls went to the powder room for an excuse to come back and sit with newcomers. At the Bali, the 'petting' that was going on at the tables included many uniformed WAVES, 'one of whom was observed to be "petting" with an Ensign'. The United States uniform was being treated even more disrespectfully at the 'rough and tumble' Spur Bar, which was packed with a crowd of semi-intoxicated sailors – one drunken CPO had already passed out on a bench.

In the early hours of the morning the investigators found that the prophylactic station near the Navy Sub-Chaser school was crowded with sailors who had presumably already found sexual satisfaction. Signs of promiscuous behaviour were evident at every corner: 'many enlisted personnel and their girls, when not in sight of the shore patrol, were observed locked in each other's arms, petting and kissing as they moved down the streets. As they progressed farther from the middle of the town, these couples were observed disappearing into the alleyways, yards, parks, and shrubbery'. Petting went on openly in 'practically all the cars, even though the lights around were bright enough to make the performance easily visible from almost every direction'. But although the survey concluded 'no actual immoral acts were observed', the inescapable impression was 'one of great immorality with no effective means being taken to prevent it. Even in instances where there were no immoral intentions, the fact that the men were up and out in the streets until all hours of the morning would appear to leave them ill-fitted for a strenuous training programme the following day.'

This survey presents a military view of the wartime hedonism that was to be found in the cities or ports of every belligerent country where servicemen sought the pleasures of female companionship, despite official efforts to control overt immorality and prostitution. But in one major American base area, soldiers and sailors enjoyed what amounted to an officially sanctioned 'red-light' district that kept them off the streets and out of the parks. Honolulu, because it served the Pacific Fleet naval base at Pearl Harbor, boasted the liveliest commercial prostitution centre of the war. It escaped the 'Brothel Blitz' until 1944, because Oahu was a military area. Its commanding general and admirals knew the contribution it was making to the morale of thousands of sailors, marines, and soldiers en route to savage battles raging on distant malaria-infested jungle-islands like Guadalcanal, so no attempt was made to take action until the tide of war had been turned against the Japanese.

The Oahu brothels were reputed to be a ten million dollar a year business – and the average fifty thousand prophylactic treatments administered each month during 1942 is indicative of the number of servicemen who went on a last sexual binge in Honolulu, anticipating the months of deprivation they would face in the Pacific campaigns. Unofficial inspections and adequate prophylaxis kept the VD rate down, as did the forced hospitalization of all girls found to be infected. The local communities – unlike those in mainland America – did not want the Hawaii brothels blitzed because they believed that they protected their daughters and wives from the huge transient male service population.

A daily ritual which took place on Waikiki beach until the summer of 1944 was a vivid illustration of how sex had become an intimate partner in the most brutal war in history. A lithe six-foot woman in her mid-twenties, seductively draped in the folds of a diaphanous Hawaiian muu-muu with her immaculate hair crowned by a broad sun-hat, would parade provocatively through the ranks of sunbathing American servicemen. She never failed to stir the men to the rhythmic chant of a marching cadence:

> One . . . Two . . . Three . . . Four
> Mamie's . . . What . . . We're Fighting . . . For.

For many GIs, Mamie Stover's famous walk was living proof of what they were fighting for. She offered them sexual consolation from the mechanical inhumanity of war. Unlike the ubiquitous pin-ups of the Hollywood sex goddesses, this former Hollywood starlet's charms were available to any GI who paid for them. Business acumen, rather than social conscience, motivated the legendary Mamie Stover, the uncrowned Queen of the Pacific. 'I think it's immoral for a woman not to accumulate money during a war,' she explained in a famous aside. 'When men are throwing twenty-dollar bills away like empty beer cans, a woman ought to be busy with a basket.' Thousands of GIs willingly forked out for their never-to-be-forgotten visit to 'Mamie's House' with its specially constructed 'Bull Ring' in the middle of an empty room. This device, which maximized her profits and time, comprised 'four pullman-sized adjacent compartments, each with a red couch – and she moved determinedly from couch to couch while her servants shuttled men in and out.' When she retired from active duty in 1944, with half-a-million dollars, the joke that went round the enlisted men of the Pacific Fleet was that, 'Never had so many men paid so much for so little.'

Mamie's competitors had less to offer, but tried doubling their rates in 1942 when US Army pay was increased – until their customers threatened a boycott to keep the average price down to three dollars a session. But even with less inflationary rates than the legendary Mamie's, many of the 'ladies' made enough to move out of the red-light district and ply their trade from smart houses in uptown Honolulu. Protests from the affronted residents brought a police crackdown – and the first recorded prostitutes' strike.

In August 1942, the staff of the brothels abandoned their couches and took to the streets with a shrill protest against police harassment because they were 'essential to the welfare of US armed forces'. All except three of the downtown bordellos closed their bedrooms. The lines that formed up outside these were so long that by the normal closing hour of three o'clock one afternoon, military police had to be called to control one hundred and eighty five angry and frustrated men who were lined up to visit the five girls still on duty. When the police agreed to end their campaign in September, the girls went back to work and it was 'business as usual' for the next two years. The 'Close Them' order was finally given in 1944 by a commanding general who enlisted the support of the Honolulu Council. That September the red lights went out for the final time as Mamie Stover and her regiment of competitors 'officially' closed their front doors and prophylactic treatments dropped dramatically. To the surprise of the police there was no increase in sexual assaults against civilians by servicemen, because most prostitutes worked clandestinely out of back doors or by walking the streets.

Attempts to shut down or limit the brothel business in the United States or Europe could not check the wartime growth of prostitution and sent its practitioners out on to the streets in larger numbers than ever before. In London, where brothels or 'disorderly houses' had been banned since the middle of the nineteenth century, little could be done about the regiments of streetwalkers and goodtime girls who plied their trade in the nightclubs and dance-halls. Hundreds of London girls responded to the national call to arms by taking men into theirs, and regiments of the so-called Piccadilly Warriors paraded around the hub of the Empire, where the statue of Eros had been taken down and the fountain boarded and sandbagged against Hitler's bombs.

The German occupiers of Paris failed to carry out their far-reaching plan to clean up and regulate the city's prostitutes. 'The disgrace of Paris these days is the cafés around the Place de la Republique, where bevies of girls from stores and offices meet German soldiers,' complained a patriotic French journalist. He blamed the situation on the Germans for failing to release the one and a third million French men captured as prisoners of war.

Keeping a quarter of the most sexually active section of the nation away from their womenfolk was obviously a Nazi ploy to drive French women into the arms of their conquerors – and hunger for love was not their only deprivation, he insisted: 'Since these girls have starving families at home, they give themselves for food.'

Yet credit for having 'basically reorganized sex life in France' was claimed in a 1941 article by a Nazi party official, who boasted, 'In France our soldiers have had the greatest success with the female population. They were, of course, not always the racially most valuable girls who approached our soldiers.' While sexual deprivation certainly encouraged some French women to 'fraternize' intimately with their conquerors, the vaunted German reorganization of France's traditional three-tier brothel system was more difficult to achieve than the Nazi theorists pretended. They succeeded in shutting down the so-called 'Houses of Appointments' where wealthy clients chose from 'photo-albums' of girls who were not full-time prostitutes but women 'moonlighting' their bodies for steep fees. Attempts to close the lowest class of slum brothels failed because they were so numerous. But the middle-tier 'bourgeois' brothels, called 'Closed Houses', which had been made famous by Guy de Maupassant's stories and whose inmates had been painted by Toulouse Lautrec, were allowed to remain in business, subject to policing and registration.

The German decision to leave much of Europe's most sophisticated brothel system intact may have made collaborators of some *sous maîtresses*, but it also provided many patriotic prostitutes with the chance to serve the Allied cause with the aid of the French underground resistance movement. The *sous maîtresses* manageresses of the 'Closed Houses' were invariably ex-prostitutes whose motherly solicitude for their girls was combined with business acumen and the toughness of a man. From long experience of the male they acquired a canny sixth sense which enabled them to spot members of the Gestapo or Vichy provocateurs from the desk where they dealt with clients.

Each girl's bedroom, which they always locked behind them and their temporary lover, was regarded as sacrosanct by the police, who subscribed to the view of the Gallic male that 'to interrupt a man in the course of his amours may do him psychological damage'. Since the 'Closed Houses', as their name implied, were close-shuttered to deny prying eyes, they were ideal hiding places for fugitive Allied airmen and with their secret exits and passages through to adjacent buildings they were well equipped for a fast escape in the event of a raid.

Since the Germans required that the prostitutes be registered with the local gendarmerie, any Gestapo requests for the papers of a particular girl or 'Closed House', which might indicate they were suspicious, could be passed on to the resistance by sympathizers on the police grape-vine. Scores of Allied flyers who came down over France or other occupied countries made their way through brothels on the escape pipeline to the Spanish border. Many owed their liberty to patriotic prostitutes who put their lives at risk. The risks were well appreciated by courageous women like Roxanne Pitt, who helped run one of the successful escape routes and who recalled that not every flyer could feign sexual intercourse when the Gestapo was expected to call:

> One day I escorted to a brothel in Montmartre a shy young English pilot who looked such an innocent Mummy's Darling that it seemed immoral to leave him there. As I heard later, he was so bashful that when *La Sous Maîtresse* showed him into the salon he caused some innocent merriment among the vistors. One of them must have retailed a description of his behaviour as a good story, for it came to the ears of the Gestapo, a member of which visited the brothel a few days later posing as a Frenchman. The manageress saw through him at once but concealed the fact. It seemed likely that a Gestapo raid was imminent. In such cases the usual procedure was to pair off the refugee with one of the girls, but this young man had been brought up so strictly that he seemed incapable of playing his part; and so he was dressed up as a prostitute instead.

Brothel girls in the French ports of Lorient, Brest, and La Pallice, from where the submarine wolf-packs sailed to ravage the Atlantic convoys, were also suspected of spying for the Allies and passing on the names of U-boats about to put to sea. Some commanders quarantined their crews for three weeks before a patrol to protect their health and prevent the disclosure of their missions, since their men always went on spree before sailing. To avoid the disease and security hazard posed by the seaport brothels, the Todt Organization built 'rest-camps' as well as the mighty concrete pens for the U-boats. Equipped with beer and dance halls, the camps were staffed with plenty of imported German females, who with the German Red Cross nurses could be persuaded to share the comfortable hotel-like accommodation provided for the crewmen.

The occupation of France made the Wehrmacht aware of the degree to which soldiers and sailors away from the homeland developed a passion for the pursuit of the native female population. This was a phenomenon long familiar to British military commanders from policing an overseas empire that reached across the globe. The wartime report of an English army physician had observed that there was a 'well-known relationship between the distance from home and VD incidence', with length of individual service abroad the chief factor.

> Among other ranks, with their more limited resources for sublimation through social and intellectual interests, the effect of long continued service overseas is seen in the increase in the venereal disease rate and, perhaps, in the type of commerce from which infection results. The sense of guilt lessens and the proportion of cases of the more sordid form of prostitution seems to increase.

The same memorandum advised that army VD rates could be cut by a third if home leave could be arranged every third year of overseas service. Such measures were clearly out of the question in wartime – and by shouldering the 'white man's burden' the British solider on long spells of overseas garrison duty had become accustomed to patronizing the 'more sordid forms of prostitution' offered by the more exotic cities from Cairo to Calcutta. Although native red-light districts were officially condemned by the military authorities with 'Out of Bounds' notices, resort to them was condoned even though the risk of disease was high.

Three generations of British soldiers fathered large numbers of Eurasian offspring all over the Indian subcontinent. Many half-caste Anglo–Indian girls had to turn to prostitution for survival, and they became much sought after in Bombay and Calcutta during World War II when these cities became the main disembarkation ports for the influx of Allied troops on their way to the distant battle-fronts in Burma and China. In advance of the arrival of the first GIs, the American Consul in Bombay reported to Washington that native brothels were certainly cheap – the usual fee was 5 rupees ($1.50 or around 5 shillings at the prevailing exchange rates) and the customers increased by four to five times at weekends, with 'call time' limited to ten minutes. Working long hours and entertaining up to ten men a night was not unusual because British military doctors charged a steep 150 rupees ($45) for the girl's regular medical examinations and prophylactic treatments.

The principal Bombay brothel district was nominally out of bounds to British military personnel, but in accordance with the principles of good order and discipline, the better houses in Grand Road were regarded by some British officers – and not always the junior ones – 'as a sort of club'. It was in one of these that a *Newsweek* reporter found 'Molly'. She wore a thin crêpe de Chine evening dress to work and was typical of the women who staffed the low-rise houses in Bombay's red-light district in World War II. 'Darkly slim', her dusky features, flashing eyes, and pearly teeth caught the attention of the American reporter, who was intrigued to discover that she wore 'a delicate necklace with a gold pendant emblem of Queen Victoria' in recognition of her Anglo-Indian heritage. 'Molly' was a 20-rupee girl in the prostitute house run by a 'Madame Marcel', a thirty-eight-year-old Detroit woman who claimed she had been 'on the game' ever since her husband deserted her. She boasted 'how she had educated two daughters at a distance in New York, putting one in hospital as a nurse and the other in a bank' on the earnings of her 'family' of seven Indian girls.

Practical considerations made it impossible even to begin policing the teeming slums of Calcutta with their estimated forty thousand prostitutes. In a city which could claim to be the vice capital of the world, *Newsweek* reported that by 1944, wartime inflation had upped the rate in even the squalid houses. American GIs and British troops in search of recreation but not rest faced a steep 10 rupees ($3 or fifteen shillings) for a brothel girl. This put Calcutta rates on a par with what streetwalkers charged in many provincial cities in the United States. In Karaya Road, one of the better streets of Calcutta's notorious brothel district, girls cost 30 rupees ($9 or £2 5s) and business was brisk for the rickshaws, taxis, and horse-drawn gharries drawn up outside the stucco houses with fake pillars and ornate grills.

The queen of the Karaya Road is a girl men begin to hear about when they reach Cairo or Karachi or on ships crossing the Indian Ocean.

Her name is Margot. She is fair, although not blonde, wears her hair brushed hastily back, shoulder length. Unexpectedly fresh-looking, with clear grey-green eyes, a profile that looks as though it is always held against a strong breeze on a grassy hilltop, and a figure that can be described as voluptuous. She wears a blue halter, a flowing skirt of figured silk, and sandals on her bare feet. All in all, I think Margot has been to a lot of movies . . . Margot's fee is 85 rupees for the shortest possible visits and at this rate – with her parlour always full of patient men of rank and determination – she is reputed to make somewhere in the neighbourhood of $1500–2000 a week. Nobody seems to know exactly where she comes from. I heard her nationality given as English, Anglo–Indian, Anglo–Burmese and French . . . There is nothing else remotely like Margot in Calcutta. There are only some thirty-odd of the plush-seat houses on the Karaya Road, with fewer than a hundred prostitutes at rates up to 50 rupees – and beyond that are Calcutta's miserable forty thousand slaves.

Clandestine streetwalking prostitutes known as 'tonga-wallahs' were common, particularly in the towns of northern Assam, near the forward Allied staging airfields for the China and Burma operations. Here 'tea-pickers' and female coolie-labourers became 'duck-soup' for black American troops. For the American aircrew who flew the dangerous Hump route into China, Indian women were preferable to the prostitutes of Chiang Kai-shek's wartime Chunking capital because army medical reports indicated that the latter were a hundred per cent disease-ridden.

For sheer variety of sexual diversions, few red-light districts in the world could match Cairo during World War II. The 'pleasures' offered by the celebrated Cairene tarts reached something of a peak of sexual exoticism in the frenzied year before the Battle of El Alamein when British and Australian troops poured in on their way to halt Rommel's advance across the western desert. 'GIVE US THE TOOLS AND WE WILL FINISH THE JOB' was the cheeky sign one Cairo brothel-keeper hung out after Churchill's famous 1942 appeal to the United States. In the back alleys of the ancient city of the pyramids there was no shortage of servicemen – or whores – who obliged. The incidence of murders and rapes, however, prompted the British military police to embark upon one of their periodic efforts to put the worst districts of the city out of bounds. But policing the squalid streets, even in the name of King Farouk, proved impractical. The legend of wild sexual practices, including squalid whore-houses which offered the spectacle of women copulating with a variety of animals – among them a donkey, according to a former member of the Black Watch Regiment – continued to lure the hard-bitten soldier and curious journalist. A British war correspondent, however, recalled that not all the sights in the notorious Wagh El Birkhet were so depraved: 'the only significant thing in a boring, rather nauseating hour – a fellah bowing in prayer to Mecca on the roof of a brothel, through the lit windows of which we could see Baudelaire's "affreuse juive".'

While Rommel's Afrika Korps was still advancing on Cairo, one prudent Cairo madam evacuated her girls to what she hoped would be the safety of Alexandria. She was doomed to disappointment: a lost Italian pilot dropped a single bomb and demolished her house of ill-repute. The incident also faced the British Army authorities with a dilemma after Cairo GHQ was told that the corpses of six British officers had been dug out of the rubble. It was decided to spare their next-of-kin painful embarrassment by camouflaging the true circumstances of their deaths. Accordingly the three officers who had been upstairs 'on the job' were posted as 'killed in action', and the three waiting downstairs for their turn were listed as 'killed on active duty'.

Italian as well as British troops appear to have found that desert fighting heightened the sexual urge. Mussolini, who was a self-proclaimed sexual adventurer, saw to it that his army in Cyrenaica was provided with mobile brothels for the forward troops and whorehouses in the rear areas. After Tobruk's surrender in 1941, the garrison brothel presented a British colonel with a difficult dilemma when, according to the war correspondent who acted as translator, the *sous maîtresse* offered to put her girls 'at the disposition of the British army':

Thousands of prisoners had been rounded up. Now ten more were taken – the ten tarts of Tobruk. They stood in line in front of the whitewashed, two-storied building which was both their home and red-light house. A woman of fifty, grey-haired, hard-faced, tawdry in attire, played the role of a very nervous CO to the girls. A motley assortment, none of them was physically attractive. Their faces were hastily daubed with paint and powder, and the best one could say of them was that they looked the part – blowsy, all of them. One, an ersatz blonde, might have been in her early twenties; a couple of others, brunettes, would have been passable had they been properly turned out. As for the others: they were human nonentities - - and very frightened.

I translated. The colonel frisked his moustache with the back of his hand.

'Tell them,' he said in anger, 'tell them to take ten paces to the rear – immediately!'

'And tell them this,' added the colonel, 'tell them they stink!'

This I managed to break down, in translation, to a milder term which conveyed to the undermistress and the girls that their offer had been rejected. Before I left we found their books, or score sheets. They had all been very industrious. One girl named Antoinette had a pretty regular batting average of fifty *per diem*, which had been topped by only a few of the others on very rare occasions. Antoinette, the undermistress told me, was the young blonde.

The landings at Casablanca, Algiers, and Oran in November 1942 confronted the American military authorities and servicemen for the first time with North African brothels and the battalions of native prostitutes whose endemic social diseases threatened to deplete front-line fighting strength. Unable to 'blitz-the-brothels' overseas, the Congress-ordained American military policy of suppressing prostitution was forced into uncomfortable compromises. Field commanders adopted a pragmatic 'off-limits' strategy which designated supervised brothels for the use of their officers and men while their headquarters and the War Department denied such a policy existed. The army corps of chaplains knew only too well that it did. Many were padres trapped in an ethical dilemma who chose to turn a blind eye rather than make themselves unpopular with their commanders and men. Those who were more concerned for morals than morale risked confrontations by penning protest letters to the Chaplain General in Washington while preaching sentimental homilies to remind GIs of their responsibilities to the women they had left behind. 'Do you see that sunset?' was a favourite theme of one chaplain. 'Over westward beyond that sunset lies America, and in my home town in one of its cottages lives the girl I love. I'm keeping myself clean for her!'

Vermont or prairie sunsets were naturally forgotten by most of the American troops who came ashore in Casablanca eager to sample the delights awaiting them in the Medina quarter, where glass-topped walls surrounded an estimated twelve thousand prostitutes. General Eisenhower ordered armed guards to enforce strictly the 'Off-limits' notices pasted on Medina's walls. On 10 December the military police were removed and GIs stormed through the single gate for three days of hedonistic exploration which came to an end when 'disturbances' were given as the official reason for the re-imposition of the ban, which had been called for by the chaplains and the medical corps. In Algiers the Casbah was also put 'off-limits', although four large brothels outside were taken over by the army. The largest was the Sphinx, which observed a strict shift system – enlisted men and civilians during the day-time, with evening hours for officers.

Monseignor Arnold, Chaplain General of the US Army, was bombarded with letters from padres in North Africa charging that 'a number of houses of prostitution formerly operated by the French, have been taken over by military authorities of the Army of the US and are now operated and managed by military personnel.' Prophylaxis stations had been set up adjacent to and in some cases inside the brothels, which one Catholic chaplain claimed, with some justification, were 'operating under the VERBAL but not written orders of my commanding officer'. In Oran it was the army doctors who demanded that the military brothel there be shut after they were threatened with a VD epidemic because French physicians were discovered to have issued false health reports for the prostitutes 'unofficially' working for the US Army. Mounting protests and the forthcoming invasion of Sicily were instrumental in General Eisenhower's decision to order the shutdown of the unofficial whorehouses in July 1943, when a strict off-limits policy was re-imposed in the theatre.

Neither closing the army brothels nor 'Off-Limits' notices could stop American GIs making out with the 'girls they met over there'. A survey of GIs' sexual habits in Italy, taken two years later, concluded, 'Army life overseas wrecks these old emotional ties when it takes a man away from his wife and sweetheart, and leaves him a set of memories and occasional letters. In its place, he has new dangers and lots of frustration and uncertainties . . . There is a new set of accepted "rights" and "wrongs" in this overseas situation.'

The Italian campaign more than any other in World War II confronted the British and American military commanders with their impotence when it came to coping with endemic prostitution. A foretaste of the problem was given by British medical officers in Sicily, who were treating forty thousand VD cases a month, twenty times more than the number treated in England. As one report advised, 'prostitution is almost universal among all but the highest class of Sicilian women.' Government-regulated brothels also existed in all of the large towns. Control had broken down, although General Patton wasted no time trying to restore it by putting US Army medical teams into Palermo's six large houses of prostitution. This did not endear him to General Montgomery, his arch rival, whose pride as well as his puritanism was offended when it was announced that the brothels were open for business again – under US Army management.

The invasion of Italy proper magnified the scale of the problem. But it was the capture of Naples in October 1943 that pitched the American and British commands into a two-year battle with an army of prostitutes – a battle Allied chaplains and doctors of both armies would later concede they lost.

Naples became the main staging port for the gruelling Italian campaign as well as the principal rest and recreation centre for thousands of Allied troops. Wine and girls were as plentiful as food was scarce for its inhabitants, who were packed into what one British officer called 'human rookeries'. K-rations became the passport to the passion GIs discovered Latin women could bring to the most transient of casual sexual encounters. 'Even when they aren't in love the Italians ape the mannerisms of the lover. Thus they can be joyous at eighty. Italian love is both articulate and silent. The lovers quickly knock down any barrier between them.'

In Naples, as one official American report put it, 'Women of all classes turned to prostitution as a means of support for themselves and their families.' A British officer recorded his surprise that Prince A. and his twenty-four-year-old sister came down from their palace to his office. 'The purpose of the visit was to inquire if we could arrange for his sister to enter an army brothel. We explained that there was no such institution in the British Army. "A pity," the Prince said. Both of them spoke excellent English, learned from an English governess. "Ah well, Luisa, I suppose if it can't be helped, it can't be." They thanked us with polite calm, and departed.'

There was an estimated female population in Naples of over a hundred and fifty thousand, many of whom became freelance whores, compounding the problems caused by the estimated fifty thousand regular prostitutes in the 'undetermined number of brothels which had previously been regulated by the civilian government and used by the German and Italian Armies.' A month after Naples had been liberated, the US 5th Army headquarters quarantined a large bordello outside the city and placed the other brothels off-limits to American troops. But the strategy that had failed in North Africa was even less able to withstand the assault of the regiments of hungry Italian women. Prostitutes refused to work in army brothels for 20–50 lira (50 cents or 2s 6d) per man when they could command fantastic prices of $10, $15, or even $20 (£5) outside. Uncontrolled prostitution sent VD rates rocketing to over a hundred per thousand men by the end of the year, and almost every infected GI gave Naples as the source of infection.

The British Army, which had no clear strategy other than the ineffective one of placing sections of Naples out of bounds, reacted to the soaring VD rate by blaming it on the Germans. A circular that arrived in all units by Christmas warned:

> From reports that have been received it is apparent that prostitution in occupied Italy, and Naples in particular, has reached a pitch greater than has ever been witnessed in Italy before. So much is this so that it has led to a suggestion that the encouragement of prostitution is part of a formulated plan arranged by the pro-Axis elements, primarily to spread venereal disease among Allied troops.

British military intelligence might have believed in a sinister Nazi plot, but a US Army doctor discerned that the dramatic rise in venereal disease was not a product of the German's corruption of Italian womanhood. 'It was not lust, but necessity, not depravity of the soul but the urge of the instinct to survive which led numerous women into the ranks of the amateur prostitute on whom regulatory legislation had little or no effect.'

The magnitude of the sexual problems that confronted the Allies in Italy was put into sharp focus when US Army medical officers conceded victory in the battle against venereal disease in Naples to the prostitutes: 'Women of all classes turned to prostitution as a means of support for themselves and their families. Small boys, little girls, and old men solicited on every street for their sisters, mother and daughters and escorted prospective customers to their homes.' When the casualties of sexual infection exceeded those from the battle front, special 'Casanova Camp' treatment centres were set up, surrounded by barbed wire to keep the men in – and the Italian women out.

The indignity of being processed through one of these American VD treatment centres was vividly described by army veteran John H. Burns. The infected GI, he reported, had to put on special fatigues:

> On the back of the jacket and on the trouser leg were painted these large and smeary letters: V D. . . . Finally it came his turn at the end of the file to enter the dispensary. Inside the screen door the line forked into two prongs and was being funnelled past two GIs, each with a hypodermic in his hand. Along the walls of the room were electric iceboxes. And many little glass ampoules of an amber liquid. Ahead of him were men with either arm bared or with their buttocks offered like steak to the needle. 'They give ya a choice on where ya want ya shot,' the blond boy said. 'If ya take it in the ass, they'll use a longer needle ta get through the fat. My advice is ta take ya shots round the clock. Then none of ya four parts gets too sore. Ya'll be hurtin anyhow.' Then . . . he felt already the stinging in his other shoulder. All his life telescoped down to three-hour periods and a hypodermic needle and yellow drops dribbling out of it. What was it called. Pncilin? Penissiclin? Pencillin?

Nor was it solely the economic facts of life in war-shattered Italy that brought together Allied soldiers and Italian girls, as Burns explained:

> To us GIs the girls of southern Italy fell into two tight classes only. That's where we got stymied. There were the girls of via Roma, whom the Neapolitans, mincing no words, called *puttane*. These girls asked fixed prices either in lira or PX rations. They satisfied us for a while as long as we had the money, but their fee was steep for a GI unless he was a big operator in the black market. And then too something in a man's vanity craves something other than a girl who's shacking-up with Tom, Dick, and Harry. American men are so sentimental that they refuse to have a whore for their girl – if they can help it. That's the schizophrenia of our civilization with its sharp distinction between the Good Girl and the Bad Girl. Consequently after a few tries, with the fear of VD always suspended over our heads, we began to look at the good women of Naples. And here entered the problem of the GI Italian Bride. I remember that Italian girls began to look sweet to us early . . . perhaps because their virginity was put on such a pedestal.

Italian women of every sort proved irresistible to Allied soldiers. 'When ya walk down the via Roma,' as one corporal observed, 'ya can tell by their eyes whether they will or won't. They make no bones about it over here . . . Christ what eyes they give ya!'

The number of tents that made up the 'Casanova Camps' that were established near the Fifth Army Rest Centre outside Naples were visible evidence of the victories scored by the city's prostitutes. So too were the thousands of pathetic mothers who crowded British and American military headquarters trying to claim paternity support. One British officer recorded how one woman came in and admitted having two lovers, one a GI and the other a Tommy. Who was going to pay her damages? The Cockney sergeant sitting next to the translator said solemnly, 'Tell her to wait until the child is born. If he says, "Thank you Mummy" when she feeds him, then he is British, but if he says "Thanks a lot Mom," he's American.'

British and American officers had the pick of the better class of Italian women who were willing to express their gratitude for their liberation by shacking-up with the officers in their comfortable billets. This made the lower ranks bitter, and one private complained:

> There are plenty of prostitutes hanging around where I work to satisfy me. Our organization has fought an officers' war for twenty-eight months. They [officers] have a fine club, whiskey, dances with civilians and US women from Rome, with nurses, with native girls. We've had nothing. I don't blame the officers as a whole. Only the organization leaders. We've had no wholesome contact with women since we've been overseas. All our relations with women we have to sneak. Naturally we aren't thrown into contact with the better females. The only women I've talked to for two years have been whores. Occasionally we see a Red Cross girl, but that doesn't ease the longing for female companionship. With a better chance at mild flirtations, a little necking possibly, I think the disease rate would fall. So far, if we want female companionship we have to resort to prostitutes. And it's rough to hear a good orchestra, laughter from the officers' club. They seem to think we can remain celibates while they bask in feminine company.

The root cause of the medical defeat that the Allied military command suffered during the Italian campaign was pin-pointed by one of the army psychologists who conducted the US Army's

wide-ranging 1945 survey into the sexual habits and attitudes of
GIs:

> Should a soldier merely want female companionship this may be easily
> had if companionship means merely being with a woman. Many write
> that they just want to dance and talk to, or be with a woman, or
> a change from the eternal male society of the Army. Here again, he is
> almost completely frustrated for a variety of reasons. British or Amer-
> ican Army girls are so few in number that he cannot hope to win one
> of them as a companion, if only for one night a week. Also, it may
> become an entangling alliance if he is one of the thirty per cent who
> are married, or of the twenty per cent who have 'loyal' sweethearts
> waiting at home. If he turns to an Italian girl for companionship, he
> generally finds himself unable to talk to her beyond a few simple
> expressions. If he maintains the companionate non-intercourse ap-
> proach to the relationship, he is almost surely a frustrated man, and
> if he is tempted to shift the relationship to a sexual one, he probably
> finds less resistance than he was accustomed to in his pre-Army
> experience. None of this is written in terms of 'guilt' or 'propriety';
> those seem to be the *facts* of the situation.

15

OVERSEXED, OVERPAID, AND OVER HERE!

Americans were 'cheeky' compared to our usual
'Mr Frigidaire Englishman', but what a boost
to the ego when one is greeted with, 'Hello
Duchess' (and you were treated like one!), or
'Hi Beautiful!' That was so GOOD! As we got to
know these boys, how generous they were; we
never lacked for chocolate or cigarettes and even
precious luxuries like nylons they could get for
us. Most of my friends had one particular GI Joe
– and so did I.

British girl

THE 'FRIENDLY INVASION' of Britain by over a million and a half GIs before D-Day faced neither the language problems nor the army of prostitutes encountered in Italy. Instead the American command had to overcome traditional reserve and downright prudery. 'The British consider sex behaviour as entirely a personal matter not subject to legislation and regulation,' reported the US Army's chief of preventative medicine. 'Public opinion frowns on brothels and so very few are known to exist, and outside London there is very little commercialized prostitution.' The average GI nonetheless found very little difficulty in satisfying the soldiers' perennial hunger for female companionship. Some American volunteers with the RAF's so-called Eagle Squadrons had fought in the Battle of Britain eighteen months before the GI invasion proper began on 26 January 1942, when Pfc Milburn H. Henke of Hutchinson, Minnesota, stepped ashore on Dufferin Quay. The local Belfast girls were waiting for the new arrivals with open arms. The welcome was to be repeated over the next two years as a tidal wave of GIs landed to discover that while the climate might be damp and the santitation primitive – 'honey buckets', as the GIs dubbed them, were still in use in some British Army camps – the native female population was not only friendly, but willing.

To British women the arrival of the Americans was a bright flash of excitement after nearly three years of blackouts and blitz. It seemed to many that these strapping, well-fed, and confident young men had stepped straight out of a Hollywood film. 'Suddenly the GIs were there,' recalled a Derby woman. 'If they'd dropped from Mars we couldn't have been more surprised.' A shy Preston girl remembered blushing when a smiling GI told her, 'Gee, you've got lovely eyes,' as his partner called out, 'She's just like a baby Betty Grable!' Another teenager from Birmingham, who described herself as 'fancy free at the time', was more explicit about the instant sexual attraction that drew British women into the arms of American soldiers:

> We were half starved and drably clothed, but the GIs said we looked good anyway. A lot was said about them being oversexed, overpaid

Love, Sex and War

and over here; maybe it applied to a few, but it was mainly a myth which was put over by Lord Haw Haw in his Nazi propaganda broadcasts from Germany to upset British soldiers overseas and try to split the Allies. That's my story anyway – and I'm sticking to it! It was just the case that the British women and the American GIs were in the same place at the same time – it was rather pleasant, really!

Many British wives and sweethearts had been deprived of their own husbands and boyfriends for so long that it was difficult to resist the affectionate enthusiasm of so many good-looking males. The GIs were outgoing to the point of freshness and generous to a fault, particularly with children, to whom they became instant heroes dispensing sweets and comics. It was not only the association of all Americans with films which endowed the GI with a special appeal, but also the finer cloth and more flattering cut of their uniforms, which set them apart from British, Canadian, and Polish troops. This difference in physical appearance, combined with their relaxed self-assurance, accounted for their glamorous attraction for most British women.

The reputation of the 'Yanks' was encouraged by wild press reports and letters from reactionary matrons like the one who expressed outrage that 'girls of thirteen and fourteen have attached themselves to coloured soldiers and others and been able to see films that only have the effect of arousing in them instincts that ought to be unknown to them for many years.'

It was not just the physical exuberance of the smartly turned-out American servicemen that provoked suspicion and hostility in the native male population. It was also a question of hard cash. British soldiers found themselves at a huge financial disadvantage when it came to competing to entertain their own womenfolk. Even a lowly American private with his $3000 (£750) average annual pay-cheque was a big spender by comparison with less than £100 pounds a year received by his British counterpart. With fifty per cent extra pay for flying duty and twenty per cent extra for overseas and sea duty, nine out of ten US servicemen were above the $50 a month earnings averaged in civilian life. Many who were single had never had as much money in their lives – and the only thing to spend it on was entertaining British girls! They were also prodigal with gifts of luxury foods passed on from their military supplies.

Even the way the Americans spoke marked them out as different, often provoking giggles from English girls when they used slang expressions such as 'bum' for a layabout and 'rubbers' for contraceptive sheaths. Many of the coarse expressions that were common parlance among American soldiers, 'Holy Cow!', 'Jeeze!' and 'Goddam!' upset the girls who operated the telephone exchanges, who complained about the 'bad language' used by GIs. British teenagers, however, relished the new oaths which so upset their parents' sensibilities. A boy recalled the adolescent enthusiasm with which he and his friends bandied about their favourite GI expletives: 'And I ain't a-shitting boy!' or 'You ain't a-tooting, boy!'

The British military authorities soon found it necessary to prepare a pamphlet for the female staff of the NAAFI military canteens advising them that the language and apparent freshness of the GIs should not always be taken at face value:

> The first time that an American soldier approaches the counter and says 'Hiya Baby!' you will probably think he is being impudent. By the time several dozen men have said it, you may have come to the conclusion that all Americans are 'fresh'. Yet to them it will be merely the normal conversational opening, just as you might say 'Lovely day, isn't it?' Remember that most Americans think that English people are 'standoffish'. If you snub them you will merely confirm this impression.

Eisenhower's headquarters had also prepared a handbook that advised American soldiers of the more staid British customs and habits. At the same time the US Provost Marshal had issued a leaflet, 'How to Stay out of Trouble', which contained stern warnings about the 'females of questionable character' who were eagerly awaiting them to get Yankee dollars. These were the very women that many GIs, of course, were hoping to encounter – and they were not to be disappointed. 'Their main aim in life,' recalled a British wartime taxi driver, quoting the American vernacular, 'seemed to be to get something to drink and 'a cute piece of "ass"'.

Too young to be called up himself, John Lazenby spent the year before D-Day driving carloads of off-duty GIs through picturesque Cotswold villages in pursuit of drink and girls. He learned all about the 'camp-followers secreted in cottage attics' and 'illicit trysts with local ladies'. Their sexual banter and adventures with women resulted in his 'rapid education in varied directions', like his 'dreadfully innocent consternation hearing a bunch of them yelling, "Just you look at Red's broad's tits – like two goddam milk bottles!"' when he picked them up one evening in the spring of 1944 'from a garden in front of the Old New Inn at Bourton-on-the-Water'. After listening to 'a lurid description of what he, the last of several, had done to the "lady", one said to me, "We'll hang on, Jimmy, while you have a go." Oh, boy! I gave rapid excuses and made a very quick exit.'

American servicemen deserved their reputation of being 'wolves in wolves' clothing' and were not always successful when it came to making passes. One ATS corporal recalled the evening she and two companions were trudging in pouring rain back to their barracks along a lonely road:

> Along came a jeep with four Yanks in it. They stopped and offered us a ride. Although there were three of us, we just didn't trust them and turned the offer down. When I tell you that we had to walk the whole five miles back to camp, and preferred this to the lift, you will appreciate just how strongly we felt. I knew quite a few civvy girls who were loved and left – literally holding the baby.

The refusal of many predatory American soldiers to take 'No!' for an answer from a pretty girl led to frequent complaints of sexual molestation. According to Mrs Anne F., the mothers on a Birmingham housing estate near a US Army base protested that they had to use physical force to fend off the GIs. She soon developed her own technique of repulsing unwanted advances:

> Almost every evening I, among others, would hear a knock on the front door and on opening it would find a GI who stated that a Greg So-and-So had sent him. When one flatly denied knowing his friend, he would calmly say, 'Come on, baby. I know your husband is away in the forces.' One would have to slam the door in their faces to keep them out. I remember one afternoon and evening the local camp was invaded by teenage girls and women from miles around. There were hundreds of them looking for Yanks. Next day the woods behind our estate were put 'out of bounds' to the GIs. But the things we found in our front gardens were unbelievable! Some of the women had a 'good time' with Americans, others just did their washing for them, while others completely ignored them. The pubs made a packet out of them and the kids went a bundle on them as they were very generous with chocolate and sweets.

For all their generosity, the GIs soon acquired a reputation for resorting to a frontal assault when it came to getting the 'cute piece of ass' they were always chasing. It was not unusual for 'Snowdrops', as the US military police were known from their distinctive white helmets, to be summoned to lift a siege at rural hostels which housed Land Girls. In London the first assault was more likely to be made by the freelance prostitutes known as 'Piccadilly Warriors'. These most brazen of wartime British 'tarts' swarmed around the entrance to the Rainbow Club that was opened for Americans in 1942 in the old Del Monico's on the corner of Shaftesbury Avenue. The sign over the reception desk indicated 'New York – 3271 miles', but the club promised a taste of home with its canteens, juke boxes, and pool-tables. 'Rainbow Corner' became a magnet not only for homesick GIs in the London blackout, but also for the regiments of streetwalkers whose opening gambit, 'Hello Yank, looking for a good time?' became a much parodied wartime joke.

Piccadilly *was* wartime London for American servicemen. Former Staff Sergeant Robert Arib recalled the standing joke in the Rainbow Club that it was 'suicide' for a GI to go out into the blacked-out streets without his buddy:

> The girls were there – everywhere. They walked along Shaftesbury Avenue and past Rainbow Corner, pausing only when there was no policeman watching. Down at the Lyons Corner House on Coventry Street they came up to soldiers waiting in doorways and whispered the age-old questions. At the underground entrance they were thickest, and as the evening grew dark, they shone torches on their ankles as they walked and bumped into the soldiers murmuring, 'Hello Yank', 'Hello Soldier', 'Hello Dearie!' Around the dark estuaries of the Circus the more elegantly clad of them would stand quietly and wait – expensive and aloof. No privates or corporals for these haughty demoiselles. They had furs and silks to pay for.

Betty Knox, a former dance-hall singer turned breezy columnist for *The Evening Standard*, related a story that was supposedly typical of the GIs' attitude to London:

> One night, as Ambassador John G. Winant left the American Embassy, he met two soldiers. Could he do anything for them, Winant inquired? 'Are there any dames in this joint?' one soldier asked. 'This is the American Embassy, and I am the Ambassador,' Winant replied. 'Say,

those Limeys must have been pulling our legs,' the soldier stammered, backing off into the blackout.

The American servicemen also discovered from the street-walkers that 'The English had a curious custom of fucking on foot, fully clothed.' It became a trademark of the Piccadilly Warriors to call 'Hey Yank, quick Marble Arch style!' But there were also many girls who were not prostitutes who believed that you couldn't get pregnant standing up, and 'wall jobs' soon became part of every GI's wartime vocabulary. One Jewish chaplain, puzzled to see so many of his men wearing their greatcoats in Birmingham on a June evening, was shocked to discover that they were wrapped around girls during alfresco couplings in parks and dark side-streets. 'There is absolutely no end to the vulgar business of soldiers making love – or should I say lust – in public places; many cases are reported of the immoral act of intercourse going on in view of the public,' complained Chaplain Frith in 1944 to his superiors in Washington. 'During morality lectures, the soldiers confessed to me, in a general way, that the reason they had thrown away all propriety was that they were away from home, where no-one knew them, and no-one seemed to interfere to prohibit their freedom of action.' The blackout, it appears, made the British policeman even more of a 'friendly bobby' who could be relied on to turn a blind eye to couples making-out in the dark sanctuary of a convenient telephone box or doorway – and US military police were more concerned with rowdy drunken GIs than with breaking up the trysting couples.

American soldiers were often surprised at the apparent lack of jealousy displayed by English males even when they flirted openly with their womenfolk. Mrs Marguerite G., who confessed that she was a 'grass widow and a pretty young miss', enjoyed 'parties galore' at the American bases. 'My husband came home occasionally, and he was always welcomed, I'm sure he regarded himself more or less as "just one of the boys".' According to some women other husbands serving overseas openly encouraged their wives not to be lonely. Margaret G. cited the example of her friend: 'One day I caught her crying and she let me read the letter from her husband. In it he said he was having a good time with the opposite sex and she should do likewise.'

But not all husbands were as tolerant of their spouses' infidelities with their American allies. A GI who was stationed in Norfolk remembers how they lost one of his company, not to the enemy but to a British soldier who returned unexpectedly to the family home and 'found one of our men in bed with his wife, threw the GI out of a second storey window and killed him. He was sent to prison.' There were other incidents of homicides motivated by sexual passion. One US Army sergeant was acquitted in November 1943 of the murder of an ATS private whose partly undressed and beaten body was discovered after a drunken dance.

It was the Canadian troops stationed in the south of England who acquired the worst wartime record as violent lovers, and who extracted the most savage vengeance on those girls who jilted them. On the night of 16 February 1943, a handsome dispatch rider, Victor Eric Gill, stormed into a Brighton pub to launch into a fierce argument with a pretty brunette at the bar. The row continued outside until a piercing scream was heard, followed by a series of shots. Ivy Ellen Eade, an eighteen-year-old hairdresser, lay sprawled in a spreading pool of blood in the car park. It turned out that she was pregnant with Gill's child and their argument began because she had dated another Canadian sergeant. Gill, who admitted he was already married, said at his trial he had never intended to kill Ivy, whom he claimed to love deeply, but had been 'overwhelmed with apprehension and jealousy'. His passionate pleas apparently convinced the jury, who found him guilty of the lesser charge of manslaughter.

A month later, a fellow Canadian, a young regimental policeman named Charles Eugene Gautier, was less fortunate. He had taken up with a Brighton housewife whose husband was a prisoner in Germany. When he discovered that Mrs Annette Pepper had taken another Canadian into her house, he blasted his way in with a Bren gun, wounded his rival and then sprayed his mistress's body full of bullets as she pleaded with him at the top of the staircase. Gautier was found guilty of murder and hanged at Wandsworth prison on 24 September 1943 after his appeal had been refused. The publicity given to the case had served to inflame the concern many British servicemen overseas had begun to feel about their wives back home. Reports were being received from field commanders that the morale of men at the fighting front was being badly undermined by stories of rape, violence, and illegitimate births.

The main sexually motivated wartime violence in Britain, however, arose not from jilted Canadians or even clashes of GIs and resentful British husbands, but between white American soldiers and their black comrades over Englishwomen who refused to subscribe to the colour bar that was enforced in the US Army. The first serious clash occurred in September 1943, when black and white GIs fought each other in the sleepy Cornish town of Launceston. It resulted in two military policemen being wounded when they tried to restore order. In Manchester the next year, the sight of a black sailor kissing a white English girl in a railway station sparked a series of race riots that brought a call for the city councillors to ban all GIs from places of entertainment for a fortnight. The censored wartime British press played down such incidents, including the fight that broke out in a pub near Kingsclere, Newbury in December 1944. After blacks were driven out of a bar by white GIs they returned with rifles to shoot their way in, killing the publican's wife in the process.

Complaints about the bigotry and feuding between the black and white American soldiers resulted in the Prime Minister being asked in the Commons to 'make friendly representations to the American military authorities asking them to instruct their men that the colour bar is not the custom in this country.' A Home Office letter of September 1942 made this official policy clear in a circular sent to all chief constables. But the Secretary of War found himself on a 'razor's edge' over the issue after a US general in Southern Command issued orders that, 'White women should not associate with coloured men. They should not walk out, dance, or drink with them.' Many British women objected strongly to the discrimination. A NAAFI counter lady explained, 'We find the coloured troops are much nicer to deal with in canteen life and such, we like serving them, they're always so courteous and have a very natural charm that most of the whites miss. Candidly, I'd rather serve a regiment of the dusky lads than a couple of whites.'

Most English people, who were not accustomed to making a distinction between people of different colour, did not appreciate that the politeness of most black troops was the result of generations of subservience to the white population of the United States. 'Some British women appear to find a peculiar fascination in associating with men of colour,' noted a Home Office circular in

1943, giving voice to deeply-rooted racial fears. 'The morale of British troops is likely to be upset by rumours that their wives and daughters are being debauched by *coloured* American troops.'

A sexual element deriving from the fascination of the exotic affected those women who had never before encountered a black man. Some gullible country girls were eager to believe a popular rumour put about by some of the Negro troops that they were GIs whose skins had been specially darkened for night operations – and that on return to the United States they would be given an injection to turn them white again. Barbara Cartland wrote from her experience as a WAAF moral welfare adviser:

> It was the white women who ran after the black troops, not vice versa. Approximately one thousand five hundred coloured babies were born in Britain during the war, but I am prepared to bet that if the truth were known it would prove in nearly every case the woman's fault. Women would queue outside the camps, they would not be turned away, they would come down from London by train, and they defeated the Military Police by sheer numbers. There were, of course, some hard cases. One girl I knew of personally married a very nice American flier. They were extremely happy, and she was delighted when she knew she was going to have a baby. She gave birth to twins; after twenty-four hours they slowly turned black. It was a third generation throwback and the young flier swore, with tears in his eyes, he had no idea that his blood was mixed.

Popular sympathy remained steadfastly on the side of the oppressed black regiments, even when the victim was a British woman. In May 1944, when a US Army court martial sentenced to death a black GI for allegedly raping a housewife in a village near Bath, his case was taken up by the *Daily Mirror* newspaper, which exposed the conflict in the woman's testimony. She claimed she had been dragged out and assaulted after answering the door to the soldier who asked directions to Bristol. His defence was that he had already paid her a pound on two previous occasions to have intercourse: when he refused her demand for double that sum she vowed she would make trouble for him. The *Mirror* campaign sent a thirty thousand-signature petition to General Eisenhower, who finally set aside the conviction in July for 'lack of evidence'.

'We were not just "an easy lay", although many of us were depressed by the war and the greyness of life in blacked-out

England,' insisted one twenty-five-year-old English housewife, whose husband had been away for three years fighting in North Africa. 'We were bruised by such accusations,' she wrote with feeling about her own wartime affair with an American army lieutenant, continuing:

> An officer's wife in California still feels her husband has a son in England. She was so wrong about it . . . My romantic memories are far too precious to go into print, but they gave me a love of America I shall take to my grave. It was as lasting and sincere as many of the wartime loves were. In fact our 'swap loves' in wartime, [when] husbands or lovers were away, were often very innocent. But as sexual appetites vary, so it was in wartime – and my only near rape was as a result of two British servicemen, not Americans. Perhaps all Yanks were not after all so 'oversexed' . . . our attitude to women's behaviour and couples courting was still rather Victorian.

Margaret Mead, the celebrated anthropologist, observed in her contemporary study, *The American Troops and the British Community* that the amatory success of the GIs with British girls had much to do with the differences in dating behaviour on the other side of the Atlantic:

> American men and boys enjoy the company of girls and women more than the British do. British boys don't go out with girls unless they have what one British boy described to me as 'an ulterior purpose, good or bad' . . . To an American eye, the absence of flirting and backchat among secondary school boys and girls is astonishing. American boys and girls start having dates with each other in their early teens, long before they are emotionally mature enough for anything really connected with sex . . . Of course this is very confusing to British girls who haven't had any practice.

She did not mention that many British children attended single sex schools.

The American servicemen had become so 'practised' in the arts of seduction that a popular joke that swept wartime Britain was, 'Heard about the new utility knickers? One Yank – and they're off.'

By no means every American serviceman succeeded as easily as many boasted. An upper-class English lady insisted, 'By and large, the Yanks all had beautiful manners, apologizing if one trod on *their* toes, but all ranks appeared to drink and get drunk.

Middle-class people would be no more likely to have mixed with coarse Yanks as coarse Englishmen – and I saw no Lady Chatterley stuff!'

Myra worked in a munitions plant at Thatcham, near the airfield at Greenham Common from where the American 82nd Airborne Division was flown to Normandy on the eve of D-Day. From her factory windows she and her workmates could see Thatcham Station. On payday, there were queues of GIs, billfolds bulging, waiting for the train to London.

> The soldiers used to line up outside a hut by the railway line where the local street ladies' lurked, while officers and the MPs turned a blind eye to the goings-on. Lorryloads of GIs would often toss out chocolate bars or VD kits containing contraceptive rubbers as they roared through the Berkshire lanes. They blew them up like balloons and would festoon their lorries with them. Officers kerb-crawled for girls, three to a jeep. I loved their parties and found Americans such good dancers. There was much jealousy by British men and their memories have not dimmed as to what English women were 'supposed to have got up to' while they were serving abroad. The Americans were so very trusting of us, wanting to be liked and be our guests. The pity of it was that enemy propaganda blew up the horrific stories of what we were up to 'in bed with GI-Joe' and encouraged the men overseas to think that they were being kept away until the Yanks were safely home again in the States.

An anonymous British versifier wrote 'The Lament of the Limey Lass', two of those bittersweet stanzas summed up the wistful sentiments of many of the women and girls who had fallen for brief affairs with Americans:

> They tell us we have teeth like pearls,
> They love our hair the way it curls,
> Our eyes could dim the brightest stars,
> Our figures beat Hedy Lamarr's
>
> And then he leaves you broken hearted,
> The camp has moved – your love departed.
> You wait for mail that doesn't come,
> Then you realize you're awful dumb

In answer to this resentful lament a GI composed a retaliatory song that unromantically stated their predicament:

> With Yankee girls you can't compare
> The difference is, You're here! They're there!

Yet many of the relationships were deep and romantic. After the American troops had departed for D-Day, a tent in the south of England was painted with the poignant message, 'Sorry Jean Had to Go – Johnny.' The US Army postal service recorded that over a quarter of the letters mailed by GIs from France during the first four weeks after 6 June 1944 were posted to addresses in the British Isles. Although scores of love affairs were to die on the battlefields of France, Belgium, and Germany, the fact that twenty thousand English girls applied to become the wives of American soldiers was testimony that a proportion of these romances endured the final year of the war.

The ubiquitous US Army jeep gave the American serviceman an advantage in the off-duty pursuit of local women that was officially dignified as 'rest and relaxation'. It helped to make a military alliance into a romantic union when the American troops launched their 'friendly' invasion of Australia in the spring of 1942.

The American military presence was to remain an ill-kept official war secret until March 1942 when General Douglas MacArthur made his dramatic escape from his besieged Manila Bay fortress of Corregidor. The first GIs had actually arrived in Brisbane on 22 December 1941. The contingent of 2385 enlisted men who disembarked from the steamer *Republic* were part of a convoy originally destined to reinforce the Philippines which had been diverted to the northern Queensland port after the Japanese invasion of Luzon.

These GIs were the first of more than a million American servicemen who arrived over the next four years. It was an invasion whose impact on the customs and social attitudes of seven million Australians was proportionally greater than the same number of 'Yanks' had on a British population seven times larger. During the spring of 1942, the southward Japanese advance led the Australian government to make desperate plans for holding the so-called 'Brisbane Line'. The threat of a Japanese attack ensured that the increasing flood of American servicemen was welcomed as saviours. This, in addition to the glamour with which a nation of avid moviegoers endowed the GIs, guaranteed that the American male received an especially warm welcome from Australian womanhood.

'It was rather fun finding ourselves comrades in arms with some of the flower of Australian womanhood,' one GI recorded of his first encounter with the Women's Auxiliary Australian Air Force, the WAAAF. 'For downright friendliness, Mom, the Aussies are the tops,' another wrote home with gusto. Lieutenant Ralf Glover, another of the early arrivals, never forgot the 'rousing welcome' he was given in Melbourne by the local female population who were 'very co-operative about getting acquainted.'

Milk bars and clubs providing raunchy entertainment quickly sprouted up along Melbourne's Collins Street. One divisional history recorded: 'To the men of the 41st Division, in those first two months, Australia was Melbourne, Melbourne was heaven, and heaven was theirs for the taking.'

'When the Boy from Alabama Meets a Girl From Gundagi' was a popular song that celebrated the liaisons that quickly sprang up between GIs and Australian girls. Although the American military authorities sought to delay for six months permission for servicemen to marry, by 29 March 1942 when Betty Laing of the Brisbane suburb of Hendra married Private Laurence Decker, she made newspaper headlines as the first GI bride, there was an epidemic of such romances sweeping Queensland. Make-up and peroxide sales soared as Australian girls transformed their appearance and camp canteens were flooded with invitations to 'parties with lots of strawberry blondes and beer.' One corporal reported home 'every household in Australia put a pot of tea on the stove and sent the younger children post-haste to catch a Yank.' In May 1942 *Newsweek* magazine described the 'all-time hospitality blitz' which had one Melbourne bus-conductress paying the fare for 33 GIs, while another Australian girl had already managed to marry two American servicemen.

The rash of romances was greatest in the townships around the army camps and air bases that were established in northern Queensland after MacArthur set up his headquarters in Brisbane. There were soon a thousand GIs ready, willing and eager to date each available local girl.

Maureen Meadows' memoir, whose title 'I Loved Those Yanks' summed up the sentiments of so many of her female contemporaries, 'swiftly learned about gum and God's Own Country' from American airmen at the Townsville base where she took a wartime job as a civilian typist. 'They possessed an "Oh Boy!" attitude towards everything, and it wasn't only beer and blondes, or candy and Coca-Cola.' The arrival of so many strapping young men, friendly by nature and determined to make the best of the meagre 'rest and recreation' facilities offered by sleepy communities such as Townsville, was going to blow away some of the cobwebs of stuffiness in a country whose bars rationed beer, shut early and where dance-halls and cinemas closed on Sundays.

'Like South Dakota by the Sea' remarked one GI scathingly of the bright lights of Townsville. Another observed that Melbourne was 'half as big as New York city's largest cemetery – and twice as dead.' As a reporter for the *Chicago Sun* commented in May 1942, 'Whether Australia keeps its six o'clock shutdown on drinking and its movieless, sometimes street-carless Sunday, matters little in a war this big.' By the summer of 1942 reluctant concessions were being made by local authorities to permit Sunday opening of cinemas. The federal government also assisted, discreetly, in meeting the shortage of women that seriously affected the quarter of a million enlisted men in the camps around Brisbane.

'The whores were so damn busy that the situation was, metaphorically speaking, red hot,' recalled a civil servant. He was one of those involved in the appeal made to the Sydney gambling establishment owners in September 1942: 'Could anyone fill a train with warm, attractive females eager to assist in the national war effort by relieving the pressures building up in Brisbane?'

Rumour had it that thanks to the intervention of a member of the government, a special train was given high priority clearance as it sped northwards to Brisbane, its carriages packed with hastily recruited prostitutes who, in addition to their fares and guaranteed wages, were promised that they could keep any additional income they made over and above the rostered call of duty!

One girl reportedly managed to save nearly four thousand pounds in the course of a year's 'contract' in Brisbane's red-light district and prostitutes were soon flocking to Sydney, Melbourne, Brisbane and Townsville from every part of the country. Unlike Britain, where brothels were illegal, Australian authorities permitted their operation and business boomed as expanding 'staff' met the needs of the long lines of enlisted men. Officer's 'girls' affronted suburban sensibilities by carrying on their profession from bungalows in residential districts near American bases.

The increase in prostitution and consequent increase in the number of cases of venereal disease was one of the factors that ended Australia's 'honeymoon' with the American servicemen. By the end of 1942 the Japanese menace had been defeated in New Guinea and much of the initial glamour had been stripped from the 'friendly invasion'. A Brisbane poet expressed the changing national mood:

> They saved us from the Japs
> Perhaps.
> But at the moment the place is too Yankful
> For us to be sufficiently thankful.

The over-warm rapture with which Australian women had welcomed the Yanks was resented by their menfolk and in Perth as early as March 1942 a reporter from *The Times* noted that when an 'American goes for a stroll down the streets in the evening with a girl on each arm, his success is somewhat resented by the Australian soldiers returning from Malaya and the Middle East . . .'

The ardour of Australian girls had also been cooled somewhat by the brutal murders of four women, casually picked up on Melbourne streets, by Private Edward J. Leonski of the 52nd Signal company stationed at Camp Pell outside the town. Leonski, a deranged former New York city foodstore worker, strangled his victims, and was executed, as was an American paratrooper convicted of a Brisbane rape in 1944. By the summer of 1942, most Australian men had forgotten that only a few months earlier a popular song had celebrated the idea that they and the Americans would soon be 'Marching Side By Side from Berlin to Tokyo'. Now the alliance was more likely to be marked by brawls which, according to one American seaman, 'made John Wayne fights look like high-school picnics.' That summer the jealousy of many husbands and boyfriends was aroused as the men of the First Australian Division returned to find their wives and sweethearts infatuated with American servicemen.

The GIs had the money, taxicabs, cigarettes – and the girls. A spot-survey conducted at a busy Brisbane intersection at six o'clock on a September evening revealed 'ninety three American service-men were in the company of 126 girls; fifty two Australian service-men in the company of 27 girls . . .' In such circumstances it was inevitable that many fights broke out in bars and dance-halls where newly returned Australian soldiers were quick to turn on the GIs some of the combat skills they had employed in the Western desert against Rommel's troops. In many instances the American serviceman was made a scapegoat for the release of wartime tensions, but as the *Chicago Sun* reported on 4 December 1942: 'Australian troops resent the fact that the Americans are better dressed, more affluent, and by reason of their manners, appearance etc., seem to have taken over an unfair share of Australian womanhood.'

That the resulting brawls – like the one that tied up Melbourne traffic on 1 December 1942 – and the battle at Bondi on the 6 February 1943 – made front-page headlines in the Australian press was indicative of a new mood of anti-Americanism already inflamed by the public debate after the so-called 'Brisbane Riot' of November 1942 which had left one Australian dead and two others wounded. Questions were tabled in the Queensland parliament and there was a spate of accusations that GIs were a menace to the female population and that WAAAFs were having to be escorted because of the threat of sexual assault by black US soldiers. The official inquiry into the riot, which had actually broken out over a row about the issue of cigarettes at the lavish American service club, attributed part of the blame to the pressures created by 'the spectacle of American troops with Australian girls, particularly the wives of absent soldiers, and the American custom of caressing girls in public.'

'When we saw our first Yanks, we were interested, not antagonistic,' recalled Alice Riddell. 'Later, we didn't like their public love-making, or the way they took out young girls, schoolgirls really.' Clergymen and politicians were quick to take up the issues of public morality, rising prostitution and VD rates. The most outspoken was the Most Reverend James Duhig, Catholic Archbishop of Brisbane who condemned 'the present decay of morals and the menace of social disease' in his 1943 Lenten letter. 'For several months now, many girls associating with Allied soldiers have shown a spirit of greed and selfishness that does little credit to Australian womanhood.' Six months later the morals issue was still very much alive when the *Sydney Morning Herald* reported 'Young girls sat on the kerbs of the city's principal streets, with their stockingless legs poised so that their knees would support their drink-sodden heads. Some sang; other argued; all shouted to every passing car.'

The local US Army provost assured the newspaper that GIs had been instructed that 'regulations forbade associating with undesirable girls, accosting women in the streets, kissing women and girls in doorways and in the streets . . .'

Moral conduct, however, proved easier to promulgate than enforce – and fostered by sexual undercurrents, anti-Americanism was to remain a problem until the end of the war. The growing public resentment against the GIs did not prevent more than 15,000 Australian girls marrying American servicemen, or the exodus of wives and babies on the trans-Pacific 'bride ships' to the United States. Not all wartime unions ended in marriage and it appears that where the mothers of illegitimate offspring of American servicemen could establish paternity, in some cases the US government did arrange some form of maintenance grant. It did not do so however in cases like that of Mrs Dawn Rigby Scott, a nineteen-year-old war bride, who returned home when her marriage broke down after eighteen months. Public concern was such that a bill was introduced in Parliament to enable Australian brides who had not yet left for the United States to sue their GI husbands for a speedy divorce.

Yet when the 'international love affair' between the American servicemen and the Australian women was terminated by departure of the remaining GIs at the end of the war, the general mood was one of sadness rather than resentment. 'How the world, ANY world, could be expected to go on without things like jeeps and orchids, chewing-gum and dates – and particularly the things like the Yanks themselves – was incredible to believe,' wrote Maureen Meadows. 'War had dramatized our lives to a large extent. Because something so great was happening in the world outside, the things which happened to us in a place like Brisbane had become great and momentous too.'

The GI invasion, did not – as Archbishop Duhig had predicted – bring about the moral 'downfall' of Australian society. Just as in Britain, most of the female population would look back on their wartime encounters with American men as one of the more positive experiences of the war. 'I'm sure they helped to bring us out of our insular shells,' one British housewife observed. 'My girlfriend and I often went out with them. They were great company, and there was an awful anticlimax when they all went home.'

The GI invasion did indeed shake some of the British out of

their blinkered attitudes to sex, because the American military obliged their hosts to educate the public to an awareness of venereal disease. The alarming consequences of the prodigious sexual activity of GIs in Britain was revealed by the VD statistics, which rose from twenty cases per thousand to almost sixty per thousand amongst American forces stationed there, by the first months of 1943. This was nearly three times the rate of troops in the United States and six times higher than the average level reported by the British Army for soldiers on home duty.

The Chief of Preventative Medicine of the US Army, in calling for action at the highest inter-governmental level, endorsed the findings of the American Social Hygiene Association's research:

> There does not exist in British law a basis for venereal disease control and prostitution of the sort that we have in this country . . . The attitude of the British public towards venereal disease and prostitution is quite dissimilar to the attitude in this country. Nothing like the public education carried on in this country has been experienced by the British public.

The first year of the American 'occupation' of Britain frustrated the US Army medical staff, because their attempts to establish prophylactic treatment centres and contact-tracing for suspected carriers were blocked by the confidentiality imposed by the 1916 Venereal Diseases Act, which made it a slander to imply that even a prostitute, who might be responsible for spreading scores of cases, was infectious. Condoms were also in critically short supply because of the scarcity of latex in the wake of the Japanese takeover of Malaya, and the British Government had given teets for infants' feeding a higher production priority. The condoms that were available in Britain were of a particularly uncomfortable design which many GIs complained, perhaps boastfully, was 'too small' to accomodate the American male anatomy.

Prophylactic posts, under American Red Cross supervision, were permitted to be set up and were discreetly signposted near the famed Rainbow Corner and at accessible locations throughout London, including each main railway station. But the only sources of information about the 'unmentionable' social disease were 'discreet little advertisements announcing the location of treatment centres in public latrines.' A US Army wartime report complained:

British sensibilities forbade the display of prominent signs and the rigid requirements of the total blackout forbade the use of the conventional green light. Perhaps the most important reason for the small use of station prophylaxis arose from the fact that the vast majority of the sexual exposures were wholly uncommercial and on a friendly basis. Surveys among soldiers revealed that under these circumstances they were much less impressed with the desirability or necessity of prophylaxis after exposure.

A high-ranking 'Joint Committee on Venereal Diseases' was set up under Ministry of Health auspices to consult the American and Canadian military authorities. Under American pressure it met in the summer of 1943, but it 'bogged down in a discussion of prostitution and was never revived'. It was months before the Ministry of Health could persuade a reluctant government to reinstate the World War I anti-VD measures embodied in section 33B of the 1939 Defence of the Realm Act. The new regulations did go part of the way to meeting the American proposals for establishing a system of contact-tracing to check on civilian women who were suspected of harbouring venereal infections. Contacts, however, could only be followed up after being named by two separate individuals – and after the case was given the go-ahead by the Ministry of Health. Investigations were to be hampered by the desperate shortage of trained civilian medical staff, though more were recruited when it was found that fewer than fifteen per cent of the women who were suspected carriers had actually applied for treatment.

One enterprising Norfolk prostitute, who had been named by no fewer than five GIs as a source of venereal infection, went so far as to ask the Ministry of Health to help her to get the American bomber station at Shipham to post a notice announcing that she had been successfully treated on the camp bulletin board. 'Request Refused' was the terse answer received from the Commanding Officer, who objected to sanctioning an advertisement to put a whore back in business!

Even the most strait-laced of Britain's town councils had been sufficiently alarmed at the rising VD rate to agree to co-operate with the crash advertising and public education programme which was launched by the Ministry of Health in 1943. After some heated debate in Parliament and racy speculations in the press, the Chief

Medical Officer of the Ministry of Health announced the launching of 'the most intensive effort in the field of health education yet undertaken in this country'. Labelled by fastidious civil servants as the 'Let Knowledge Grow' campaign, its purpose was to make the public aware of the dangers and symptoms of the disease, for which free treatment had already been available for a quarter of a century. Initially it had been feared that the public would react squeamishly to words such as 'intercourse' and 'sexual organs' appearing in the press, on the radio, and in the films and lectures that were shown in factories, clubs, and even some schools. The problem was not to be quite so serious as they had feared. One British girl, a doctor's daughter, remarked, 'It was a hoot really,' when she heard one of these broadcasts put out by the BBC after the nine o'clock news. Government surveys, contrary to anticipation, revealed that there was no squeamishness about the anti-VD campaign which by the end of the war had made the public thoroughly familiar with the disease, through artfully explicit posters of which ninety per cent of the people interviewed approved. The posters were designed to shock – like the women's veiled hat jauntily perched atop a skull with the dangers of VD implied in its attention-catching headline, 'Hello boyfriend, coming MY way?' above a warning that, 'The "easy" girlfriend spreads Syphilis and Gonorrhoea, which *unless properly treated* may result in blindness, insanity, paralysis, premature death.' 'It is hard to realize that even at the beginning of this war, the words syphilis and gonorrhoea were taboo,' noted the London correspondent of the *New York Herald Tribune*.

The wartime VD campaign unleashed an enormous public response. Eighty thousand letters were received by the Ministry of Health, mostly from women, revealing that VD was most prevalent in the nineteen to twenty-three year olds and that 'infection often results from a romantic love affair or a single act of promiscuity with an apparently "respectable" man.' The wartime health education campaign was responsible for the erosion of the Victorian taboos against explicit public discussion of the other aspects of sex besides health.

In the military context, the decline of VD cases in both the civilian population and in American troops pouring into England for the crucial cross-channel assault was dramatic. US Army statistics reveal that in the months leading up to May 1944, the rate of infection fell by nearly two thirds – although 'final-fling' pre-battle promiscuity must have increased sexual activity. The statistical data, moreover, indicates that the health campaign prevented around fifteen thousand GIs – or enough men to man a front-line infantry division – from falling victim to syphilis or gonorrhoea during the months before and after the invasion of France. The Allied ground forces proved to be only just sufficient to tip the military balance during the June battle for Normandy. It is therefore not difficult to appreciate the concern of its planners that the greatest amphibious assault of the war should not be put at risk by a pre-invasion *VD*-Day.

16

YIELDING TO
THE CONQUERORS

The average soldier who landed at Utah beach
and survived to take Germany, the man who was
neither stud nor sissy, probably slept with
something like twenty-five women during the
war – and few of them were, I might add,
prostitutes.

GI with 4th Armoured Div.

It seems to me that while the American Forces
are doing their big part in the invasion of
Europe in a temporal way, we are also invading
other lands in a moral and spiritual way, and the
imprint we are leaving on the invaded peoples is
not too good a picture.

US Army Chaplain, June 1944

'YOU WILL GO THERE AS LIBERATING HEROES and those women will be eager and urgent in the solicitation of you. Now bear these facts in mind,' American troops embarking for the D-Day invasion were warned. 'The women who will be soliciting your attentions are prostitutes of the most promiscuous type.' Mindful of the degree to which the strength of the Allied armies in Italy had been sapped by VD spread by prostitutes, and fearful that medical services in France had been run down by the German occupation, Allied medical and military planners had taken unprecedented measures to keep the troops spearheading the liberation of Europe from becoming casualties of sexual disease.

A fleet of mobile VD treatment centres staffed by two medical officers and six orderlies had been mounted on three-ton trucks 'to treat as far forward as possible all cases of primary and recurrent venereal diseases'. Equipped with thousands of high-strength penicillin doses, they were to provide quick treatment injections to keep up strength at the fighting front. The hitherto limited supplies of the 'wonder-drug' that was to prove a potent weapon in the Allies' arsenal during the 'Crusade for Europe' had already saved thousands of battle casualties from serious infection. Some medical experts were against using the 'magic bullet' of penicillin as a fast cure for venereal disease on the grounds that it would remove a powerful incentive to restraint by the troops. But strategic rather than moral considerations enabled the D-Day planners to overcome such objections.

The easy availability of a quick cure for the wages of sin was reassuring for those members of the Allied forces who were encouraged by the enthusiastic reception they received from the women of the towns and villages of Normandy to join an intimate celebration of the liberation. Nor did their commanders interfere. Within hours of the American capture of Cherbourg, two houses of prostitution were doing a roaring trade 'run for, and indirectly by, American troops, with the familiar pattern of the designation of one brothel for negro troops and the other for white, with a military patrol stationed at the doors to keep order in the queues which formed.' The SHAEF medical inspectors might protest at this infraction of military regulations, but they could do little more than insist that 'Off-Limits' notices were pasted on the French-run 'Closed Houses' that re-opened for business even before the shelling had stopped. Battling the Germans was of more concern to the Allied commanders than French whores, and they regarded posting military guards outside the brothels as a waste of manpower. It also did little to sustain the morale of troops in search of 'rest and recreation' between bouts of fierce fighting in the Normandy hedgerows.

'Approximately sixty per cent of my company had relations at one time or another with professional prostitutes or pick-up girls,' noted a sociologist who fought in Normandy – and it was the same story for the British and Canadian troops. One English soldier recalled with amusement his first-ever visit to a brothel, shortly after D-Day, when his colleague 'smelled out' one of the houses they had been ordered to avoid:

> We went in and there was a small bar full of ladies hanging about in their underwear. 'Act natural!' I said to Knobby. 'Pretend you have gone into one of these all your life.' I went across to a beautiful blonde girl who was holding a poodle and boldly asked, *'Voulez-vous couchez avec moi et combien?'* I had two hundred francs, which I reckoned to be more than enough, and to my delight and Knobby's surprise, she agreed and took us up to her room. To my dismay she insisted on getting out a basin and washing my privates. In the cold water my anticipation withered so rapidly that she tickled it with her finger and said, *'Alors, c'est un petit patron.'* I said, 'Just you wait a moment!'

When the Germans were finally put to headlong flight across the Seine in August, SHAEF's Chief of Preventative Medicine acknowledged that because of some Allied generals' 'firm conviction that the operation of brothels was a duty which the Army owed the individual soldier', they were losing the battle against French whores:

> The history of venereal disease control problems in France has been largely one of difference of opinion between those who favoured segregation and licensing of prostitution and those who opposed it. Unfortunately, the subject being what it is, it has never been possible to gain a free and open discussion; it is generally accounted that since the War Department policy is clearly stated and specifically directs

the repression of prostitution, it is necessary to give apparent support to such a policy, even while doing the contrary.

George S. Patton was one of the generals who persisted with the 'contrary policies' he had followed during the Sicily campaign. He infurated the chaplains in his 3rd Army by encouraging the opening of a string of brothels that were supervised by military medical personnel. 'I realize that our Commanding General is not a typical officer, and if I thought for a moment that he was I would be tempted to reconsider my decision to stay in the regular army,' wrote Father H. F. Donovan of the 29th Infantry Division to the War Department, in a report which detailed the extent of Patton's transgressions:

> After my last Mass yesterday I drove to the house of prostitution, received the information from the MP on duty that forty-four men had made use of the house between 2 p.m. (opening time) and 4.27 p.m., took a picture of the sign 'Blue & Grey Corral Riding Lessons – 100 Francs' and a picture of the forty-fifth customer, whose name, rank, and number I have . . . I passed by the House again and was present when an MP officer closed it and put it 'Off-Limits' at 6.57 p.m. – seventy-six men had made use of the House.

American officers were not moral exemplars. Their activities brought charges from the French town council in Bayeux that they had made 'a public pastime' of whoring, according to another army chaplain:

> German officers had run their brothels quietly. They did not demand that the owners of private billets *couchez avec* as American officers did. The French Welcome Societies stopped furnishing girls to American Army camps for dances because of immoral treatment. I personally saw about a dozen officers taking French girls into their billets during the dance, turning off the lights and being there from one half to one hour at a time.

Even before the first Allied troops entered the French capital, it was appreciated that any attempt to put the hundreds of Parisian brothels off-limits to Allied soldiers would be doomed to futility. Accordingly, on 2 September 1944, the Provost Marshal of the Seine Section US Army toured the city brothels accompanied by a representative of the Brigade Mondaine, 'for the express purpose of selecting certain houses of prostitution to be set aside for officers, others for white enlisted men, and still others for coloured enlisted men'. American headquarters in France faced up to the situation with which they were confronted, even if their policy was 'somewhat interfered with' three days later by an order from the Chief Surgeon of the US Army which unrealistically insisted that the French Ministry of the Interior direct all prefects of police to exclude all US military personnel from the brothels or close them! The 'unofficial policy' nevertheless prevailed, in the face of repeated protests from the War Department, because the local military commanders were 'unable or unwilling' to assist in the policing of the red-light areas which the French authorities regarded as a necessary social convenience that helped keep down the numbers of sexual assaults on the female population.

Parisian brothels enjoyed their second wartime boom as American and other Allied troops, their fear of venereal disease assuaged by the one-shot penicillin cure, crowded into the narrow streets of Montmartre and the other red-light areas. In the smarter sections of the city, its liberators were not safe from the repeated assaults of the less respectable segment of the city's women. The US Army headquarters at the Hotel Scribe, according to a *Newsweek* correspondent, 'had all the better aspects of Custer's last stand', with the street lined with jeeps whose embattled drivers were assaulted by streetwalkers. 'The women of Paris are still very smart. They dress fit to kill and make up thickly but on the whole artistically . . . but Chanel No. 5 doesn't smell the same as it did in 1940, although the "feelthy picture man" is still there.'

Paris became the Mecca for GIs for 'rest and recreation' during the final months of the war in Europe. The city became, in the words of an American colonel, 'the natural objective of every soldier on pass or furlough; and countless numbers of soldiers in groups all the way from one or two to entire convoys "got lost" on their way from hither to yon and would end up in Paris for a bit of sightseeing. The German occupation had done nothing to improve the morals and behaviour of the Parisian women of the brothels and boulevards, and the lack of food, and later of fuel, gave the American soldier with a K-ration an unbeatable bargaining position.'

Those soldiers lucky enough to get to the city which had long had the reputation of being the sex-capital of the Continent were not usually disappointed, as one GI enthusiastically explained in a letter to his father back in San Francisco:

French girls are easy to get, what with American cigarettes and chocolate and us being heroes in their eyes, so I'm not going to be choosey from now on and get my fun where I can get it while I'm still alive. And to hell with tomorrow – it may never come . . . I hear penicillin will cure ninety-five per cent of VD cases in one day. Do any of your doctors use it yet? But don't worry about me, I'll try to be careful.

That '*Voulez-vous couchez avec moi?*' had become the one French phrase practised by every Allied soldier in France during the autumn of 1944 was evident from the upward leap in the VD statistics. Euphemistically referred to as the 'Hit Parade', the graphs indicating the sixfold increase in the number of cases were posted up in the regimental headquarters of every US Army unit. There was no surprise amongst the medical staff that two thirds of all those troops who contracted VD in France gave their stay in Paris as the source of their infection.

The British Army suffered the same rocketing VD casualty rate in liberated Belgium – mainly contracted from whores. Ghent alone was reported to have some two hundred registered and seven hundred unregistered prostitutes, and nearly all of its hundred and forty-eight small cafés functioned as brothels.

Not every sexual encounter was with a prostitute, as one Scottish sergeant fondly recalled of his night of passion with a young girl called Janine just after Brussels were liberated:

A warmth and pleasurable joy swept over me as I lay in the arms of the loveliest girl in the world, her long hair falling like silken water over my shoulders. Her lips filled me with gasping urgency and my stroking hands reached for some joy I never knew existed. The girl Janine, in my arms, whispered to me, stroking my head, kissing my face and reaching for the happiness that eludes men and women in time of war, never knowing if this day is going to be your last on this earth. Her insistent hushing as we made love lulled me into another sleep, till in a rushing dream I was roused by her strident tones, '*Allez Jock . . . Six heures . . . Allez!*' All that day I was filled with one aim, to get off duty as quickly as possible and return to the Avenue du Canada. My heart was thumping like a child at his first party as I jumped from the tram at the terminus, my small pack bumping heavily on me with its load of cigarettes and chocolate . . . then I saw the house . . . Janine's house . . . Its walls were now daubed with obscenities and rough painted swastikas. Above the door were two large scrawls, '*Traiteur Collaborateur*'. There was no movement within the silent rooms, only the whispering of a torn curtain in the window of her bedroom. A tear fell from my eye as I thought of Janine – then I walked into the war once more.

In Brussels, it became impossible for a British soldier to walk 'more than ten to twenty yards' without being accosted by a fresh streetwalker. By March 1945, the VD rate had climbed to such an alarming level that SHAEF headquarters shipped penicillin supplies to civilian hospitals in the Belgian cities to treat the prostitutes who were suspected of harbouring sexual infections. With the push across the frontiers of the Third Reich now gathering pace, it had become essential to cut down the VD rate and maintain the strength of front-line units. When German cities and towns began falling to the Allied advance, SHAEF headquarters counted on Eisenhower's 'non-fraternization' policy to check the epidemic of promiscuity which afflicted the 'Crusaders for Democracy'.

The chaos into which the Thousand Year Reich crumbled during the final months of World War II combined with the sexual and physical hunger of a large number of German women defeated any strict enforcement of non-fraternization. With so many of their men in the Wehrmacht, many German girls had already defied the Nazi laws against fraternizing with foreign prisoners and war workers. The penalties, even for suspected intimacy with non-Aryan males, were swift and severe, as 'Anneliese', a teenager from northern Germany, discovered when she was imprisoned after befriending a young Belgian:

> According to the radio, I had signed a file an inch thick which said that every night the prisoners took turns sleeping with my mother and me, that I was pregnant and had sex relations with every one of the POWs. The reputation of my mother as a God-fearing soul was reason enough for the townspeople not to believe any part of the sordid so-called confession.

Prostitution had also been made illegal in the Third Reich. But wartime conditions forced even the totalitarian Nazi regime eventually to sanction red-light districts in seaports and in other cities like Berlin and Frankfurt where there was a large transient military population. Soldiers on leave had spread infection in rural areas, and the clandestine brothels and the reaction to Allied air bombing had sent up VD rates in the cities. By the third year of the war, sexual disease was a growing menace in the cities. The syphilis rate had increased by a hundred per cent over 1939 levels in Hamburg, a hundred and seventy per cent in Munich, and a whopping two hundred per cent in Frankfurt. The bombing of Hamburg's dock area had reduced the prostitute population in the nearby red-light district by half. Prices, at 2.50 to 10 Reichmarks, were low, but as the number of brothels was reduced the number of customers per girl per day increased from twenty to thirty, and the shortage of condoms inevitably increased the VD rate.

Other forms of prophylaxis were freely dispensed by first-aid stations, but the Nazis surpassed the Vatican in denouncing birth control to encourage the Master Race to prove its genetic superiority by outbreeding the subject nations. Rubber was too scarce to waste on providing German soldiers with contraceptive sheaths, and the Wehrmacht relied on ineffective warnings to troops not to indulge in sexual relations with foreign females except in the militarily supervised brothels. In deference to the Fuehrer's concern not to dilute the Aryan bloodstock, fraternization with foreign females was actively discouraged.

'At home, hundreds of thousands of vivacious German girls – and numerous war-widows too, unfortunately – are waiting for our returning soldiers,' proclaimed the directive prohibiting members of the Reich's armed forces from marrying non-Aryans. Unofficial 'liaisons' were, however, tolerated – except in the elite SS, who were forbidden by a 1941 directive to engage in 'intercourse with women of alien blood'. Officers were expected to bring all transgressions to the personal attention of the Reichsfuehrer himself. The obsession of the former chicken farmer with eugenics encouraged Himmler to take a personal interest in promoting the notorious *Lebensborn* programme. The so-called 'Fount of Life' homes for unmarried women had originally been started by the SS before the war to 'care for racially and genetically valuable mothers of whom it may be assumed, after careful investigation of their own family and that of the father, that they will give birth to equally valuable children'. During the war the intention was to turn the homes into 'baby factories', and by 1945 German gossip and Allied propaganda had made *Lebensborn* synonymous with stud farms where SS officers on 'rest and recreation' helped breed a new generation of Nazi supermen.

Proposals were discussed for legitimizing babies born to unmarried fathers who were killed in action. Generous child allowances were given to the single mother and Himmler, who practised what he preached by starting a family with his mistress as well as his wife, almost persuaded the Fuehrer to approve legalized bigamy to mop up the anticipated post-war surplus of German women. But despite Himmler's bizarre experimentation with *Lebensborn* mothers – he fed them on porridge to encourage greater baby production – and Hitler's repeated exhortation for parents to have more babies, the vast mass of German men and women did not produce more offspring to compensate for the men getting killed in action. The *Lebensborn* homes proved more successful at spawning ribald humour than babies. '*Rekrutsmachen*' – 'making recruits' – became popular wartime slang for sexual intercourse in the Third Reich, and factory workers risked imprisonment to deface propaganda posters that urged, 'Wheels Must turn for Victory' by adding, 'And pram-wheels for the next war!'

World War II had also brought to Germany the problems of teenage sex-delinquency that plagued the Allied nations. The steady wartime rise in what the Third Reich's bureaucrats primly labelled 'juvenile demoralization' was carefully plotted in the surveys conducted by the Reich Security Police. These revealed that the increased Allied air raids sent up the number of illegitimate births and VD rates among German teenagers. Just as in Britain and the United States, men in uniform appeared to have a special attraction for promiscuous teenage girls. Himmler was especially troubled to find that his plans for a new puritanical social order for the masses were threatened by his own black-uniformed SS troops, who appeared to have a particular attraction for adolescent females. Court records indicate that as the war advanced, an increasing number of the Reich's elite troops were being prosecuted for unlawful relationships with under-age girls. One fifteen-year-old girl, who was charged with repeatedly importuning SS men, unrepentantly told the judge that if she became pregnant she would 'only be doing what the Fuehrer wanted by becoming a German mother'.

A Munich court concluded in 1944 that the principal reason for the rising VD rate and teenage pregnancies in Bavaria was the decline of moral standards due to 'inadequate parental control in wartime'. But another wartime study, no doubt because it was ordered by the Fuehrer's secretary, Martin Bormann, blamed the rising tide of immoral behaviour on young people who had shirked their Hitler Youth duty, charging, 'Their ideal is democratic freedom and American laxity.'

When the Allies fought their way through to the Rhineland towns in the spring of 1945, they found bands of youngsters calling themselves Edelweiss gangs who sported pink shirts and bobby-sox. They roamed the rubble hurling insults and stones at the Hitler Youth – when they were not trading sexual favours with willing girls. 'Nazism has so poisoned the nation that neither marriage nor chastity is respected. Soldiers' wives have lovers. Married women are unfaithful to their husbands. Husbands openly sport mistresses,' was the rationale offered by one gang-leader in Dusseldorf for his group's sexual promiscuity. Parental as well as administrative discipline had collapsed under the Allied land and air assault, and by the time American forces reached Berlin, the problem was so pervasive that GIs were astonished to be accosted by young girls plying the world's oldest trade in the city's ruined streets.

When Germany surrendered on 7 May 1945, an estimated four million fathers and elder brothers of the defeated male population remained in Russian captivity. This only increased the pressures on a sexually starved female population to yield to their conquerors in an 'unofficial polygamy' with the men of the occupying armies that was to send the post-war bastard population soaring – in 1945, one out of every five German births was estimated to be illegitimate!

That a large percentage of these children were fathered by Allied soldiers was an indication of the rapidity with which General Eisenhower's original 'non-fraternization' policy had broken down. The erosion had begun when Hitler's vaunted Westwal defence cracked in March 1945 and the 'liberation' of German women began – despite a US Army decree that contracting VD inside the German frontier would be taken as *prima facie* evidence of fraternization, entailing a $65 fine. Neither the policy nor the stiff penalty were effective. Officers and soldiers in every Allied army were soon fraternizing openly. As an American intelligence officer reported from Aachen, one of the first towns in the Third Reich to fall under Allied control, it was difficult for the average GI to regard the native women as hostile:

The essential kindness of the American soldier was in evidence. Soldiers helped German housewives with their chores, played with the children and through other small acts of friendship made living more tolerable through the creation of a friendly atmosphere. Conversation with some of those soldiers evoked such comments as, 'These Germans aren't bad people. We get along with them OK. All you've got to do is to treat them good and you have no trouble.'

Germany's female population did not resist the demands of the occupying soldiers. As one American report put it, 'Women were told that it was right and patriotic to bear children for any soldiers desiring the same.' They soon discovered that sex could be traded for food and cigarettes from the GIs, who found it easy to forgive the Germans, unlike their British comrades who had suffered the bombing of their homes by the Luftwaffe. The average GI could also identify with the cleanliness and domestic values espoused by the conquered but still house-proud womenfolk. 'Despite living in cellars and bombed buildings, the German civilians had kept clean,' one US Army intelligence officer noted. 'The girls, in particular, look out of place amid the debris. They wear bobby-sox and pigtails with gay coloured ribbons. They wear thin dresses, and they are fond of standing in the sun.'

Soaring VD rates were disturbing proof that 'getting-together' increased in the first weeks of peace. Now there was no longer any fighting, the sexual hunger of Allied troops feasted on that of German women separated from their husbands, many of whom had risked imprisonment in concentration camps to solicit the favours of Polish and Russian slave workers. Negro regiments were especially susceptible to fraternization. There were many white women who were eager to exorcize Hitler's racial myths in the most intimate manner.

'We cannot expect the GI to behave differently,' observed an American officer who urged the abandonment of the unworkable 'non-fraternization' policy'. 'After all he is human. He wants companionship – he's lonely, and the Germans are pastmasters at getting around men who feel that way.' Physical and sexual hunger combined with a flourishing black market to make sex a commodity to be traded for the necessities of life. 'In this economic set-up, sex relations, which function like any other commodity, assume a very low value,' explained one US Army survey. 'Because of this situation, plus the fact that every American soldier is a relative millionaire by virtue of his access to PX rations, the average young man in the occupation army is afforded an unparallelled opportunity for sexual exposure.' In Berlin immediately after the end of the war, German girls considered 'four cigarettes good pay for all night. A can of corned beef means true love.'

The lifting of censorship in the summer of 1945 encouraged newspapers in America and Britain to run sensational stories that ridiculed the failure of the non-fraternization policy. 'Have six years of war not taught us to call a spade a spade rather than a digging implement?' an English army captain in Germany wrote anonymously to *The Spectator*. 'It would be better to confess our sexual trespasses, as our European neighbours so blithely do theirs, than to risk alienating our friends by denying the true basis of "Fraternization", which is primarily sexual and not a social impulse, a get-together with German womankind and not with the German race.' Wives and sweethearts, impatiently waiting for their Johnny or Tommy to come marching home, were outraged at the very idea that the alien 'womankind' of a defeated foe might be stealing the affection of their husbands and boyfriends.

American war correspondent Julian Bach reported on what he called a 'vast social, ideological, and moral upheaval' that was taking place in the ruins of the Thousand Year Reich:

> When a pack of king-size cigarettes brings $18.50 on the Berlin black market, then the economy is sick. When a buxom fraulein, taught by Hitler to loathe and despise all 'North American Apes', turns around and, for the sake of a handful of Hersheys, cuddles up to a GI whose name she does not know (and probably could not conveniently pronounce), then moral values are in travail.

So much fraternization was taking place in Germany during the spring and summer of 1945 that GIs jokingly compared it to prohibition. One staff sergeant in the 30th Infantry Division explained the difference between non-fraternization and prohibition: 'In the old days a guy could hide a bottle inside his coat for days at a time, but it is hard to keep a German girl quiet in there for more than a couple of hours.' A tank driver commented, 'Fraternization? Yeh, I suppose it's all right. Anyway I've been doing it right along. But every now and then I wake up in a cold sweat. I dream that we are at war again and the German bastards I'm fighting this time are my own!'

The hostile press publicity brought an exchange of top-level communications between General Marshall and SHAEF headquarters followed by an official relaxation which began in June 1945 with the directive that the non-fraternization order was 'obviously not expected to be applied to small children'. Social contact with women was soon allowed because of what Eisenhower assured correspondents was 'the rapid progress which has been made in carrying out Allied de-Nazification policies'. As one philosophical American soldier/writer observed, 'Women are always the first to un-make the conquest and betray the conqueror – and properly, else the males' preposterous wars would continue for ever, unrelieved by sanity.'

In Heidelberg and other cities ex-Wehrmacht servicemen did not share this sentiment. Die-hard Nazi groups began a surreptitious campaign against fraternization, threatening vengeance with posters that proclaimed:

> What German women and girls do
> Makes a man weep, not laugh
> One bar of chocolate or one piece of gum
> Gives her the name German whore.

A very different attitude was encountered in Japan where, to the embarrassment of General MacArthur and the delight of the GIs, more than adequate provision had been made for occupying soldiers. In accordance with the oriental view of sex as a necessity, uncomplicated by the taboos and inhibitions of Christian doctrine, the nation that had dispatched medically inspected whores to army bordellos on the Pacific outposts of its empire also set up 'rest and recreation' centres for the American army. To forestall a wholesale violation of Japanese women, plans had been made even before the first American soldier had set foot in Tokyo to build a six million dollar bar and café complex to house five thousand women who, according to the coy announcement in the *Nippon Times*, 'will entertain Allied troops'.

When the first GIs arrived, they found temporary 'Special Recreation Centres' had already been set up in the surviving unbombed factories – only nine of the three hundred and ten brothels that had packed Tokyo's celebrated Yoshiwara red-light district had survived the American firestorm raids. Price-lists for these 'establishments' were posted on the quartermaster bulletin boards in all US Army camps – with the ever-present reminder about the need for prophylaxis to avoid infection:

> 20 Yen – a buck and a quarter – for the first hour, 10 yen for each additional hour and all night for 50 yen. If you pay more, you spoil it for all the rest. The MPs will be stationed at the doors to enforce these prices. Trucks will leave here each hour, on the hour. NO MATTER HOW GOOD IT FEELS WITHOUT ONE, BE SURE TO WEAR ONE.

In addition to the 'Special Recreation Centres', the street corners of the bombed-out Yoshiwara district were soon crowded with young Japanese girls sporting gaudy rayon pyjamas and crude attempts at Western make-up and hairstyles. These freelance whores were hardly the inheritors of Japan's cultivated geisha tradition, but the myth of Madame Butterfly was revamped by the ribald ballad of 'Gertie the Geisha' who was forsaken by her heartless 'cavalier in khaki', which appeared in *Stars and Stripes* in November 1945:

> Yes her Geisha *hear* was dipsy
> For a soldier from Poughkeepsie
> For a lad with winning smile had thrilled her through.
> And she quarantined her fanny
> To all men excepting Danny
> And she wore his dog tags just to keep her true.

Outraged chaplains protested that the US Army was sanctioning 'licensed houses of prostitution' – and with VD rates rocketing up to the near epidemic levels in Europe, medical supervision was being unofficially supplied to the 'recreation centres'. Some Catholic officers made themselves unpopular with the GIs and MacArthur's staff by insisting on hewing to a stricter moral line. A veritable typhoon broke in the American press after a navy chaplain had complained to *Newsweek* magazine that the liberty men on his ship were directed to 'houses of prostitution' in the Yokosuka area where there were separate 'geisha houses' for officers and chiefs. He had personally watched 'a line of enlisted men, four abreast, almost a block long, waiting their turn', and his letter continued:

> MPs kept the lines orderly. As the men were admitted into the lobby, they would select a prostitute (113 on duty that day), pay 10 yen to

the Jap operator, then go with the girl to her room. When the men returned they were registered and administered prophylaxis by Navy corpsmen.

'The Navy neither authorizes nor forbids patronage of houses of prostitution, but takes all practical measures to safeguard the health of personnel,' was the equivocal denial issued by Admiral Nimitz. The Commander in Chief of the US Navy, Pacific was obliged publicly to acknowledge for the first time the hypocrisy of the Allied military policy, which had provided discreet medical supervision for the local whorehouse while turning deaf ears to the protests of zealous chaplains and the indignation of self-righteous politicians.

The willingness of the female population of a defeated enemy to give themselves to the occupying troops demonstrated the ascendancy of human nature over military policy. But the tacit approval of relationships that it signalled did not please the keepers of America's moral conscience, as a service chaplain spelled out:

> We have won the victory of arms. We believed that the civilization for which we fought was immensely superior to the *Kultur* of the German, who under Hitler's leadership placed boys' and girls' camps near together with obvious expectation. We have read with horror the Japanese concept of women as men's playthings. But will the parents and families to whom American servicemen return, their thinking warped by 'take-a-pro' morality, will these families be convinced that the better civilization has won? Or that we lost our civilization in winning the war?

While the majority of soldiers' affairs were as transient as their military service, for some of the men in the US armed forces the romances and affairs with the girls they met overseas became permanent. Many GIs were first generation Americans, the children of European immigrants, and marriage to an Italian, French, or even German girl was a romantic adventure that renewed links with the ancestral homeland. The excitement of wartime had prompted Americans stationed in Britain to take as their brides over sixty thousand English girls. Many had left their new wives pregnant, others had left their girlfriends unwed and 'in the family way' with promises of returning for the marriage that would bring a passport to America. A song which had gained in popularity in the weeks before D-Day, 'Oh give me something to remember you by,' was suggestive of the way British girls might make their wartime romances into a permanent affair.

One wounded GI who had promised to come back and marry an English girl was shipped back to the United States. He mailed the engagement ring, and to speed her application for a visa she agreed to a proxy marriage. 'It was held in a Roman Catholic Church where all the family worshipped and was heard over the American radio network and reported in all the local papers. I listened in over the transatlantic telephone and could even hear the organ playing in the church and the giving of vows.' But after all the publicity the newly 'wedded' couple were disappointed to find that the state of North Carolina did not recognize the legality of their proxy marriage, and this particular GI bride never saw the United States.

Many other European women who thought they were going to marry a Yank would never see the promised land. 'There were, I remember, American GIs and officers who most cruelly betrayed and seduced Neapolitan girls, concealing from them and their families that back in the United States they'd a wife and kids,' wrote Sergeant James H. Burns.

Such was the appeal of America as the land of 'many' British girl's wartime dreams that 'some' of them married on trust. By early 1946, the US immigration department was snowed under dealing with permits for eight thousand French, Italian, and Dutch war brides in addition to the four thousand residency applications submitted by Australia and New Zealand women and over sixty thousand from Britain. A transit camp had to be set up in the south of England to process the British migration, which the War Department called 'Operation War Bride', and early in 1946 the first six hundred sailed for the United States aboard the steamship *Argentina*, which had been specially fitted out as a nursery ship. It was the start of what was to be the largest single influx of mothers and children into the United States in two centuries.

For many GI brides the dream came true, as it did for one British girl once she had recovered from the shock of finding that the United States really was the land of plenty:

My first impression of America was all food. It was absolutely sickening to see the amount of food. We went out to dinner the first night I arrived in New York and I remember a steak that was the size of my plate, it was more than I had had in England during the entire war! We had been hungry for a long time. Everybody there was so tired by the end of the war, but here was a country teeming with vitality. It took me a time to catch my breath and become part of it.

America proved to be the promised land for many of these new immigrants, including the English wife of a US Army sergeant who went through with her wedding even though her parents were against it because her future husband had said he was a fisherman. She went to the United States after the war expecting to have to work as a secretary in hard times. When she arrived at Redondo beach, California she discovered that he really was a fisherman – but what he hadn't told her was that he 'owned a fleet of five boats and was in a very good line of business'.

Not every GI bride found the glamour and excitement that her wartime romance had led her to expect. 'Peggy' was one of the unfortunate ones who realized, too late, that she had made a terrible mistake. She came to the end of her long journey to find herself and her two children face to face with her husband, out of uniform for the first time, and not in glamorous Hollywood or exciting New York, but in a grimy town in the Pennsylvania boondocks:

> It was getting dark when I got off the train. He was wearing one of those long overcoats like I'd seen people wearing in the old movies. He looked like Himmler. I stared at him and thought, 'Lord! What have you married?' And his mother! I was shocked to find that she was German to the hilt. The first thing she said was, '*Ach die Leber-sehen!* when she saw the two children. I looked at him and said, 'Am I really in America?' I woke up next morning and I told him, 'I'm going home. I don't like it here.' He said to me, 'You're not getting away. You're mine, you belong to me!' – and he meant it.

It was twenty-five years before Peggy was able to get a divorce, but other war brides became so homesick that they had to come home. 'Like many young girls at that time, they were infatuated with the GIs, and who could blame them?' observed a British woman whose best friend had married an American soldier only to return.

The majority of European war brides did make their future in the United States. But it was not just those that the GIs married and brought back who made an impact on the American male. Three out of every four American servicemen had sexual encounters overseas that were to influence the national image of romantic womanhood back home. 'My husband says the girls in Europe aren't like us. They're more human and understanding,' became a common complaint of the American wives of veterans in the year after the war ended. *Ladies Home Journal* went to one of the new arrivals for an answer:

I am surprised in this country, where you put so much emphasis on all the surface aspects of sex, that you shy away from the real meaning behind them. Your movies, your ads, your magazine illustrations, are full of allure and romance. Yet you shy away from the real relationship between men and women, which can be the richest, finest experience of your life. You make jokes about it instead. Like the European girls, all your young girls want to get married. But when they do, so many of them act as though they'd achieved their goal and finished a job. They seem to think everything should now come their way. I'd say European women don't feel this way about marriage. They feel it's the beginning of a job, at which they must keep working. They're happy to work at it, because they know it can be the most rewarding job in the world.

17

THE SEEDS OF SEXUAL REVOLUTION

World War II affected women profoundly.
Before the war, unless the job was something
very special, married women left work and the
man was expected to provide. All that changed
with the war – so did women's attitudes. Many
of us were earning almost as much as the men
and we learned to be not so dependent. Life spent
sweating over a hot stove became a thing of the
past for many.

A British housewife

Like You, Mrs America, Eureka will put aside
its uniform and return to the ways of peace . . .
building household appliances.

Eureka vacuum cleaner advertisement, 1943

'WAS THE PERMISSIVE SOCIETY set at this time?' mused one of the first British war brides of 1939. On reflection she agreed the collective wartime experience of her generation played its part in shaping the 'sexual revolution' two decades later:

> It was all there then, not quite so obvious as now. Whenever young, vital people meet in unusual and unsettling circumstances, there will always be a permissive group. Togetherness in the blackout was the car seat or doorway. We were brought together that way by the pressures of time and shortage of accommodation and a sense of unsettling uncertainty, in fact nothing was positive. Our generation, through sex education in the forces and all the 'free talk', learnt a thing or two about birth control. Few of us lived mentally or physically for tomorrow – or even next week. Many relationships were set for as long as war lasted – or the posting arrived for elsewhere. A free and easy, in some ways a slightly mad style of living took over. Many girls were married or spoken for, but husbands and boyfriends were not there. Company relieved the tension of what was about to happen. In the background a slight fear hid behind the bravado. The then current saying – given with a grin – was, 'Don't worry, it may never happen.' It often did! Many girls were left pregnant with no hope of marriage because of death, overseas posting, or rejection. Wartime work was plentiful for us and men were there for the taking. Girls were now able to walk into a public house and order their own drinks and buy cigarettes. We paid for our own cinema tickets and the days of sharing costs had begun. No-one would have thought of a date paying her own way before the war. But we didn't feel obliged to allow favours if we didn't fancy the escort in 'that' way.

The lives and moral attitudes of millions of people had undergone an extensive emotional trauma, and in the unsettled conditions of wartime many social inhibitions had lost their restraining force. Making the best of the present without thinking about the future had led to pleasure seeking and increased promiscuity. A British woman summed up in 1945 the personal impact that the war had on her life and that of her contemporaries:

> We have known terror and heartbreak, frustration, strain, the unbearable joy which unexpected happiness amid war can mean, in all a

world-wide testing of limb and spirit which has never been imposed on any earlier generation. We have matured more rapidly, emotionally, than any previous generation – including even the last war's, for then war was localized and women did not play a direct part in it.

Even before World War II had ended, its social costs were being measured not just in the lives lost and the destruction of homes, but by the continued upswing in the barometer of illegitimacy, venereal disease, and divorce. This was taken as an indication that there had been a wartime breakdown in public and private sexual conduct and something approaching moral panic overtook church and lay organizations on both sides of the Atlantic. They began calling for firm and fast action to restore the old moral values of 'The Married Way' and sexual continence. Indeed so many marriages were threatened by wartime adultery that one English bishop proposed a blanket indulgence for war-separated couples who went through another religious ceremony to renew their marriage vows. This was too radical a proposal to be taken seriously even by the Church of England, whose spiritual head, the Arch-bishop of Canterbury, launched a crusade of moral reconstruction two months after the death of Hitler had signalled the final destruction of the Nazi evil. Addressing the nation from the pulpit of his ancient cathedral on Sunday 12 July 1945, the Archbishop called upon people to reject 'wartime morality' and return to living Christian lives. 'People are not conscious of injuring the war effort by dishonesty or sexual indulgence,' he warned.

There was general public agreement that the Archbishop was right in denouncing the 'breakdown of morals'. Another high-ranking British churchman ever gave a catalogue of what he described as 'the grim facts' of a national malaise which cited:

. . . the increase in divorce, the declining birthrate, the spread of venereal disease, and the number of young couples who, as always in war time, wed in haste without any intention of fulfilling the primary purposes of marriage. This is partly due to the influence of war-time conditions, and partly to the flaunting sale of contraceptives. Life is so uncertain that young people are apt at the same time to snatch at the immediate satisfaction of sex, and also to be unduly cautious as to taking any risks in life. The throwing together of men and women in close proximity in war work has created a whole host of new problems . . . It is to be feared that promiscuous sex is on the increase. Here the alarming factor is the growth of amateur prostitution, especially among younger girls.

'Are We Facing a Moral Breakdown?' also became the subject of national concern in America, where the sky-rocketing divorce and juvenile delinquency rates made it the hot topic of the WOR radio network's popular 'Forum of the Air'. The debate, which was aired within weeks of Japan's formal surrender, reflected a significant difference in the moral climates of the victorious Anglo-Saxon powers. In Britian the decline in national *mores* was equated with the doom-laden prophecy that unless it was arrested the British Empire would crash like Imperial Rome, while in the United States the moral aftermath of the war was regarded as part of the ongoing process of social evolution. The consensus of American church leaders, educationalists, and labour officials was that while there had been a 'loss of moral tone', there was broad agreement that 'war has accelerated changes already taking place in courtship, marriage, family life, and the inter-relationship of the sexes. These changes, though rapid and disrupting, do not necessarily mean "breakdown".'

Even the French, who had prided themselves on their country's liberality in sexual affairs, succumbed to post-war moral fervour. With impeccable Gallic logic the forces of reaction set about changing the law to make brothels illegal. Led by the formidable campaigner Madame Marthe Richard, the challenge to the *maisons tolerées* quickly drew public support with charges that the brothel-keepers had profited from collaboration during the German occupation. By 1946, the ancient trade which had helped make Paris the erotic capital of Europe was proscribed and the brothels were obliged to close their doors for ever – thereby forcing French prostitutes to pursue their profession in the streets and by telephone.

The post-war moral crusade intensified after the wild abandon of the peace celebrations. Sober Victorian principles were offered as the panacea which would repair the damage that the war had wrought on the family and married life. The call to put back the moral clock had been started in the United States a full year earlier in April 1944, when ex-President Herbert Hoover had warned that 'the moral life of America is in danger . . . We must accept the fact that total war relaxes moral standards on the home front and that this imperils the whole front of human decency,' he wrote in a magazine article which drew attention to the emptiness of a military victory unless accompanied by a 'moral victory'.

Military victory, however, had only been won by millions of American and British citizens sacrificing the trappings of a civilized morality. Moral and social taboos, once broken, were not to be easily restored, especially when the traditional patterns of life had been disrupted for so many for so long. It was beyond even the propaganda resources of governments to recondition the wartime mass psychology overnight. The brutalizing and dislocative effects of war had left many individuals reacting to the cessation of hostilities as another interruption in the transient pattern of existence to which they had become accustomed. Millions of demobilized servicemen had grown used to an adventurous existence which did not reach beyond tomorrow. It took months and even years for many of them to accustom themselves again to a routine civilian existence. The transition was especially hard for those who had entered the services straight from school and to whom the mundane world of everyday work was as great a shock as joining the army had been.

The extent to which the attitudes of servicemen had been deeply affected by the war was only to become apparent in the decade after 1945, when a new generation of American writers, led by Norman Mailer, James Jones, and Irwin Shaw, began chronicling their experiences with a force and conviction which shocked the literary establishment. Unlike the English war novelists, who tended to romanticize the rather more genteel experience of the officer, *The Naked and the Dead*, *From Here to Eternity*, and *The Young Lions* were drawn with the brutally honest and often sexually explicit language of the enlisted man. The instant success and huge sales they achieved was due in no small measure to the huge market they found among the millions of servicemen who wanted to read about themselves.

It was not just the immediacy of the war experience that made these books – and their subsequent imitators – perennial bestsellers, but also the way in which their authors had boldly portrayed the relationship between violence, sex, and the role of the individual in a mechanistic war. Action and psychology were combined in intense, essentially humourless plots, which dealt with the loves, friendships, and hatreds of combat soldiers struggling to survive and find a rationality for their existence in the face of the grim irrationality of death. Sex, machines, and power were the underlying preoccupations of the plots.

Combat was presented, according to the authors' viewpoint, as either the sublimation of sexual energy or its direct release. The characters battled their way through the pages of these books in search of an emotional catharsis on the field of battle, making their choices between heroism, wanton butchery, or cowardice. Homosexuality was dealt with both candidly and unsympathetically, reflecting the not insignificant part it had played in the respective authors' military lives. In another echo of their military conditioning, male potency was usually equated with an individual's prowess as a warrior – and comparisons were frequently drawn between a soldier's ungovernable sexual impulse and the war itself.

The pattern for World War II fiction established by the 1948 publication of *The Naked and the Dead* was to prove a progressively liberalizing influence on post-war literature's treatment of explicit sexual themes. Despite the protests of the moral reformers, there were sufficient readers to know that these novels told it like it was, and that modern warfare was not to be romanticized as it had been in the past. Not only did these books play an important part in preparing the public for the language necessary for a more open and explicit discussion, but one of their main themes – the confrontation between human sexuality and man's technological capacity for self-destruction – was to become the focus of much contemporary literature.

Very few veterans were to exorcize their wartime emotional traumas by writing about them, and the many who were psychologically disturbed enough to warrant hospitalization laid their ghosts with the help of consoling wives and girlfriends. After enduring the anxieties of separation, the female population was expected to heal the emotional as well as the physical casualties of the men who finally came home. It was a not inconsiderable post-war burden. Three out of five women had husbands, brothers, fathers, and sons in the armed forces. A profound impact was made on the psyche of the female population by the loss of 292,131 Americans and 271,311 men of Britain in addition to the 671,278 men of the US armed forces and 277,077 British servicemen who returned home mentally and physically maimed by the war.

Many more wives, mothers, and girlfriends were to discover that the experience of battle left mental scars which often took longer to heal than physical wounds. Marriage counsellors advised American women anticipating the return of a veteran to 'let him know you are tired of living alone, that you want him to take charge'. A sociologist suggested they give 'more than the wife's usual responsibility for her marriage', by offering husbands 'lavish and – and undemanding – affection'. It was not just the coarse language that shocked some wives: many men were disturbed by bouts of impotence or sadistic over-aggressiveness.

For most wives and sweethearts, World War II did not end when the shooting stopped. It was many months before the majority of troops could be brought home and demobbed, and even before they arrived to rebuild old relationships, the press had revealed the extent to which Allied troops had fraternized with the Italian, German, and Japanese women. Although the military authorities in both Britain and America took care to issue strong official denials, the secret US Army sex surveys of 1945 indicated that three out of four veterans returned from overseas service more sexually experienced than when they had left.

For many war brides there was also the shock of discovering that the man who returned was not the romantic hero of a hasty embarkation wedding. One American observer concluded that as many as one in three war marriages were not worth saving: 'we may as well reconcile ourselves to that fact, and accept a thumping increase in the divorce rate as one of the costs of war.' Many of these marriages were quickly dissolved in the twelve months after 1945 which brought over half a million divorces in the United States and thirty-four thousand in Britain. But by no means all wartime brides resorted to legal processes. It was a reflection of the strength of the traditional moral standards that once peace came 'Phyllis' – and many others like her – decided that for better or worse they had no choice but to learn to live with their mistakes:

When my husband finally came home we discovered we were two different people, so much had happened in those years apart. My husband, older than myself, was time-conscious, critical, and came back with the attitude of a regimental sergeant major; I am sure he expected me to jump up and salute when he entered a room. We had to take it that the men were faithful while away, but my in-laws were very quick to tell tales of my friendships with the opposite sex. My

husband later threw this at me when I complained of the years I had
spent alone. I realized that settling down was going to be hard, but
by this time I had two babies, quickly, and I was stuck. In a strange
area, strange faces, and for hours on my own. He was finding it hard
to get a civilian job and having to take orders after having had some
measure of authority. I missed going to work and the companionship
and intelligent conversation. After a while we settled to some sort of
married life, but there were times when I thought that if there was a
hell on earth, I was living it. I did not want a divorce, I could never
have left the children.

If the soaring post-war divorce rates became one of the most
debated manifestations of the 'sexual fallout' of the war, the impact
of female mobilization proved to be another, more permanent,
catalyst in the post-war equation. Women had made a critical
contribution to the Allied war effort, but in the year after the war,
three million American women and over a million British women
were laid-off or voluntarily left their wartime jobs.

At the height of the manpower crisis in 1943, the percentage of
women in Britain's engineering industry had risen to thirty-one
per cent compared to less than ten per cent in 1939 – but this was
to fall to thirteen per cent after the war. Similarly American
women's share of the lucrative jobs on Detroit assembly lines was
to fall from a wartime high of twenty-five per cent to only seven
and a half. In the United States and Britain, although almost three
quarters of the wartime female labour force managed to stay in
work, nine out of ten suffered a sharp decrease in earnings as
weekly wages fell by as much as a fifth.

The post World War II downgrading of the economic status of
working women was a repetition of what had happened after
World War I. In 1919, the leaders of the suffragette movement
had tried to link voting rights to equal pay. 'The time has come
now when we women have a right to ask that we shall be free to
labour where our labour is needed, that we shall be free to serve
in the capacity for which we are fitted,' declared the veteran
American suffragist Anna Howard Shaw. But the right to vote
was to prove an easier goal to achieve than the right to equal pay.

Only in Germany did World War I bring the issues of sexual
discrimination and women's rights into the centre of the political
forum. The 'New Woman' proposed by the radical feminists of
the Weimar Republic was to be liberated from her traditional

baby-bearing and infant-rearing role through state-funded contraception and abortion and government-sponsored child-care programmes. Equal employment opportunities in industry and the professions were to be guaranteed. Hitler's rise to power blocked the rise of the liberated 'New Woman' as envisaged by the Weimar reformers, but she was to prove a far more enduring model for female liberation than the American flapper. It was to be one of the great ironies of history that the ultimate realization of the Weimar model of the liberated woman was the very one which the Nazis so assiduously and successfully repressed. That she was to be revitalized and reborn through the wartime experience of the female populations of the United States and Britain was one legacy that Hitler most certainly did not intend when he began his war in 1939.

The breakdown of the traditional sex roles of a large section of the Allied female population was the most profound sexual consequence of World War II – even though its full impact was to take two decades to manifest itself. The female labour force, in Britain and the United States, expanded by over forty per cent during the war years. Its significance was not so much that the industrial sex-segregation barriers had been breached by women who made ships and aircraft, but that by the final year of the war three quarters of the new women workers were married. Many of these were mothers of young children who entered the workplace for the first time. In answering the urgent call to join the production battle demanded by a 'total war', this large section of the female population had finally broken down the resistance to employing wives and mothers. While almost ninety per cent of women eventually married, eighty-five per cent of pre-war working women were single, whereas by 1944 a quarter of all female workers were wives and mothers.

The wartime labour shortage that was instrumental in helping break down the reluctance of employers to hiring married and older women and brought a general extension of the economic contribution did not, however, change the attitudes of management and unions to 'women's work'. The wartime female labour force was paid far less than the male rate for the job. Women were paid on average only sixty per cent of what men earned in the same job in the United States and fifty per cent in Britain. This was in spite of a continuous campaign for equal pay. In the

United States women's organizations had received the Roosevelt administration's support for the principal of equal pay for equal work. In 1941, the Supreme Court upheld federal non-discriminatory legislation on wages and hours, but the male-dominated unions and management contrived artificial sex-related scales for women doing wartime 'men's work' like welding. They justified the lower pay for women by asserting that the female workers had not served long apprenticeships and were therefore less skilled and productive than men.

In Britain the barriers to equal pay for women proved just as rigid. While women were praised for doing 'men's jobs' like crane driving and welding, which showed 'they were capable of greater things than tradition put into their hands', they were employed as semi-skilled workers – and paid correspondingly low wages. Britain's restrictive craft unions only reluctantly admitted women to skilled trades on a temporary wartime basis, at a percentage of the normal rate unless they proved able to work 'without special assistance and guidance'. This left plenty of latitude for the shop stewards and employers to carefully regulate female pay scales well below the men's. The wartime Transport and General Workers Union Workers organizer in Coventry, Jack Jones, was not alone in insisting that women were not in engineering 'to cheapen the industry or to take the jobs of the men for the whole of the future, but just for the duration of the war'. The unions therefore sided with the management in drawing up special 'women's work' categories which assigned them 'work of a very light kind'.

Many British women became union members under the naive impression that organized labour was committed to the struggle for equal pay. One girl who had left her job in a grocer's shop to become a mechanic and who hoped to keep her wartime job finally realized that she had been trapped by the system:

> If they hadn't let us in and didn't make a fuss to raise our wages, we'd be as skilled as the men by the end of the war and yet working for smaller wages. See? And the boss would want to keep us on after the war instead of taking the men back. If we get into the unions and get the men's pay, the boss will prefer to take on the men after the war. There wouldn't be a proper reason to keep us on, now would there?

Such overt sexual discrimination in job classification generated resentment between the British workers, leading to disputes and strikes that threatened production in several vital war plants. The government Royal Ordinance Factories, which manufactured most of Britain's shells and bombs, eventually abandoned discriminatory pay rates because 'they found this business of sorting out men's work from women's work quite impossible'. But private industry proved more reactionary. At the Glasgow factory which built many of the Merlin engines for Spitfire fighters and Lancaster bombers, management's insistence on sticking to the inequitable dual rates resulted in a week-long strike in October 1943. But the compromise which settled what could have been a war-threatening stoppage side-stepped the issue of equal pay by fixing a rate for individual machines regardless of the sex of the operator. Nor was the real issue mentioned in the strike announcement, which merely proclaimed that 'Rolls Royce workers are determined to achieve their demands and in doing so realize they are defending the wages of their husbands, brothers, and sweethearts and other workers in the armed forces.'

Throughout the war Churchill resisted the growing demands from the female labour force for equal pay with the same stubbornness he had marshalled to defy Hitler in 1940. Since all able-bodied British women were conscripted into some form of war-work, his coalition government saw no need to make any concessions. A Royal Commission on Equal Pay was only set up after a parliamentary impasse was reached over remuneration scales for male and female teachers proposed by the 1944 Education Bill – and its majority report two years later came down firmly against making equal pay a guideline for post-war British industrial policy.

Women workers had invaded 'men's' jobs as welders, riveters, and crane drivers in heavy industry in wartime, but they lost them when the approach of the Allied victory brought a rapid return to the traditional sex discrimination. Long before the last shot had been fired, 'Rosy the Riveter' had become an extinct species in the shipyards as production rapidly declined and veterans returned to reclaim their old jobs. Women were also forced to withdraw from the engineering and aircraft industries. Those who needed to continue working had little choice but to accept lower paid 'women's work' in the traditional industries such as textiles and food. Only in the electrical industries did the female work force hold on to its wartime gains as production geared up for the peacetime market.

In politics, as in industry, there was a growing post-war reassertion of deeply embedded social beliefs about gender roles. Symbolic of this reaction was an anti-feminist backlash which had emerged in the United States in June 1944 when Congress approved the bill which ejected female pilots who ferried planes to their destination from the cockpits of army planes. It was as much an economic as a sexual reaction, a response to pessimistic predictions on both sides of the Atlantic that the end of the war would bring an end to full production and a return to the Depression, with men being thrown out of work in favour of lower-paid women.

Lavish tributes continued to be paid by American and British government spokesmen to the magnificent job that women had done, but behind the scenes their male-dominated bureaucracies were casting post-war plans on the assumption that most of the women would meekly return to their ageless mission as wives and mothers. It was an assumption shared by most male factory workers. 'Women still enjoy raising families, and the way to a man's heart is still through cooking,' one foreman insisted. 'Most of our women war workers will want to get back to housework as soon as we win the war.'

Not until American women were actually asked – by an official 1944 survey of the War Manpower Commission – did the policy-makers in Washington realize how wrong their assumptions had been. Many women certainly did not want to go back to housework after the war. 'I'd stay if they want me without taking a man's place away from him,' was the typical response heard from women who were reluctant to deprive a returning veteran of his job, but who wanted to continue working. Surveys of thousands of female factory workers in the United States found that 61–85 per cent of all women war-workers wanted to continue their employment in peacetime, and that more than half of all married women wanted to keep their jobs and new-found economic prosperity.

For many thousands of women, work was not a matter of choice, but of economic necessity

> Rose Carson, who used to work in a five-and-dime store, got a war job as a riveter in an aircraft plant and says she expected to keep on working until her fiancé was out of the service, had completed his education, and was able to marry. Mrs Martin, a candy-store clerk, who had recently lost her husband, had to keep a job indefinitely to support herself and three children. Mrs Simmons, a saleswoman in a

department store, was supporting an invalid husband suffering from rheumatic heart disease. Caroline Smith, a single woman and a stenographer, said she would have to continue in her position as she was the only wage earner in the family, which included a disabled father. Mrs Cartwright had taken a war job as a machine operator to help her husband buy a home and would have to keep on working after the war to meet monthly payments. Another woman, a school teacher, was contributing to the support of her crippled brother's children.

'Will the Factory Girls Want to Stay Put or Go Home?' was the question that Britain's semi-official Mass Observation survey attempted to answer in the final year of the war. In contrast to the United States, only a quarter of British factory workers polled unequivocally answered yes to the loaded question 'Should women be allowed to go on doing men's jobs?' Another twenty-eight per cent said that it 'depends on post-war conditions', leaving the pollsters to conclude, 'The most general opinion seems to be that women will want to go back home, or take up jobs which were considered suitable for women before the war, while waiting for marriage.'

The Ministry of Labour, unwilling to put its trust in opinion polls, began weighing the introduction of legislation to force women out of their wartime jobs to forestall possible unemployment when four million servicemen were demobbed. This would have reneged on the pledge Labour Minister Ernest Bevin had given in 1942, when he proclaimed, 'it will become the bounden duty of every one of us to arrive at proper conclusions as to the right use and place that women must find in the post-war world'.

In the ambitious social engineering planned by Sir William Beveridge for the creation of the post-war welfare state in Britain, equal pay was deliberately excluded. The Womens' Advisory Committee on Post-War Reconstruction made its dissatisfaction felt by directing the greatly increased female union membership to persuade the Trades Union Congress and the Labour Party to support their resolution calling for the rate for the job: 'Women have established their claim to a share in the economic life of the nation. By having shared equally with men the tremendous task of producing for the needs of war, they have an equal right to employment after the war.'

In the USA, a report by the US Department of Labour in 1944 stated, 'The American people, therefore, must demand consideration of the status of women in all post-war plans.' Like British feminists' call for equal pay, the Americans' claim for equal employment opportunities was a measure of the extent to which women's participation in the war effort had given them a new sense of their economic importance and political force as well as the confidence to call on the male legislatures to recognize their rights.

'Surely we will not refuse to our own that which we purchased for strangers with the blood of our sons,' was a convincing argument used to persuade the wartime Congress to accept the 1923 Equal Rights Amendment, which proposed making all sexual discrimination constitutionally illegal. But not until 1945 did the supporters of the bill receive presidential encouragement from the Judiciary Committees of both houses. But it was a measure of the post-war anti-feminist reaction to women's wartime activities that the following year the Senate passed the bill by only a three-vote majority, far short of the two thirds necessary to submit a constitutional amendment to the individual states.

The Congress rebuff to ERA came within months of the British Parliamentary Commission coming out against equal pay for women workers. These defeats were a sharp setback to hopes for liberation which had acquired a new momentum and purpose through women coming together in the wartime workplace. But the failure of both Congress and Parliament to approve the equal economic rights that many women felt they had fought for in World War II was only partly attributable to an anti-feminist backlash whipped up by men. The majority of American and British women were still ambivalent about claiming a new role in society. Most regarded their wartime gains as 'time out' for the duration from their traditional role centred on marriage, home, and dependency on the male breadwinner.

'Americans may no longer believe that a woman's place *is* in the home,' *Time Magazine* had observed early in 1945. It soon became apparent that most women did not subscribe to this view, and neither did the vast majority of men: 'There are two things I want to be sure of after the war,' a typical soldier wrote from the South Pacific. 'I want my wife waiting for me and I want my job waiting for me. I don't want to find my wife busy with a job that some returning soldier needs, and I don't want to find that some other man's wife has my job.'

To counter fears that American soldiers would return to an employment market saturated by women in spite of the GI Bill of Rights, which guaranteed them their old jobs, the US Army distributed a booklet entitled 'Do You Want Your Wife To Work After The War?' In slick Madison Avenue style it employed cheerful cartoons to show that the war had not dramatically shifted the demarcation between the sexes in the workplace. The record indicated that the female share of the United States workforce had been growing steadily from thirteen per cent to thirty-four per cent since 1873. 'The war has merely speeded up a march that has been under way for a century and a half.' GIs were reminded that 'women are not made only for having babies,' as the Nazi's had dogmatically insisted. The leaflet continued:

> Women are not all alike, and there are many who have long felt restive and rebellious about housework to whom the war has brought the first opportunity for release. To them dishwashing and baby-tending are dull drudgery compared with the interest and excitement and sociability of working in a war plant.

To explain why so many women opted for domestic drudgery in the aftermath of World War II became the mission, twenty years later, of militant apostles of women's liberation who invented the phrase 'feminine mystique'. This was the title of the influential book by Betty Friedan which expounded on the success of the 1945 version of the male confidence trick:

> When the men came back, there was a headlong rush into marriage. The lonely years when husbands or husbands-to-be were away at war – or could be sent away at a bomb's fall – made women particularly vulnerable to the feminine mystique. They were told that the cold dimension of loneliness was the necessary price they had to pay for a career, for any interests outside the home. The mystique spelled out a choice – love, home, children, or other goals and purposes in life. Given such a choice, was it any wonder that so many American women chose love as their whole purpose?

By making jobs like wartime welding seem glamorous, American propaganda fostered the impression that such work increased the chances of finding a husband and becoming a better homekeeper in peacetime. The trend was particularly apparent in the American wartime media. Women's magazines, newspaper features on female war workers, and advertising for wartime housewives all stressed the feminine attributes. 'She does a man's work in the ground crew servicing airplanes, but she hasn't lost any of her glamour, sweetness, and charm,' ran a *McCalls* headline. A cosmetic company advertised that the war could not be won by lipstick, 'But it symbolizes one of the reasons why we are fighting . . . the precious right of women to be feminine and lovely.'

Women were also lured away from the masculine clothes of wartime work with the 'New Look', which promoted the return to a more traditional and restrictive style of female dressing. Its instigator was Christian Dior, who admitted that he had hated seeing women who 'looked and dressed like Amazons. But I designed clothes for flowerlike women, clothes with rounded shoulders, full feminine busts, and willowy waists above enormous spreading skirts.'

The fact that many women responded so rapidly and eagerly to the revival of the myth of fragile femininity may have been less to do with their seduction by the so-called feminine mystique than with the exhaustion of a large percentage of the female population after their wartime burdens. Anxiety and deprivation made a retreat to post-war domesticity a very attractive option for many women. The notion that somehow they were tricked out of the freedom they had won during the war raises questions about just how 'liberating' their wartime experience really had been and how far it had redefined the individual woman's attitudes to their unique role of wife and mother.

Social welfare workers and child-care experts, moreover, blamed the lack of parental supervision in wartime for the high levels of juvenile delinquency. These accusations stirred the collective guilt of large numbers of working mothers. It was reinforced by the emphasis laid on maternal responsibilities by the fashionable post-war theories of educators like Dr Benjamin Spock and others whose writings sought to put motherhood and child-rearing in a modern context. Women were advised to devote far more time to their children and to indulge them more, which necessarily decreased their opportunities to do work outside the home.

The tremendous increase in the numbers of couples getting married was another factor that checked the move towards greater women's liberation in the immediate post-war years. Men and women were not only marrying at a younger age during the war and after, but the marriage rate jumped by nearly fifty per cent in 1946 and remained over twenty per cent above pre-war levels throughout the decade. Two out of three men who returned from the war were still single, and those couples whose marriages had survived the test of war wanted to make up for lost time by starting or expanding their families. Child-rearing became a national pre-occupation and homemaking became a feature of women's magazines.

That so many women responded to the post-war call to their ageless mission was to result in a larger than expected generation of post-war children who were to make a significant contribution to furthering the 'sexual revolution' when they matured. The 'baby boom' children, raised to adolescence according to the permissive 'Spock doctrine', were to become participants in the sexual liberation movements which emerged in the late 1960s in the United States and had spread by the early 1970s throughout the Western world. Raised in the increasing affluence of the fifties, they had not only reached puberty earlier in their teens than any other generation but they also wielded economic power. It was teenage spending which fuelled the phenomenon of Rock 'n' Roll, whose ostentatious eroticism ensured its wide appeal amongst a sexually mature and rebellious younger generation and provided the emotional context for their dating, courtship and generally permissive life-style.

After the immediate post-war reaction, the trend to permissiveness was firmly established with the commercialization of eroticism in the films, television, and advertising industries which had followed the lead of the wartime pin-ups and girlie magazines. Sex-appeal was to become an important element in marketing the consumer boom of the fifties.

A generation after World War II had ended, the seal was to be set on the 'Permissive Society' when the old definitions of obscenity were successfully challenged in Britain and the United States. By the early 1970s, homosexuality was no longer a criminal offence and the laws against prostitution were relaxed or less stringently enforced. Abortions became legal for the first time, representing a significant increase in the freedom of choice for the female population – although only in the face of vehement opposition by the churches and moral purity campaigners.

The development of more reliable and less intrusive means of effective birth control such as the contraceptive pill encouraged sexual experimentation by the younger generation and under-mined the moral compulsion towards virginity. The right to abortion represented a political triumph for a revived Women's Liberation Movement, whose emergence in the sixties signalled that a large cross-section of female population had finally mobilized to make the most serious challenge since the war to their continued subordination.

The women's movement that spread its influence across the Atlantic was to become one of the most important cultural and political events of the decade. Significantly, it drew part of its inspiration and inheritance from women who had experienced a transient liberation during World War II. Now that they had raised their families and become bored with the post-war ideal of suburban domesticity, they had the time and energy to march shoulder-to-shoulder with their daughters to campaign vocifer-ously for equal pay and legal rights, free birth control, abortions, and adequate nursery care.

Many of these issues were familiar causes to the women of the war generation, who were more united and determined this time to press for the status and rights which they had been denied in 1945. Although the movement succeeded in closing the wage rate and the gender gap, full equal rights and pay were still elusive. Nonetheless another major step had been taken in 1970 to put men and women on a more equal footing with the passing of the Equal Pay Act, which was not, however, enforced until 1975. The consumer economy had expanded to the point where it depended not only on women's spending power, but also on the labour of married women, who were working in larger numbers than at any time since the war.

The steady advance of the female population towards full equal economic and social status with men may well prove to be the most significant social revolution of the twentieth century – a revolution that is far from over. World War I, because it came at the more critical point, may have produced the sharpest changes in the status of women, but it was World War II, because it mobilized a far greater percentage of the female population, that was eventually to bring about the greatest transformation in West-ern society.

While many of women's wartime economic gains were to be given up in the retreat to post-war domesticity after 1945, the seeds of a profound sexual revolution had already been sown. They were to germinate and flower two decades later into a movement for female liberation that won many of the rights for which the women of World War II had been fighting.

ACKNOWLEDGEMENTS

The genesis of this project is rooted in a 'war baby's' curiosity that his mother had 'done her bit' with hoe and milking stool in the Land Army, while his father fought with the Royal Navy.

It was an idea that grew out of many personal interviews during a decade of writing about World War II. During the filming of a D-Day anniversary documentary there were the Frenchwomen who still cherished romantic memories of their allied liberators; the veterans who told of their amorous adventures; and the discovery from official documents of the contribution penicillin made to the success of the 1944 invasion. It was, however, while assembling material for *The Battle of the Atlantic* that official data and pictures graphically brought home the staggering contribution that the women of the United States and Britain made to the allied victory.

The hundreds of former 'Rosy the Riveters' who responded to a *New York Post* item on the Battle of the Atlantic book confirmed my belief that the full story of the sexual impact of the war had yet to be told.

The 'war baby' was soon enthusiastically adopted by Little, Brown and Company. To Chris Coffin in Boston—as well as to Sonny Mehta and Simon Masters at Pan Books in London—I owe an enormous debt of gratitude for their confidence and support of what turned into an extended and complex project. A special contribution had been made by Teresa Sacco, whose own youthful wartime memories brought a unique addition to the final manuscript. To Tess and Chris, as well as Carol O'Brien at Collins, I am enormously grateful for the skilled editorial management that has brought the project to the printed page.

Love, Sex and War would not have been possible without all the personal wartime accounts to which I have had access. So my principal acknowledgement is to all those men and women whose published and unpublished accounts are the documentary backbone of this book. Particular thanks are due to all the listed people who corresponded as a result of the co-operation of the radio and television stations, newspapers and magazines which broadcast my appeal on both sides of the Atlantic.

In the United States I have been able to tap the extensive collections of books, magazines and wartime memorabilia in the New York Public Library, the Library of Congress in Washington and Columbia University

Library. Without the friendly and efficient assistance of their staffs this book would not have been possible. I am also grateful to the Public Records Office, Imperial War Museum as well as the Cambridge University and British Libraries for the research facilities they provided.

Much of the original research in this work—as in my previous books—has been facilitated by the knowledgeable encouragement of the staff of the National Archives in Washington. Especial mention must be made of John Taylor and Edward Reese who, along with Wilbert Mahoney, Terri Hammett and William H. Lewis, make research in the modern military section such a rewarding adventure. My thanks are also extended to Jerry Hess and Dr Virginia Purdy for guiding me through the voluminous wartime files of the Labour Bureau, the War Manpower Administration and the Women's Bureau. Richard von Doerhnof and George Chaloux were instrumental in turning up fascinating documentation, and Jim Trimble provided expert assistance in locating photographs.

Over the four years that it has taken to research and assemble the material in this book I have received logistical assistance, wise advice and professional help from old friends and many new acquaintances all of whom have been unstinting in their support. Acknowledgement must be made, therefore, to the contributions made by: John Alston, Ed Anderson, Anthony Batten, Linda Aness, Ann Balery, Betty Blackman, John Boileau, Larry Collins, Susan Costello, Irena Czaposa, Professor Christie Davies, Jonathan Copus, Robert Crowley, Captain Thomas Dyer, Admiral Sir Morgan Giles, Jim Gough, Dagmar Henne, Cherry Hughes, Terry Hughes, David Ireland, Gerald P. Jantzi, David Kagan, Alan Kelly, Professor Warren Kimball, Harold Ketzer, Admiral Edwin T. Layton, Gary Lazarus, Bruce Lee, Charles Lowdness, Jill Lowry, Jimmy Mack, Jim MacDougal, Barry Meanwell, Vic Meyers, Rob Michaels, John D. Montgomery, Diane Newman, Milo O'Sullivan, Mary Pett, Captain and Mrs Roger Pineau, Colonel Harry Pozner, Harry Chapman Pincher, Murray Pollinger, Lawrence Pratt, General Sir Frank Richardson, Peter Rhodes, Karen Ross, David Rowley, Dr A. L. Rowse, Gregory Saunders, Captain Raymond Schmidt, Robert L. Sherrod, Graham Sergeant, Professor Norman Stone, Chauncey W. Smith, Linda Wade, Tom Wallace, Nigel West, Robin Wight, Robert Wolf, Robert L. Young and Hans Zellweger.

Orlando Figes, Brendan Lemon and Andrew Lownie contributed valuable material and criticism during their spells as research assistants. My thanks are due once more to Diane and John Moore for their efficient collection of illustrations. To my trusty Morrow computer and its 'senior partner' go all the customary accolades for typing and manuscript preparation made possible by the 'magic' of Wordstar.

Last, but in no way least, I owe a considerable debt of gratitude to Anna

Del Valle and William C. Bodie for their personal banking expertise which has underpinned the whole project.

John Costello   New York
April 1985   London

Grateful acknowledgement is made to the following for their response to the author's appeals in Britain and the United States:

'A Grandma', Robert L. Abel, Dolly Ackerman, Jimmy Adams, R. Adams, W. Adams, Joy Adland, Agnes Allen, Jesse Allman, Eugene Anderson, Earl L. Archer Jr, E. M. P. Arnold, V. Bannell, J. E. Barrington, H. U. Bell, Sarah Bell, Barbara Bennet, J. Beverley-Smith, Joseph E. Biernacki, Gewn Bingham, Doris Bish, O. M. Blewitt, Ethel Botting, James A. Boyd, Elizabeth Bradbury, Betty M. Bryan, J. W. Bryant, Frederick T. Budde, C. A. Burke, Dorothy Callaghan, Philip Candilière, R. Carpenter, James F. Champ, Knowlton A. Chandler, E. H. Churchill, Frank Clear, P. Climie, J. Collins, Evelyn Colyer, Wyn Costello, Patrick E. Creamer, E. T. Crees, D. M. Crompton, Carmine Cusmano, I. M. Cuthbert, Susan P. Daddo-Longlois, E. Davies, Ruby Davies, Lillian Davitt, Edward J. De Havilland, G. L. Dean, R. W. Dobie, Daphne Dodey, I. Dunn, Lucy M. Elliot, Jeremiah F. Enright, Alta M. Evans, Ruth Farnham, Richard L. Felman, A. Finch, Hilda Forrest, Zena Forster, Alden Francis, Terry Frier, John D. Fulgenzi, John O. Gallup, Arthur R. Gill, Hugh J. Greecham, E. C. Green, Myra Constance Griffin, V. Guzenda, S. Gwillim, Melvin E. Hawkes, Eileen Hayward, Joseph E. Hecht, Vicky Henton, Molly Higgs, Jean Howard, B. A. Humphrey, Stella Jarvis, Eileen Jones, Patricia Jordan, J. B. Keene, Jean M. Keitch, Helen Kerr-Green, V. E. King, Malcolm D. Kunes, M. Lauer, Joseph L. LeBlanc, Effie C. Lettle, Ben Levinson, Grace S. Love, W. Ludwig, Norma Mann, Jean Marston, J. S. Martin, Laurence N. Mason, M. Mason, Jean Mason, M. A. Mason, M. McBride, Jean McCallan, Philip M. McGhee, William G. McGuire, A. A. McInnes, E. Miles, Marietta L. Moellar, John D. Montgomery, L. Montgomery, Arthur Moore, Olive Morgan, Phyllis Moss, Geoffrey W. G. Munnery, Olive New, R. Oxley, Kathleen Parker, Anna Parkhurst, U. L. Patterson, J. Peek, Joyce Peters, B. Phillips, Christine Pitman, Harry Pozner, Barbara Prutton, Carlos Radcliffe, N. K. Radford, J. W. Ramsay, G. Reid, G. M. Reilly, Sir Frank Richardson, Irene Ritter, Beryl J. Robertson, Dennis A. Roland, Patience Saunders, D. Scharf, Lynn Scott-Southall, Donald Seebold, Michael Senko, Patricia A. Sexton, W. Shephard, Allan J. Simpson, M. Smalley, Gerald F. Smith, I. F. Smith, Babs Smith, Joyce Smith, Ruth King Spark, S. R. Sparks, Trixie B. Sparrow, D. Spencer, Ivy Stanier, Barbara S. Staton, D. Stephens, William Steward, Bernice Stoddard, Daureen H. Stover, O. G. Sutterly, Henry Swyers, Jean Tabor, Eve Taylor, Sherrie Thompson, Wilfred J. Toczko, Joan Tole, J. G. R. Trasker, Walter W. Tripp, R. C. Tynes, Thomas R. Upshaw, Anne Valery, Nelson E. Walker, C. B. Ward, L. Watson, M. E. Watts, E. D. White, M. Whyte, Phyllis D. Williams, Joan Williams, Thomas Henry Wood, Ruth F. Wright, Agnes Young.

BIBLIOGRAPHY

Anderson, Karen, *Wartime Women: Sex Roles, Family Relations and the Status of Women During World War II*, Greenwood Press, Connecticut, 1976.

Archibald, Katherine, *Wartime Shipyard*, University of California, Berkeley, 1947.

Babcock, Myles, *A Guy Who Knows*, Benidji, Minnesota, 1946.

Balfour, Michael, *Propaganda in World War II*, Routledge and Kegan Paul, London, 1979.

Baxandall, Rosalyn, *America's Working Women—A Documentary History*, Vantage Books, New York, 1976.

Beck, C. L., *Fighter Pilot*, privately published, California, 1946.

Berkin, Carol R. and Clara M. Lovett (eds), *Women, War and Revolution*, Holmes and Meier, New York, 1980.

Bidwell, Brigadier Shelford, *The Women's Royal Army Corps*, Leo Cooper, London, 1977.

Binder, Jean Patterson, *One Crowded Hour*, William Frederick Press, New York, 1946.

Bleuel, Hans P., *Sex and Society in Nazi Germany*, P. J. Lippincott, Philadelphia, 1973.

Bloch, I., *The Sexual Life of Our Time*, Falstaff Publishers, New York, 1937.

Blum, John Morton, *V Was For Victory: Politics and American Culture During World War II*, Harcourt Brace Jovanovich, New York, 1976.

Bowker, Benjamin C., *Out of Uniform*, W. W. Norton, New York, 1945.

Braybon, G., *Women Workers in the First World War: The British Experience*, Croom Helm, London, 1981.

Briggs, Susan, *Keep Smiling Through*, Weidenfeld & Nicolson, London, 1975.

Bullock, Alan, *The Life and Times of Ernest Bevin—Vol II: Minister of Labour 1941–1945*, Heinemann, London, 1981.

Bullough, V. L., *A History of Prostitution*, University Books, New York, 1964.

Burns, John Horn, *The Gallery*, Harper Bros., New York, 1947.

Burton, E., *What of the Women? A Study of Women in Wartime*, Frederick Muller, London, 1941.

Calder, Angus, *The People's War*, Jonathan Cape, London, 1969.

Cartland, Barbara, *The Years of Opportunity*, Hutchinson, London, 1948.

Statistical Digest of the War, HMSO, London, 1951.

Chafe, William Henry, *The American Woman: Her Changing Social, Economic and Political Role, 1920–1970*, Oxford University Press, 1972.

Gillespie, D. M., *The Psychological Effects of War*, Chapman Hall, London, 1944.

Civil History Series (Ferguson S. M. & Fitzgerald H.), *Studies in the Social Services*, HMSO, London, 1954.

Clawson, Augusta, *Shipyard Diary of a Woman Welder*, Penguin, New York, 1944.

Colett, Wadge D., *Women in Uniform*, Sampson & Low, London, 1946.

Cox, M. D., *British Women at War*, John Murray, London, 1941.

Crew, F. A. E. (ed), *The Army Medical Services: Campaigns* (5 Vols), HMSO, London, 1955–6.

Davies, Christie, *Permissive Britain—Social Change in the Sixties and Seventies*, Pitman, London, 1975.

Davies, R., *Women and Work*, Arrow, London, 1975.

Delmer, Sefton, *Black Boomerang*, Viking Press, New York, 1962.

Deutrich, Mabel E. and Virginia C. Purdy, *And Clio was a Woman: Studies in the History of American Women*, Howard University Press, Washington DC, 1980.

Duus, Masayo, *Tokyo Rose—Orphan of the Pacific*, Kodansha International, Tokyo, 1983.

Ellis, John, *The Sharp End of World War—The Fighting Man of World War II*, David and Charles, London, 1980.

Enloe, Cynthia, *Does Khaki Become You? The Militarization of Women's Lives*, South End Press, Boston, 1983.

Fischer, H. C. and Dr E. Dubois, *Sexual Life During the World War*, Francis Aldor Publishers, London, 1937.

Forster, Anneliese, *Wooden Monkeys*, Academy Press, Chicago, 1961.

Fraenkel, Nat with Larry Smith, *Patton's Best*, Hawthorn Books, New York, 1961.

Freud, Sigmund (Translated A. A. Brill and A. B. Kuttner), *Reflections on War and Death*, W. W. Norton, New York, 1950.

Friedan, Betty, *The Feminine Mystique*, Dell Publishing Co., New York, 1963.

Gabor, Mark, *The Pin-Up—A Modest History*, Universe Books, New York, 1972.

Gardner, Brian, *The Terrible Rain—The War Poets 1939–45*, Eyre Methuen, London, 1966.

Garthaus, Ils, *The Way We Lived*, Australia, 1961.

Ginter, Maria, *Life in Both Hands*, Hodder & Stoughton, London, 1960.

Gittins, D., *Fair Sex, Family Size and Structure 1900–1939*, Hutchinson, London, 1982.

Goodman, Jack, *While You Were Gone: A Report on Wartime Life in the United States*, Simon and Schuster, New York, 1974.

Grafton, Pete, *You, You and YOU!*, Pluto Press, London, 1981.

Graves, C., *Women in Green: The Story of the Women's Voluntary Service*, Heinemann, London, 1949.

Green, G. F., *A Skilled Hand*, Macmillan, London, 1980.

Greer, Germaine, *The Female Eunuch*, McGraw-Hill, New York, 1971.

Hale, Edwin R. and John Frayn Turner, *The Yanks Are Coming*, Midas Books, Kent, 1983.

Hartmann, Susan M., *The Home Front and Beyond*, Twayne Publishers, Boston, 1982.

Heger, Heinz, *The Men with the Pink Triangle*, Alyson Publications, Boston, 1980.

Higham, Charles, *Trading With the Enemy*, Dell, New York, 1983.

Hirschfeld, Dr Magnus, *The Sexual History of the World War*, Panurge Press, New York, 1934.

Hodson, J. L., *The Home Front*, London, 1944.

Hoehling, A. A., *Home Front, U.S.A.*, Thomas Y. Crowell, New York, 1966.

Hoopes, Roy, *Americans Remember The Home Front—An Oral Narrative*, Hawthorn Books, New York, 1973.

Hovespin, Aramis, *Your Son and Mine*, Duell, Sloan & Pearce, New York, 1944.

Hughie, William Bradford, *The Legend of Mamie Stover*, New York, 1963.

Hughie, William B., *From Omaha to Okinawa—The Story of the Seabees*, E. P. Dutton, New York, 1945.

Hull, David Stewart, *Film in the Third Reich*, Berkley, New York, 1969.

Hyde, H. Montgomery, *Secret Intelligence Agent*, Constable, London, 1982.

Jewell, Derek (ed), *El Alamein and the Desert War*, Sphere/*Sunday Times*, London, 1967.

Jones, James, *WWII*, Ballantine Books, New York, 1975.

Jones, Peter G., *War and the Novelist*, University of Missouri, Columbia, 1976.

Joseph, S., *If Their Mothers Only Knew: An Official Account of Life in the Women's Land Army*, Faber, London, 1945.

Katchadourian, Herant A. and **Donald T. Lunde**, *Fundamentals of Human Sexuality*, Holt, Rinehart and Winston, 1975.

Kee, Robert, *We'll Meet Again— Photographs of Daily Life During World War Two*, J. M. Dent, London, 1984.

Keil, Sally Van Wegegen, *Those Wonderful Women in Their Flying Machines: The Unknown Heroines of World War II*, Rawson Wade Publishers, New York, 1979.

Kertzer, Morris N., *With an H on My Dogtag*, Random House, New York, 1947.

Kinsey, Alfred C. (*et al*), *Sexual Behavior in the Human Female*, W. B. Saunders, Philadelphia, 1953.

Kinsey, Alfred C. (*et al*), *Sexual Behavior in the Human Male*, W. B. Saunders, Philadelphia, 1948.

Klink, Gertrud Scholtz, *Einsatz der Frau in der Nation*, Berlin, 1937.

Leizer, Erwin, *The Nazi Cinema*, London, 1974.

Lerner, David, *Sykewar: Psychological Warfare Against Germany*, MIT Press, Cambridge, 1971.

Longmate, Norman, *How We Lived Then: A History of Everyday Life During the Second World War*, Arrow, London, 1973.

Longmate, Norman, *The GIs—The Americans in Britain 1942–5*, Hutchinson, London, 1975.

Longmate, Norman, *The Home Front: An Anthology*, Chatto & Windus, London, 1981.

Lynd, Robert S. and **Helen Merrill**, *Middletown: A Study in Cultural Conflicts*, Harvest/Harcourt Brace Jovanovich, New York, 1965 (1937).

MacNalty, A. S. and **W. F. Mellor** (eds), *Medical Services in War*, HMSO London, 1968.

Malkin, Richard, *Marriage, Morals and War*, Arden Book Company, New York, 1943.

Marshall, Brigadier General S. L. A., *Men Against Fire*, Dept. of the Army, Washington DC, 1947.

Martin, Ralph G. (ed), *The GI War*, Little, Brown & Co, Boston,

Mass Observation Reports, *War Factory*, Gollancz, London, 1943.

Mass Observation Reports, *People in Production*, John Murray, London, 1942.

Maudlin, Bill, *Up Front*, Bantam Books, New York, 1983 (1945).

Mead, James M., *Tell it To the Folks Back Home*, Appleton-Century, New York, 1944.

Meade, Margaret, *And Keep Your Powder Dry*, Morrow-Quill, New York, 1965 (1942).

Melly, George, *Rum, Bum and Concertina*, Weidenfeld & Nicolson, London, 1977.

Merril, Francis E., *Social Problems on the Home Front*, Harper Bros, New York, 1947.

Meyer, Agnes E., *Journey Through Chaos*, Harcourt Brace, New York, 1944.

Miklos, Josephine von, *I Took A War Job*, Simon & Schuster, New York, 1943.

Millett, Kate, *Sexual Politics*, Doubleday, New York, 1969.

Milward, A. S., *War, Economy and Society 1939–1945*, Allen Lane, London, 1977.

Ministry of Health, *Report on the State of the Public Health During Six Years of War: Report of the Chief Medical Officer*, HMSO, London, 1946.

Minney, R. J., *I Shall Fear No Evil—The Story of Dr Alina Brewda*, William Kimber, London, 1962.

Minns, Raynes, *Bombers & Mash—The Domestic Front 1939–1945*, Virago, London, 1980.

Moore, John Hammond, *Over-Sexed, Over-Paid and Over Here!*, University of Queensland Press, Australia, 1981.

Morella, Joe (*et al*), *The Films of World War II*, Citadel Press, New Jersey, 1973.

Myles, Bruce, *The Night Witches—The Untold Story of Soviet Women in Combat*, Presidio Press, California, 1981.

Overseas Press Club of America, *Deadline Delayed*, E. P. Dutton, New York, 1947.

Padover, Saul K., *Psychologist in Germany—The Story of an American Intelligence Officer*, Phoenix House, London, 1946.

Page, Martin, *The Songs and Ballads of World War II*, Granada Publishing, London, 1975.

Statistics Relating to the War Effort of the United Kingdom, HMSO, London, 1945.

Pelling, H., *Britain and the Second World War*, Collins, London, 1970.

Pendleton, Ann (Mary Beatty Trask), *Hit the Rivet, Sister!*, Howell, Soskin Publishers, New York, 1943.

Perrett, Geoffrey, *Days of Sadness, Years of Triumph: The American People 1939–1945*, Coward, McCann & Geoghegan, New York, 1973.

Plummer, Douglas, *Queer People*, W. H. Allen, London, 1963.

Polenberg, Richard, *War and Society: The U.S., 1941–1945*, Lippincott, Philadelphia, 1972.

Priestley, J. B., *British Women Go To War*, Collins, London, 1944.

Pruller, Wilhelm, *Diary of a German Soldier*, Coward, McCann & Geoghegan, New York.

Rhodes, Anthony, *Propaganda: The Art of Persuasion: World War II*, Chelsea House, New York, 1976.

Richardson, Major-General Sir Frank, *Mars Without Venus*, Blackwood, Edinburgh, 1981.

Robinson, Victor (ed), *Morals in Wartime*, Publishers Foundation, New York, 1943.

Rosen, Marjori, *Popcorn Venus—Women, Movies and the American Dream*, Peter Owen, London, 1975.

Rowse, A. L., *Homosexuals in History*, Macmillan, New York, 1977.

Rupp, Leila J., *Mobilizing Women for War*, Princeton University, New Jersey, 1978.

Sackville-West, V., *The Women's Land Army*, Michael Joseph, London, 1944.

Satterfield, Archie, *The Home Front*, Playboy Press, Chicago, 1976.

Schimanski, Stefan and Henry Treece (eds), *Leaves in The Storm—A Book of Diaries*, Lindsay Drummond, London, 1947.

Schindler, Colin, *Hollywood Goes to War*, Routledge and Kegan Paul, London, 1979.

Scott, P., *British Women in War*, Hutchinson, London, 1940.

Seidler, Franz W., *Blitzmaedchen—Die Geschichte der Helferinnen der Deutschen, Wehrmacht im Zweiten Weltkrieg*, Wehr & Wiseen, Hamburg, 1968.

Seidler, Franz W., *Prostitution, Homosexualitat, Selbstverstummelung*, Kurt Vowinkel, Neckarmund, 1977.

Sherman, Allan, *The Rape of the Ape*, Playboy Press, Chicago, 1973.

Smart, Charles Allen, *The Long Watch*, World, Cleveland, 1967.

Snyder, Louis L. (ed.), *Masterpieces of War Reporting—Great Moments of World War II*, Julian Messner, New York, 1964.

Somerhausen, Ann, *Written in Darkness*, Alfred Knopf, New York, 1946.

St George, Thomas R., *C/O Postmaster*, Crowell, New York, 1946.

Stearn, James (translator of anonymous diary), *A Woman in Berlin*, Harcourt Brace Jovanovich, New York.

Stein, Ralph, *The Pin-Up—From 1852 to Today*, Crescent Books, New York, 1984.

Steinbeck, John, *Once There Was A War*, Pan Books, London, 1961 (1943).

Stephenson, Jill, *Women in Nazi Society*, Barnes & Noble, New York, 1975.

Stouffer, S. A. *et al*, *The American Soldier* (2 Vols), Princeton University, New Jersey, 1949.

Straubel, James H., *Air Force Diary*, Simon & Schuster, New York, 1947.

Summerfield, Penny, *Women Workers in The Second World War*, Croom Helm, Kent, 1984.

Titmus, R. M., *Problems of Social Policy*, HMSO, London, 1950.

Treadwell, Mattie, *The US Army in World War II—The Women's Army Corps*, US Army, Washington DC, 1954.

Tripp, C. A., *The Homosexual Matrix*, McGraw Hill, New York, 1975.

US War Department, *What the Soldier Thinks* (2 Vols), Princeton University Press, 195

Wakeman, Frederick, *Shore Leave*, Farrar & Rhinehart, New York, 1944.

Waller, Willard, *The Veteran Comes Back*, The Dryden Press, New York, 1944.

War Histories—Civil Series (Parker, H. H. D.), *Manpower—A Study of Wartime Policy and Administration*, HMSO, London, 1957.

Wechter, Dixon, *When Johnny Comes Marching Home*, Greenwood Press, Connecticut, 1945.

Welker, Robert H., *A Different Drummer*, Beacon Hill Press, Boston, 1958.

Wendel, Else, *Hausfrau at War: A German Woman's Account of Life In Hitler's Reich"*, Odhams Press, London 1957.

Wilder, Margaret Buell, *Since You Went Away*, McGraw-Hill, New York, 1943.

Wilkerson, Tichi and **Borie, Marcia**, *The Golden Age of the Hollywood Reporter*, Coward-McCann, New York 1984.

Williams-Ellis, Anable, *Women in War Factories*, Gollancz, London, 1946.

Wilson, E., *Only Halfway to Paradise: Women in Postwar Britain 1945–1968*, Tavistock, London, 1980.

Winnick, Charles C. and **Kinsie, Paul M.**, *The Lively Commerce—Prostitution in the United States*, Quadrangle Books, Chicago, 1971.

Woll, Allen L., *The Hollywood Musical Goes To War*, Nelson Hall, Chicago, 1983.

Wolsey, Serge J., *Call House Madam*, Berkley Davis, New York.

Young, Wayland, *Eros Denied—Sex in Western Society*, Grove Press, New York, 1964.

INDEX